IN GARAGELAND

Seeking to understand youth culture through its visual and musical expression, *In Garageland* presents a pioneering ethnographic study of rock bands and their fans.

The authors explore the functions of rock playing within three socially different peer groups, investigating how their activities relate to the external demands and resources of a postmodern world. Presented in 'dialogic' format – the authorial text juxtaposed on the page with the remarks of those interviewed – the authors analyse the objective, social, symbolic and subjective sources and meanings of rock playing, relating these to theories on modernity, social groups and the production and reception of cultural symbols.

In Garageland develops the notion of youth culture research in a way of mirroring our own grown-up identities and of staking out the limits of late modern culture in general.

Johan Fornäs is Associate Professor of Musicology and Reader in Media and Communication Studies at Stockholm University.

Ulf Lindberg is a secondary school teacher and youth researcher in Lund, Sweden.

Ove Sernhede is a lecturer and research assistant in the Department of Social Work at the University of Göteborg.

Communication and Society
General Editor: James Curran

What News?
The Market, Politics and the Local Press
Bob Franklin and David Murphy

Glasnost, Perestroika and the Soviet Media
Brian McNair

Pluralism, Politics and the Marketplace
The Regulation of German Broadcasting
Vincent Porter and Suzanne Hasselbach

Potboilers
Methods, Concepts and Case Studies in Popular Fiction
Jerry Palmer

Communication and Citizenship
Journalism and the Public Sphere
Edited by Peter Dahlgren and Colin Sparks

Images of the Enemy
Brian McNair

Seeing and Believing
The Influence of Television
Greg Philo

Critical Communication Studies
Communication, History and Theory in America
Hanno Hardt

Media Moguls
Jeremy Tunstall and Michael Palmer

Media Cultures
Reappraising Transnational Media
Edited by Michael Skovmand and Kim Christian Schroder

Fields in Vision
Television Sport and Cultural Transformation
Garry Whannel

Getting the Message
News, Truth and Power
The Glasgow Media Group

Advertising, the Uneasy Persuasion
Its Dubious Impact on American Society
Michael Schudson

Nation, Culture, Text
Australian Cultural and Media Studies
Edited by Graeme Turner

Television Producers
Jeremy Tunstall

News and Journalism in the UK
A Textbook, Second Edition
Brian McNair

News Content, Language and Visuals
Glasgow University Media Reader, Volume I
Edited by John Eldridge

Industry, Economy, War and Politics
Glasgow University Media Reader, Volume II
Edited by Greg Philo

IN GARAGELAND

ROCK, YOUTH AND MODERNITY

JOHAN FORNÄS, ULF LINDBERG AND OVE SERNHEDE

Translated by Jan Teeland

London and New York

First published 1995
by Routledge
11 New Fetter Lane, London EC4P 4EE

Transferred to Digital Printing 2004

Simultaneously published in the USA and Canada
by Routledge
29 West 35th Street, New York, NY 10001

Typeset in Sabon by Florencetype Ltd, Stoodleigh, Devon

British Library Cataloguing in Publication Data
In Garageland: Rock, Youth and Modernity. –
  (Communication & Society Series)
  I. Fornäs, Johan II. Series
  306.484

Library of Congress Cataloging in Publication Data
In garageland: rock, youth and modernity / edited by Johan Fornäs,
  Ulf Lindberg and Ove Sernhede.
     p. cm. -- (Communication and society)
  Includes bibliographical references and index.
    1. Rock music--Sweden--History and criticism. 2. Music and
society. 3. Popular culture. 4. Music and youth. 5. Rock
groups--Sweden. I. Fornäs, Johan, 1952–   . II. Lindberg, Ulf,
1941–   . III. Sernhede, Ove. IV. Series: Communication and
society
  ML3534.15   1995
  306.4'84--dc20   94-29091

ISBN 0-415-08501-2
     0-415-08502-0 pbk

CONTENTS

LIST OF FIGURES viii
PREFACE ix

INTRODUCTION 1
 The Authors 3
 The Project 5
 The Theoretical Fields 7
 Qualitative Methods 10
 To the Reader 16

THREE BANDS – THREE CULTURES 19

OH – IN BETWEEN 21
 Facts about OH 21
 Introduction 22
 History 32
 The OH Culture 39
  Being yourself 39
  Power and powerlessness 41
  Us and them 43
  Order and chaos 46
 Style 48
  Appearance 48
  Interaction 49
 Music 51
  Musical taste 51
  OH's own music 52

FROM THE SUBURBS – LAM GAM 59
 Facts about Lam Gam 59
 An early meeting 60
 Bergslunden 63
  The situation of youth in Bergslunden 65

The Ark	67
The Ark culture	67
A concert at the Ark	76
The history of Lam Gam	77
A rehearsal with Lam Gam	85
Dissolution	86
Lam Gam's music	88
DETACHED – CHANS	94
Facts about Chans	94
Commuting to the cottage	95
Villaholmen	101
History	104
The Chans culture	111
Cultural tastes	124
Chans' own music	128
OBJECTIVE LIFE CONDITIONS	**141**
LIVING IN THE LATE MODERN PERIOD	143
Prehistory	143
The children of the boom	147
The Late Modern crises	150
THREE SPHERES	155
The family	158
The school	163
Leisure	167
Spaces for identity work	171
SUBJECTIVE DRIVING FORCES	**173**
KURRE	176
THREE THEMES	190
Authority	191
Work	192
Sexuality and living together	194
THE GROUPS AND THEIR ROCK MUSIC	**199**
THE BAND AS A GROUP	**201**

SEARCHING THROUGH SYMBOLIC PRAXIS   207
  Searching   207
  Rock as symbolic praxis   210
    Objective sources   210
    Socio-cultural sources   212
    Subjective sources   222
    Excursus: Adolescence as a second birth   227

LEARNING PROCESSES IN MAKING
ROCK MUSIC   229
  Learning types   230
    Learning in the external world   231
    Learning in the shared world   234
    Learning in the inner world   238
    The complexity of learning   242
    Excursus: communication   244
  Modern possibilities   245
  Resistance and alternative public spheres   247

CONCLUSION   250
  Why rock?   251
    Collective autonomy   251
    Alternative ideals   252
    Narcissistic enjoyment   253
  The youth debate   255
    Serious play   255
    Active searching   256
    Necessary norm experiments   256
  Youth work   257
    The complexities of learning   258
    Communications between different spheres   259
    Learning to resist   259
  Youth research   260
    Polydimensional content   260
    Theoretical openness   262
    Strategic self-reflection   263

NOTES   264

BIBLIOGRAPHY   272

INDEX   279

FIGURES

1 OH: *Just a Dream*   57
2 OH humour   58
3 Lam Gam: *Money and Dead Nature*   92
4 Lam Gam, sketched by a 12-year-old fan   93
5 The Chans culture   117
6 Chans:*Teheran*   133
7 Illustration from *Chans Mag*, autumn 1982   139
8 Daily life, the state and the market   144
9 Experience of youth and parents   153
10 Bands' home districts compared   156
11 Types of learning   242
12 Functions of aesthetic expressions   245

PREFACE TO THE ENGLISH EDITION

This book, originally published in Swedish in 1988, has been slightly revised for the present English edition. All books have limitations, but we think this one remains pioneering, with its combination of vivid depictions of ordinary teenagers' music-making with recent theories of rock and modernity, symbols and styles, identities and adolescence.

Sweden is at once similar to and different from other Western industrialised nations; but despite the differences, we think our analysis and the cultural phenomena we describe will be easily recognised by non-Swedish readers. Recent modernisation processes are world-wide; rock, youth culture and adolescence have important international traits and tendencies, and our theoretical tools are used in trans-national discussions. What is specific in our presentation will be indicated in due course; at this point we wish to point to a few details that might facilitate the understanding of some of our ethnographical material.

Several aspects of the social and cultural history of Sweden are discussed in the book: Sweden's relatively late industrialisation (starting in the 1870s); its strong national popular movements (nonconformist, temperance, working-class trade union movements); a powerful Social Democratic welfare state (from the 1930s); a Lutheran state church (though secularisation is extremely high). Also, since the 1940s Sweden has had a fairly good employment record, and in the period when the book was researched and written, the 1980s, there was very little unemployment.

Our educational system is discussed later in the book, but it might be well to mention here that we have had nine years of compulsory schooling since the 1960s, starting at seven years of age. Almost all go on to the upper secondary school, the 'gymnasium', where students can specialise (two years for vocational courses, three for theoretical, four for technical studies). Education, including university and college levels, is mostly free, financed by taxes.

Youth culture in Sweden is pretty similar to that of other countries. A special Swedish subculture known as the *raggare* evolved in the 1950s around big American cars and rock 'n' roll music. Otherwise, most Western cultural styles have had their Swedish variants, including mods, rockers, hippies, disco, heavy metal, punk, rasta, skinhead, hip-hop and acid. For the vast majority of Swedish youth, lifestyles are an individual mixture of mainstream, media and subcultural elements – as they are in all other countries.

Until the late 1960s, Swedish rock music was seldom original. Most artists followed Anglo-American models (Jerry Williams was one of the best, and is still active today). Around 1970 an unusually strong and well-organized youthful music movement arose, with bands, clubs and associations, record companies and distributors providing alternative scenes and channels for domestic rock with realist or progressive lyrics (Pugh Rogefelt, Peps, Blå Tåget, Hoola Bandoola Band, Nynningen, National-teatern). The journal *Musikens Makt* (The Power of Music, 1973-80) reflected this movement; the organization of music clubs, Kontaktnätet (Contact Network), was founded in 1974 and still lives on. The culmination of this movement was reached just as punk rock gave voice to a new generation: in Stockholm the best known bands were KSMB and Ebba Grön (the latter developing in the 1980s into Imperiet); in Gothenburg there was Attentat. Some of the old counter-culture institutions survived (together with artists such as the rock troubadours Björn Afzelius and Mikael Wiehe), others changed radically. Yet as a whole Swedish rock has not only persisted but expanded: today, internationally famous professional artists, from ABBA to Roxette, are the crown of a rock music tree with more than 100,000 rocking grass roots out of a total population of 8.5 million people, and of an infrastructure of rock clubs, recording companies and rock festivals. Rock and pop music is also the greatest and most evenly distributed leisure interest and activity among the population. Swedish teenagers are among the most avid buyers and listeners of recorded music in the world.

What has happened since late 1987, when we wrote our book? The main trends in youth culture look much the same, although the hip-hop scene has grown in importance, and, of course, our boys and girls have grown considerably. This became evident when we discussed the book after publication with our band members – an illuminating experience for both them and us, the full evaluation of which will have to wait for another context.

As expected, most of our by then 18–22-year-old informants mainly read the chapters about themselves, glanced through the sections on the other two bands, and found it difficult to penetrate the more theoretical parts. Nevertheless, some tried and they had several interesting comments.

On the whole, they directly or indirectly confirmed our interpretations and appreciated the descriptive parts. The Chans group, for instance, declared our summary of life in their middle-class bungalow area and of their own culture to be quite to the point. Where they protested, their criticism in a way rather confirmed than contradicted our analysis. Frasse, for example, claimed that his family was not at all lacking in 'cultural capital', but a second check showed that they still seldom visited or used the institutions or cultural forms associated with 'cultivated' life. His own protest can be seen as typical for his class: anxiety about being exposed as superficial economic climbers in the social hierarchy.

The new interviews have provided some material to bolster continued interpretations of the long-term development of personal and group identities through later phases of adolescence and post-adolescence as well as of the development of amateur bands and peer groups. Late adolescence into post-adolescence is a phase of rapid change. Much could be said about the further adventures of our rock band members, some of whom have become parents by now. However, we will conclude by adding a few remarks on their reception of the book. There was a sharp difference between the reactions of Lam Gam and those of OH and Chans. With some exceptions, Lam Gam seemed overwhelmed by reading difficulties and a feeling of being socially stigmatised compared with the other groups. Chans and OH, on the other hand, contributed interesting counter-readings of our interpretations of them as well as comments on the impact of the research project on their lives.

Much could be learned by studying how the youths handled our 'mirroring provocations'. Being subjected to our research seemed to have been useful for the identity work of Chans and OH members especially, by contributing to their reflexivity, mirroring and enlarging their identities, and by offering tools to be used in internal conflicts and self-constructions. They used our concepts in their own way and tested them on each other – and on us. Some of these concepts, metaphors and images were rejected, while others seemed extremely productive. For instance, Micke picked up the concept of *project*, characterising Kurre's current girlfriend as 'another of his projects', obviously as part of a strategy to emancipate himself from subordination to his old mate. Micke's remark occurred in one of the interviews which ended with a clever brainstorming session devoted to applying expressions from the book to Ulf's everyday life.

Such transference and reflexion processes ought to be studied in more detail, through dialogic research based on a paradigm of understanding rather than by conventional objectifying methods. Youth culture research is also a way of mirroring our own adult identities and of staking out the limits of late modern culture and life forms in general.

Some important new references have been included in this edition, even though the Bibliography is not nearly as exhaustive as it would have been if we had written the book today. Such is the fate of late modern youth culture – and of studies of it: they are in a state of dynamic flux, and every text is but a preliminary – and rapidly dating – one on the road to something different. But we invite you to step off at this station for a while and make your own use of what it offers.

Stockholm, March 1993
Johan Fornäs, Ulf Lindberg, Ove Sernhede

Editors' note:
This book was originally published in Sweden by Brutus Östlings Bokförlag Symposion in 1988 and this translation has been financed by the Swedish Council for Research in the Humanities and Social Sciences (HSFR).

INTRODUCTION

Youth culture is a new and exciting research area. In debates and work on youth, insights into the cultural forms of young people are sought after, and in this connection the central position of rock music is repeatedly noted. Why is it that rock music seems to mean so much to youth just now?

There are good reasons for an adult to be interested in theories of youth culture: we have all been young but we inexorably get older. Times change; the culture of our own youth is soon history. Songs, hairstyles, jargon and views of the world: as adults we might giggle with nostalgia, embarrassment or amused indulgence at all that, while at the same time we have difficulty understanding the youth we see around us.

To understand the world – our own and others' – is neither simple nor trivial. It is important not only to study other modes of living, the past, or the celebrated 'high' culture, but also to reflect over and conceptualise one's own culture, one's own times and media-based popular culture. In order to be 'scientific', the observer/researcher often tries to study what lies far from him- or herself – to establish 'nonpartisan distance', to avoid 'subjective values'. Middle-class youth researchers tend to prefer to examine the cultures of working-class youth, leaving middle-class youth shrouded in mystery – but then the latter seldom cause any problems for the authorities involved with control and funding.

However, it is worthwhile also to examine 'oneself'; the culture of one's own youth and to contemplate what it actually meant. Historical knowledge provides invaluable tools for understanding and acting in the present, but cultural scholars could also very well devote more direct attention to present-day culture. Furthermore, popular culture dominates the everyday life of the majority. Like high culture, popular culture is permeated by commodity forms, but nonetheless has a use value worth trying to understand. Everyday culture is more motley than one would at first suppose.

It is also important to see beyond what language normally conveys. One key to a richer understanding of youth culture lies in visual and musical expression: in styles and in rock. Moreover, it is important to be interested in class as well as sexual conflicts in youth culture and to take heed of their many different levels: the visible styles and hidden identities, mainstream and deviant subcultures, social, psychological and ethical relationships, the production and reception of cultural symbols, traditions and changes, power and resistance.

We can only illuminate a few important areas. There are other vital questions outside our field, which remain for others to discover. And there are insights into our own territory which the youths themselves or other researchers would be able to express better.

We are especially curious about the functions of rock music because rock is so important, both for us and for most contemporary youth. The world of rock poses a challenge to our rational self-understanding and to our theoretical work. What is it about rock that defies all theorising and makes it so difficult to express in words? *What is hidden under the surface of rock?*

The relation between rock and theory is problematic. Rock-loving youth seem satisfied with living in the myths of their own culture. And to study rock practitioners scientifically poses special problems, one of which is the resistance of the representatives of the genre. Musicians tend to maintain that the music should do the talking and not to want to question something which is for them uncomplicated, natural – simply rock 'n' roll. Critics and others in the music industry are liable to defend rock's mass cultural character and their own roles as part of the initiated. This resistance is understandable and often sympathetic, at least to the degree that it has to do with defending boundaries against highbrow culture and theoretical encroachments from above. Against such a background, research quite rightly appears as a form of power, an instrument of integration which threatens the very grounds of rock culture – rowdiness, sensuality, immediacy. Unfortunately, experience has shown that research often functions in such a way. Time and again researchers and writers cater to the powers-that-be and deliver results and arguments which either make the young more manageable or define them as a special problem group.

We have also experienced this resistance, but it has been counterbalanced by other forces. It would be a serious drawback if we denied the possibility of 'solidaristic' research, oriented towards understanding; such a denial would mean that the world of knowledge is a homogeneous, static, subservient bloc. But it is not so simple, and if one does not view knowledge in such terms, it is imperative that one tries to demonstrate in practice that research can be used in other ways. For instance, theoretical analysis could be linked with practical criticism like that carried on by young people themselves in social movements, subcultures, music associations, or in demonstrations and other actions. Critical theory could thereby acquire use value as an orientation in the field of music, in formulating personal identities, as a defence against the intervention of those in power, and in exploring openings towards a better future.

In addition, there is a practical need for understanding, anchored in what is for two of the authors our daily work. Working with youth is similar to research: it can, but should not be, done manipulatively and integratively. Other motivating forces may be less pure and in part, unconscious, but it would be dishonest to pretend they did not exist. It is a matter of satisfying a need for collective creativity in research, of developing instead of treading water, of capturing or demarcating a position in the field of youth research, and of acquiring a perspective *vis à vis* one's own experience.

THE AUTHORS

We three, authors, friends and colleagues, all have one foot in each camp.

Ulf Lindberg (b. 1941) listened to jazz during the 1950s, when Elvis and Tommy Steele competed for the favours of other teenagers. Ulf became Kalmar's (a town in southeast

Sweden) one and only beatnik at the turn of the decade, and came to rock music via underground outposts such as Mothers of Invention. He worked in the music movement during the 1970s, began to play by practising in secret on his daughter's guitar, and since the year of punk, 1977, has played rock music in various local amateur bands. At the time of writing, he is a gymnasium teacher and has taken part in a school research project under the auspices of the Pedagogiska gruppen in Lund, a Swedish alternative educational group that aroused his interest in teenagers' lives outside school.

Ove Sernhede (b. 1951) has been devoted to rock music ever since as a young teenager he formed an intimate relationship with the Rolling Stones, Small Faces and the Animals. A number of more or less passionate affairs with soul, blues and jazz never seriously threatened this relationship. Like Ulf, Ove also plays in a local rock band – with no ambitions of earning his daily bread by means of music. Between 1979 and 1984 Ove worked as a field social worker with the rock music project, Låt Tusen Stenar Rulla (Let a Thousand Stones Roll) in Gothenburg (Göteborg).[1] At present he is working as a psychotherapist.

Johan Fornäs (b. 1952) grew up in a 'folk high school'[2] on the plains some 200 kilometers south of Stockholm. He read and thought and listened to classical music, protest songs and the Beatles, but became seriously interested in both rock music and cultural theory through the burgeoning Left and music movement in Lund at the beginning of the 1970s. A winding career path led over maths studies, industrial jobs, and the magazine *Musikens Makt*, to the Musicology Department at Gothenburg University, where he completed his PhD in 1985 with a dissertation on the progressive music theatre show, Tältprojektet (The Tent Project), which toured Sweden in 1977. The length of Johan's hair and his 'shade of red' have varied somewhat belatedly with the trends. Through punk's ·liberating influence, the piano keys were finally challenged by rock groups' freer synth in various small music associations within Kontaktnätet. In 1984 Johan was drawn to Stockholm by Hillevi Ganetz, whose interest in female rock lyrics and feminist textual theory has even infected the present project. Johan now works at the Unit of Media and

Cultural Theory in the Department of Journalism, Media and Communication at the University of Stockholm as an associate professor of musicology and Reader in Media and Communication studies.

The three of us were brought together by common experience and engagement. All of us were in amateur rock bands, moved in the same undogmatic leftist intellectual circles and, in contrast to many political comrades, shared a positive view of the ostensibly de-politicized 1970s and 1980s youth, punk and the European BZ movement (squatters' movement). We began to work together concretely in 1982 when each of us was asked to contribute to a rock issue of the Swedish critical educational journal, *Krut*. Early the following year, we wrote an article for Sweden's largest daily newspaper *Dagens Nyheter*, and put together an anthology on youth culture.[3]

THE PROJECT

When we began to work together, each of us, separated geographically and with different points of departure, was interested in rock music's counter-cultural and liberating possibilities.[4] Ove's youth work in Gothenburg had also demonstrated what revolutionary learning processes were initiated in the youth groups involved with building up Låt Tusen Stenar Rulla – now a project led by social workers and music teachers. But what happens in ordinary rock-playing youth gangs – are comparable learning processes going on there?

We were all critical of the prevalent picture of teenage rock enthusiasts as mere passive victims of the manipulations of the culture industry. We were equally critical of the view – one purveyed not only by the mass media – of youth culture and rock music as a destructive force, a threat to civilisation and morality. We had already argued for an alternative way to understand and relate to youth culture. It was clear very early on that what was lacking – and thus necessary – in order to push the discussion forward was a serious close study of a number of groups of youth. We wanted to broaden the understanding of – and thereby create respect for – the many-faceted work with identity and the dynamic learning processes which take place in youth groups in general and in involvement with rock music in particular.

So we began the research project which resulted in the present book. We hope it will be read not only by youth researchers but also by anyone interested in youth culture. The book should be considered, first, as a contribution to an ongoing debate on youth, in which we argue in favour of abandoning the old, narrow perception of youth culture and instead seeing its many and various connections to large, central social issues. Second, the book is conceived as a constructive contribution to critical and radical youth work, as a way for us to work with and reflect on our own experiences and at the same time inspire others working with or in contact with young people to do the same. And, third, we have tried to develop theoretical concepts for a youth research which addresses itself to the function of cultural symbols in learning processes and identity work in modern society.

The project was entitled 'Cultural Production and Reception in Three Youth Groups' and continued, after a few months planning in autumn 1984, for over two years – from January 1985 to July 1987. It was mainly financed by HSFR (Research Council for the Humanities and the Social Sciences). Formally, the project was under the auspices of the Institute of Arts and Cultural Administration, Gothenburg University.

We selected three groups of youth: one mixed-gender group, Chans, from a middle-class residential suburb of Stockholm; a group of boys from Helsingborg, OH, from the upper strata of the working class; and a group of boys from a Gothenburg suburb, Lam Gam, who were predominantly from the lower strata of the working class. Most of the twenty-odd youth were around 15 years old when the project started (the members of OH were slightly older). Most entered a practical or theoretical course in gymnasium (upper secondary school) during our two years together. All of the bands had been influenced first by punk and then hard rock, but during the period of the project, they played fairly heterogeneous rock music.[5]

Each of us followed his band closely and documented its culture through participatory observation during rehearsals, concerts, and, as far as possible, in other circumstances as well. We recorded group discussions and in-depth individual interviews as well as the bands' music, and we collected diverse documents from the groups' activities and interviewed people close to band members (parents, teachers, youth club leaders, friends, etc.). As the conception of the project implied, our contact with the youths was an extension of our professional roles as teacher (Ulf) or social worker (Ove), or through our own unprofessional participation in local rock music life (all of us).

Most of our material was collected in 1985–6; we recorded and transcribed around 150 hours of interviews before concentrating on the analysis of interviews, documents and music recordings.

THE THEORETICAL FIELDS

The project was empirical, but it had clear theoretical contexts and implications. In the 1980s, an extensive and multi-dimensional Swedish research was finally developed in the field of youth culture. In particular, British cultural studies, German modernity and socialisation theory (Ziehe, Habermas) and French cultural sociology (Bourdieu) received well-deserved attention.[6] The present book is an attempt to proceed from internationally discussed theoretical traditions, to develop and relate them to each other and to our qualitative ethnographic study.

Our work is unique in many ways. There are very few qualified ethnographic studies of teenage peer groups or amateur bands.[7] Although almost 10 percent of all Swedish teenagers play in rock bands, most books on rock deal only with the professional end of the spectrum, while many studies of youth cultures are badly informed on precisely that music which is so central to them.[8] We differ by concentrating on amateur and everyday practice in peer groups rather than on professionals in the music business, and by diving into deep qualitative levels instead of collecting statistical data. Few of the rock studies we know of use their material to develop an advanced systematic combination of recent theories of modernity, style and subjectivity in the use and meaning of symbolic forms in adolescent identity formation.[9] We try to give modernity theories a concrete empirical grounding while raising the level of youth culture ethnography to the standards of present-day theoretical discussions.

In the field of cultural theory, we attempt to further discussion of modernity: that is, of current cultural trans-formation processes. It is important to continue to observe long and deep traditions, for example, how power, social relations, sexual roles and generation conflicts are repro-duced from generation to generation. However, it is also vital to be attentive to the shifts, movements and dynamics of history. This is particularly timely today, when so many aspects of youth culture indicate such modernisation processes.

In this we have been especially inspired by Jürgen Habermas' and Thomas Ziehe's theories, even though we also take up somewhat parallel ideas from a number of contemporary (post-) modern cultural theoreticians (Berman, Jameson, Lyotard, Sennett et al.). Like Ziehe and Habermas, we emphasise the ambivalence of modernis-ation – that it exists, like it or not, and that it is irreversible. Modern culture is neither better nor worse than past tradi-tions, but it is unavoidably different.

Our contribution to this field is that we ground our theoretical arguments on our own empirical material, and on the connection of general concepts of modernisation with specific analyses of youth culture and music forms. The debates on postmodernism often lack analyses of popular culture's forms of expression and of people's real daily lives. This is unfortunate since a central point in the current wave of modernisation is that, more than before, it affects everyone's daily life and changes the relations between elite and mass culture.

Our analyses of our groups' immediate social environ-ments are inspired by several different sociological and social anthropological traditions. We are unabashedly eclectic and combine models from Habermas (system-life world, communication, public sphere, etc.) and Oskar Negt (counter-public sphere) with certain concepts of Pierre Bourdieu (social fields, economic/cultural capital, etc.) and others from British youth culture research (sub-cultures, style, homology, bricolage, etc. It is a matter of finding the best way to understand and describe the antipodean energy fields our young bands move within, where different concepts function on different levels. It is essential to examine contradictions and conflicts, power and resistance, instead of viewing cultures as homogeneous, closed and stable systems.

Hence our study contains an argument for comparisons and new connections between hitherto separate theory traditions, for an independent work of bricolage in the field of theory.[10] There are elements in, for instance, French (Bourdieu) or British (the Birmingham Centre of Contemporary Cultural Studies) cultural sociology which we think deserve to be linked up with the cultural theories of Habermas and Ziehe. We depart from the works on subculture (Willis, Hebdige, and others) by studying how 'common', relatively 'normal' young people produce cultural expressions and identities instead of concentrating upon specific, deviant subcultural styles. We also introduce psychodynamic levels of analysis into ethnography and cultural sociology (a valid point for a comparison with Bourdieu and many other cultural sociologists).

Also as regards theories and symbols and their functions we call for a bold combination of different theory traditions. We investigate youth culture styles and means of expression in a wide context, which *inter alia* brings in semiotic and linguistic theories, the Birmingham researchers' style analyses and various psychoanalytical theories of symbols. Cultural symbols and expressions function concurrently on several different levels and this requires a multi-layered analysis. It was, for example, fruitful as well as necessary for us to see how the music and styles produced and used by our teenagers could be interpreted multi-dimensionally: they pointed towards objective social positions in terms of class, gender and geography, towards cultural fields with other aesthetic objects and traditions, and towards internal, subjective deep structures. It is also important to understand the function of cultural symbols in two opposite directions: backwards – as an expression, symptom and way of handling problems whose roots lie in the history of the individual or of society (styles as putative solutions to social problems, symbols as a way of repairing inner conflicts from early childhood); and forwards – as concrete utopias (experiments with new experiential and life forms, the creation of unique and changeable identities).

Finally, we also avail ourselves of theories of subjectivity. We enter into a field of psychoanalytically oriented socialisation research, primarily from the German Frankfurt School tradition (Alfred Lorenzer, Thomas Ziehe, *et al.*), but we also include ideas from other schools of psychoanalysis such as the French Lacan school (for example, Julia Kristeva), the British object relation theory (Melanie Klein, D.W. Winnicott and Hanna Segal), and also the American tradition of Ernst Kris, and Heinz Kohut. We realise, of course, that such a blending runs great risks as there are open conflicts among these approaches. To examine thoroughly such conflicts is an interesting task – but one for the future; for the present, it is a matter of suggesting different interpretative possibilities for our youths as generously as possible.

We try to contribute to this theoretical field by making concrete and putting into focus young people's cultural expressions.[11] Further, it is important for us to underline subjectivity as neither given by nature nor an illusion, but something socio-culturally produced – yet no less real for that. Subjectivity is intrinsically contradictory, and in our society, it stands in contentious relations with the surrounding social units.

In summary, we ascribe to a number of theoretical fields without claiming to be able to present a conclusive theoretical argumentation. We utilise comprehensive cultural theories of modernity, social theories of spheres and fields, style and symbol and language theories as well as theories of socialisation and subjectivity.

QUALITATIVE METHODS

Our study is an empirical and qualitative field study. We have closely followed three exemplary rather than statistically selected groups and empathetically interpreted rather than objectively calculated when we analysed our material.

Ulf already had connections with his group as a couple of its members were his pupils in school. Ove found his group through his social work contacts in Gothenburg suburb music clubs. Johan used contacts with local music

Kurre: I think it's – it gives us a helluva lot to talk to you and that, 'cause we – it's a good way to get into contact with each other, get to know each other. You don't do that instinctively, or whatever it's called – otherwise you don't, you know.
Bobo: We don't start discussions like this in our place,

you know, when we sit up there.

Ulf: No, you can't when you know each other too well, you show more or less the same sides all the time.

Kurre: No, but we do that now. That name, artistic manager [what Ulf called himself], is terrific – even though you don't decide for us artistically.

Ulf: It's only a joke.

Kurre: Yeah, but it's still right. We talk a lot about artistic matters when we talk with you. Right?

Ulf: What's special about me actually, in comparison with other adults you know?

Finn: The fact [?] that you're none of us's parents.

Kurre: No, you act like a mate. You're just like any old pal. For one thing, you're much more experienced. We – we respect you in different way from a pal maybe. Could say you're in between a pal and a parent. And there's hardly anybody we know like that, in the middle, you're the only one I know who's like that [. . .].

Micke: It's great that you have the same interest as us.

Kurre: Yeah, we know that we can talk straight with you – and know that we won't get a lot of flack.

Håkan: When you came, you know, we never thought you'd choose us. We were really proud when you chose us as you had several other bands [. . .] It's cool to be involved, it's a different deal, sort of, not many people get to be in something like this.

Björn: I think it's been terrific to have you around, a new pal! [. . .] It's been great – you get to talk things through [. . .] It's cool to be helping research along [laughter].[. . .] And you've asked different things about music that we've not thought about so much before, and then you think 'ah-ha, maybe we should try something like that anyhow?' [. . .] I've seen you more as a mate than a researcher who's going to

clubs and with friends who were gymnasium teachers around Stockholm. In this way, our contacts acquired a certain personal touch. The bands were not *only* research material for us and we were not *only* researchers for them, but the researcher–informant relationship was openly articulated right from the start. The differences among us as regards when and how we set up contacts with our respective bands affected the continuation of the project. Johan and Ove never gained the kind of close and strong contact with their bands that Ulf achieved with his. Ulf was more or less adopted as an important, supportive father figure to OH; Johan became a welcome and somewhat fascinating guest of Chans whereas Ove's relations with Lam Gam remained more problematic.[12]

As Ulf had already set up contacts with his band, we began a preliminary analysis of his first interviews in spring 1985. The following autumn a complete series of interviews with and participatory observations of all three bands was compiled. We all made notes, went along to rehearsals and concerts and conducted at least one group interview and at least one individual interview with each band member. In the spring of 1986 we augmented our interview material with a few more group interviews. In the first, we played a cassette tape with ten recorded rock songs, partly the same songs for all the bands, partly chosen in light of the particular characteristics of each band. The music was a mix of different periods and styles, and we recorded the discussions afterwards. We each saw a film with OH and Chans – *Purple Rain* and *Absolute Beginners* – and documented the discussions of the films. We also carried out one more round of individual interviews, so that each band member was interviewed at least twice. In addition we interviewed several parents, teachers, friends and others in the bands' surroundings. Our material comprises a total of 60 transcribed interviews.

All the interviews were recorded and transcribed literally. We all worked on the transcriptions and members of Chans and OH read them and had the opportunity to comment on them (members of Lam Gam were less interested in this). OH also read parts of the analyses, which they appreciated but had few opinions about. The three authors met together regularly to discuss and analyse the interviews and decide on questions to pursue further with the three bands. Feedback reading was very useful, even if it seldom entailed any substantial interventions in the text.

We made several recordings of the bands, some in rehearsal, some at concerts, and we had access to the concert and demo recordings made by the bands themselves. Their current repertoire was analysed during the period of investigation, and we chose three songs from each band, which we examined especially thoroughly (with transcriptions of the texts and music, and analyses of various levels of form and content). Chans was given a questionnaire about how they spent their time. Only a small part of all this material is directly evident in the present book.[13]

In our interpretations of the cultural artefacts made or used by the groups, we worked in three dimensions. On the cultural level proper, we looked for the positions of their music, lyrics, images and styles in the aesthetic and stylistic field itself: genre types, influences from other artists, etc. On a more objective or social level, we discussed how their cultural expressions related to various social hierarchies and positions such as class, gender, age, ethnicity or geography. We tried to note how the three bands positioned themselves socially through their music-making and how their objectively given positions were reflected in their music. Thirdly, the subjective level led us to consider psychological meanings in their use of media and aesthetic expressions: how their music pointed towards internal need and motive structures which were shaped through life-long socialisation processes. In this way we differentiated our interpretation of meanings into three dimensions, which we felt should not simply be reduced into one another.

The cooperation between and among the three researchers has been enormously irritating and stimulating. Each of us has contributed with his special knowledge and expertise, with criticial comments about the others' texts and ideas, and with support and encouragement. Working like this is, of course, rather cumbersome, especially when we live so far away from each other.

The groups involved have the right to be anonymous in this sort of investigation. This is easier said than done. We have changed all the personal, place, group and song names that we thought might reveal their identities to

explore every nook and cranny of me [laughter].
Gustav: I think that probably this has turned into a bit more of an inspiration for us, yeah I think so [...] We can see that someone is sort of keeping tabs on us, interests himself in what we do, like that.
Gösta: Partly it's something to remember and recall sort of, and it's also interesting ... to see how you, an outsider, see the band, as it's rare we get to listen to someone who says so much. Mostly it's like: 'Yeah, this was good', or 'Where're you at?', but you ask questions that get us to think and that.
Olof: It's good to talk to someone else about how it is. It's interesting. To talk about things you don't talk to the others about.
Betty: I think this has been a positive experience – talking over relations within the band a bit, how we've developed, etc. because this is something we maybe don't discuss with our friends, but still I think it's useful.
Barbara-Ann: I got a real kick, you know, since you're interested, and I thought, 'Let's get going and practise'. [...] I like that, that you start thinking maybe you're doing something good. [...] This has got us to mature in a way, actually. Our relationship to each other, I mean. Not that we're better pals, but we realise how it is and how we feel about each other. [...] You've got us to grow up a little in some way.

Ove: How have you felt about me coming in and checking out your rehearsals and so on?
Ola: Hasn't mattered, it's OK. You've even contributed one or two ideas.

readers. This is a delicate task as it involves retaining at least something of the ambience of the original names. However, with this we have had excellent help from the bands themselves, who came up with good proposals for pseudonyms. Unfortunately, we have also had to avoid certain kinds of concrete illustrative material (photos, detailed presentations of songs, etc.).

We have also discussed the effects of the project on the three bands. For both OH and Chans, our close attention had a status-raising effect; they have enjoyed and been fascinated with being research subjects and have been very obliging. For understandable reasons, Lam Gam's members' positive reactions have been mixed with indifference or suspicion *vis à vis* being subjects of (yet another) investigation.

However, for all the bands, we have been significant as adults who have listened and discussed but not exercised control, and because of this, we have influenced both the music and relations within the groups. In qualitative close studies it is impossible to avoid such influence: this type of research does not establish any straight up and down subject–object relationships. Our own subjectivity interacts with the young people's in the construction of the empirical material as well as in our interpretations. This can indeed be viewed as a problem, considering all the methods we use that are based on closeness rather than distance to their objects – transference mechanisms easily arise, for instance. Already during the first spring, we detected, for example, mutual transference between Ulf and OH's central figure, Kurre. Ulf's initial interpretations of his interviews with Kurre contained clear projections of his (Ulf's) own desires and ideals. Equally, it was clear to us that Kurre himself was aware of Ulf's ideals and tried to fulfil them through playing the rebel role they required. Because two of us were not in the same transference situation with Kurre, we could discover these mechanisms in discussions together and improve the analyses; and indeed, once we became aware of the transference mechanism, it could be used to improve our insights into Kurre. What first was conceived of as a problem from the point of view of traditional, objectifying scholarship, became transformed through conscious and collective interpretation and self-examination into a resource.[14]

We have experienced the qualitative approach as productive theoretically. Closeness to young people's concrete
cultural forms has given us access to insights which a
greater distance would never have allowed. It is, of course,
also important to recall the method's limits. For example,
it is impossible to draw generalising conclusions from
our observations. We cannot 'prove' anything about the
influence of locality, age, class or gender on the involvement with music in general – our examples are unique.
Through our analysis, we can suggest how various factors
affect our bands, but to what extent these are typical for
other bands with comparable backgrounds remains to be
shown. Gender, locality, class, age, etc. can have different
effects on groups in other contexts. We can claim that the
middle-class character of Chans creates a flexibility – but
also a willingness to compromise; however, there are certainly other middle-class groups that are, for other reasons,
rigid and/or rebellious.

Neither is it our ambition to reveal the whole truth
about these three unique bands. We do not provide any
sort of total explanation. We combine different theoretical
tools to illuminate certain aspects of our groups' realities,
to reconstruct a picture of the learning processes of three
modern group cultures and their making of rock music.
Other aspects of these groups remain in the dark. What
we say about the groups and about youth culture and rock
music in general does not therefore constitute any final
truths but should be taken as provisional interpretations
to be considered and worked on.

The task of interpretation entails major problems, both
practical and as regards principles.[15] One problem lies
with language itself. What we said above about research
as a social field applies also to the language of theory,
which in our society tends to function repressively and
conflict with the way youth culture and rock express
themselves. However, the language of theory has valuable
strengths – to survey, penetrate and reflect, which give it
emancipatory possibilities if its users are open to inquisitive contact with non-discursive language and aware of
their own limitations. In interviews and group discussions,
we have not only registered what the band members normally say but also stubbornly provoked verbal reflections
and symbolising of experiences which would otherwise

remain discursively unformulated (this has been confirmed by the band members themselves). In our analyses it has been a major problem to understand the interaction between our presence and their subjectivity in discussions, and to detect how the discussion itself creates expressions for these experiences.

We interpret the youths' different verbal expressions, that is, 1) texts in the form of interviews, 2) texts and documents which the bands themselves wrote down, 3) the bands' lyrics and music, 4) signs and symbols in their visual styles. We have not had anything more radical than texts (in the sense of symbolic expressions) to interpret; but there are different types of texts, in different media and channels, which we have made use of. We have sought relations between different texts and by this means looked for underlying, possibly unconscious processes. Not least, it has been important to combine interview analyses with music analyses and direct observations of our groups.

The language of youth – both silence and profuse expressiveness – encompassing verbal language, music and visual style can be problematic. Young people cannot explicitly articulate aspects of their lives, at least not in what are for us interpretable symbols. Here we are forced into reconstructions on the basis of contradictions and obvious 'lacunae' in the texts we have had access to. From inconsistencies, ambiguities and infractions – everything that is in contrast to a 'normal' or anticipated way of talking – we can construct concepts for underlying unconscious tendencies; concepts that transcend the bands' own self-image but which exist implicitly in their mode of living.

The opposite problem arises when in certain areas of their lives, the groups throw out messages all too fervently. This complicates analysis by making it difficult to distinguish the essentials in the flood of information, and requires the ability to discriminate in order to concentrate on the central, meaningful elements in their cultures.

Interpretation is never unbiased. To a degree we have been able to augment our insights by recalling our own experiences. We have also had access to coded experiences, scientific and/or aesthetic (youth culture theory, the universe of rock, etc.). As mentioned above, our ambition has never been to achieve a total interpretation, but we have chosen to 'expose' ourselves as broadly as possible to the groups' life forms. On the other hand, from the start we have had ideas and goals which have directed our interest towards decided aspects of the cultures (learning processes in playing rock music). This was essential – otherwise we would have been buried in empirical material – but it has often involved painful choices, and much material and many lines of thought have had to be left unattended to. There has been no way to accomplish everything we would have wanted to do, and what we have included in this book has entailed the exclusion of other important areas. For example, we are all men and there were girls in only one of the bands, so the aspect of gender requires other studies. Like our groups, we play the music ourselves, so there is a study of the reception of rock music waiting to be done. All this should be kept in mind when reading this book.

TO THE READER

We have written this book *together*. We have sent drafts back and forth to each other, exchanged sections and worked on each other's ideas. Obviously, each of us has had the main responsibility for everything having to do with his 'own' band, even though we have commented on each other's analyses. However, as regards the analytical sections of the book, we hardly know ourselves who has written what; in any case, it is futile to try to indicate division of work since we all three stand for the whole.

The book consists of two main sections. The first section comprises 'Three Bands – Three Cultures' in which central features of each of the three groups are presented in turn.[16] Each group analysis is accompanied by an insert containing basic facts about the group.

The second section contains three more theoretical chapters: one on the the groups' external life conditions, one on individual subjectivity, and one on the groups themselves and learning processes in their music-making.

We conclude by summarising our work and commenting on current research and debates on youth, and youth work in Sweden.

Parallel to, and set alongside, our text are quotations from our interviews with band members, which accompany and illustrate the main text. The content and nature of these interviews is spontaneous and they capture the vocabulary of the individual group members. There are also notes to accompany each chapter and a bibliography.

Stockholm, Lund and Gothenburg,
September 1987/March 1993
Johan Fornäs, Ulf Lindberg and Ove Sernhede

THREE BANDS –
THREE CULTURES

OH – IN BETWEEN

FACTS ABOUT OH

Name: One Hand Beats Five Fingers (OH).
Date of formation: beginning of 1984.
Home: Helsingborg, a town on the south coast of Sweden with over 100,000 inhabitants. Half the group lives in a high-rise housing estate in town, half in a nearby residential neighbourhood with detached houses just on the outskirts.
Number of members: originally 5.
Line-up: originally a singer, two guitars, bass, drums; later also synth.
Quarters and instruments: own rehearsal quarters in a storehouse (the 'Barn'); own instruments, some collectively owned, having a value of about SEK 70,000 (1985).
Members:
Finn (b. 1967) vocals, lyrics. Father lorry driver, mother nursing assistant; both parents early immigrants. Finn has three years of gymnasium, one on the natural science course, two in social science. Aims at being a parish assistant. Engaged in church youth organisation, music, diving and judo. Moved away from home in 1986. Music preferences: U2, Saga, Alan Parsons, Simple Minds, Toto.
Bamse (b. 1966) lead guitar, previously song writer. Father sanitation worker, died in 1985; mother an immigrant and hospital cleaner. Two years gymnasium studies in metal work, short-term unemployed, youth work in the church, part-time work, night courses. Aims at being a parish assistant, engaged in church youth organisation and music. Was not in the group in 1986. Former music preferences: Jimi Hendrix and hard rock.
Kurre (b. 1966) rhythm guitar, song writer, the group's musical driving-force. Father an immigrant, cook and supervisor, mother part-time shop assistant and cleaner. Has two years gymnasium in metalwork – welding and plumbing; dreams of being professional musician. Engaged in music and, earlier, politics (Social Democratic Youth organisation). Musical tastes: from Clash, Alarm, Jam and other punk groups to U2, Simple Minds, Toto, Saga, Alan Parsons.
Bobo (b. 1968) bass. Father plumber, mother cashier. Two years in gymnasium (electrical engineering), works as electrician. Engaged in music and motorcycles and previously in a church youth organisation. Music tastes range from Clash and hard rock to a broader range.
Micke (b. 1965) drums, song writer. Father immigrant, small businessman; parents divorced, lived with father until 1987. Two years metalwork course in gymnasium, worked part-time (30 hours per week) in a department store, did military service. Took welding course and is a plumber, but works as a storeman. Engaged in music (several instruments), previously, in football. Wide music tastes from Clash via Simple Minds, Alan Parsons, Toto to Agnetha Fältskog.

INTRODUCTION

> 'My good Adso', my Master
> said, 'during our whole journey
> I have been teaching you to
> recognize the evidence through
> which the world speaks to us
> like a great book.'
> Umberto Eco, *The Name of
> the Rose.*

Just outside Helsingborg lies the Village: a centre with older buildings and a hamburger stand, a gathering place for local youth surrounded by a residential area of detached houses. About 4500 people live here, with an average income of about SEK 76,000 in 1985 – according to local authority statistics, about on par with the rest of the municipality. Over 70% of the employed inhabitants commute to work somewhere else. The area has a surplus of families with children and a deficit of older people. There is little overcrowding – 2%. Emigration frequency, the number of non-Swedish residents, and the number of people on social welfare or unemployment lie well below the average for the municipality.[1]

Half of OH – Bobo, Kurre and Micke – live in one of the Village's bungalow areas. Micke's parents are divorced. He lives with his father who is an immigrant and a small businessman; his younger brother lives with his mother. Born in 1965, Micke is the oldest of the group, and plays the drums. The guitarist and driving force in the group, Kurre, is not only a neighbour but also Micke's best mate. Like Micke's family, Kurre's parents are young, his father is also an immigrant and works as a cook with managerial duties. Kurre's mother has contented herself with part-time work as a cleaner and shop assistant. The family has three children, of whom Kurre is the eldest. Bobo is the group's bassist and youngest member, born in 1968. His mother is a cashier, his father is employed as a municipal sanitation worker. Bobo's elder brother has moved away from home. When this book was written all three band members had graduated from two-year trade courses at gymnasium (upper secondary school) and had jobs. After a period of unemployment, part-time employment and military service, Micke joined Kurre, working as a plumber in the same firm. Bobo got a job as an electrician.

A detour from the Village into the town takes you past a residential area dominated by modern blocks in red or yellow brick. The other two original members of OH come from here – the lead guitarist, Bamse, and the singer, Finn. This neighbourhood does not give the same impression of prosperity as the Village, but neither is it considered a problem area. The district has about the same population as the Village, of which 3% are classified as overcrowded – just below the municipal average. Age distribution is about even, with a slightly higher proportion of families with children. The district's average income is a few thousand kronor below that of the Village. Emigration frequency, the proportion of non-Swedish citizens and the number receiving social welfare or unemployment benefit are higher than the municipal average. Politically the district has a clear working-class profile: more than 60% of its votes went to the socialist bloc in the parliamentary election of 1985. In the Village, the bourgeois bloc dominated to a more or less equal extent.[2]

Finn's family lives in one of the residential blocks. At the time of writing, only his parents live there, both of them immigrants. Finn's father drives a lorry and his mother is a nurse. An elder brother started to study in the nearby university town of Lund and in 1986 Finn also moved away from home. Finn is the only member of the band who has tried any of the academic courses in gymnasium. He studied the natural sciences for awhile, but changed to the two-year social studies course which he completed in spring 1986. Bamse's female-dominated family – he has four older sisters – live in a detached house in the district. His father, who was a sanitation worker before he was given an early pension for health reasons, died at the end of 1985. His mother is a nursing assistant. At present Bamse is the only child living at home. He graduated in metal trades from the gymnasium in 1984, was unemployed for a time, but finally got work through job creation programmes, in among other places, the church. The church brought Finn and Bamse together and encouraged them to educate themselves to be parish assistants.

Thus OH was not a gang or peer group from the beginning but a mixed group – in more ways than one. Socially, their parents belong to a borderline group, between a stable working class and the lower middle class. The music the group plays defines the members as 'synth-based rock', that is as a hybrid form. And by coincidence, the group's base, the 'Barn', geographically lies right in the middle between the Village and the District, in a large green area.

Visitors to the Barn find themselves standing outside a storehouse.[3] The door is secured with a horizontal iron bar and two padlocks. If in doubt, one has only to read the sign: 'Our Home – OH'. Anyone who manages to force the door sets off an alarm, which can only be shut off by those who know where the switch is. The room inside looks roughly square, and is rather dark, the only source of light being a small barred window in the left-hand wall. The floor space might be about 20 square metres. When your eyes get used to the dimness, or when the electricity is switched on, you see that the walls have been sound-insulated with grey egg cartons. Head-high by the door are coat hooks and a shelf with a sign saying 'Shelf for shoes', and you simply remove your shoes lest you sully the wall-to-wall felt carpeting.

What dominates the room is a large white Shiro drum-set, with four tom-toms and three cymbals, and two black, obviously home-made speakers, resembling a pair of Frankenstein-like ankles with feet. Between these 'legs' are the voice amplifiers on a low wooden bench. Cables hang above. The drums are right under the window and the sound system directly opposite, along the right-hand wall. Both walls are equipped with lighting systems with different coloured lights, presumably to create 'stage atmosphere'. The walls also have compartments for pedals, microphones, etc.

Again on the left is a bass system, a Peavey-combo, in the corner. Previously this stood on the other side of the drums and lead guitarist Bamse's amplifier was here. In the middle of the wall opposite the door is another guitar amplifier, a Marshall-combo. The space in the middle of the room has been left empty for the musicians. The only definite sign that the group contains a vocalist and a keyboard player is a mounted microphone and a collapsible stand for the synth on the right of the door. A note on the inside of the door reveals a certain familiarity with religious expressions: at the top there is the caption, 'Olle's Ten Commandments', clearly referring to the landlord. A few of these commandments are:

Micke: The beat is rock, it's not exactly a waltz [laughter] [. . .] It's more smarmy pop [. . .] Synth-based rock, though not with synthesisers.

Kurre: Black is very hip, black coats, black pants, black berets, all that. We have a lot of black too. Micke has white drums, Bobo and me have black instruments.

I Thou shalt always clean up after yourself when you have finished your daily tasks [. . .]
IV Thou shalt always close Olle's gate [. . .]
VI Thou shalt never pee in Olle's garden [. . .]
X Thou shalt place coins in the collection box after using the phone. Price Kr. 1.

Opposite the door, in the left-hand corner, a metal ladder leads up to a hatch in the roof. Crossing the room towards the ladder, you cannot help noticing that the place is not just functional, but clean and tidy. At most, there might be a used matchstick on the floor. To get up the ladder and open the hatch, you can be neither fat nor rheumatic: you have to get on your knees; and to see into the attic, you have to hunch over, since the roof, covered on the inside with perforated white plastic sheeting with yellow fibre insulation showing through, slopes steeply towards the ladder. The hatch can be closed from inside the attic so it is possible to talk without being too disturbed by the noise from below. The attic, too, also has a wall-to-wall carpet; but there the resemblance stops: downstairs you work, upstairs you lounge.

The attic is much smaller than the ground floor. Even so, the band has managed to stuff in a whole suite of furniture – heaven knows how – sofa, table, armchairs at the far end, and put a small window in the wall. The table is low and black, and decorated with maxims such as 'Think, if we all were a bit more tired, no one would have had the energy to go to war', signed 'Figini'.

The window wall is dominated by a white banderole with the group's initials in red and blue, and a bookcase of chipboard planks. On the top shelf is a cassette tape recorder, and below, files and a double coffee machine among other things. Water is supplied from a large plastic container with a tap and a short tube mounted on the wall. In the opposite corner, on the other side of the sofa, stands the 'pig can', another plastic container for rubbish. This one has been decorated with two large, bulging eyes, so that it looks a bit like a snowman. Half the wall is covered with small posters from the group's gigs, the other is more or less covered with a noticeboard full of picture postcards. Along the wall is a small TV and on its right, a crate of soft drinks. Above the crate a sign says 'LIST über SPRUDELWAN', containing strange aliases, inspired by a variety of foreign languages: Figini, Wollwie, Derball, etc.

Finn: No, we just don't think it's cool [. . .] a mass of broads on the wall and that . . . pin-ups [. . .] Everywhere you

After each name is a row of strokes indicating who is presently consuming the most. When the crate is empty there is another one in reserve across the room.

The opposite wall is also decorated, but differently. There are a few large posters in bright green, yellow and pink which the eye is unavoidably drawn to – they look like some sort of advertisements for horror films. On the ceiling above the hatch is a U2 monogram. Otherwise there are no signs of idols, nor for that matter of cars or pin-up girls, despite the fact that, strictly speaking, this is a boys' room. Perhaps what denotes gender most clearly is the table – cluttered with unwashed coffee mugs, full ashtrays and all manner of junk – and, not least, the sight of the season's first mouse, taped by the tail to the lamp above.

Having come so far, you cannot help admiring the care and thought the group has given to its 'home'. You understand that the text on the door is not a joke. If the ground floor represents the group's commitment to music, the attic stands for a corresponding commitment to something more: in the group's own language, to 'gemenskap' – a spirit of community or group solidarity, often abbreviated by OH to a single big 'G', and inspired by the popular youth film G by Staffan Hildebrand (1982).

If you are so bold as to take Kurre's file out of the bookcase and look through it, you will come upon a headline which awakens immediate and genuine curiosity: *A vile presentation of 1985. 'Oh Story' presents*. Automatically the eye wanders, stopping here and there in the text:

> *Year's best song*, in my opinion, *The Rain* – it has everything
> [. . .]
> *Year's worst month is May* – one gig together
> 1985 was the year we became men, 'Whoopie, we are men!'
> [. . .]
> 1985's the year when Bobo got his own set
> 1985 was the year when OH had their international breakthrough in Helsingborg
> [. . .]
> 1985 was the year when we had 3 keyboard players in the group Kokos
> JAN-FEB Ludde March/Nov Moltas DEC-
> [. . .]
> *Year's rarest sweat fleck* is Finn's, under his nose
> 1985 was the year nobody knew anything about Chile
> *Year's most meaningless thing* was when Finn cleared the notice board and then put everything back up again
> *Year's worst pedals* are two phasers and of course, the heavy metal pedal

go it's there. It's a real pain to look at all the time. OK, it's slick too, there's good-looking girls there too.

Bamse: You're not a human being there, in the Barn. You're like an animal, really.

Ulf: What do you mean?

Bamse: Well, you've got to keep to rules here, but you don't at the Barn – you say and do what you please.

Bobo: It sounds really strange, but I think this is more like home than home, if you know what I mean [pause]. It looks a little more amateur . . . a bit . . .

Finn: [laughing] Yeah, it's my family, my other family, that's it.

Kurre: You think, damm it this is something we've created, nobody can ruin it. It's like real 'G', a bloody fine togetherness. That's what's most important.

Kurre: It's the same as when you play a concert, I think it's wrong to say, 'Now on the guitar, there's Bamse, on percussion it's Michael, on the bass, Bobo, on vocals it's Finn and here on the guitar, Kurre.' It's better to say '*We are OH*', yeah? It's we, it's not him and him and him, it's us. That's the way it is at our place, there it's us – there's no one person stepping up and saying, 'I'm best' . . .

Bobo: Well, I don't know, I think it feels better to play your own material. Instead of keeping on picking out a song here and there, we might just as well try to do our own thing.

Sound of the year – Figini's drums [. . .]
Rehearsal quarters of the year – ours of course
Visit of the year – a madman, a police crazy. Uffe etc.
Discussion of the year – Christianity, girls, songs, problems in the group, Chile, Derball's belly, Figini's memory, Bobo's girl-friend, Wolle's – so that's done, brrr
[. . .]
Bird nests of the year – our old descants
and finally, some of the year's most popular expressions: oiya, now that's done, Müde, brruv, hell what a smell, Dodda Daiffty, Currats, so vider schön, schadde, we're playing now, oops I forgot

The Cash Book reveals, among other things, monthly payments to a Lutheran charity. Finn's file contains a thick collection of song lyrics, most of them typewritten and in English – nothing recognizable, obviously his own. The most common subjects seem to be war and peace, social injustice and love. Curiosity requires a pause at what must be the group's signature tune, *One Hand Beats Five Fingers* (Like all OH songs in this chapter, originally written in English):

1 When you're born you yell because you're frightened
   Your only hope is the others faith for you.

   You don't know! How shure you are!
   People are kind when your small.

2 But you grew up like everybody else
   You starting walking a way of your own.
   That's the main thing for you.
   Oh Lord! You don't know it's true.

Kurre: What OH is, it's not the name but . . . what we are together. For a start I don't know what we are – we aren't musicians, but a bunch . . . kids that get along well together [. . .] One little dream is that we can keep together for a long time, yeah? That's a dream we all have. A bigger dream is, well, that we could get a record contract, that we could support ourselves on it, and an even bigger dream is that we want – like everybody else – we want peace and that, yeah? we're trying to do something for peace, a little at least.

Bamse: Some groups think like, 'Now we've got to practise, now we'll get famous.' We don't think like that.

Refrain I We're not fooling you
           We know a better way
           We're not fooling you
           You got to understand

Refrain II We all know one hand beats five fingers
            And it's hard for you to stand there all alone.

3 It doesn't matter where you are
   It doesn't matter what you stand for.

   Where know it's right! Listen to us!
   We'll see the light! Open your eyes!

4 You got to belive in yourself
   You had walked a way of your own.
   That was the main thing for you.

   Oh Lord
   You don't know it's true.

Leafing through the files, you find two complete personal 'interviews' with group members, carried out as questionnaires, and dated October 1984. If you are to believe these documents, everyone in the band smokes, and takes snuff

(Prince cigarettes, General); they drink, they are against money and politics, they hate war and racism but love girls, peace, OH and, among other bands, especially U2 and the Clash, and they admire Martin Luther King and either Che Guevara or Jesus. However, you also begin to suspect a division in the group which makes some of the solidarity rhetoric sound more like invocation. In the following, Bamse presents as a deviant in his answers:

Name : Bamse
Age : 18
[...]
Smoke : sometimes
Snuff : yes
Drink : yes
Politics : shit
Hobby : OH, the church youth group
Money : yes
Think of life : mmm, he he
Think of me : yes
Favourite : myself
Favourite food : food's good
Favourite group : Def Leppard, Jimi Hendrix and OH
Favourite drink : beer (milk)
Cigarettes : White Blend.
Snuff : General
Hate : Kurre, untuned guitars, bad press, girls
Love : everything
Favourite song : *Wasted* with Def Leppard, *Hey Joe*, Jimi Hendrix
OH's best song : none are good
Admire : myself
Write most often on the walls : Bamse, Heavy Metal, OH
What you want to be : Bigger
Why : because
Think of parents : fine
Are you together with anybody : yes
Say whatever you want : long live Jesus and God, hope we meet soon. OH must be better Fuck interviews
Where do you think OH will end up : in the shit

Finn: He was the only one who came in with muddy shoes, it was only him who made everything dirty up here, it was only him who did things, yeah? [...] It all runs better now, sort of. There's more music you like yourself, and when you play music you dig yourself, it's all much better, right? It was difficult to do when we had his, sort of [giggle] 'grater' around.

Kurre: We'd be sitting up here rapping in peace and quiet, then he'd go down, sometimes he'd go down half an hour before us and jam, sometimes he'd come up again and go home much earlier than anyone else. And then sometimes he wouldn't come at all, and when he did he'd hardly say Hi or anything. Stuff like that's a bit disturbing, it makes you think, 'What the hell's up with him?', and you had to ask him all the time, like 'How's it going, how is it with you?' You always had to take it easy so he wouldn't have a bloody fit and just disappear.

Of course, you can never browse undisturbed in OH's Barn because it is accessible only two evenings a week and the band rehearses there. On the other hand, you don't need to sneak a read or ask permission to look in the files. OH 'have no secrets'. Usually, if you arrive early when the boys are rehearsing you find some of them downstairs and others upstairs. You exchange a few words with the boys downstairs, perhaps listen to a demonstration of new idea, and climb the ladder to the attic in the knowledge that the band normally assembles up there. This time,[4] it is the group's 'mamma', Finn, who is nesting up there with Bobo. Finn is broad-shouldered, somewhat stocky, with dark lanky hair, brown eyes under bushy eyebrows, and a large mouth which easily breaks into a wolfish grin. His clothes are sloppy-comfortable – a white long-sleeved sweatshirt, maroon jogging pants marked Adidas and a pair of well-worn trainers with socks rolled up over his pants legs. Bobo looks a bit more child-like, with round cheeks, lightish hair, a faded black T-shirt and blue jeans mostly consisting of patches. He has an unopened bag of buns in front of him.

The door slams downstairs. It is Micke, whom everyone is waiting for. His arrival is the signal for a general gathering around the coffee table. Bamse heaves himself up through the hatch, a little thinner than the others and with a ball of snuff under his downy mustache. The mandatory trainers and blue jeans are topped by a long- sleeved baby-blue sweatshirt. Bamse's hair is light and shoulder-length. After him comes Kurre, heavily built like Bobo, with a great shock of hair, somnolent blue eyes and heavy features – there is something lion-like about his head. And finally, Micke, who is somewhat different from the rest: his jeans are black and in one piece, and his cropped hair raises itself over his head like a coarse brush. Perhaps to fend off complaints about his being late, the first thing he says is that he has sold his old drumset. Since he has some cash, he can take the request for his pound fine, which someone reminds him about, with equilibrium. During this exchange, the bag of buns has been opened, the contents inspected and approved.

The talk goes on. Bobo does not say much, Kurre is much more voluble. In the band's argot, this 'priming' is their counterpart to the gathering that goes on in the dressing room of a football stadium before a match. During the 'priming', Micke, who is keeping watch at the window, signals that more visitors are coming. The visitors turn out to be Kurre's father, a small man with thinning hair in his 40s, and Kurre's 7-year-old brother. They are immediately taken in and given places to sit – it seems to be the most natural thing in the world.

Bamse has already announced that he wants to go down and play, and indeed he disappears through the opening. Soon a great roar soars through the floorboards. One after another the band members climb down. When the group is finally assembled, the instruments must be tuned, the

Finn: Yeah, I want to be a sort of humble type, a servant [laughter]

Bobo: Well, I don't know if it's a style exactly, but I like it when . . . yeah, I don't want to be like everybody else. Make your mark. And you do that if you get into [. . .] But then [inaudible] . . . like if someone meets me for the first time and I come in with those patched jeans and a denim jacket and that, well they'll think I'm one of those . . . tough guys in a gang [. . .] – most people would.

Bamse: But I'm still like that, still confused. I'm a child, you know, I'm not grown up. Even though people say I should be grown up, I can't be, I can't be an adult. I can only try to make the best of the situation.

Kurre: I could think of being some sort of leader for something special. Take responsibility for something, to make it good or . . . I want change, and I want to get that over to other people.

Micke: I know I think first before I speak and the others don't usually do that. They shoot off their mouths all the time.

Kurre: Turning on is the most important. So we can act out, jump and scream and do whatever – flip out, yeah? And begin with a cup of coffee and a smoke – a cigarette – and sit and rap a little.

Kurre: And then we just start, like suddenly somebody says 'In volume adjusted, etc. All goes smoothly. Kurre's little brother sits himself down at the drums and tries to keep time with Bamse and Bobo in a blues number. Micke then takes his place and the group begins to practise, obviously with some rather new material. The song is not quite right and it is interrupted after a few minutes. However, you can hear that the guitarists have worked hard with their riffs. After a little individual polishing, OH get going with *One Hand Beats Five Fingers*.

The song opens with a guitar riff, which sounds very much like the Clash and which is played more or less in unison on heavily distorted guitars. The riff remains during the first two lines of the verse, and the following two are played with hacking guitars and in harmony. The second verse repeats the first. The first chorus is also based on a guitar riff, but it sounds more like hard rock. The second, true chorus, however, is played with longer, straighter chords and more harmony. The *da capo* contains two solos, the first by Kurre, the second by Bamse. Bamse's solo consists of a series of rapid figures, played with both hands on the fingerboard, which reveals that he has listened to guitar virtuosos like Eddie van Halen. In this song, the synth is right in the background while the guitars spread themselves out. It sounds quite tough, heavy and ambitious, but against the guitar-dominated rock breaks a melancholic tone which seems to emanate from the singers' voices and the melodies.

The final chord is hardly struck before the guests begin to applaud. Very good, very good, says Kurre's father with an unmistakable German accent. No one in the band seems dissatisfied either. A little chatting, adjusting the sound, and it all breaks loose again. Ludde is reprimanded for not keeping pace when he alters the sound. (Ludde played synth in the band during 1985.) The first song is gone through again, this time with the singers. Gradually one realises that a concert is coming up and the whole set is to be rehearsed; Bamse starts it up.

At this point Kurre's father and brother take their leave. Micke seems to have an idea for an introduction to the first number, which the group decides to test. Much later, they finally slow down to a break. Finn says he is exhausted. Up to the attic again. The talk is initially about problems with jobs – Micke, who works part-time, launches the subject.

that song, should we do this or that instead?' and, 'Yeah, we can.' And so we try it . . . then we do the song. We try it again if it sounds good, or maybe try something else. Then we run through it again. Finally maybe someone says, 'Let's go through all the songs', and so we do that. And then somebody when he's playing thinks, 'This sounds pretty cool, maybe we can do something with this?' Like me, I usually do the words at home, make a little music too, which we work out in the group later on.

Finn: Often we don't begin with any words, we just start up. 'Right, this sounds good, or this sounds good.' Then they all play. And I improvise to it. I try to find a good melody line to sing to.
Ulf: And eventually add words which are usable?
Finn: Yeah, eventually some words too. Then I might find a chorus that I think sounds good and I try to build on that and come up with the rest of the words.

Kurre: We want to sound both/and. We want a good heavy beat with raunchy guitar sounds, heavy guitar, raspy bass, yeah? and not a hollering singer, but a singer that goes . . . not lalala, like. But – if we have something sweet in there, it's better, I think it's better. So, if you thrash a guitar, like dooooo, and you have a synth, dididudu, you've got both the raw and the sweet. Then it's like the sweet lies over the raw underneath. Certain people would say it should be the other way around, but we don't, and that's it.

Micke: Yeah, but it's our sound, you know, Finn's voice . . . and that – I stay on a tone in the background like in the chorus . . .

Kurre: Anyway – there are always people who say to me 'You should have bloody well been a politician' [. . .] I know I talk a lot of shit, but [. . .] the more you talk, the easier it is to find out what you want.

Kurre: The most fun thing there is getting into it, letting go. Not just on stage, but – I think it's cool with the work before, you know, packing everything, taking off, the group's together all day, eating together – living together for a whole day – it's fucking great.

Ulf: But you're so terribly nervous before you get up on stage.
Bamse: Yeah, I've got stage fright, I'm scared like that people will think different [. . .] If the interaction in the group works [. . .] then it's positive. But if you feel that the first chord goes wrong, then you might just as well pack your things and go, because there's no point then in playing the next five songs.

But the coming concert edges into the discussion. When Ludde reveals he is still unclear about the order of the songs, it is written down for him. While this is going on, someone starts on new questions – the possibility of loaning their instruments to people in the audience and whether the concert should be divided into two parts with a break in between. Bamse brings up the problem of keeping to the rehearsal times because of his job in the church youth group. Again, it is Kurre who tends to fall into the role of leader of the discussion.

Towards the end, it begins to get a little heated. Bamse, supported by Finn, argues that the group should give thanks to God after playing and not only pray together that it will go well before-hand. Kurre cannot see the point – neither, it seems, can Micke. Bobo and Ludde lie low. In the end, the 'heathens' give in, and finally all go down for a new run-through.

The concert is held a week later in an unusual venue, the parish house in the 'Village' – as OH call it – where half the group lives. The event is documented, if summarily, in the following notes taken by Ulf:

I ring Ludde in the morning and find out that OH will gather to transport their gear between 3 and 4 p.m. So after school I drive to the Barn. Bamse comes up and shakes hands – Are you coming? Clearly a positive surprise. Most of the stuff is already loaded. A neighbour has loaned them a trailer. I give them rope to secure their gear and am allowed to drive the guitars plus a few boxes. Kurre, Bamse and Finn have obviously done the most work and there is some grumbling, both now and later, about people who don't do their part. The parish house is a large old building with outhouses. Inside is a large room with questionable acoustics. A long discussion ensues concerning where the gear should be set up – inside or outside, and if outside, where. One possibility is outside a garage which is only a few steps from the house if it should rain. But the garage is locked and the [church youth] leader, A, who is believed to have the key, won't arrive for an hour. I suggest that it's possible to break the lock (and replace it later) and get some support from Kurre and Micke, but Finn and the others are definitely against it. Bamse seems stressed – he's going off later in the evening to a church camp and has his things with him – and repeatedly threatens to take off if it's going to go on like this. The atmosphere is actually uncomfortable and everybody is whinging. At last, there is a sort of vote, which also includes the probable votes of those absent (Bobo, Ludde), ending up in a clear majority for being inside. This causes a great rush to get everything in and set up. The absent members arrive and Ludde appropriates me to drive his gear twice tonight (he's going to play twice, first accompanying a singer, then in OH). [. . .]
Later I am present for a second sound check, a sandwich

and a chat before the whole thing starts. I also exchange a few words with the leader A [. . .]. Most of the boys know her well. Finn gets a hug because the band is really taking off. And indeed it sounds good during the second sound check. People begin to come in, the majority of them of confirmation age and girls. Kurre introduces me to a female fan while we sit outside in the car and wait. His entire family arrives, and I am introduced to his mother and middle brother whom I have not met before. Later in the evening I also see Micke's dad stick his head into the sanctuary, so there's a bit of a family gathering about the whole thing, even if the adults, parents and church youth leader only comprise a few per cent of the public.

First Ludde accompanies his singer [. . .]. Then a few church youth put on a pantomime, an absurd, artless play, sometimes funny, sometimes ridiculous, without a trace of piety. When OH go on after a 15-minute pause, there are between 60 and 80 people in the room – crowded, in other words. I have been instructed by Micke to take pictures, and I get into the role of photographer during the concert – change camera angles etc. and finish the roll.

The concert goes well. The group seems relaxed. Finn takes care of the chatting to the public. He leads in with something that later arouses strong reactions from Kurre and Micke. He says, more or less: 'There is one person we want to thank for our being here tonight. It is Jesus.' Several times during the evening Kurre and Micke have underlined that they have nothing to do with the church, so Finn naturally got skinned for having made the statement in the group's name. But the public show their thanks and are in fact enthusiastic, so afterwards everyone feels pleased.

The group splits up: Kurre and his family, Micke and I sit upstairs having a bite to eat while the rest of the band follow the public underground – that is, to the crypt – for evensong. Afterwards, people pour in upstairs and the leader A and a lightly bearded youth begin to fiddle around, strumming guitars and singing. It feels a little awkward, and I am reminded of a vision I had during the concert but suppressed – of rock as spineless folk music for all ages, deprived of all subversive content. In short, I began to long for a smokey basement with a vicious public. But of course it isn't so simple. It felt good to exchange glances with Kurre's little brother sitting in the first row, clapping hands and joining in with the chorus.

After having transported Ludde's stuff also, Ludde and I join the rest in the Barn. Kurre's dad and his little brother are also there. We listen to the concert tape, which holds quite good sound quality. Kurre's father likes to comment on the songs – like 'that went down well' – and has views on this and that – not always to the point in my opinion [. . .]

It's about time to go home – it's almost 1 o'clock. When we part Kurre suggests that we meet in Lund next time and go out somewhere. I promise to see what's going on.[5]

HISTORY

To understand the formation of OH it is impossible to ignore punk music. Punk did not merely represent something new – a trend like any other: it embodied an uproar

Kurre: We also put in a few things, like du-dat-dat-da-da [singing together with the audience], things like . . . so people will laugh – what in the hell is that, huh? [. . .] Lots of groups think, 'We can't bloody well destroy that song with that shit,' but we don't think so.

Micke: Bobo's really – like with him, you might just as well have a machine as . . . you can't get any contact with him when you play [inaudible]. You look at him and laugh like – just a little . . . he's like totally dead, like a stone. Bamse, he's funny. He goes up to the drums, he hangs over them, you know like that. It's an incredible feeling then [inaudible] when that happens or when you look at each other.

Kurre: There aren't any sour faces, nothing put on either. I suppose that's our nature. It may seem spineless but I don't give a shit. If the whole world had been like that, we might have avoided a hell of a lot.

Kurre: It was Clash that did it. We were so bloody in love with Clash, there's no word for it. We loved them more than anything else. It's like, 'Shit, we've got to start playing,' we saw them and thought, 'We've got to start.' Like that rebel instinct, everybody got it then. OK, it sounded like crap in the beginning, but we didn't want anybody's help.

Kurre: I went to the local music school half a year, and I thought it was so damn dull I wanted to quit.

Bamse: Just because . . . yeah, I stopped too because it was notes. You just had notes in your head after.

Bobo: Then I began a guitar course, I think I went a term and a half [. . .] study circle course. I thought it was boring . . . 'cause I thought what I learned there was meaningless. You know, sitting there and picking out melodies. I could read music and that, so I quit, and then we began to get together and play.

Micke: It was his brother, him on the bottom floor, he had masses of records. Anyway, we heard it when we were in his room one day, and we asked who it was, and it was Clash. Then, it was like only that record, like it was the only record in the world. I taped it then.

Finn: Yeah, it was cool we could do something ourselves. Like if you heard something on a record that wasn't too hard, you could probably do something better than that.

and did so under the aegis of programmatic amateurism. Playing was easy; the step from being a member of the public to being a musician, small.

Two members of OH had learned to play instruments as children – the drummer Micke, and Ludde, who played synth for a while in the group. But the majority were pure beginners when they started in their first bands at the age of 14–16. Only after OH was formed did they become interested in the optional music instruction in the schools or courses on the side. Most of the formally regulated educational processes were a disappointment, but the informal education obtained through listening, tips from mates and their own tinkering around was fruitful. 'All I have learned I have taught myself', says Kurre, and Bamse especially refers to the influence of two older mates who admired Jimi Hendrix.

The sudden burning interest in learning to play was naturally associated with personal maturation processes. For Kurre, who more clearly than anyone else in OH expressed such a connection, the turning point occurred in the eighth class.[6] When OH's most important source of inspiration, the London punk group Clash, entered Kurre's life, he was ready to receive it:

> In the eighth class I began to wake up, so to speak [. . .] Like, what's the meaning of all this . . . of life, what's it for. It's not simple – there's no simple answer [. . .]
> It was at the end of the eighth, the summer between the eighth and ninth year, I think. Then . . . we coloured our hair green when we played sometimes, you know, and wore torn jackets and clothes and that and played. It sounded lousy, but shit, we had fun, real fun. That's the main thing, to have fun when you play. So we called ourselves 'Anti'. We wrote words about Clash or about . . . one was called 'The Egotist'. And then we made songs about where we lived – we thought it was the pits, nothing ever happened. [. . .]
> *Ulf:* What was it that you admired in Clash?
> *Kurre:* Their aggressiveness. Joe Strummer's – his whole childhood, his whole way of just having survived [. . .] It's a symbol for my development, yeah. When Clash came on the scene, then it was like I got big, I could talk for myself [. . .]

The contact with Clash occurred in a way that has parallels with our other two bands. An older brother of a mate played a Clash LP for the younger suburban boys, Micke, Bobo and Kurre. Kurre also listened to other punk bands – he went to a Ramones concert – but it was Clash and Clash alone that inspired him to play.

Kurre's strong identification with Clash, and especially with the singer Joe Strummer, seemed not to have any counterpart among the other band members, possibly excepting Micke. For Finn, who began to sing in a band at the peak of Swedish punk in the beginning of the 1980s, the focus was on competing with what he heard on records. For Bobo, punk seemed simply to have been an entrée to playing; the attraction of why punk in the beginning had to do with lack of technique. If punk was significant as an incitement, presumably a stronger identification with punk culture was required for the suburban group Anti to be able to continue in the same style. According to Micke, Anti were never true punks despite the outward signs: bold, cheeky words, brazen guitars, 'rebellious' clothes and hair-styles. Most also listened to other music than punk – sometimes preferred other music.

One style that lay close at hand was hard rock, which demands more of its executors and expresses more controlled aggression. In Sweden, the advent of hard rock on a broad front occurred at the beginning of the 1980s and at present it dominates the rock scene in Helsingborg. Hard rock came to mean a great deal to the boys in OH, especially Bamse, who early on was attracted to blues rock, which provided him with models and an outlet for his interest in developing as a guitarist. If OH's early hardcore songs were inspired by 'classic' hard rock, the later OH was not free from influences of a 'modern' European variant of hard rock, with strong synth elements and an androgynous image.

To the external forces that drove OH so wholeheartedly into rock must be added parental attitudes. In some cases it is easy to see that encouragement from home was important on various levels: the fathers who played a little guitar themselves (Kurre); the mothers who supplied a loan for a drumset (Micke); parents who simply approved of a hobby that kept their offspring off the streets. However the whole picture is not so straightforward. The opposite can have the same effects: one can also begin to play rock music in order to distance oneself from both parents or one of them. As we shall see, OH's music-making is very much about showing – particularly to their fathers – that they are good at something.

For the boys from the suburb, the route to OH went

Bobo: The first bass wasn't so bad, but then I was going to change and that: 'What's so good about that one?' and 'Why do you want that one?' And like when I bought amplifiers, I got 'you already got an amplifier, why do you want a new one?' and . . . well [. . .] Now the last demo recording we did, they thought it was really good, they said so, but before they thought it sounded terrible. But they haven't heard, they haven't listened to us since we played in Anti [laughter][. . .] It's so bloody pathetic, I mean you got to show them that it's gonna lead somewhere [. . .] No, I want to be there on the day you can come home and throw a record on the table and say, 'Here you are.'

Micke: Oh yeah – that was the best music we've played – in that band. It's never gone as well as that since. But we weren't much of a group, no feeling of togetherness as he decided everything. 'Here's the way it should be, you shouldn't go on the drums there but . . .' But he was a musical genius, he was, so it sounded terrific.

Micke: It sounded very good actually, but it was boring music, you know, just ti-ti-ti-tit, like that. You shouldn't bang the kettle drums too much 'cause then it sounded too raw.

Bamse: They think a lot about money too the whole time, getting ahead in your career. It never lasts. [. . .] Yes, I did the same. Money, [. . .] be famous . . . [. . .] But it doesn't work. I think you have to just play at it.

Micke: Togetherness. You get a warm feeling when you take communion. You were in a lot of camps and that too. You sing a lot and . . . [. . .] You played a lot of games, went out in the forest at night and the girls screamed and . . . [. . .] But then the vicar quit and then I quit too – I didn't like the one that came after.

over a number of other bands. The honeymoon with punk came more or less to an end when Bobo, who then played guitar, was manoeuvred out of Anti and replaced by a better guitarist with training in hard rock. At the same time a singer was recruited, only to be replaced by another. Dynamite, the band that arose out of the ashes of the old one, worked harder on their music, and soon a new and very competent member set his stamp on the band, now renamed Mercy. However, after a dispute, he had had enough and the band split up. Micke and Kurre, who at this time played bass, stuck together. This time they landed in a band called Basic that played dance pop – about as far from Clash as one can get. In the end, this became intolerable for Kurre, who had not thrived either in the period of flirtation with hard rock in Dynamite and Mercy ('I can tolerate playing it, for a while, OK? but then I get into a sort of panic when I can't get my own songs out'). In the beginning of 1984, Kurre and Micke, who once again stuck with his mate, assembled what would become OH. They brought with them a fair amount of hard-won experience. On the one hand, they had been able to test various genres; on the other, they had seen how difficult it can be to keep a band together, that loyalty to one's mates and the demand for quality are not always compatible. And they had understood that in the long run, it may be difficult to subordinate oneself to a style one is not at home with, regardless of how good it sounds.

Bamse had had similar experiences. He had seven or eight bands behind him – 'either you've been kicked out or you've quit'. Just before joining OH he played in Bloody Mary, whose music he described as 'Swedish charts pop'. The attraction of Bloody Mary was the opportunity to play in a studio. It never developed: Bloody Mary never contacted him again. Bamse felt little either for the music or the band members, ('Tories all of them'), but he had learned a lesson.

Before that, Bamse played with friends in a Christian rock band; he left it for the sake of playing in a studio. He also performed sporadically in a duet with OH's future vocalist, Finn. They had met in school and were recruited into the church youth group when they were confirmed. Their repertoire consisted of 'camp songs'; they performed publicly, to the extent they had a public at all, in church camps.

The church youth groups and school have contributed a great deal to bringing the members of OH together. Bobo, Micke and Kurre were also in the church youth group for a time after confirmation (Bobo later returned to his father's house), and most of the group met each other at one of the annual summer camps – only Micke was missing. Kurre, especially, made a strong impression on Finn: 'Yeah, there at the youth camp, when we met, it took about five minutes and we knew each other inside out.' However, Kurre was already taken up with Dynamite, so it was the others who started loosely to discuss playing together. But nothing came of this until later. In the meantime, the missing link was forged: Kurre and Bamse met each other through landing in the metalwork course in the same school.

In addition to serving as a meeting-place, the church youth organisation seems to have satisfied certain deeper needs. This is partly because the parish priests have functioned as father figures and partly because the church has legitimatised serious discussions and the search for solidarity or communality. There is no doubt that the church youth group has had an enormous influence on the band's culture. The role of the school is less clear. In Kurre and Bamse, negative school experiences seem to have contributed to a rebellious identity, but the same is not true for the others.

When the five original members of OH agreed to play together in February 1984, they had the advantage of having their own premises which they obtained on good terms through contacts. We have already stressed the position the Barn soon came to occupy in the band's life, but the conditions were unusually favourable in general. There was a sense of something special with this band already in the initial interviews – the sense of their hitting home or being born again – a sense of 'everything is possible'.

The word they use most is 'fun': in OH you play because it is fun. This attitude leaves its mark also on their understanding of the band's music – they play 'fun' rock. Against 'fun' stands playing to be famous and make money. To have fun is first and foremost associated with being a gang, with solidarity – the famous 'G'. How the

Bamse: I think that more and more people will become Christian. The way the world is today and . . . everything will, the world's going under. So people will want protection somewhere, yeah [. . .] You get so when you get into puberty that you think about death, what it is and 'What am I?' You should do something with your life, you know.

Bamse: It really is a fantastic group. I wish we . . . were younger [laughs]. It just flows.

Bamse: The idea was that they'd ditch him. But then we changed that, me and Finn, to ditch – we don't want that word in this group. Even if it takes time to learn, you know from the beginning, everything [...] But it's better we learn together, all of us.

music sounds is less important; instead, the band members stress the joy of collective creativity. Especially Bamse promotes 'developing together', and asserts that it was he and Finn who saw to it that Bobo came into the group.

The ideology of solidarity can be seen as a response to previous experience of playing in bands. It can also be seen in relation to the individuals' technical expertise, which was not very advanced in the beginning.

The group member more capable than the others was Bamse (and to a degree, Micke). So when Bamse advocates keeping together and learning together, he is speaking from a leading position as an instrumentalist, a position of power which he doubtless has good grounds for maintaining. But when, for example, Kurre agrees, and repeatedly celebrates 'G', he is expressing another, and deeper, dependence on the group. The group is *his* instrument: he neither saw himself then nor sees himself now as principally a guitar player. So regardless of one's position in the internal hierarchy, there was a strong interest in a solidaristic ideology.

It is no accident that we contrast Kurre with Bamse. They soon became the moving forces of the band, and in their persons the antagonisms within the group were crystallised. Against Bamse's technical lead, Kurre had something which in time turned out to his advantage: his wealth of ideas, his absolute commitment to the band, and perhaps most of all, a superior social competence – what the others called, not without a trace of envy, his 'big mouth'. During his time in OH, Bamse managed neither to acquire any of Kurre's diplomacy nor to prioritise the group to the same degree. On the contrary, he was gradually isolated, and as we shall see, was perceived as increasingly unreliable. His attempt to combine OH with a steady relationship, a job and evening classes (part of his plan to become a parish assistant) was mistrusted by the others. Both the church and his girlfriend took a great deal of time and energy. When Bamse – and Bobo, who also had a girlfriend and was continually unsure of his place in the band – left rehearsals at 11, the rest stayed on. The schism was not lessened by Bamse and Bobo's orientation towards traditional rock, whereas Kurre and the others based their ideas on having their 'own style'. Nor was the conflict resolved by Bamse and Bobo's submitting to

Bamse: It was Kurre I think that put me down. And I couldn't let that asshole do that. So I got myself going on the guitar, got good on it, and he got himself togetherness and togetherness won the day [...] It means more. I was the one who was stupid there, who didn't realise it.

Kurre: We say we're going to have fun, right? We're going to have a helluva good group feeling, togetherness, first.

the majority taste within OH and playing hard rock on the side in a hobby band, which is what they did for a time.

Initially Bamse's engagement in the church and his girl-friend had a positive effect: both directed him towards lyrics with serious messages. This went well with the punk tradition which had been absorbed by the others. Music was viewed as a weapon, a way to mediate feelings and ideas to others, and a way to influence people. Songs should be about something, should have a message – this was mandatory in OH. But after ideas on music as a potential career took root in the band, Bamse was trans-formed into a nit-picking crank. This development can (with a certain amount of corroboration from the mem-bers themselves) be described in three phases.

The first period, from the band's formation to Ludde's arrival as a synth player in spring 1985, covered about one year. During this time OH developed greatly, performed a bit and introduced a new sound: in autumn 1984 the band tested out pitting the guitars against a synth. But not until Ludde joined the band did the synth acquire a prominent role. Their progress prompted Kurre, among others, to imagine a future for OH as rock musicians. The conflicts in the band were under control.

During the second period, which ended with Bamse's leaving the band in January 1986, the synth was estab-lished as an indispensable element in what began to be the 'OH sound'. Increasing technical skill fortified dreams of a future in music for several members. Their efforts led to their first demo tape in the summer of 1985; it also led to conflicts in the band becoming acute – to the extent that Ulf was called in to try to settle them. A 'we four' attitude arose when Ludde joined those who stayed on late after rehearsals: if Finn were to realise his dream of playing bass and singing, the band could dispense with both Bobo and Bamse. However, the 'G' ideology was still strong enough to counter such temptations. Instead, Ludde fell to the attractions of a dance band, which did not work out with OH's rehearsal schedule. In December he was replaced by a new keyboard player, Moltas.

During the third period, OH became more ambitious and more professional. Without Bamse's lead and solo guitar, the sound and division of labour were changed so that the synth mainly dominated during the songs, the

Second . . . the lyrics should be good, like they should be about something, not that 'Oh I love him true' and so on.

Kurre: Before, when Bamse was with, in the beginning, let's say the first year, the first year and a half, then, you know, there wasn't as much, there wasn't as much going on, like not much going down, yeah, not so much playing maybe either and . . . so you had more time to talk about other things, yeah? So you talked a lot more . . .

song-writing was increasingly left to Finn, and Kurre became the band's undisputed leader. Subjects such as love, banned from the repertoire after the songs that Finn and Bamse contributed were put on ice, were again available. In spring 1986, OH made their second demo, this time assisted by a producer. This was a decisive step, considering the fact that DIY had always been a cornerstone of their ideology, which explained the absence of covers in their repertoire. At the time of writing (autumn 1986), OH has won for itself a position in the rock scene in Helsingborg and performed in a few places outside their native city. This has involved increasing administration and PR tasks, which have come to occupy time in the attic discussions and, to an extent, overshadowed discussions of the type that Kurre listed in the introductory citation from *A vile presentation of 1985*. In short, OH is entering the field of rock; but this does not mean that the band has lost all contact with its previous ideals or that this development is devoid of conflict.[7]

THE OH CULTURE

As implied in the introduction, there is not much difference between OH on and off stage. Their stage dress basically consists of spiffing up their ordinary clothes – a slouch hat, a skullcap, a leather jacket. Communication with the public has gradually become more relaxed and non-authoritarian, and been given more weight. You have the impression that some of us common mortals have happened to go up on stage and take up instruments: for the sake of comparison, a Bruce Springsteen image of ordinary boys from the working class. In private, the boys seem open, pleasant, easy to get into contact with – in short, 'good guys' – which is exactly the impression they give on stage.

BEING YOURSELF

To 'be yourself' is important for the members of OH, but it is difficult. One must 'find oneself', acquire an acceptable identity, and defend oneself against threats like the 'herd mentality' (Finn) and the need 'to be seen' (Bamse). One of OH's songs, *The Rain*, is about being dependent – how easily people bend with the wind, bow to the dictates of fashion. For OH the risk of such submission is constantly present. The rock scene easily supplies examples of idols who suddenly start to perform in order to get known and make money, betraying their ideals to become commercialised in a way reminiscent of a natural law.

Initially OH also experienced another tendency in the rock world as problematic, namely, the expansion of technology. Playing was seen as a craft and linked to the concert form. Music should be heard in the here and now, played before an audience. Music is the result of what you manage to do with refractory material. You should not be able to fake or hide what you are behind computer programming and therefore several members of OH initially distrusted synthesisers. The strongest purists were those members most influenced by a traditional working-class socialisation, Bobo and Bamse. Kurre also distanced himself from music technology, but in his case, distrust was more associated with a 'humanistic' fear of the cold, dead, the inhuman, which relates to his pessimism about the future.

The member of the group who had the greatest problem with 'finding himself' was Bamse. His reflections on his development – with its elements of delinquency, smoking dope, etc. – concern a phase in which he was almost exclusively trying 'to be seen'. He regards his father's illness and death, meeting his girlfriend, and his contact with the church as providing the impulse to strive consciously towards 'becoming an adult'. However, a similar struggle may be traced in the others. Finn also smoked dope for a time; it taught him how vulnerable he was to group pressure. But when he succeeded in quitting by himself, he also learned something about his own resources. Self-discipline is a concept that means a great deal to him now. Bobo has had difficulties coming to terms with his physical image. On stage, he gives an impression of inertia, for which he has suffered some shame. It also tends to frighten people when such a large figure is combined with long hair, patched jeans and a motorcycle. Nonetheless, Bobo defends his style. Micke's proven 'indolence' is clearly connected with both bonds to and contradictory demands

Kurre: If you've seen on TV when they showed the time before Frankie Goes to Hollywood, when they began as a band, they began like any old bloody band. It's just they've developed, they've given in to development.
Bobo: I don't like it, I think it's wrong. Yeah, I do . . . it should be drums, real drums, real bass and real guitars. [. . .] I don't like it when a machine does all those instruments.

Bamse: People who want to be seen all the time, you don't pay any attention to those people. And then I tried, I tried to impress her, do things, show how tough I was, show how much I could drink. Then she said, 'Oh, how tough you are', she said, 'It's childish to drink.' So I never did it again. Later it was a bit difficult. But then, one day I was myself, suddenly. Then she began to like me.

Ulf: Umm – is it a specially important dimension, what you're talking about, a good psyche and that [. . .]?
Finn[emphatically]: I think it's

bloody important today, it's just crucial. Because it's typical today, this 'Take care of yourself.' And if you can't, well, you can't reckon on any help.

Kurre: I don't want to meet a chick at a disco, I want to meet someone when I'm out travelling, when I'm in France or . . . When I'm out playing somewhere or when I'm working, or whatever shit I do, go to school – anyway, meet a chick in a normal situation. It's such a bloody cattle market at the discos.

Kurre's mother: To be honest, it doesn't matter if you go around in the most expensive car, the most expensive caravan, all that stuff, it doesn't interest me. [. . .] What I think is important is that you're healthy and [. . .] that you relate to each other and . . .

from his parents. And Kurre, finally, who on the surface seems to be the one with the most stable identity, has fought many hard battles for the right to be a bit odd and still be accepted.

In short, there are efforts to be authentic in OH, which also set their stamp on sexual roles and the group's language. OH members collectively have dissociated themselves from the ostentatious masculinity of most other working-class males their age. Sex is subordinated in the word 'co-habitation'. The 'inner' in general is asserted at the expense of the physical and 'outer', but this does not exclude a keen awareness of and a certain amount of experimenting with the impression that hairstyles and clothes makes on others. Signs of material success are rather uninteresting. Traces of the influence of the church youth group are not irrelevant here: to take responsibility, stand for what one believes in and not only look after oneself are, according to the youth leader, important precepts which the church wants to convey. However, the same leader has underlined that the church youth recruits many young people who are already seekers and who concern themselves with existential questions.[8] And as regards Kurre and Micke, who had the least connection with the church, it is easy to see that similar precepts were mediated by their families. Kurre's mother cares about life quality, and even if Micke's father gave his son contradictory messages, they included being honest and caring about others.

POWER AND POWERLESSNESS

Finn: I think it's good that we have someone who's like a real mover. It can be difficult, like Kurre's always pushy, the 'Oh, oh, oh' thing, a real pain. But it's good too, 'cause when Kurre hurt his hand, then it was like nothing got done. You know, like 'What should we play now,' and 'What's happening' and that. Kurre, he's like our engine.

Actually, *self-determination* would be a more appropriate term than power; the 'power' OH strove for was rather the power to rule themselves within reasonable limits. One side of this has already been mentioned: power is *inter alia* to model oneself after an ideal. Power is also, of course, to be able to set others in motion, to influence by means of a combination of music and words. However, in this respect, their aspirations have waned. On the surface, only Bamse seems to have had – and abandoned – dreams of being a star. The aim is 'to be able to live on music', which is hard enough in practice, certainly not to reach for the moon. In fact, already by 1985 the group had rejected an, admittedly bad, offer of a record contract.

This pragmatic realism also suffuses the group's internal democracy. During the period when solidarity ruled, no leader should exist – 'who has written that song? *We* have.' Two of them who were at odds with each other actually did write a song together, but it did not work very well. Kurre's later assumption of leadership seemed to be a relatively painless process.

In general, OH associate power with the collective; as the message in the song *One Hand Beats Five Fingers* tells us, the first person singular is not strong. Here one can detect a melding of several different influences. The idea is central in the church and equally, albeit more defensively, in traditional working-class ideology. Moreover, it is probably experienced as an everyday truth by youth groups all over the world. Musically, one could claim that OH learned to make a virtue of necessity. No particularly prominent instrumentalist has ever established himself in the band, but the band can 'play up to' seemingly better equipped competitors in concerts through their ability to sound good as a group – and communicate with the public.

Their rehearsal quarters, as we have seen, are considered by the band as a symbolic expression of autonomy. The Barn represents, at least up to the band's third, hard-working phase, a refuge, a space without heavy everyday demands, but also a place for self-chosen activities. If 'do it together' is one of OH's maxims, 'do it yourself' is another – words, music, arrangements, style. Neither can participating in externally organised activities – playing club football, going to discotheques, dance or guitar classes – be compared with creating one's own music or with other, equally informal, activities.

At first, the band's quarters meant, among other things, an imaginary liberation from parents. During the documentation of this book, everyone in OH except Finn began to work; they became economically independent, their real autonomy increased. Still a student, Finn's conflicts over 'doing the right thing for oneself' were conducted with his parents as opposite party until, in the autumn of 1986, he acquired another form of autonomy through obtaining his own digs. To Micke, economic

Bamse: If they didn't, if they didn't follow my line, then I got angry. But they have, it's the church that's changed me on that, it's Hans [parish assistant] who's impressed on me that 'You . . . are a little shit, you can't just do what you want.'

Ulf: But is music more important than football?
Micke: Oh yeah [. . .] Much, as we . . . with football, you don't do anything more than practise and pay your member-ship fee and play matches. It's like got nothing to do with yourself. Here, we've got our place and you do your thing, and . . . here we are, in the group we're like bosses, we're all bosses, if you know what I mean – we decide things a little.

Kurre: When we play football at home now – I do that almost every night. So the telephone rings, could be the kids next door, little nippers – not more than 8, 10, 12. 'Hello, want to play football?' 'Hell, yes', I say, 'sure I'll come and play football.' And my Dad's there, and my brother, and apart from we three big oafs it's just kids, the rest.

'The starvation in the world/curls into your living-room/You turn your TV off/ And you keep wondering all the night'
        from *Like the Night*.

Kurre: I want – even if I had zero IQ, I can be something, right? So I think everybody should have a chance. You should never – those that have an idea – you should never oppress them and their idea.

independence is especially important as it takes the wind out of some of his father's criticism. Otherwise, jobs mean rather little to the boys in OH: they are primarily a safety net in case the boys do not become musicians. Jobs mean that one has a place in society.

In the interviews with the band members, it has been difficult to detect any particular anxiety about their personal futures. However, consciousness about worldwide problems – starvation, war, environmental destruction – has always been near the surface. The song lyrics are different. Although the problems of the world are very much present, they sometimes seem to be images for other problems closer to home. Also, some of the lyrics depict rather more manageable problems – marginalised people, the falsely accused, prisoners, the draft, the lonely . . . One song, *Toni's*, delves into the breach between major injustices that circumvent the law and small misdemeanors that are immediately punished. In most of the lyrics, society is portrayed as a capricious, impersonal power. Identification is with the victims in a manner that has strong links with punk. The mixture of aggressiveness and melancholy conveyed by the 'OH sound' clearly also suggests that the group's belief in the possibilities of controlling their own fate is, to put it mildly, wavering.

The 'victim' songs attest to an ability to empathise with others. Especially with Kurre, who has strongly influenced the band's repertoire, there are hints of a connection between empathy and an ideology of tolerance anchored in the personal experience of being a victim of circumstances.

US AND THEM

Bobo: I almost think it was the togetherness [. . .] If we can't get along then we can't get any response from the audience and we can't be famous. Everything depends on it.

In the middle of 1986, OH still thought of itself as a gang, not as a group of musicians – 'a bunch . . . who gets along well together' (Kurre). The project they shared was to convey a message, to have fun or be able to live on music; for most of the band, all this was inseparable from the group. Only Micke might conceive of a separate career if he got a very good offer, and during the time Bamse was separated from the band, he made his longing to return movingly clear.

'We' are first and foremost the group – which contains

your best mates and in which you can be yourself and just enjoy. Intimacy is considered the foundation of music-making. Apart from music OH no longer functions as a group; the members associate mostly in pairs, which leaves out Bobo somewhat. The converse seems equally true: group cohesion presumes music, or in any case, a common project. Security in the group has not been equally established for all; Finn and Bobo especially have felt the lash, and as late as at the time of Bamse's departure from the group, Bobo felt an old threat of dismissal in the air. Cohesion has required a certain amount of hocus-pocus – talk about solidarity, Kurre's pep talks, his biographical notes on the group, the psychological charge of their Barn, etc. OH do not boast about how good the band is, at least not in my presence. It is their solidarity, their sharing rather than their musical performance which is inflated.

I think this is symptomatic – and important. It would be wrong to reduce the ideology of solidarity to a defence mechanism in the service of musical progress and to ignore the fact that this ideology satisfies deep individual needs for closeness and security. To OH, the concept of solidarity is coupled with other concepts in such a way that the idealised group represents a sort of model for the world. Solidarity is contrasted with egoism, faction and isolation; the latter encompasses two main representations, 'Svensson' (the grey, ordinary 'Smiths' of this world) and the outcasts. The majority of OH members consider their parents' generation to be 'Svenssons' who live in their prescribed routines, chary of too much socialising outside the family, and who have lost all links to their own youth. Kurre particularly emphasises gaps in biographical continuity, much in the same way as he accuses certain bands of betraying their ideals. The positive alternative consists of the here and now, the teenage years with their expansive network of friends and opportunities. In short, there is a great fear of growing up – at least in the 'wrong way' (Kurre).

This fear also affects relations with the opposite sex. On the one hand, the boys in OH do not want superficial sexual relations; on the other, each relationship contains threats – to the group and of a premature future as a 'Svensson'. Membership of OH requires that the group comes first: 'A girl cannot replace our group. You have my

Kurre: Mmm [laughter] I couldn't have said it better myself. That's right. I've never thought of it, but there's a lot in it. Like we are towards others maybe when we're on a gig, with other bands – you know, we never do shit for anybody.

Finn: Yeah, I wouldn't cope. Like he has practically nobody, no mates to be with. He never goes out, you know. Nor does his mother, but when they go out they go together. It's really boring as both have had lots of mates here in Sweden, in Helsingborg, when they were young.

Kurre: I've a helluva – I've almost too many mates. I had a party the other day and there were 40 people . . . I invited 30 [. . .] but I could just as well have invited a hundred, I can tell you.

Finn: I'm a very good psy-chiatrist, I think [giggle] as I often listen to people's problems [. . .] I see myself as a good 'catcher in the rye' I guess you'd say.

word on that' (Kurre). For these reasons, a girl in the group is inconceivable.

When this single-sexed 'G' is projected onto the world, the vision is one of humanity living in peace, justice and democracy. It is more a Christian than a political image. Most of the band members totally dissociate themselves from (party) politics, but this does not preclude strong objections to the 'Tories'. Kurre has the broadest political perspective, but then he also has a legacy from his 'red' grandparents to preserve.

OH's solidarity is directed downwards in world society; it may be quite simply expressed in terms of a working-class dichotomy ('them up there – us down here'). However, solidarity associates a better world less with struggle than with help. To help, or 'share' is an important concept in the band; thus, for example, the New York female band, Unknown Gender, can be labelled as 'egotists' because they play such 'difficult' music. As has been mentioned, OH have their own 'Band Aid' in the form of contributions to a church charity. Other concrete expressions of solidarity are found in the song lyrics.

The group itself is one of the 'we's in the songs. This 'we' often demarcates its distinctiveness; a typical example is 'We gonna be/someone who can care' in the chorus of the song, *The Rain*, which is about daring to stand on one's own two feet. 'Them' here corresponds to people in general, a reference which remarkably often has negative tones. Otherwise, 'them' refers to the representatives of power – politicians, the police, the courts, the military, the rich; in these cases, 'we' stands for the people, the poor, or the young. *Too Young* concerns a young American who is forced to go to Vietnam and lands in conflict with his fellow soldiers – one of many characteristic victims in OH's songs. However, victims can also be depicted exter-nally, for instance the subject of *Streetman*:

> A woman and a child were walking on that street
> and the child asked who's that man
> The mother said as mothers say:
> 'Beware my child and don't go there.'
> And don't you ever dare go near such a man
> 'cos that stinking man is just a streetman.

With OH's own entrance into the adult world, the per-spective becomes somewhat changed. Their views of the older generation, for example, become more positive, and sexual relations less threatening. There is quite a distance between the 'fat cats who destroy our world' in *Toni's* and *Words of Wisdom* from 1986:

> The elder and the dead keep telling us
> words of wisdom
> If anyone should know it's they, they've
> been through it

ORDER AND CHAOS

In OH's later music the synth is a prominent part of the sound. Under the pure synth sounds scratches Kurre's distorted guitar: the beautiful should rise above the raw. To me this also indicates a shift in the group's world view – a gradual emphasis on control. In the early OH the borders between acting out and musical composition were more indeterminate, and as long as Bamse was in the band, he stood for an element of 'party' – spontaneity and rawness in the music, particularly in his solos. The beautiful and the raw, the disciplined and the wild were pitted against each other without either one really winning. Today, OH is a band that 'tinkers around', which is more about 'working on' – letting many small bits run together into a single flow – than about 'giving all'.

This change doubtless reflects the band members' growing up, but in fact OH have never been a disorderly group. Many times I have been surprised at the discipline at rehearsals. What I have seen resembles work more than play: jam sessions have been few and far between. There is much greater orderliness in their Barn than in other groups' quarters. The disruptive factor, the group's *enfant terrible*, was Bamse. When he left, musical aggression was relegated to a place where presumably most of the rest of the group had long wanted it. Aggressiveness is still admitted as a necessity in the group's artistic *gestalt*, but in their world picture it is purely associated with a threat to central values such as solidarity and peace: it is associated with destructiveness and war. Losing self-control exposes one to evil, to chaos. Aggression is a feeling that must be suppressed. Hence OH are openly against violence, and in

Kurre: I can't get it into my head why people can't agree [. . .] If I really think about it – I mean that's the point, that it should be spread to everybody. Everybody should be . . . yeah, not have this [. . .] warring in themselves.

Micke: When I got beaten up – in school, for instance, there was this idiot who stood with his leg outstretched and I tripped over it, and he kicked me from behind, and then I turned and asked what he was doing, right? Got angry but not like over the top, yeah? And then he hit me, punched out a tooth, here. But most of the rest had got up and knocked him down, or at least tried [...] but I just went away.

Micke: We're [...] not really like – yeah, lots of people aren't like us. But anyway, like that stuff in school, if you know what I mean, standing there and yelling, 'Wow, check out those tits and ...' [...] I never hear such stuff at our place and I think that's great.[...]

Bobo: Of course, if you pass by a chick who [inaudible], sure you look, but you don't think 'Cripes, like to have that one in bed' or suchlike.

Kurre: You sort of ... sometimes I get this feeling when I watch Finn sing, yeah? When he gets like this perfect ... sound ... Hollers out something that's so bloody good with all the rest, right? And it's like ... 'Christ, you're good.' You know, together ... its ... catching each other's eye, like keeping contact the whole time. And after we rap, it's like, 'Bloody hell, that was good.' It's all feelings. And I think I show those feelings best with a guitar across my navel.

Finn[laughing]: Yeah, it was during my first communion which we had there at the camp. And it was, yeah, you were just filled. [laughs] Yeah, it's hard to describe. You know, like when you play guitar and you get a super sound. It feels like that, your whole body trembles and you feel it's all wonderful.

Micke: It shouldn't look put on either.

Kurre: No, but it isn't either. It starts with doing a show, right, that's a demand, but it goes over into feelings. It's pure feelings.

the song *Last Fight*, even against boxing. Bobo experiences his image as problematic because he does not wish to be assumed to be a 'fighter', and Finn strives for a 'strong psyche', which he associates with ju-jitsu training, among other things. Micke's inability to react aggressively can take on masochistic elements and transform him into a veritable victim. And Kurre has never 'hit' anyone; instead has learned to curb, to 'chew on' his anger so that he does nothing he normally would not want to do. Verbal aggression too tends to be repressed, at least in my presence.

However, discipline takes its toll. Both Finn and Micke, even Kurre, have had reason to wonder whether the price they have had to pay for their musical success has not been too high. There is also a perceptible longing to give way, to have the courage to fall into the opposite, into 'pure feeling'. In the early interviews, band members several times described ecstatic experiences in playing. A reggae number, *Oh Yea*, introduced to the band by the church youth members, Finn and Bamse, expresses just such an experience ('When I dance God touches me'), coloured by rasta religion. On another occasion, Finn drew a parallel between being 'filled by Jesus' and a guitar sound. OH's later, more elaborated music hardly allows any surprises; instead, the demand for 'acting-out' increasingly has been satisfied by stage performances. 'We want to be more than anything else, the best live band in Helsingborg' (Kurre). Kurre especially seems to dream of a coalescence between show and authentic experience, but this assumes mastery of one's instrument. 'Ego-tripping under the aegis of the collective' could describe this side of the band's efforts.

Thus, to OH, playing rock music is to navigate between Scylla and Charybdis, to be able to control oneself but not too much – to avoid becoming 'stiff as a poker' (criticism of Bobo) or a 'lemon' (criticism of Micke) on stage. At the same time, this voyage symbolises another, greater problem in the band. The boys want to be neither outcasts nor 'Svenssons', and further education is not the most attractive alternative right after eleven years in school, not to speak of the economic consequences of that alternative. To be a rock musician is a tempting solution as it involves 'side-stepping', living unconventionally, but remaining part of the community – even being celebrated. In addition, you increase your prospects of ensuring autobiographical continuity and remaining young if you can drag your mates along. It is not surprising that a career in rock music has had such magnetism for working-class youth, who have had difficulties adapting themselves both to educational institutions and to a future in their fathers' footsteps. Kurre, OH's driving force, is in essence one such 'working-class freak'.

STYLE

APPEARANCE

> Kurre's clothes today: trainers, white sports socks, a white band tied in the wide space between trouser leg and socks on one leg, jeans made of at least two pairs – the bottom green and the top faded blue – sewn together with various patches, including a white patch on the crotch, belt of jeans denim, an *ace* attached on the right buttock, a white T-shirt and over it a blue shirt in blanket-like cloth, with cut-off arms, a white 'scarf' with a little hard knot at the throat, and a green beret (interview, summer 1984).

Like many other youth, OH are very conscious of 'image' – the impression one makes on others. One's appearance may be shaped; one's appearance is a language. When asked in 1986 how he viewed his former rebel role, Kurre responded by beginning to talk about hairstyle and clothes on the same level of seriousness that he discusses his ideas.

In the beginning of our acquaintanceship, Kurre's dress, as described above, gave somewhat contradictory messages, more or less summarised by 'a young man in rags'. We normally associate rags with poverty, but poverty also usually implies slovenliness. We do not first and foremost associate poverty with youth, and so the experience of symbolic dress among the young leads us to believe that the poverty must be feigned. But why should anyone pretend to be poor? The dress code activates a myth of normality while at same time it criticises this myth. 'In Sweden there is no poverty' is one such myth which is questioned by Kurre. What is provocative in the code lies in its seeming to assert that the material prosperity that 'Svensson' is so proud of is in fact hollow or meaningless: it is not what counts.

Kurre: Maybe I'm a nicer rebel, not one of these RRR rebels, now I can formulate more . . . what I think than I could then. Then it was only 'I don't give a shit' and then, you know, I'd turn around and stick out my ass with the ace on it and go like that. [. . .] But I got my driver's licence in the end.

Micke: No, I'm like generally interested in clothes, if I may

say so. And I feel like shit –
what shall I say, when people
go out wearing sleaze – it's
enough, you know, if you have
a pair of awful shoes, to make
you feel insecure. So it means a
lot actually.

However, the individual signs in the code, the details or
accessories, do not point in exactly the same direction.
Kurre's beret, for example, has both military and
bohemian connotations. Like the cloth band on his leg, the
scarf seems pointless; possibly it is meant as a sarcastic
comment on ties or a part of a uniform. Some of the
signs are not distinguishing, for instance, the T-shirt and
trainers, which are worn by a large number of youth with
very diverse cultural backgrounds. Neither is Kurre's dress
as a whole punk's antithetical bricolage: the code's syntax
is based rather on shifts of meaning. His clothes accentuate class as deviance (lumpenproletariat/bohemian) and
imply militancy – a covert threat. It is, in his own words,
a rebel image.

Two years later, this rebel has begun to dress more normally and on stage, has exchanged his beret for a 'cult'
black slouch hat. In general, he has inclined more towards
the bohemian and toned down the lumpenproletarian and
militant. Parallel with OH's proceeding into rock, Kurre
started to become fascinated with the external attributes
of 1980s aestheticism.

Apart from the militant overtones, Kurre represents the
group's development. This means that there are still limits
to how far adaptation to normality can go. If one of
the limits is suits, another is short hair. What long hair
actually means to OH is difficult to say; at a guess, self-
determination, youth, nature, sensuality. But it is no uniform. Micke has always cultivated a more conformist
image – the 'enemy within', so to speak.

INTERACTION

Bamse: Also there's the fact that
I'm bloody negative to Boom
Boom [Bobo], 'cause he stands
there like a bloody fig tree
[laughter]. Now when we play
on Tuesday, if he doesn't move
himself, I'm going to go right
up and kick his balls and stand
and poke him and that. He
should be clear about that.

Kurre: No one says that to
Finn, I could say it, like

Boys usually wrestle, fight, pretend to attack each other as
part of their normal relations. Such physical aggression
hardly ever occurs in OH; it is replaced by verbal and
musical actions. As might be expected, only Bamse cannot
really control his impulses. On one occasion, he furtively
set fire to a few loose threads in the normally tolerant
Kurre's jeans right in the middle of a group discussion.
However, usually Bamse compensates for his rhetorical
inferiority with his guitar and a sharp heavy metal pedal,
his 'grater' (Finn). Several times when I was present,

Bamse used a rehearsal for his own purposes, for example, practising riffs whenever he felt the urge upon him, or trying to gain attention by doing something totally out of place on the guitar. Verbally Bamse is also different: he picks at the others and is sexually more outspoken. Otherwise, much criticism is mild or left unsaid; improving one's singing or getting a new instrument is up to oneself. Bamse's sexual relations seemingly also lead to open confrontation more often than do the others'.

These differences contain elements of class conflict. Bamse has grown up in a fairly traditional, patriarchal working-class family, under conditions favouring an aggression that settles things. In OH this inherited rigidity confronts the flexibility of a more modern, mobile social stratum that stands with one foot in the working-class and the other slightly higher. These young people's behaviour is 'softer'; they do not exaggerate their masculinity, they are often articulate and have a 'feminine' ability to talk about feelings within the single-sex confines of the group. They are not interested in discotheque 'cattle markets' and seek contacts with girls under 'normal' circumstances, that is, circumstances in which no one tries to be anything other than what he/she is – and they stress the importance of being able to trust each other in a relationship.

The group's argot has changed somewhat since its inception. Initially, verbally expressed insights into others were not always on par with actions. Bamse probably had good grounds for worrying that someone would quit because such 'gross language' could be used in the group: for instance, Micke had to tolerate being called 'spag' ('spaghetti'). Coarse jokes, sometimes with racist overtones, were not that rare. In time, the group humour developed in a lighter, more absurd, *Black Adder* direction, which sometimes broke through on stage. As the introduction indicates, the group idiom is often imaginative, witty, concrete and exact, tending towards the physical, and in writing, rather disdainful of formal rules. Sometimes it gets lost in spontaneous extravaganzas:

> *Kurre:* I can't tell the difference between this and ZZ Top, and Tottas Bluesband, and Bengts Bluesband and Svens Bluesband, and ZZ Down and ZZ Up, and . . . Sven-Ingvars Bluesband, and . . . Blues a la Bengt [general laughter]. Yeah, for it is verily all the same *crap*.

kidding, 'Now you damn well get a good mike,' right? It's only a joke and we all laugh. But – he does it anyway because he wants to. We don't pressure each other.

Finn: It's just that, you're frightened both of hurting her and yourself.
Kurre: You don't only hurt yourself when you do it, you hurt her too, but you feel it most.
Finn: It hurts you most. And it's like you go along and . . . you feel like shit and get full of anxiety and that.

As usual in long-standing groups, there is a tendency in OH towards fixed roles, which the boys are very aware of. For example, Micke is called (rather justifiably) 'the UN'. In his own eyes, he is a 'pessimist and realist' and recognises that to an extent he is Kurre's shadow. Finn is the freedom-loving 'mum', the religious and psychological expert; Kurre is naturally the 'father', and Bamse, the *enfant terrible*, the black sheep. Micke a big brother and Bobo a truculent 'Benjamin', the family picture is complete. For a time, Bamse had no place in the group, and the others sometimes find the roles problematic, but they seem to have learned to live with them.

MUSIC

MUSICAL TASTE

As one might expect, OH members listen to music a lot – on the radio, TV and recordings. However, they seldom go to concerts and when they do, it is to performances of less known, most often local bands. Proximity to larger arenas like Copenhagen is not usually taken advantage of. It would seem as if OH use concerts mainly to compare themselves with others who are on about the same level.

Possibly excepting Micke, no one in the band is much of a dancer, though informal dancing will occur at private parties, less often at discotheques. In Kurre's case, as in his learning to play, negative experiences of formal instruction are present here. The band members read the music press only sporadically. Kurre, who tends to look for objects to identify with among rock heroes, is the one who most refers to such reading material.

As listeners, the band members are rather finicky; they pick and choose, even at work. Their listening has something of a dual purpose: music at once functions as a dream factory and as a source of ideas from co-musicians. Finn explains that if something sounds good, they try to figure out how it is done. In such cases, each concentrates on his own instrument – the bassist listens to the bass, etc. This analytical and instrumental listening has gradually become so entrenched that it is sometimes felt like an obligation.

Kurre: No, I don't want to learn it. I quit because I didn't have any of those patent–leather shoes, and you know they didn't like you having gym . . . [. . .] The youth club was *closed* if you didn't go along and dance later. Bloody cheek.

Kurre: One day when I'm at the firm working, right? I begin to listen about half eight [. . .] I put on the radio and listen to the local station first, from Helsingborg. That goes to nine. Then I switch over to P3 and listen to *Radioapparaten* till eleven. Then around eleven to twelve it's usually just crap. Then at twelve the local radio programme *Prairieexpressen* starts, and he plays Björn Lundqvist [. . .]. I listen to

Members of OH also differentiate between types of music for different situations. At a party there should be danceable music, pure and simple, even if one can get 'high as a kite' (Kurre) when something is played that one has a personal relationship to. As goodnight music, a bit of everything can be tolerated. This functional attitude is fairly typical of working-class boys.[9]

The listening interviews that I conducted with OH show that the group's genre spectrum is rather narrow: wider than Lam Gam's but much more limited than Chans'. Experimental music is dismissed, idiosyncracies crop up (against female singers, Mick Jagger's looks, etc.). However, the majority like the hits of Simple Minds and Frankie Goes to Hollywood; their views coincide fairly well – only Bamse differs.

Generally, OH's taste development parallels that of their music. It begins with a quite broad rock base but shifts gradually towards more melodic and elaborated music. From Clash, Alarm, Jimi Hendrix and Def Leppard, the band moves, via U2, towards synth-dominated groups such as Simple Minds, Saga and Toto. On the way, Bamse leaves and Bobo says that he really doesn't know where the impulses for the band's present style come from since he doesn't listen to 'that stuff'. On the other hand, the same pattern has meant that Micke has edged closer to something he was ashamed of in the beginning: a fascination with 'commercial songs like Agneta Fältskog [ex ABBA] puts out'.

that till three, but I work till a quarter to four so I'm bloody unlucky as I get only half an hour, maybe a bit more of *Måndagsspecialen*, one of the best programmes, I think. With Håkan Persson – he plays local bands and such.

Finn: Yeah, it's a bit sick, you know, I can't go to a concert without checking out their equipment, like and 'Ah ha, not quite right there' and that – there it is [...] I regret I ever became a musician [laughter].

OH'S OWN MUSIC

> *Kurre:* I want to do my own thing. I don't want to have to say when they ask, what do you play? Hard rock.

Right or Wrong from spring 1984 was OH's first 'hit'. It opens with an introduction – all OH songs have introductions – in which Bamse's lead guitar plays the main role. The verse builds on a hard-rock riff; in the chorus, straight chords (punk) go out under the song towards two alternating accompanying figures which, like the verses, have a hard-rock sound. The singing is loud, a bit on the shouting side, and succeeds in rising above the guitars.

Kurre: Well, then I thought: 'Those are heavy strings, you can try something brilliant with them.' And so it went [...] Like it sounded so bloody hip that [sings the verse riff], like it went 'here am I dit-di-di-dit, oh it's you,' it was an answer, right?

Give me, give me a reason/why should I believe in you/Take me, take me to prison/But I don't think you know what to do//The judge knows if you're right or wrong (×2)//Leave me, leave me alone/You don't know what it's like/Have you, have you been charged/Charged to, put in jail//The judge knows (etc.)//Why do, why do you look so/Look so boring at me/Do you think it's fun/You don't know what it's like//The judge knows (etc.)//He think he knows/He think he knows. etc. . . .

Kurre: The theme I've had in my head for a long time, that there are people who judge other people, there are people who execute other people, right? Who in the hell says that they've got the right to do that [. . .]? Maybe it's got something to do, maybe from bullying, with why I've been oppressed. Like 'Why me?'

Bamse: OH. It's OH . . .
Kurre: First-class material.
Finn: Helluva war there was around that song. A huge war over the lyrics.
Ulf: What did you fight about then?
Bamse: Everything [. . .]
Kurre: The text is by OH and the song . . . I was going to teach Kokos to play the synth. And I ran some chords and then Finn came, and he said: Shit, that sounds good. So we developed it.

The melody largely follows the basic chords. In addition to the verses and chorus and introduction, *Right or Wrong* includes an instrumental break, a short Bamse solo, middle 8, and coda. Through the defendant's monologue, the English lyrics depict a court scene and smoulders with the same aggressiveness as the music. The object of the aggression is the judge, the autocratic representative of power: 'The judge knows if you're right or wrong'. But the aggression is impotent – the defendant is, in principle, already doomed. *Right or Wrong* is a protest song, played by a rough cellar band with certain ambitions, but the work put into it shows potential.

The song *Just a Dream* occupies a central place in the band's production. It was written six months after *Right or Wrong* and, together with the sing-along song *Toni's*, remained in the repertoire throughout 1986. The raw material for *Right or Wrong* was delivered by Kurre and Micke; the music to *Just a Dream* was written by Kurre alone and the lyrics were, for once, written collectively. At this time (autumn 1985), U2 was the number one band with the members of OH, and this is evident in, among other things, the toning down of the blues element in favour of other traditions. *Just a Dream* uses an ordinary major scale and functional European harmony. Formally, the song is rather less complicated than *Right or Wrong*, but more care has been taken with the arrangement. The song includes percussion backing, harmonising in the chorus and a recitative section. The melodies are beginning to liberate themselves from the basic chord tones, and the presence of a synth indicates that the supremacy of the guitars is broken, even though Bamse still dominates along with the vocalist. Micke's drumming, which would never carry much weight with a rock drummer, combines with the synth to form a pop-style undercurrent. In short, OH is proceeding to abandon its hard core, the unsophisticated blend of punk and hard rock which characterised the band's first period, and to approach that style of their own which Kurre was seeking in the quote at the beginning of this section.

The lyrics of *Just A Dream* open dramatically, depicting a scene in which a white man and a black face execution by a platoon, but are saved at the last minute when peace in the world is declared. According to Kurre, the song was inspired by a Tintin album. It is not uncommon for OH to search for material among the media – from the news to other rock music. The story consists of a monologue related by one of the freed prisoners – also representative of OH. Very few OH songs are lyrical or refer directly to their own experiences; projections such as *Right or Wrong* or *Just a Dream* are the norm. Gradually, it is all shown to be a dream, a revelation conveyed in recitative – a finesse for the sake of emphasis. The final verse establishes the song's protest-song character when the narrator/group turns to the audience: 'Let's make this real/Come on!' Such direct appeals are, of course, expressions of the desire to 'mediate' and influence, but they occur so often in OH's production that one might wonder if they do not also stand for a fundamental contextual idea.

The history of *Just a Dream* indicates an unusual amount of work on the lyrics. OH's school English, prevailing in all but three of their songs, has its faults, but the story hangs together and the message is conveyed partly through rhyme and the repetition of the key word, 'together' in the chorus. What makes the lyrics special, however, is the use of antitheses: dreams are contrasted with reality, black with white, war with peace, the present with memories. Over half of the twenty-four OH songs examined have been composed around such pairs of opposites (one–all, men–women, the people–the powers-that-be, etc.), but none really resembles *Just a Dream*. I would connect its uniqueness with what I mentioned above, namely, that it is their only truly collectively produced lyric.

Micke: There's something else too [with *Just a Dream*], sort of hidden, you might say – it's our lives too. At least I think so.

The semantic function of antitheses is confirmed to the degree that it reveals given and seemingly irreconcilable differences which accentuate clarity in a way that 'belongs in a dualistic, static and theological universe', in contrast to, for example, paradoxes.[10] However, it is true that the antitheses in *Just a Dream* seem to strive after the paradox's levelling of differences in a tension-filled unity. If black and white join together to fight for freedom, the dream and reality, then and now, will merge. In other lyrics the oppositions are maintained so that the antitheses acquire a subjectively clarifying function in line with the group's 'realism'. Here it is more a question of 'sharing' a common daydream:[11] a vision in which freedom takes on the character of a vague, symbiotic coalescence.

I first heard *The Rain*, which also became something of a hit, on OH's demo cassette from the summer of 1985. It is a peculiar song, reminiscent of film music, despite the fact that as usual the words were written last. The sound has changed further, so that, along with the singing, the synth is most prominent. Bamse does not have his obligatory solo. In this sense, *The Rain* anticipates the third period's emphasis on a dominant synth, pitted against the punk elements of a distorted guitar, or doubling the guitar part. In *The Rain* OH play synth rock for the first time. If one includes the rest of the songs on the demo, it is evident that the genre spectrum has narrowed. The uniformity also applies to tempos and song length.

The Rain was written by Micke, Kurre and Finn – an increasingly common combination. Ludde comes in on the drums when Micke plays the synth. The demo version begins with a synth glissando, followed by a recurrent interlude of the verse chords (A and G), a triad, which is also played on the synth. After the song verse, there is a repeated middle 8 with a sound-painting character, which is moderated by a figure on a damped guitar. The chorus is based on heavy beats that break against the quiet, lyrical and melancholy character of the verse and middle 8. In one of the interludes the synth spreads a shimmer of sound while the guitars are silent. In general, efforts to achieve dynamics are very marked. Tension is only partly bound up with differences between the formal sections; it has been built into the total sound.

The singing also sounds more professional. Finn's assertion of his importance for the so-called OH sound has a certain validity. He produces the melody lines which, with his stress on descending motifs, contribute greatly to the melancholic ground tones (the band members think it sounds a bit gloomy sometimes). Also, the song has acquired a leading role; Finn performs like some sort of relaxed shouter who sounds neither caustic nor screechy, but sings legato with a full head sound – just a bit deeper than his idol Bono of U2. The new style favours such a way of singing, but training and investment in technical equipment have also helped: Finn no longer has to scream.

Finn has exercised increasing influence over the words, which has made them more subjective. *In The Rain* he cultivates his lyrical gifts. The words are again based on

Ulf: Just this [imitates the glissando in the intro] in the beginning, it could be a change of weather, yeah? It sort of begins to blow, like wind . . .
Kurre: Yeah, that's – hell, we had a wind when we first wrote the song [. . .] When I played it [the triads] on the guitar, he had wind [. . .] So, pssssch and then it came on the guitar. We gave it over to the synth because it sounded too thin on the guitar.
Finn: Yes, I would say it's me [. . .] I have very strange melodies when I sing [. . .], yeah, I'd say that [laughter].

Kurre: Yeah, in minor key. Unfortunately. But there you go, so that's the way it is.

Finn: I was into this period that I wanted to analyse everything, analyse everything from the beginning and paint it all over with comparisons [. . .] And then we rapped, in a way that – I don't remember what it was, it was something, we quarrelled about something, and then it was 'Yeah, you just go along with the tide.' Just like that. In the rain I try to hide away/And in the wind I'll fly away/In the rain, yes, I'll be myself/But in the wind I'd be like someone else/People are like leaves in the wind/No one can stand against the storm/and face the reality/No way, no way//We gonna be! (×3)/Someone, someone who can care//Snow on the mountain tops/It's lying all the year/And the rain is falling from above/And the rain is falling from the sky (×2)//We antitheses, with the oppositions symbolised by natural phenomena – the rain stands for independence, the wind for the 'herd mentality'. Otherwise, lyricism is a rather obscure element in OH's music. The music of *The Rain* reinforces the contrast in the words between verse and chorus; the tone of the verses is pessimistic whereas the tone of the chorus is the opposite. However, this is hardly intentional; it is mainly due to the fact that the chorus is Kurre's and the rest is Finn's.

During my period with OH the band underwent two remarkable development processes. Most of the members ceased to be teenagers and entered into adult working life, and their music changed. It is perhaps appropriate to conclude by speculating on the relationship between these two processes. I think that OH's musical development can only be attributed to personal factors to a certain extent. At least as significant is the role of music in personality development: to OH music functioned as a bridge to the mainstream and established adult attitudes. In the beginning music awakened clear associations with youth, masculinity, the lower strata and deviant subcultures like punk and hard rock. Gradually these associations ceded to broader perceptions of the 'aware young musicians' type, which heavily permeated the texts. The local music scene began to enter the picture and exerted increasing pressure towards professionalism. Yet this is not a direction that is given in the biographies of the individuals; it is very much due to, *inter alia*, the absence of a young counter-authority such as that of the Swedish progressive music movement, punk, or the Ark. It is in the space created by this absence that OH enters into the market, where rebellious elements are considered a burden – at least according to OH's own view of things. Or as the realist Micke explains the producer's role in the group:

> Because . . . I don't think any band – yeah, style-setters can manage themselves, the ones that can change style altogether, they have their style and they break through with that. But if you don't exactly have your own [. . .] well, you have anyway to – it's like with the *Words of Wisdom* – he knows so much more than we do.

gonna be etc.//When the sun is breakin' thru the cloud/and the rain dries from the ground/The wind is still there and we are following it/Following it, yes we are following it//We gonna be [etc.]

Kurre: Yeah, a synth hits the mark better than just a vrrr, a raw guitar, right? Like hard rock, for example, there's a recession in hard rock now. Absolutely not so with . . . rather more synth groups like Toto and Simple Minds.

Ulf: Is there really such competition among Helsingborg bands?

Micke: Oh yeah, there is [. . .] And it seems it's stepping up the whole time . . . Anyway, the only band we have any contact with is Red Hot [. . .] And every time we meet it's 'Have you got a record contract yet?' and 'You'll never get anywhere' and [. . .] Mostly in fun, but still – it's always the same. If one of us ever got a record contract, the other band would probably die [laughter].

Figure 1   OH: Just a Dream

Verse 1 It was nine o'clock, Friday morning / We stood with
our backs against the wall / A military squad with their guns
pointed towards us / The leader screamed: 'Lay on, aim!' /
STOP DON'T SHOOT//
Chorus Together we can fight / We'll make peace over a
night / Together (together) black and white//
Verse 2   (with more guitar and voice)//
Chorus Verse 3 . . .
Chorus (as above) (guitar solo)
[Break (intro)]
Verse 4
Chorus [coda]

NB. Transcriptions only include the melody, solo instrument passages
and certain prominent aspects of the accompaniment. Performances
varied. This version was played during the period of investigation.

Figure 2   OH humour

Hey garlic-head, This is a picture of last year's Christmas party. You are invited to this year's rave up, 21st Dec. See you Sunday.

FROM THE SUBURBS –
LAM GAM

FACTS ABOUT LAM GAM

Name: Lam Gam.
Date of formation: winter 1984/85.
Home: Gothenburg (Sweden's second city, half a million inhabitants, situated on the west coast), in Bergslunden, one of Gothenburg's northern suburbs, with about 12,000 inhabitants. The district mainly contains 8–12-storey blocks built during the 1960s.
Number of members: 6
Line-up: singer, two guitars, bass, drums and synth.
Quarters and instruments: The group shares rehearsal quarters with some other bands in the Ark, a municipally owned youth centre in Bergslunden. One of the members has his own guitar, the others use equipment provided by the municipal recreation department.
Members:
Ola (b. 1969) singer. Father driver, mother part-time shop assistant; both parents emigrated from Norway in the early 1960s. Two-year food technology course at gymnasium. Listens mostly to disco and synth music, but also to Afzelius and Imperiet.
Sigge (b. 1969) guitar. Father factory worker, mother shop assistant. Two-year metalwork course in gymnasium. Listens almost exclusively to hard rock – Scorpions, Whitesnake, etc.
Lollo (b. 1969) guitar. Father sailor, mother unemployed. Two-year metalwork course in gymnasium. Prefers 'straight Swedish rock': Imperiet, Attentat, etc.
Jonna (b. 1969) bass. No contact with father, mother has had a variety of jobs, periodically out of work. Two-year food technology course. Listens to both hard-rock and punk: Iron Maiden, Whitesnake, Ebba Grön, Attentat, etc.
Seppo (b. 1969) drums. Father factory worker, mother cleaner; both parents came to Bergslunden from Finland in the mid-1960s. Two-year food technology course. Hard-rock fanatic: Whitesnake, Scorpions, etc. Is also active in a judo club.
Conny (b. 1969) synth. The only one who does not live in the high-rise blocks around Bergslunden's centre, Conny lives in the area's single-row house neighbourhood. Father a department manager, mother a part-time office worker. Two-year economics course at gymnasium. Listens to almost all rock music, but prefers Swedish punk such as Ebba Grön and KSMB. Is also a successful football and handball player.

AN EARLY MEETING

> What can a poor boy do,
> except to play in a rock'n'roll
> band?
> Jagger and Richards: *Street
> Fighting Man*

It's Sunday, the first of September, and it's ten to five when
I [Ove] park the car outside the youth centre, the Ark.[1] I
have arranged to interview the rock band Lam Gam at five
o'clock. This is my first proper interview, with a tape
recorder and all that. The band rehearses twice a week,
Wednesdays and Sundays. On Wednesdays they are in one
of the Ark's two rehearsal rooms and on Sundays they use
an old abandoned cottage which actually is an annexe of
the youth club in the area. I had been told that the cottage
was 'only a few hundred metres from the Ark – just go along
the path and you can't miss it'. Despite this description, I
can't find it. Only after wandering around residential
blocks and football fields for about half an hour do I finally
arrive at something resembling an old shack. The whole
gang is sitting or lounging in front. 'Oh, there you are, we
thought you'd forgotten us.' There's a new band going to
practise and they're already there, so we decide to go to the
Ark for the interview. During the walk there is a discussion
of what happened during the weekend. Conny, Lollo and
Sigge are the most talkative and say they've been in town
and bought booze from a liquor peddlar. Then they went
to a rock club and 'had a great time', missed the last bus
and had to walk all the way home. Jonna and Seppo don't
say much and seem to have some doubts about the veracity
of the others' bravado. Ola has to go home for a while, but
he promises to come to the Ark soon.

Rather as a joke, I ask if anybody is nervous about the interviews, but I only get sardonic grins in response. Conny peers
at me and says he is 'dead nervous' and that he 'couldn't sleep
all night.' Once again I explain why I want to interview
them, but I hardly get started before Lollo interrupts in a
way that shows that he can't stand hearing all this again.
'Yeah, yeah, it's legit, 'course we'll talk to you.' The
encounters I've had so far with the band have led to good
contacts with Lollo, Conny, Ola and Jonna. Seppo and
Sigge seem a bit more distant; they have never asked what

I'm doing or what I want the interviews for. When I turn to them they are obviously bothered, nod and pretend to understand, look in another direction, or make some sort of move to distract my attention to something else. My relations with them feel difficult, as if I'm pressing myself upon them.

Having arrived at the Ark, which is a detached, single-storey building in the midst of all the high-rises, we find that it is closed. Outside is a gang of boys and girls, possibly fifteen people. 'What the hell, isn't it open?' wonders Lollo. 'No, what d'ya think we're standing here for . . . you fucking nerd?' replies someone in the gang. 'Örjan's supposed to come with the keys at five, but now it's about six so he'll show up soon.' Nobody seems all that upset at having to wait. They chat, smoke, somebody rides around on an old bicycle, others just stare into nothing listening to their Walkmans. A few amuse themselves by target spitting. Clearly this has happened many times before. After ten minutes, however, the boys in Lam Gam start to get a bit restless, a bit nervy on my behalf. Somebody discovers that a window is open. Lollo fixes a few old wooden boxes and a table he's found in an open storage area. With help from Sigge and Jonna, he manages to crawl through the window and then opens the main door with a grin, saying that since he has now fixed it so we can get in, 'it's our job to make coffee.' Before I've even managed to sit down, Jonna has put a cassette in the tape recorder. He points at me, saying 'This is our song I talked to you about.' The whole group gathers around a table, no one says anything, they all listen attentively. Seppo, the drummer, misses a bit after a break and everyone laughs, including Seppo himself. After a while, three boys come up to our table and ask if it's Lam Gam playing on the tape. The band members nod and wait nervously for comments. To Lam Gam's great chagrin the three don't seem very impressed, but extend themselves enough to praise Conny on the synth. 'But if you're gonna be a band, you've gotta do more than just play.' Jonna reacts strongly and directly: 'Don't come here talking shit, your fucking band's crap. You do a couple of fucking Rolling Stones numbers, we play our own music. And, you don't get, you don't understand what we're doing. It's *supposed* to sound like that, understand!' There's no further discussion; the three go off to another table and take out a deck of cards.

Conny seems almost embarrassed by the praise, but the others aren't slow to come in and confirm his importance: 'It was when Conny came along that it started to take off.' The camaraderie feels very good. It is obvious they've known each other a long time, there's a sort of natural flow and openness among the boys. Despite the tough language and rough tones, there's a great deal of sensitivity to and consideration for each other. Someone takes out the Lam Gam tape and puts in another cassette with a hard-rock band, the Scorpions. Two young boys of 12 or 13 come up and cadge fags. No one says anything, no one does anything. Sigge, who has just lit up, gives the cigarette to one of the boys without even looking in their direction. Then, on the sly, he starts to strum a non-existent guitar to the guitar solo coming out of the loudspeakers until he realises that I've noticed what he's doing.

People drop in all the time, some for a coffee, others only to 'check out the scene'. When we have been sitting for a while and chatted about this and that, Lollo wonders if it isn't time for the interview. 'We can go into the quiet room where we can lock the door,' he says.

Lollo, who plays the guitar, is without doubt the group's spokesman. He organises most of the gigs and he comes up with the most advanced, brazen jargon. Ola, who is the band's singer, seems somewhat different from the rest: he gives a more orderly impression. Conny is considered tantamount to a genius by the others, 'he's fantastic with notes and that.' The drummer, Seppo, is shy and doesn't say much, seems apathetic or indolent. He also plays the guitar. The bassist, Jonna, is in this respect Seppo's opposite, he has an explosive temper and is incredibly wilful.

When we get up to go to the quiet room, Ronny comes up. Ronny is one of the detached youth workers in the area. Lollo, who's been a bit distant and quiet today, goes straight up to him. Choking down tears, he later comes to me when I am rigging up the tape recorder and microphone and says that he has to talk to Ronny before we do the interview. I ask him what it's about, but he answers rather sweepingly that 'it'll be OK soon.' Jonna confides that Lollo 'isn't in very good shape right now, it's a bad scene, so go easy with him.' He goes on to say that Lollo doesn't get on with his mother and that he's left home.

'He's living here and there, with different friends and that. Ronny has promised to fix him up with something, his own place or somewhere to live. So he talks a lot with Ronny about what to do and that.'

We go out to the café again. I go up to order something and suddenly the door to the kitchen flies open and hits Togga, who's standing at the cash register, in the back. He shrieks Tarzan-like 'AIHIJIAA', and there is wild tumult behind the counter. Since this is only in fun, the fight goes on without anyone intervening. As usual there are mostly boys in the Ark tonight. What girls there are either play cards or leaf through photo books. In the concert room a table tennis tournament is going on – with a few girls involved. All the café can offer tonight is inky coffee and a few half-frozen cinnamon buns – but at such times anything goes down. I get out my evening paper and scan it without reading. Lollo and Ronny sit in Ronny's car and talk. Seppo and Jonna get into the ping-pong tournament. The others sit and smoke, drink coffee and listen to music. After half an hour Lollo returns and we go into the quiet room and have our interview.

BERGSLUNDEN

When describing Bergslunden, our focus is primarily on the area around the central mall.[2] Both the members of Lam Gam and the majority of Ark visitors come from this area. In many ways Bergslunden is a typical 1960s suburb. It covers a large area: to walk through all its districts would take nearly a whole day. You walk along pedestrian paths through rather dilapidated high-rise blocks which are built in and surrounded by bits of forest. Football fields, large grassy areas, forested rocky outcrops and heavily trafficked roads create natural boundaries between the districts. Walking through the area you are struck by how few people – almost only pensioners and schoolchildren – you meet. There are very few shops and other services in the residential areas. In fact, there are only people out and about around the centre, which is actually a very large two-storey mall. This is the heart of the area: there is life and movement here from early in the morning to late at night. Adjacent to the mall, with its shops and restaurants, is a library, a gym, a dental and health clinic. The mall is the hub of communications, which has meant that since it was built, it has attracted people who for various reasons have been marginalised by society.

Socially, the area as a whole is a relatively homogeneous working-class area where the population is decreasing in all age groups except those over 65. Emigration frequency in the area around the mall is about 20%; in the rest of the districts it is about half of that. In one district adjacent to the mall, a district called Pilot, emigration frequency is one of the highest in Gothenburg, nearly 30%. The residential districts around the mall are also the most densely populated; they have the most families and consequently the highest youth population. Somewhat over one third of all the inhabitants of Bergslunden live around the mall. Almost 40% of the families are single-parent families – the comparable figure for Gothenburg as a whole is 22%. The child care case index for the districts around the mall in the beginning of the 1980s was between 200 and 210 (for Gothenburg as a whole, 100). The predominant flat size in Bergslunden is one or two bedrooms – about 70% of all flats. Only 15% of the flats have three or four bedrooms.

The average income in Bergslunden is below the average for the whole municipality (index: 85,100 SEK per annum for Gothenburg). Most residents work outside the area, and most work in manufacturing, building or service industries, or in trade.

Unemployment in Bergslunden is higher than in Gothenburg as a whole. Around the mall, the unemployed comprise about 10% of the population between 18 and 64 years of age. Those involved in job-creation programmes are included in this figure. As is generally the case, youth, women and immigrants are hardest hit by unemployment.

According to figures from the social services, 12–15% of the population around the mall have active social service files. Social services involvement primarily concerns economic assistance in accordance with the social welfare laws.

Bergslunden is culturally and politically fairly homogeneous. In the local elections in 1985 the Social Democrats won 60% of the votes from the mall districts and the Swedish Communist Party received 10%; voter

Ubbe [old Ark regular, now music instructor at the Ark]: Yeah, those cellars, they were all over Bergslunden, round the mall, everywhere. I don't think it's the same today, there's another attitude towards drugs and all that. It was like . . . you know, big gangs then. I was born in 1962 and there were alotta kids born out here then. And it was like you had masses of mates your own age and you can hardly sit at home with fifty pals – just not on. But you want to be with them, so what d'ya do? you either hang around the mall, but that's dull as hell, and like it's not yours. No, so we went down and took over cellars and shelters, on the sly like. We had a good deal on this street as we had a shelter with nine rooms. We rented pinball machines and we had a ping-pong room and a music room. We did it all ourselves. Then we fixed a bar and sold beer and wine. We had tables and chairs and we painted the walls and fixed it up good. Then the police came and chucked us out, but that was because there were alotta people there on the run, people we didn't really know . . . that had loot, and junkies and that. It was a fuckin' pity 'cause it was a great time.

participation was 84%. This has been the voting profile of the area since it was built, but voter participation has been steadily decreasing. The number of immigrants in Bergslunden is relatively small: the mall districts have the largest proportion, but there immigrants comprise only 9% of the population, which is the same as the municipal average. However, 37 nationalities are represented, of which Turks and Finns are by far the most numerous.

THE SITUATION OF YOUTH IN BERGSLUNDEN

By the mid 1960s Bergslunden was more or less completed.[3] As in most of the newly built suburbs at that time, the residents were primarily families with children. During the 1960s Bergslunden had a relatively high status; it was considered an attractive area. Neither local authority agencies nor the owners/landlords had anything to complain about.

This relatively harmonious picture began to change during the first half of the 1970s. It became increasingly clear that, after all, there was a fair amount of social problems, and it was at this time that Bergslunden became marked as an area with problem youth, drugs and teenage gangs – a label that lasted a long time. Especially in the area around the mall, the baby boom of the early 1960s grew up into several large youth gangs. Between 1973 and 1978 the subject of these gangs dominated discussion about the area's social problems. The lack of natural places to meet drove youth into storage areas, air-raid shelters and cellars. The gangs were considered disturbing – vandalism, and misuse of drugs and alcohol were common. The authorities were not prepared for this development; neither the newly opened youth club nor sports activities attracted these youths during the 1970s.

The youth in Bergslunden did not travel to the city centre very much, despite good transport communications. The gangs remained in the district in which they grew up, where they knew every cellar and every stairway, where they felt secure. The gangs were dependent upon the area – the arena for their actions. The function of the gangs as regards outsiders and their importance for their members were linked in various ways to the area.

Conny: Lollo, he's like a typical Bergslund kid. He's only seen Bergslunden, McDonald's, the mall and that and the kiosk, that's all he's seen [. . .] He can't even get to Brunnsparken [centre of town] by himself.

Demands on the authorities to do something about the situation intensified in step with the press coverage. Neither the police nor the social services were successful in their efforts to get to grips with the Bergslunden gangs. Detached youth workers tried in various ways to channel the youth into existing recreational activities. This did not work very well as the young people disliked the local authority youth clubs. However, in addition to these clubs there was one place where conditions were easier to accept – the Ark. During the 1970s the Ark was run by a religious youth group with support from the youth workers in the area. 'Here there was no one on your back, nobody nagging you to do this or that, or not to do this or that. Here it was more us who decided things.' The Ark clearly had a higher tolerance threshold – one was not thrown out if one was drunk, for example. When the police started closing cellar hangouts between 1975 and 1977, thus forcing young people up into the daylight, the social workers placed many of them in the Ark.

In 1977 the Ark was shut down for lack of funds. The Ark regulars responded by occupying the place (similar actions occurred at that time in other places in Gothenburg as well). The sit-ins got a good press and were supported by parents and other adults in the area who contributed food and sleeping bags. The sit-ins were successful and the local authority (Recreation Department) was forced to take over the house. An association was formed and in the beginning, the young people themselves ran the place. However, the enthusiasm and visions generated by the sit-in gradually waned.

Towards the end of the 1970s, the situation of young people in the area stabilised. The products of the baby boom became young adults. Gangs were dispersed, their members trained for employment, created families, etc. All this meant that the Ark's clientele diminished and in 1980 it was decided to shut it down.

However, in 1979 a few detached youth workers initiated a rock music project with a gang of teenagers who hung around a mall in the centre of Gothenburg. When in 1980 the project, 'Let a Thousand Stones Roll', began to be spread to the suburbs, it was decided to reopen the Ark and make the whole house into a youth centre focusing on music. There was no money for this so the rebuilding was

Ove: Did you never go to the youth club?
Ubbe: The youth club? Na, I don't know . . . it felt dumb to be there. It felt like there was nothin for us there, there was just rules and that there – rather like going to school . . .

Ove: What happened during the sit-ins?
Ubbe: What happened was that people got aware that there were people who didn't have anywhere to go [. . .] We did masses of things and were there the whole time, at night too, and we were there only so they wouldn't close it down. We were like a big stumbling-block, because they can't shut it down with people in the way.

Ove: Can you say what it was like when the Ark was rebuilt?
Jonna: It was great, there were so many people, you met a lot of people . . . and we were the youngest, only like about 11 or 12 [. . .] and so we built, really got into it. It was cool to do all that, though that's maybe something other people didn't think about much . . .

done by the social workers and the young people themselves. In the spring of 1983, the Ark was basically ready and its musical activities involved almost one hundred youth.

THE ARK

The Ark has a somewhat tarnished reputation for being an arena for problem teenagers. It is true that in the 1970s some of the Ark regulars were on police as well as social service files. During the rebuilding and just after, a comprehensive changed occurred in the Ark's clientele. The older youth were thinned out and younger ones streamed in. The young people who today have the Ark as their second home have similar social backgrounds and attitudes to school as those preceding them, but as regards criminality and drug use, the present situation is very different.

Ove: Why aren't there more people here?
Misse: Some of my mates think it's a bad place ... that there's a mass of junkies and that here.
Putte: Yeah, the word's gone round that there's alotta weed here.
Gurkan: Lots of people think the Ark's chaotic and the social's here and that.
Putte: But that's what we want to get rid of, that label.

Ove: How much are you at the Ark?
Purdie [member of house committee and core group]: Every day, straight after school, but sometimes I go home and have a sandwich first.

Lollo: It's like they try to be a bit more refined like, grown-up and that ... go around in those fuckin' jackets and flannels, bloody hell!

The core of the Ark, or the group that is more or less continually there, consists of 30–35 youth. About one hundred frequent the house on a regular basis – for a coffee or because they use the house for band rehearsals.

The Ark is owned by the Gothenburg Recreation Department and the house is part of a preventive/remedial programme managed by the area youth workers. The musical activities are run through an educational association. However, neither the social services nor the educational association decides what happens in the house. It is managed by a committee of four to six with one vote each; the committee is elected by the young people involved in the house.

THE ARK CULTURE

The Ark is not just a house; it possesses a specific culture. What comprises the 'Ark culture', that is, the 'Ark gang's' special character, stems from the young people's negative and contentious attitudes towards school as a compulsory institution, from their working-class parents' lifestyles and values, and last but by no means least, from their great interest and engagement in rock music.[4]

At the Ark there is a widespread and unambiguous aversion to intellectual work. Those who concentrate on getting good marks in school are 'wimps', they have 'no balls'; they are total bores, who think they are something 'just because their dads have money'. Even if the Ark regulars go to school, they devote a minimum amount of energy to learning anything offered by the school and their teachers. One went to school to meet mates, 'to hassle the teachers and have fun with the gang'. There are innumerable stories about how various teachers were 'psyched and shattered'. In the interviews with Lam Gam, school is presented as an information centre, a place where one checks things out and plans the coming evening's activities. Their attitudes towards school are part of their repudiation of the intellectual and 'soppy' middle-class life which the teachers represent. This rejection is also expressed in the Ark regulars' style of dress – usually tattered jeans, trainers, a sloppy T-shirt, and some sort of short jacket, usually a denim jacket. Their hair tends to be well cared for, but long, usually shoulder-length. Studded belts and leather jackets are rare. In general, there are relatively few signs of the products of the teenage market or identification with any particular subculture. This lack of style is still a style, however. Their dress code clearly distinguishes the Ark gang from the 'well-dressed, attaché case' crowd and 'those yukky flannels and button-downs', as it does from the 'flakies' or 'post-romantics' – people with aesthetic, bohemian and new-wave orientations and interests.

However, the Ark gang's style approaches what could be called the Gothenburg 'hard-rock look': jeans, a leather or denim jacket and long hair. Ark attitudes towards the real hard-rock freaks with their studded belts, pounds of arm and neck metal, curled or frizzed hair are not dismissive, even if such freaks are considered somewhat ridiculous. True punks are also accepted provided that they 'don't talk too much politics and don't look *too* shitty'. In general, Ark regulars have little time for anyone with too great an interest in his or her appearance. There is some difference between the dress of the Ark regulars who are in school and those who go to gymnasium. School kids' jeans are more tattered, their hair is more unkempt, their denim jackets are scribbled all over with names of their favourite groups. This more demonstratively scraggy style is con-

Ove: Why did you go to school?
Sigge: To meet my mates and slag off the teachers.
Ove: Did you do that often?
Sigge: Yeah, we cracked a few . . . went out blubbering . . . got the headmaster . . . that was the best.

Jonna: . . . long hair and torn jeans, then you were feared in school.

Sigge: Most people like hard rock or Imperiet, but nobody dresses for it . . . but if you go to a concert you can see freaky kids with studs and pants in shreds [. . .] We're more ordinary.

nected to rebelliousness towards and rejection of school. When they begin gymnasium, attitudes towards education change: they are positive, at least in the beginning. They have *chosen* to go to gymnasium, where academic subjects do not dominate as much as they did in school. Many relate how liberating it is not have to deal with subjects like history and religion and instead be able to learn welding and lathe work, and how much they like the teachers, especially in the vocational subjects. In gymnasium they do not play truant nearly as much. Gymnasium tends to tone down the rebellious element in dress. Presumably this is a compromise and an adaptation to impending labour market demands as well as an expression of fear of making a fool of oneself in one's placement or apprenticeship or before one's teachers. My interviews show that these teachers (of vocational subjects) are often idealised and become identification objects, especially for boys lacking fathers or male figures at home.

Jonna: Many people say that going to gymnasium's the shits, they think it's worse than ordinary school. But I don't think so 'cause here you can do other things, yeah, it's not the same thing the whole time. The teachers [. . .], like they're not teachers, they're more ordinary people.

Ove: You and Mona are sort of leaders of the band?
Karina [guitarist and singer in the mixed band, History]: Yeah, we are, even more so before – they [the boys] had nothing to say . . . but now they've started to come up with things.

Ronny: Almost all the girls that came here last spring have disappeared. A few regulars are left, some are still playing here . . . yeah they've met boys that hang out somewhere else, they look for steady relationships with older boys and they don't have the same 'herd mentality' as boys do at the same age.

The Ark culture is dominated in various ways by boys; girls comprise only 20–25 per cent of the core group. The Ark culture may be characterised as largely a traditional and relatively circumscribed male-dominated working-class culture. Having said that, there are in fact several elements which contradict this description. Work in the kitchen, particularly making coffee and baking, is done primarily by boys. Equally, cleaning is by no means a female task – everyone helps out. The girls frequenting the house participate rather little in its daily upkeep, regardless of whether this has to do with the economy, shopping or cleaning. Even if the boys command a certain amount of sexist jargon, it has very little bearing on the real communal life in the house. Neither have any of the girls complained of being exposed to derisive treatment; on the contrary, they have emphasised that boys do not 'put it on' or 'lord it' over them. Several of the bands using the house are also 'mixed' bands with both boys and girls. However, girls do not remain in the Ark as long as do boys. They do not identify with the house and the gang in the same way. The girls are more mobile, they frequent the house with one or two girl friends, stay one or two terms and then disappear – some other context beckons. Only a few girls have been in the core group longer than one year. For the boys in the core group, the gang, the Ark and music

comprise their entire environment outside their jobs and
school. The same is not true of the girls: they clearly have
more irons in the fire. Girls tend not to associate in large
gangs, instead they move in smaller, more mobile constel-
lations. One of the reasons why the girls do not stay on at
the Ark could be that the traditional female tasks have
been taken over by the boys. The girls seem to have no
appropriate function or roles; quite simply they have difficulties finding a niche in the Ark gang, who mainly 'sit
around drinking coffee'.

In interviews with the youth, all have stressed the
importance of having their own place, where they can be
at ease. They are not happy in youth clubs where the
leader, always 'hearty', 'runs around' with bunches of
keys and demands participation in various activities.
Nothing spontaneous can happen there – it is always prim,
proper and dull. Some of the Ark youth even prefer the
streets or malls to youth clubs, not because the streets are
fun to be on, but compared with the alternatives – an
evening at home in front of the TV or 'basket-weaving' at
the youth club – the streets are at least somewhere something can happen: police patrols, adults to pester, someone
coming up with a 'slick idea', like smashing windows.
Better than the street, of course, is having your own place,
and the most important thing about your own place is that
you do not *have* to *do* anything, that you can be with your
friends, undisturbed.

Most of the time at the Ark is spent 'not doing anything'
– killing time, drinking coffee, smoking, listening to music
and, above all, talking. Life in the Ark largely circles
around these 'activities'. 'Not having to do anything'[5] in
this context primarily means to talk, to 'bullshit'. It is
not mainly about discussing ideas, politics, etc, but the
experience and enjoyment of hearing your own voice,
expressing and 'training' yourself verbally. It is about
broadening yourself before a group of listeners, holding
forth, showing that you are really in the gang, that you
know the jargon, the slang, etc. Identity and gang membership are palpably linked with the vernacular cultivated
and maintained at the Ark. There is a clear connection
between the language used by the Ark regulars and the
traditional verbal idiom which flourishes on the factory
floor, building site and other work-places. Certain linguis-

Ove: What is it that's good with
the Ark?
Lollo: Well, there's no stupid
rules. The rules here we've like
made ourselves. There's no
asshole swankin' around, no
smartass sayin', 'Hey, hey, you
can't do that' . . . like.

Seppo: You come here in your
free time, drink coffee, play
cards, listen to music, and do
things.
Ove: But can't you do that at
the youth club too?
Seppo: I don't know . . . there's
so fuckin' many rules there . . .
[. . .] We're not allowed to be
there, just be there, like we are
here – the Ark's like ours.

Ove: How would you describe
the Ark?
Conny: . . . it's like a shelter for
the working-class.

Ove: You're not specially shy, I
mean I've seen how you get into
the house meetings at the Ark,
for instance. Where've you got
the confidence from, do you
think?
Lollo: I don't know, but I think
I've had to think so fuckin'
much, so I think I've learned a
lot in that way . . . . I've had to
think a lot . . .
Ove: What do you mean?
Lollo: Well, like I've had to
take care of myself . . . If I've
had problems I couldn't go to
my mum with them.
Ove: Who've you gone to?
Lollo: No, but I haven't gone to
anybody . . . I've had them
inside me like . . . I've had to do
for myself and I still do.

Ove: Do any of you have a steady relationship?
Lollo: No, we have it off with different chicks, ya know.
Conny: Yeah, on my bathroom floor there's a lot of fucking . . . was she fourteen or . . . ?
Lollo: Yeah, Ola said she was 'a good fuck'.
Conny: Yeah, yeah . . . but Sigge, he's the worst, he takes them over when they're worn out.

Ove: What do you want to do?
Conny: Smoke, drink coffee and write songs . . . [. . .], be like free, be in a band [. . .] you can work when you want, nobody says that you start at 7 and stop at 4.43, or whatever it is now at the bloody firm. To clock in and have that fuckin' pling pling, that's not much fun.

Putte [member of house committee]: . . . The last few days have been a bit hard, we've been here till after twelve 'cause people won't go home. I don't get home till one or so and then I've got to get up for work or go to my placement next day, and I start early as hell. But it's like we're turned on to doing something. And then if you see somebody coming and ruining it all, you just blow up. It's like when a little kid's got a new bike and along comes a bigger kid and slashes the tyres.

Ubbe: I'd rather set up a tent under some tree here in Bergslunden than move to another part of town.

Lollo: We're the powerhouse in Bergslunden.

tic influences from the local rock culture can also be detected. One does not acquire status and respect at the Ark by driving a fast motorcycle or dressing in flash or shocking clothes, or by showing a broad criminal register. No, there are primarily two ways of obtaining status: mastering an instrument and verbal competence. To never be at a loss for words, to be able to come up with a crushing comment in any situation, to always have the last word is what gains respect among the Ark youth. You show through language how experienced in the ways of the world you are; language reveals what you have gone through, in what circles you move, etc. The ability to handle language, to do all the talking and be entertaining also determines your position in the group since much of the life at the Ark has to do with killing time. The person who has the ability to capture his or her listeners and get them to laugh is greatly valued.[6] The prevailing tone is raw and punctuated by insinuations, often of a sexual nature, but the language is never seriously hurtful. Everyone knows the limits and sensitive questions are rarely discussed openly; should such questions surface, the discussion usually becomes savage and competitive.

In our society, time is costly; it is something we must learn to budget. This is obviously not a concept shared by the youth at the Ark. In my discussions with teachers and social workers, one of their main reservations about the Ark was the young people's regard for time: 'They lose so many opportunities by *wasting their time* just sitting in that café.' But time is something young people want to have power over and control themselves, and this is only possible at the Ark, where they are free from school schedules and clocks. Time is not something to invest in or bookkeep in order to reap benefits from in the future.[7] Time is the here and now, it is being with the gang. The young would prefer to stop time, not to have to go home and leave their mates: every evening going home involves a painful separation.

Relations to the Ark are mixed with strong feelings of ownership. It is their house. Something of the same exists in the young people's bonds with Bergslunden; they have great difficulties imagining moving away from the area. Some who have been forced to move with their parents return to the area every evening, even if they live on the other side of town. Their identities and self-images are heavily dependent upon and linked to the area, to the Ark and to the gang. But this local patriotism does not exclude complaining about how boring it is in Bergslunden, how 'dumb' the youth club is, how 'ding-a-ling' the adults are or how 'worthless' the social workers are, etc. Sometimes this identification with their own district has other expressions. The locals are uncertain of outsiders who visit – 'they're weird' – and the language used is naive and self-assertive. On those rare occasions when a gang from Bergslunden find themselves in another part of town, they not infrequently land in fights with other youth. The myth of Bergslunden superiority which is cultivated in the gang is materialised in the use of fists on these occasions. Even if it has happened that a member of the gang has been tried for assault – even in the first degree – most of these sorts of gang fights have been relatively mild. The Ark gang maintains a self-sufficiency and an insularity *vis à vis* the rest of the world.

Connected to this strong territorial feeling is also an expressed interest in the history of previous generations of youth in the area. Everyone at the Ark is well versed in the exploits of the cellar gangs and the events around the occupation of the Ark. When one of the older ones who participated in these events relates stories about them, there is a respectful silence in the café and everyone listens. Old newspaper clippings and flyers from the sit-in period are mounted on the walls and in the telephone room there is a scrapbook of press clippings. The Ark youth see themselves as carrying on a specific Bergslund tradition, in which youthful unruliness and freedom from the guardianship of the authorities are important ingredients.

This picture of the Ark as a place where nothing special happens other than drinking coffee, smoking, playing cards and talking is not quite the whole picture – though for the occasional visitor it may seem to be. To discover the gaps in that picture it is necessary visit the Ark often and over a fairly long period of time. Nevertheless, to describe the main aspects of the Ark culture in terms of defensive categories is correct. The Ark is a free zone, a haven, where you can withdraw, be with your mates, shut out all the demands – from parents, the school, even the teenage industry – concerning how you should be and

Örjan [member of house committee]: The sit-in was a long time ago, but everybody knows what happened. My brother was there, he's 23 now and he's still got articles from the newspaper . . . pictures too.

Conny: . . . Some of the old guard think we've taken over the house now, yeah . . . they think it was more fun before. But we thought there should be a little order, the Ark must be something, we have to want something . . . not just a lot of fuckin' talk.

behave. When one has been with the Ark youth for a while, one discovers that even if the core of 30–35 teenagers is a homogeneous group, it still contains internal oppositions. The fundamental antagonism, which is present in all contexts, is between activity and passivity. The core group could be roughly divided into three tendencies. One would turn the Ark into a well-functioning all-activity house, a youth project which revolved around rock music. This tendency is of a relatively late date and expanded during the time I frequented the house. The young people representing this tendency are the most active and responsible and in certain ways most of them are in the process of withdrawing from identification with the more traditional forms of working-class life described above. Instead, they orient themselves more towards attempting to get into the more established rock culture in Gothenburg. They want the Ark to be more open and accessible to other groups of youth than those traditionally frequenting the place. This could be accomplished by, for example, arranging concerts where Ark bands could play together with bands having a very different audience from that normally attending the Ark. Spokesmen for this tendency in the core group are primarily those with the greatest interest in music and those oriented towards punk and Swedish rock.

Among those promoting these ideas are also youth who are not in any band, but who like to organise, take responsibility, work in the café, fix up the house, etc. During the time I visited the Ark, it was from this group that most of the house committee members were recruited. Among these activists were those who worked hardest and most concentratedly on playing their instruments well, and they also tended to be the ones who had the most developed contacts with other young rock music enthusiasts outside the Ark.

In opposition to this activist tendency is the passive, which encompasses the majority of the youth at the Ark, among whom the 'do nothing' mentality dominates. As with the activists, there are also passive rock musicians and non-musicians, but their preference is for hard-rock music. The most energetic of the activists are viewed by the passivists as 'climbers' – interested in raising themselves socially, becoming 'bosses' in the house. This could

Sigge: I think it's got boring here at the Ark, alotta new people've come who think they should decide what goes on . . . so I'm not here so much anymore.

Seppo: Other people can do politics, those who were good in school.

Freddy [old Ark regular]: We workers must stick together, otherwise the bosses will ride right over us.

almost be interpreted to mean that the activist vision undermines one of the fundamental elements of Ark culture, namely, the aversion to 'making something special' of oneself and all forms of 'climber' mentality. However, it is important to mention that the boundaries between these tendencies are fluid. Even if tensions between different groups exist, the youths are all members of the same gang.

The third tendency could be called the 'deviant' tendency. It is represented by a number of youths who have particularly problematic social situations (drugs, criminality, etc). Representatives of this tendency stand with one foot in the Ark and one in the mall, or on the street. They are always welcome in the gang, but they stay away from the Ark for periods. The third tendency also encompasses rock-playing and non rock-playing youth, but interest in music is least developed in this group.

One might think that political views would be dependent upon what tendency one adhered to. The core of the activists consists of a small group, at one time involved in the management of the house in various ways. To an extent, this group is more open to and more interested in society and social problems, but this is not to say that they are more interested in politics in a traditional sense, that is, in party politics.. Everyone I talked to demonstrated indifference to what we normally mean by politics. They do not want to talk politics because they do not think they understand what it is about. In principle all parties are considered equally hopeless and dull – 'just mouthing off'. However, the views and attitudes towards trade unions are not equally negative. Several of the older youth at the Ark are union members and on several occasions I heard them saying how important it was to be organised – and the subject did not always concern unemployment benefits.

With few exceptions, no visions of a different society were conveyed in the interviews. Most, including Lam Gam, aim at getting on the labour market as quickly as possible, not because they want to work but because they want to earn money. Their goals are to be able to buy a car, good guitars, decorate a flat, etc. Somewhat further along, there are hints of wives and children, but they are more reserved about that. The future in general looms a

Ove: What's a good society like?
Jonna: I don't know, I've never thought about it. [. . .] The problem is that you can't go to the pub when you want, drive a car . . . go buy booze.

Ove: What do you want for the future?

Lollo: I want good wages, a cool flat and I want everything to function . . . nice around me, orderly and that.

little frightening, not least because it involves separation from the gang: 'you're without your mates . . . alone like my old man' (Sigge). What is absolutely crucial is that you are with the gang. The future as a 'nine to five' existence is by no means the ideal, but what alternative exists 'for us with bad marks who don't like to study'? To many, a steady job, decent wages and a 'nice' home mean rising socially in comparison with the conditions under which they grew up. The only way out of waged work is music, but everyone is painfully aware that even if you are very good, it is difficult to support yourself on rock music. At the Ark there are very few having the requisite romantic, bohemian attitudes which would enable them to imagine compromising their living standards in order to devote themselves to their art. Most of the active musicians at the Ark have a double strategy – vocational education and dreams of being musicians.

To enter the Ark on an ordinary weekday night is like going into a simple, cheap bar in Greece, for example: cards, music, spartan furnishings, a little messy and noisy, people just sitting around. Coffee, cigarettes, card games, loud, intense conversations are succeeded by a half-stifled silence. People look in only to find out if there is anything going on. The Ark is a meeting-place, an information centre. The core group, those who are always there, know everything about what is going to happen at the weekend, who is home alone, who is currently at odds with their parents, who is with whom, etc.

A casual visitor sitting in the Ark in the evening may find it difficult to imagine that these young people rebuilt the whole house. But after periods of passivity, the house can suddenly break out into a flurry of activity. The fact that in principle everyone is going to or has attended two-year vocational courses in gymnasium, and is able to show visitors the results of their work, doubtless has a great deal to do with all the building projects at the Ark.

The detached youth workers bear the formal responsibility for the Ark's activities. Their ways of relating to the young people were, during the period when I regularly visited the house, fairly unconventional. The premise was that the youths themselves would manage and take care of the house. The Ark was open daily except for Fridays and Saturdays. The youth workers were there Mondays and

Thursdays – the rest of the week the place was run by the young people themselves. The house committee opened and closed the place, cleaned up and ran the café. This extensive self-management was fairly new; previously the social services had been more involved in running the house.

A CONCERT AT THE ARK

When I arrive around three activities are in full swing.[8] Some 15 kids are busy preparing for the evening's event – cleaning, baking, building the stage, etc. I hang up my coat on the newly mounted coat hanger and chat a bit with Ammi, who is, along with Ronny, one of the youth workers at the Ark. Patrik comes up and asks if I feel like helping with the stage construction, which is a fairly large and sophisticated project. Previously they have had a mobile stage which was dismantled after every performance, but it wasn't very 'hip'. The new one is much larger and has a real drum podium. Four or five boys are hammering and sawing away. Two girls are tacking down a full-cover carpet on the stage. It all looks very good. There's actually nothing for me to do. Patrik had asked mainly to ensure that I'd come and check out their work. Not without pride he tells me how they've gone about it. In the kitchen Örjan has been in charge of the baking – cinnamon buns and rye rolls for sandwiches. They've also made masses of sponges, oatmeal biscuits and chocolate balls. The fridge has been filled with things to drink, coffee's been made and put into flasks. And now the main attraction of the evening arrives – the band Camouflage. They carry in their gear and do a quick sound check. It's getting close to six o'clock and people start coming in – the black-clad rock folk from town, come to listen to Camouflage, mixed with hard-rock fans from the suburbs. The atmosphere is calm and pleasant and the Ark gang are beaming as they count entrance money and sell buns. Gullet and Putte sit at the door and take the entré: '10 kronor, yeah, too bloody cheap. At a club in town this would have cost at least 30.'

   To my surprise, the Lam Gam boys aren't especially active. They're all here, except Conny who has a handball match. Only Jonna is helping out. Lollo mostly runs around trying to look busy and involved. Ola's sleeping in the quiet room. Sigge and Seppo play cards and take it easy.

   First band out tonight is Heavy Power, a hard-rock group consisting of four boys from 10 to 12 years old, and they're bloody good. Especially the guitarist and drummer. They're wearing studs, knives, shades, scarves, shredded jeans and God knows what. Lots of people have arrived and they're all raving. The band plays five numbers and puts on a real show. The Lam Gam boys stand right at the front near the stage and are digging it in a sort of big brotherly way. The fact is that Heavy Power sound appreciably better than Lam Gam, but I don't think the Lam Gam boys realise it. Super Natural from the Ark are the next band – they play a sort of melodious hard-rock. The best thing with them is that there are two girls in the band who sing and play guitars, while the boys play bass and drums. The girls are very sure of their instruments, but somehow it never takes off. However, since the band is an Ark band, they get fantastic applause and two curtain calls. In contrast, Camouflage doesn't go down particularly well with the Ark gang. When Camouflage were playing and the whole room was packed out, half the core group sat in the café.

Previously, when the Ark has arranged concerts, they've primarily been directed towards the local rock public in Bergslunden. This was the first time they've put up posters in town and tried to attract a somewhat different audience. I had thought that this might cause friction in the Ark gang. A few provocative remarks about the 'black-clad' were made of course, but it was surprising how much pride in the Ark was shown. They just beamed, 'Yeah, this is our house, this is where we hang out . . . It's great, isn't it?'

After the concert the money was counted meticulously. There'd been about a hundred paying, and this meant that there were 130– 140 people there that evening. All the sandwiches and buns had been sold, a clear profit just in the café of 1400 kronor. Nobody had the energy to stay around and clean up, everybody just sat collapsed in a heap. A successful but extremely exhausting evening.

THE HISTORY OF LAM GAM

Jonna: We've always been together . . . I've known Sigge since the first year, Seppo too and Lollo since the second year, so I've known them quite a few years.

Lollo: . . . I don't think she's given me what a mother should . . . I've never hugged her . . . never felt like it, you know what I mean . . . she's had her problems, but I've never cared about her.

In August 1984, Lollo, Jonna, Seppo and Sigge began their last year in the same class in comprehensive school. About the same time they decided to form a rock band. When Sigge and Seppo agreed to Lollo and Jonna's proposal, they had never played an instrument. Lollo and Jonna, however, had been regularly visiting the Ark for about a year; they had helped with the rebuilding and developed a taste for playing themselves. Together with two somewhat older boys they had a functioning band. However, since the older boys were more advanced musically than Lollo and Jonna, the band split up. But Lollo and Jonna had been the driving forces, they had written their own songs – which the band played – and Lollo was not only a guitarist but also the group's vocalist.

Other than as classmates, the future Lam Gam quartet did not spend much time together. Seppo and Sigge were members of a larger gang of younger youth who hung out around an arcade in the area. Lollo and Jonna were mostly together with a gang dominated by somewhat older youth who frequented the Ark. The school authorities considered Lollo and Jonna very difficult and problematic pupils. Their attendance was bad and when they were there, they were disturbing and provocative. The school also knew that they were in the notorious Ark crowd. All this led

to Lollo being accused of selling hash at school. Both
Jonna and Lollo come from economically and culturally
impoverished split-up families. However, whereas Lollo
has a contentious and aggressive relationship with his
mother, Jonna has an extremely friendly and tender relationship with his. In both cases the father is totally
absent. Both boys have had high absenteeism in the upper
form and consequently disastrous marks. By the time they
were 10 or 11 they had begun to stay out late at night and
came in contact with older boys who hung around the
mall and at the Ark. Seppo and Sigge are sons of factory
workers. Seppo's parents came from Finland and moved to
Sweden and Bergslunden in the middle of the 1960s. Even
if neither Seppo nor Sigge showed any great interest in
school, they were mostly physically present. They had generally below-average marks. They never got on particularly
well in school, but they were never exposed to the sort of
special treatment given to Jonna and Lollo – observation
classes for students with behavioural problems and special
study programmes. Both Sigge and Seppo have fairly chilly
relationships with their shift-working fathers, but get on
much better with their mothers, a shop assistant and a
cleaner respectively.

What enabled the four classmates to start playing
together was that the school purchased drums, guitars and
amplifiers which made it possible to choose rock as an
elective subject for study. At the same time the group
registered themselves as a study circle at the Ark. No one
had his own instrument, not even an acoustic guitar. Lollo
and Jonna taught all the chords they knew to Sigge and,
assisted by the music instructor at the Ark, Seppo learned
the fundamentals of drumming. They played the few
three-chord tunes that Lollo and Jonna had played earlier.
They also tried a few Ebba Grön covers. At the school's
St. Lucia Day the same autumn, they were ready for their
first performance. The show was a hit, not only because
the lyrics were outspoken, but also because one after
another the teachers crept out of the auditorium with their
hands over their ears. During this first autumn the boys
practised at the Ark as well as at school. Their links with
the school became increasingly weak and by the end of the
term they played only at the Ark.

None of the four original members had previously

Ove: Your last year in school,
you played hookey most of the
time – why?
Jonna: Na, but it was so fuckin'
boring, and you were so fuckin'
tired – you'd gone nine years
straight.

Jonna: It was those crappy
songs.
Conny: No, but they were cool!
Lollo [singing]: 'I went to the
city an' found a li'l' kitty'
[laughter]. You can't begin with
anything else.

Conny: I remember when I
heard you in the assembly, on
St. Lucia Day, shit it sounded
bad! I busted my gut for an
hour after.

had any developed or passionate interest in music. They naturally listened to music on the radio, records and cassettes, but none had an expressed music interest in terms of buying records or going to concerts. Neither had any of the boys much of a music background at home – from parents or siblings. Sigge has an older brother and Jonna an elder sister who listen to hard rock and Swedish punk. Even if all this is not decisive for starting to play music, it is not insignificant as regards the boys' future music-making. In my interviews with them all four were convinced that had the opportunities at the Ark not existed, none of them would have played at all. This was not only because it costs next to nothing, but primarily because at the Ark an entirely different musical pedagogics is applied from that of their school or the municipal music school. At the Ark the whole group is worked with from the start, even if all are beginners. It is about respecting the young people's desire to be in a group, and the learning process is steered by their musical interests and needs. Scales, harmony and other music theory enter at a later stage, and are often taught individually when the need arises and when the individual is ready for them. Hence one does not learn the instrument first, but instead begins directly to play together with others while learning the instrument. When the foundations have been laid, the music instructor removes himself and the group develops on its own.

Ove: Before you began to play, did you listen much to music?
Jonna: No, I didn't, don't think I listened to music much then. Now not one day goes by without gettin' up and puttin' a record on first thing, or a tape.

Ove: What do you use to impress people now?
Jonna: I don't know, yeah, I play in Lam Gam – that's bloody big. 'What do you do?' they say. 'I play in a band.' [. . .] That's really fantastic, that's groovier than just about anything else.

How did it happen that these boys chose to play rock music? The answer in part lies outside the music itself. To be in a rock band is a way of acquiring respect and social position. For these boys rock presented an opportunity for social revenge. Backed by a band one can show that one can do something, that one is not a 'thickhead' just because one has not done well at school. For these boys rock became an alternative strategy for obtaining identity and self-respect. The usual or normal means for attaining these things for youth who are successful in neither school nor sports is often to define themselves as deviates or outsiders of some sort. Making rock music involves a third alternative; one need not battle with a middle-class scale of values and performance demands, and neither is one threatened by lumpenproletarian criminality. Another important element on the threshold of puberty is relations with the opposite sex. One of the motives mentioned in the interviews was that as a musician one 'rates' in the girls' eyes, which indicates rock's social status. This also figures in the dream of being a rock idol, a dream which is definitely part of the boys' motivation and which is openly discussed, even if to the question why one plays, the answer is usually only 'because it's fun'. To anyone who has seen Lam Gam, it is also clear that a very important motive behind their playing is simply to 'get a kick' out of performing and being seen. Being in a rock band is synonymous with being tough, 'hip' and 'cool': it is quite simply a continuation and development of the attitudes and behaviour developed in confrontations with the teachers in school.

Seppo: Why it's cool to play . . . lots of chicks [embarrassed laughter].
Ove: So playing's a way of getting girls?
Seppo: Yeah, that's right . . . it's easier when you play in a band.

Ove: Who do you think you are when you're up there on stage?
Lollo: I'm Lollo and I'm doing a good job . . . I want to show I'm something.

In addition, the local amateur rock culture which grew up around the Gothenburg suburbs during the first half of the 1980s has had a decisive influence on the formation of Lam Gam. The project 'Let a Thousand Stones Roll' suddenly opened musical opportunities for a new category of youth for whom playing music had not previously been a self-evident option. A great many bands were formed, concerts and playing live out in various districts became a part of daily life. In almost every district of town, shelters and storage areas were made into rehearsal quarters.

The first phase of Lam Gam's development was the autumn of 1984. The band sounded fairly bad and they knew it.

Shortly after the St. Lucia Day performance, Ola, who was in the same class as the others, was asked if he would be in the band and sing. Ola was flattered and accepted. He had neither sung nor played an instrument before. Ola was not only in the same class, he also lived in the same block as Seppo and Jonna. Ola's parents are from Norway; they moved to Gothenburg in the 1960s and started a tobacconists in central Gothenburg. At first the family lived in an older bungalow area south of Bergslunden. When the shop went bankrupt in the mid-1970s, the family was forced to move to rented accommodation in Bergslunden. In Norway Ola's father had been an ordinary worker, an occupation he was forced to return to. Ola is the youngest of five, of whom all but Ola have left home. Like the others in Lam Gam, Ola was not interested in school and had bad marks.

Ola also listened to Ebba Grön, Attentat and other

Swedish punk bands, but unlike the others in Lam Gam he preferred more mainstream-oriented and synth-based music. He had difficulties with punk's socially critical texts. Seppo and Sigge had nothing against punk, but preferred English and American hard rock. Lollo and Jonna were the ones who felt the strongest bonds with Swedish suburban punk; Ebba Grön and Thåström had become the main models, especially for Lollo. Ola differs from the others in more than just musical tastes: he has difficulties accepting life in Bergslunden, he is the only one who does not identify himself with the area. He is in the Ark gang, but he dreams of moving back to the bungalow area or another area with 'class'. He is strongly aware of having a somewhat different background from the others, and this is demonstrated in his image – his hair is shorter and he seldom wears jeans and a T-shirt. However, this is not to say that he dresses nicely or is 'stylish' in any other way. Ola's first period in the band was difficult: he had trouble finding himself, experienced himself as stiff and had problems letting go. Ola felt 'out of it' and decided to concentrate on acting-out and giving his all in every song. He got results and worked himself into the band. Ola knew Conny, who played piano and was in a parallel class, so Ola had the task of asking Conny if he would 'test' for Lam Gam. Conny immediately answered yes and Lam Gam became a sextet.

With the addition of Conny, the band acquired something of a new sound and entered its second phase. In contrast to the others Conny had a relatively decent musical education behind him. The music that moved him most however was Swedish punk and groups like Ebba Grön and KSMB. Conny comes from a relatively well-off family; his father is a department head in a small company in Bergslunden's industrial area. His father, who also plays piano, has worked his way up from the factory floor. Conny's mother works in an office. The family had formerly lived in one of the high-rise blocks in Bergslunden. Conny has had no problems with school; even if he did not thrive, he obtained good marks with no difficulty. In addition to music, he is also interested in sports and is said to have a glowing future in both football and handball; unlike the others in Lam Gam, Conny never gave up his interest in sports.

Ove: Do you think Ebba Grön's lyrics are too political?
Ola: Yeah . . . they go on too much.

Ove: What role do you think you have in the group?
Ola: I feel pretty unimportant, really . . . I can't play any instrument – anybody could get up and sing.

Conny: I've played a long time, I don't know how old I was when I started . . . I was in the third year when I began the piano. Had teachers and all that, but then I quit, it was so bloody boring to play Beethoven, so I just laid off. I began to play my own music and learned from that.

When Conny arrived, the band began to sound better. And although he had never played with a group, Conny rapidly acquired an important role, socially as well as musically. He could also add nuances and load the music through 'fill-ins' as well as playing brilliant solos. From having been a guitar-dominated group, Lam Gam gradually allowed the synth an increasingly prominent role. To an extent Conny became the band's musical leader. This is noticeable not least in the rehearsals: Conny 'knows how it should be', he can improvise tunes, he makes the rehearsals efficient, he notes when the tempo slows, etc. Lam Gam's repertoire expanded to six or seven songs. The old originals disappeared, and were replaced by covers like *The State and Capital*, *Young and Horny* by Ebba Grön, *Boat Song* by Attentat and *I Don't Give a Shit* by the satirical pop singer, Magnus Uggla. During the spring of 1985 the band played live at the Ark, in the youth club and at school. The group developed musically, putting together a strong show and becoming something of a cult band at Bergslund school. Lam Gam's popularity led to more schoolkids becoming aware of the Ark; during that spring, when there were performances or concerts, the house was more or less invaded.

The spring of 1985 was an expansive and intense period in Lam Gam's history. Since they were in a milieu with a lot of live music, they became conscious that there were bands that sounded a good deal better. This did not prevent Lam Gam from 'going in there and putting on a show that blew the ceiling off'. Possibly as a compensation for their erratic musical quality, they created a most singular stage show. They gradually developed a 'band ideology', which asserted that what was important was not to play correctly, but every time they were on stage, to be a 'rock 'n' roll rumble', and that they played to 'have a ball on stage'. The stage shows could be like the one which was given as an internal gig at the Ark in April 1985. The band members had put on loose penises filled with yogurt which was squirted over a jubilant public between numbers. Even if all performances were not as spectacular as that one, the boys always hopped and bounced around intensively in time with the music. Some of them often dressed in wide-brimmed hats, old jackets and the like. The band was mainly marked, however, by their ambition

Lollo: You feel collective creativity in music in a different way from in football . . . if you're five that like have the same feeling for life then it's better [. . .] you're you, you're Lam Gam.

Conny: We're actually not so good if you compare us with other bands, but we've like been raised sky high here at the Ark, got a lot of gigs. And then we're really hip on stage . . . with hats and standing there hollering.

Lollo Take Downtown, they're great, but on stage they're real nerds . . . it's more fuckin' important to give a good show than play well. [. . .] If we didn't have the show and played like shit poor then we'd be total rubbish, wouldn't we?

Lollo: You get a real buzz standin' there havin' the whole audience with you, it's like Scandinavium [a stadium in Gothenburg], right? Especially when they light cigarette lighters and sing along.

Sigge: You can't bump a pal, he's [Seppo] got just as much right to be here as anybody else. He's been with us from the start.

Lollo: There wouldn't be any Lam Gam without me, I'm the one who started the band, and I've set up 70 per cent of all the gigs. When we began I did everything, like I knew most then.

to always be in contact with the public. This could be brought about in various ways, by Ola and Lollo jumping down into the audience during the playing, or by Ola using the old ploy of holding out the mike, inviting the audience to sing along. They always had at least one song with a passage for just drums and public singing. In these passages the band members clapped their hands with the public while they led the singing with the microphone. They have all talked rapturously about just these occasions when they have 'got the public going'.

During this spring (1985), the friendships among the band members were greatly strengthened. They went around together more than before, weekday evenings as well as weekends. The Ark became the second home for the whole band. Ola and Conny came into the core group easily, and there were few conflicts in the group. However, also at this time the first signs of what would later split the group could be detected. As they developed greater competence on their instruments, Sigge and Seppo began to try to play the hard-rock music they preferred listening to. In addition to the irritation created by Sigge's hard-rock riffs during rehearsals, Seppo's lagging tempo was a frequent topic of discussion. They did not tell Seppo he was 'hopeless', but everyone knew that he knew that they all thought he was bad. Yet there was never any talk about replacing him.

During this time Lollo became more and more the group's manager, continually chasing new gigs. This role in the band coincided well with his being one of the most driving and active forces in the Ark house committee. Lam Gam's fan club was formed on the initiative of Ola, who also became the club's treasurer. Membership cost 3 kronor and in return members received nothing more than an illegible membership card. Ola had difficulty keeping the club's finances separate from his own. One day when he was broke, he took 67 members' paid fees to invite his girlfriend for hamburgers. The other members of the band were livid, but there were no reprisals.

In the interviews recorded after the band broke up, this spring is described as 'the best time': the members were mates and they had 'a hell of a good time'. The band had many gigs and were the focus of a great deal of interest. Wherever they played, they were followed by a loyal public, mainly young girls from Bergslund school. Each performance was preceded by preparing the stage show. Future plans were sketched: 'If we just keep together, we'll be something one day.'

The group profile during this period was clearly punk-influenced. In addition to playing Swedish punk classics, the band strove for punk acting-out and intensity. They had a reputation for being a 'rave' band, but they were also labelled 'communist' and 'progressive' especially by the most committed hard-rockers outside the Ark. Only Ola had difficulties accepting this label; Lollo, the band's 'front man', also adopted the guise of 'red rebel'. In fact, Conny was the band's ideologist, even if he never openly performed as such, but he comprehended in a different way from the others what the texts actually said.

To Lollo and Jonna – and also Sigge and Seppo – punk was associated with a boldness and rebellion against school and middle-class values which they could easily support. Song titles such as *Hang God, Shoot a Cop*, etc. were totally unambiguous, whereas *The State and Capital* and *Every Wise Man* were rather more difficult to understand. At rehearsals Conny tried to get the others to realise how important it was that they understood and endorsed the messages in the songs, but Lollo was the only one who made an effort. Ola was fascinated by punk's fervour (*à la* Thåström, Ebba Grön/Imperiet's charismatic singer and probably the most famous artist to emerge out of the Swedish punk movement), but alienated by its message. That Ola did not resist Conny and Lollo's more political stance was partly because he was uncertain of his place in the band and partly because he did not want to provoke conflicts when the band was doing so well. Jonna, Seppo and Sigge had nothing directly against being labelled a 'prog' band; what was important to them was that the band's image was tough and brazen. Lollo and Conny were Lam Gam's central figures, and to the extent that the group had a political image, it was because of them. In practice they also decided the band's repertoire. Even if Conny was more familiar with the political message of Swedish punk than the others, he was far from politically aware or interested. He did not see himself as a socialist, but neither was he 'conservative at any rate'. Like most others at the Ark, he thought all politics was 'a load of

Lollo: It was all a buzz with the old Lam Gam, everybody had ideas and everybody thought it was fun. Hell, we got up and played even if we couldn't play a thing really . . . we played anyway, like it was cool. Not like that any more, not so much fun now and I think that's a bummer.

Ove: Your brother likes hard rock?
Sigge: Yeah, he thought Lam Gam was a fuckin' communist band . . . 'Turn off those fuckin' revolutionary songs', he'd say when I put on a Lam Gam tape at home.
Ove: Did you also think they were a bit too much?
Sigge: No, I didn't think it was difficult . . . didn't matter to me so long as it sounded good.
Ove: So you didn't have anything against being called a communist?
Sigge: Ha, ha, no, no . . .

Ove: What do you think of *The State and Capital*? What do you think the song's about?
Lollo: Yeah, mmm . . . well, it's about the state and all that shit. I don't know, haven't thought about that song so . . . it's like an inborn song. I've played it since I began to play, it was the first song I learned . . . I've played that song for two years.

Ola: . . . shit POLITICS.' I DON'T GIVE A SHIT FOR IT, IT'S THE PITS, I wouldn't get involved in it for tuppence.

crap'. To Conny, punk was about 'us down here versus them up there'. The group agreed with this interpretation, which also correlated well with the basic view of society developed among the youth at the Ark.

A REHEARSAL WITH LAM GAM

It's Thursday, the day for a Lam Gam rehearsal – at 4 o'clock to be precise.[9] I get to the Ark at 3.30 and have a coffee while waiting for the boys. Örjan is alone in the house, and piddles about tidying up, solders electric cords and makes coffee. He gives me a cup before the coffee is finished brewing and I sit down at his table in the middle of the flexes and soldering equipment. The place looks a bit grotty today. Örjan says that order in the house's somewhat up and down at the moment. Like so many others, he studies metalwork at school and likes it. He's been with the Ark gang about a year and is now a member of the house committee and in charge of the keys. His image or style is somewhat different from the other boys in the house. Despite the fact that he's studying metalwork, he hasn't the workers' argot so characteristic of the Ark regulars, and he isn't as masculine. All this as regards his way of talking, his relations with the girls and his style of dress – slightly baggy grey cotton trousers, red basket-ball shoes and a matching shirt. His hair isn't so long either, but he has a little plait down his neck. His movements are rather stiff, making one think of a well-permed lady. We talk about Bergslunden, I drink coffee and he solders. Conny arrives and joins us, lights a cigarette and says, 'So I'm first again today. They can't tell the bleeding time or there's something else wrong with 'em.' After a while, Jonna comes in with Masken, Bosse and Anna-Karin. There's a sort of self-evident atmos-phere, one is simply here and chews the rag. They've all come directly either from school or work, only gone home for a sandwich. The way they are in the Ark makes one think of the way one is at home. More and more people drop in. Örjan starts more coffee and Masken rounds up people to play cards. The tape recorder plays Dire Straits today – must be the youth workers' cassette. Most of Lam Gam has arrived, all except Sigge and Seppo. Before we go into the rehearsal room, Lollo says that he hopes that 'all the gear works'. When we go in, one of the boys in the Ark core group, who isn't in any band, is sitting at the drums playing with a knife and fork as drum-sticks. The Lam Gam boys blow up at him and he removes himself with a sneer. The room looks like hell, but the gear works and everyone helps to clean up. Lollo tells me that it's like this everywhere at the Ark. There are times when it's a total mess, but suddenly people get going and tidy up. While waiting for Sigge and Seppo the rest jam. A drummer from another band is called in to play until Seppo comes. They start with rock classics like *Under My Thumb*, *Smoke on the Water*, etc. They don't know the whole song, but can manage the first eight bars, the riff, a verse and a chorus here and there. They have a great time and let each other flip out. In truth, I must say it sounds pretty decrepit. But then they play an old Ebba number they had in the repertoire last spring, and the music immediately improves. Seppo arrives and so the rehearsal can really begin. There are two new songs on the cards for today. They decide the arrangements together, even if Lollo and Conny lead. They are all allowed to try out things until they get what they want. Jonna has problems finding the rhythm and it sounds like he doesn't hear what he's playing, because sometimes he's totally 'out'. It's a bit chaotic but Ola struggles on and thanks to him Lollo, Jonna and Seppo know where they are in the song. Conny has problems with the synth which has stopped working, so he goes around and helps the others. It's not easy for Lollo – he struggles on rather clumsily and unrhythmically, but after an hour or so he gets a beat he's happy with – he grins and looks pleased. Seppo's quiet but occasionally mumbles something nobody hears. Conny goes around and encourages the others – he's done most of the work on these four songs. He doesn't direct, he's no conductor, and he's careful not to tread on anyone's toes.

At half six Sigge looks in. He's got another kid with him whom he wants to test out on hard-rock. 'We're going to make a new band', says Sigge, 'but I'll still be with Lam Gam.' They go into the other music room and start up a hard rock riff so it bounces off the walls. I go into the second room and listen. After a while, the others come in – no bad vibes as far as I can tell. Later, when I go into the café, the Gams are there talking. 'He can't fucking think he can skive off and still be in the band', says Ola. Lollo fills in that 'he really only wants to play hard rock with other people but he's with us 'cause we're so well known.' Jonna tries to calm the situation by saying that 'nothin' will come of him anyway, he's such a bummer.'

DISSOLUTION

During the summer of 1985 the band was forced to break off playing since the Ark's instruments were loaned out to a municipal summer camp. The band entered its third phase when they started rehearsing again at the end of August. They began with great enthusiasm and signed themselves up for a rock band competition taking place that autumn. One of the conditions of entry was that the bands had to play three of their own songs. Lam Gam had one already, and everyone was committed to working hard to compose two more. After stormy discussions they also decided to decline all performances until the first of November. The rock band competition was a common goal which placed demands on and kept the band together. However, despite this, after about a month the rehearsals began to go badly. It became clear that Seppo and Sigge had developed most during the summer. Seppo was a transformed drummer: he had sat and mimed drumming to gramophone records nearly all summer. Sigge had bought an electric guitar with which he had spent the

Lollo: In the long run, I think somebody's gonna quit.
Ove: Who?
Lollo: I think Sigge . . . he only wants to play hard rock.
Ove: Have you all talked about it?
Lollo: No . . . sometimes we take it up, but it's so fuckin' painful, such things.

Conny: I care, you know, like if I see that Lollo's on his way out, then I take him with me somewhere [. . .] then if I see the junkies coming, then I know they'll drag Lollo along, so then I've got to make him stay . . . But the last time they came, he was here when I saw them, then he came up and said, 'Conny, I'm staying, I can handle it myself this time.' He knew I'd go and talk to him.

Jonna: ... It's got more fun to play ... In Lam Gam it was always somethin' to do with capital or how bad society is and that ... Nothin' wrong with that kind of music, but hell, not just that kind [...] In the old band Sigge, Seppo and I never got to do anything ... Sigge, he got sick of just pumpin' away, he never got anything cool to do – he wanted that, you know.

Ola: It was the gigs that were so great ... you miss that time when you were in such a gang of real mates.

summer. In addition, Sigge began to make it increasingly clear that he was not as interested in Lam Gam's music as he had been. He missed rehearsals and demonstrated in various ways that he was involved with other projects.

Another problem which loomed large for the band was Lollo's difficult situation. He had come to a dead end with his mother, and had lived most of the summer with friends whose parents were away. In the autumn he got temporary accommodation in the home of one of the youth workers, but the conflicts with his mother had taken their toll and his enthusiasm for the Ark and the band increasingly gave way to 'reefers' and the old gang at the mall. Many at the Ark tried to talk to him, but he wanted contact with no one except Conny and the social workers. For a few months Conny had more or less regular 'supportive conversations' with him and a warm friendship developed between the two. However, despite this support, Lollo began to drift out of the band.

Yet up to the rock band competition the band functioned fairly well, even if they never revived the solidarity and happiness of the spring. The band went forward in the competition, but not even that success resuscitated the old Lam Gam spirit; on the contrary, around Christmas the band fell apart. Lollo's difficult social situation, which was only getting worse, meant that he never came to rehearsals; Sigge thought the band's music boring and missed rehearsals. A listlessness permeated the atmosphere.

Then Sigge, Seppo and Jonna started a new band. There was never any discussion of this with the other members of Lam Gam. Initially, they intended to play in both bands, but when they felt the new band was functioning, they abandoned Lam Gam. Jonna, who never actually had anything against Lam Gam's music, was attracted by the power of the new band. The three were absent from Lam Gam rehearsals, but never openly declared they had left and there were never any conflicts with the remaining members. Everyone realised that a split in the band was unavoidable. However, a certain amount of disappointment that the three had simply gone could be detected. Immediately after the split, Conny and Ola decided to 'lie low', partly to wait for Lollo, partly to find new members for the band. Lam Gam reappeared a few months later with the three original members plus three new recruits.

The new group, however, never really got off the ground and broke up after three or four months. Ola and Lollo continued to play in several loose groups, but at present neither is playing in any band. Conny has been sucked into the semi-professional Gothenburg rock establishment and plays in several bands, yet has not left the Ark gang. The breakaway group, Sigge, Seppo and Jonna, have developed enormously. Unleashing an astonishing creativity, they have become a real song-writing team. Confidence in their instruments has been strengthened by intensive practice, and with their melodious blues-based hard rock, they are presently one of the most interesting bands at the Ark.

LAM GAM'S MUSIC

During the period Ove followed Lam Gam's activities, the band's repertoire consisted of seven or eight songs. Of these three were their own; the rest were classic Swedish punk covers – Ebba Grön, Magnus Uggla and Attentat. When the band began to do its own material in the autumn of 1985, they devoted all their rehearsal time to it. Their intention was to build a whole repertoire of their own songs, all of which – both music and lyrics – tended to be written in the same genre as the covers. Their first song, *The Sun*, was written by Lollo and Ola and could be described as a sort of traditional Swedish sing-along. It is clearly modelled on Attentat's *Boat Song*, which is a rock version of *The Sloop John B*. Despite the fact that *The Sun* is a rather plodding rock ballad, there is an underlying aggression and menace in the group's performance of the song. The drums are restrained and straight to the beat, even in the chorus at the end when the intensity increases. Conny's synth is also extremely disciplined and plays a single-chord background harmony through the whole song. The aggression partly lies in the dominating guitar distortions. However, it is primarily Ola's singing that makes the song something other than an ordinary sing-along ballad. In contrast to the restrained accompaniment, Ola tears into the song. Like Lam Gam's other songs, including covers, the lyrics are in Swedish. *The Sun* was written by Lollo and Ola after they had seen a TV

The Sun
The sun it will rise over the grey sky/ and light up your grey home/ Money is their weapon, power's not ours on our earth./ The fear it was theirs, but it's worth nothing now, no, worth nothing now./ See their courage, see their toil, they can't live like this their whole life.// Na, na, na, nana, na, na, na, nana, na . . . // But one day the people said stop./ You won't take our lives, no you won't take our lives./ For soon we'll have a free world, without a mass of rules/ where people can think and feel what they want. Yeah, what they want. Yeah, what they want. Yeah, yeah, what they want, yeah, yeah what they want . . . // Na,na,na . . . Na,na . . . yeah, yeah what they want.

programme on El Salvador and Nicaragua. The song is about a people living without hope and under oppression, but who one day rise up and create the conditions for 'a free world'. The text is devoid of historicism, neither does it refer to any particular people or country. This makes it ambiguous: Conny thought the text was about growing up in Bergslunden. The song is a monologue in which the narrator addresses a group of oppressed people and relates a story about a successful rebellion. Its message is that it is possible to change society by collective action. The chorus, which is like a repeated chant – na, na, na, na – breaks against the insurrectionary content and dampens the song's revolutionary-song character. The whole song has a mythic aspect – to console and give hope. The chorus helps to lend prophetic, religious overtones; otherwise, in concerts the main function of the chorus was to get the public singing along and clapping.

The musical influences behind Lam Gam's next song, *How Did We Get Here?* came from Imperiet. The bass melody is very like that of Imperiet's *Kicks*. The middle 8 is more or less lifted from another Imperiet song, *What Do You Think She Wants*. Needless to say, Conny, who wrote the song, is a great Imperiet fan. As in *The Sun*, *How Did We Get Here?* has a Swedish heaviness or melancholy combined with a pent-up and unreleased aggressiveness which conveys a sense of menace. The fairly fervent tempo, distorted guitars, the dominant and somewhat noisy and jagged synth, the simple, straight percussion and the intense, passionate vocals make this song sound rather like beginner's punk. The lyric is episodic and impressionistic. Its theme is the little man as victim of power – the ruthlessness of power and the dominance of money in life. The narrator asks his listeners how they can have allowed social development to go so wrong, why they have allowed themselves to be ruled by power. Like *The Sun*, this song has no specific time/place references, but it is obvious that it refers to the present. Power, which is addressed as YOU, is prepared to put our whole civilisation at risk in order to augment itself and increase its economic profits. The first-person narrator in the song perceives the injustices but has been rendered powerless. However, the lyric also wants to make us aware that we are all involved since we support this state of affairs

How'd We Get Here?
How'd we get here, was it by our own toil,/ was there really anyone wanting to get here,/ now we're here and 'war is everywhere',/ so much and so little we learn.// I've my contribution so I'll be glad/I think of other poor children/do you think, do you think, do you think I feel well// you got power by chasing money,/ you call it splendid, I call it slaughter,/ you got our support and our livelihood,/ but you pay us with war and death/ If you got a chance to make a million/you'd take it rather than let the world be/ do you think, do you think, do you think it feels good.

through our work and by adapting. This gives rise to a
sort of uneven exchange. People work and subordinate
themselves, but power responds by creating suffering and
ruin. In this way, guilt for the situation rests on both sides:
power is culpable when it is negligent and the people are
culpable through their passivity.

The words express a need to analyse, conceptualise and
try to comprehend what happens in society and in the
world. It fleshes out Lam Gam's punk rebel image and
links in well with the type of protest songs which were
common among Gothenburg's young suburban punks
in the early 1980s. The direct influences on Lam Gam, in
addition to bands like Ebba Grön and KSMB, were bands
of the progressive music movement of the 1970s. Despite
the accusations in the analysis of society, the enemy
(power) is not the object of any direct and open aggression
– there are no exhortations to revolt. In *The Sun*, the
narrator is outside the events he describes; in *How Did We
Get Here?* the narrator is a participant, he is one of us.
This indicates self-reflexion and a desire to act: despite
everything, to defy impotence and do something about our
inadequacies.

Lam Gam's third original song, also mainly Conny's
work, was entitled *Money And Dead Nature*. Musically,
this song is also fairly conventional suburban punk *à la*
Ebba Grön. Conny leads in by imitating the sound of a
helicopter on his synth, which gradually begins to sound
like a machine gun. The song has a driving tempo and the
song is strong, desperate and fervent. The synth dominates
the sound. *Money and Dead Nature*, like its predecessor,
resembles a form of protest song, with influences from
Swedish punk and progressive rock. The chorus is clearly
a paraphrase of Imperiet's *Gold And Green Woods*, but
there are also traditional stereotypes and symbols which
come, via Imperiet, from folktales and the Bible (wolves,
sacrificial lamb). The narrator depicts a society in which
the people have had hopes of welfare and happiness, but
development has led to oppression, war, injustice and
environmental destruction. The words are more aggressive
and desperate than that of *How Did We Get Here?*, but
equally lacking in hope for change. Identification with the
victims and the oppressed is palpable.

The three lyrics hardly offer any rational political

analysis; they express rather a search for symbols which can identify how one experiences the condition of the world and one's own situation. Even though they deal with social and political problems, it seems reasonable to assume they also deal with inner concerns. The impotence which is so marked in the last two texts may be seen as an expression of the author's own puniness when facing his parent's demands for success in school and in sports. The guilt, culpability in the encroachment of power, may be related to Conny's deep awareness of not really being one of 'them down there'.

If we consider Lam Gam's repertoire, their own songs as well as the covers, we find a striving for unity and a fidelity to the genre they have chosen. All the songs contain a very Swedish-sounding melancholy, a heaviness, which also exists in Lam Gam's models. The songs are usually written in a minor key and the melodies move in descending and plaintive legato patterns.

Compared with their models, aggressiveness and energy are not as marked in the Bergslund boys' music, partly because technical competence is lacking. Lam Gam's music, not only in comparison with their models, but also with other bands at the Ark, is hardly polished. This lack of finesse was one of the reasons that Sigge, for one, thought the music too uniform and dull. The low degree of working on, practising and polishing was also obvious in the covers, which did not quite plagiarise the originals. The covers were performed in simplified versions in which the nuances and playing finesse of the originals more or less disappeared. However, Lam Gam did not stint on special effects such as breaks with the audience singing along and clapping to the beat together with the public. Lam Gam's music is characterised by the guitars, together with the bass and the straight drumming, laying a heavy foundation which is then countered by the vocalist and the synth. The aggressive undertones are created by the singer's intensity and a fairly monotonous 'hard core hacking' by the guitars – a sound resembling hard rock as well as punk. Most important seemed to be to sound heavy, raw, and to have a song that showed feeling and passion. In short, the music should reflect a picture of a gang of tough boys who have rejected the middle-class values of school. Hence the fidelity to a style and reluctance to experiment with musical genres that, to Lam Gam, stood for other values. Hence also the demand for authenticity, that the music should represent and be a part of both the individual and collective identity. Lam Gam's music-making, therefore, should not be taken as any old recreational activity. The group constitutes a forum for working on the members' own experiences and impressions of the world; it occupies a central position in Lam Gam's identity-formation.

Figure 3 Lam Gam: *Money and Dead Nature*

Money And Dead Nature

1 You came to give us something/ A new time, an extinct people/ It's all about money and monster egos./ I can cope without capitalism/ For you crying's a disgrace/ We're your lambs, going to be sacrificed/ on our last trip through the free world.//

Chorus
For you get money and dead animals/ money and dead nature/ You get money and dead animals/ money and dead nature.//

2 You make bombs and grenades/ that are put in soldiers' hands/ but they don't want to kill but clasp hands/ but they'll kill with courage/ when they kill for their land./ What disgrace for your land/ When you hunt us like wolves hunt

lambs./ We've lost control of the journey/ can no one change the free world?//

Chorus
3   You came to power with a lot of laws/ that I don't understand/ So I can't complain/ But I know I can count my days/ Give to the rich and take from the poor/ Have you ever thought of the word disgrace/ when you hunt us like wolves hunt lambs/ We've lost control of the journey/ We're going to die in the free world.//

Figure 4   Lam Gam, sketched by a 12-year-old fan

DETACHED – CHANS

FACTS ABOUT CHANS
Name: Chans
Date of Formation: 1981
Home: Stockholm (capital city on the east coast, population over 1 million), in Villaholmen – a pleasant, old-established, densely populated district of mainly detached houses with about 10,000 inhabitants.
Number of members: 9.
Line up: lead vocalist, two backing singers, two guitars, bass, drums, synth, and manager.
Quarters and instruments: The band has its own rehearsal quarters in an old cottage in one of the members' back garden. Their equipment is worth about SEK 40,000; what they own collectively is valued at about SEK 5000 (1986).
Members:
Björn 'Valle' Wallin (b. 1969) vocals. Writes most of the lyrics. Like all the boys in the band, resident since birth in Villaholmen just outside Stockholm. Father a machine programmer, mother a PA. The cottage is on the Wallins' land. Like most of the other band members, chose an academic course in gymnasium (natural sciences). Was an exchange student in the USA in 1986–1987. Fond of comics and Talking Heads.
Håkan Bengtsson (b. 1969) solo guitar. Writes and arranges most of the music and also writes lyrics. Also plays in another group with a younger cousin. Father works for the local authority as an engineer, mother pre-school teacher. Started a technical course in gymnasium but changed to the social sciences. More hard rock influenced than the others and listens to a great deal of recent British ('cult') rock. Draws well and contributed to the group's fanzine, *Chans Mag*.
Gösta 'Talle' Tallgren (b. 1969) drummer. Was a cornerstone of the band, especially during its formation. Father a section head at the Board of Education, mother a primary school teacher. Technical studies in gymnasium. The only member with a steady relationship. Christian and involved in the church (grandfather a vicar). Participates in many different activities, and has danced breakdance and played music with two older boys in the area. An older brother has supplied Chans with many musical influences. Quite broad musical tastes.
Pär 'Olof' Olofsson (b. 1969) bass, sometimes also trumpet. In charge of the band's economy. Parents have their own computer company. Technical studies at gymnasium. Has been occupied with various small business deals with Frasse (buys and sells through newspaper adverts, etc.). Enjoys being cheeky and clowning about. Especially interested in punk (Dead Kennedys etc.) and funk.
Gustav Bergman (b. 1969) synth. Finnish origins, father school caretaker, mother works for the Cooperative Union and Wholesale Society. Technical course at gymnasium. Like Gösta, plays football.
Per 'Frasse' Fransson (b. 1969) guitar, vocals when Björn is away.

Also sings in a choir. Father economist with his own company, mother primary school teacher. Economics course at gymnasium. Lives in a somewhat 'posher' part of Boviken, a district of Villaholmen. Joined the band a few months after it was formed. In the summer of 1985 was together with Barbara-Ann.

Karl Gran (b. 1969) manager of the group. Takes care of PR and bookings, the *Chans Mag* and the fan club, both of which were disbanded after a couple of years. Mother a divorced primary school teacher, lives with an engineer. Economics course at gymnasium. Very involved in athletics.

Barbara-Ann, 'B-A' Sjöberg (b. 1970) backing singer (dua-dua). Plays a little piano and saxophone, but not in Chans. Has previously sung barbershop with Elisabeth. Divorced mother who works in second husband's business. Lives in the centre of Stockholm. Went to a comprehensive school specializing in music with Elisabeth and began to study economics in gymnasium in 1986. Barbara-Ann and Elisabeth joined the band after the winter break in 1985 after having met the boys on a skiing holiday in Austria. B-A is a keen skier and likes symphonic synth music à la Jarrre.

Elisabeth 'Betty' Österberg (b. 1970) backing singer. Has also played jazz piano and sung barbershop. Lives in an inner suburb alone with her mother, a journalist, who has a steady relationship with Betty's 'extra' father, who has his own engineering firm. Went to the music comprehensive and then in 1986 studied natural sciences in gymnasium. Interested in theatre and style. Her idol is Annie Lennox from Eurythmics.

COMMUTING TO THE COTTAGE

> School is a preparation for life, says Lector Barfot at a weak moment when he no longer has the wherewithall to give our questions sensible answers. Well, I'll be damned! responds Ljung (in discussions with our teacher in the Swedish language we always try to use authentic Swedish expressions). Preparation for life? Am I not living? Am I not living right now? Who knows if I will be living tomorrow?
> Hjalmar Bergman: *Jag, Ljung och Medardus* [Ljung, Medardus and Myself]

When the commuter train from central Stockholm arrives at Villaholmen, the immigrant families, hard-rock gangs and *Mirror* readers have long since got off, and I [Johan] feel ill-dressed and unkempt in the remaining company.[1] The sun shines invitingly on the rich vegetation – so close to the city and yet so idyllic! Along the winding lane I walk down are houses of varying size and age – neither mansions nor mass-produced boxes. Pears, apples and plums provide clumps of colour in the foliage along the fences. An established residential neighbourhood that feels like a private oasis – clean air and unspoiled by traffic noise.

The boys in Chans have lived here all their lives, at a comfortable distance from each other. And here, in a corner of a garden, they have their own 'home', a little red cottage with white trim. Björn's parents have put the old cottage – older than most of the houses in the district – at the band's disposal for a token annual rent of SEK 500. The band pays the electricity.

I go through a dilapidated wooden gate and look around at the tiny garden in front of the cottage. A few new bicycles are parked on the grass and from the cottage I hear sounds of talking, music, warm-up noises from the bass and drums. Near the gate are two graves marked with crosses: one for a pigeon which was found dead, the other for two white mice which the drummer, Gösta, forgot to feed while their owner, Björn, was on holiday in June. On a tree trunk is nailed an old LP – another is nailed up in the cottage.

The cottage has two small rooms, each at most 15 metres square, with a tiny hall between them. The attic formerly contained what was designated the 'grotto', but now it is given over to storing junk. The cottage has very low ceilings; it is necessary to duck going through the door. As I come in, band members emerge from both rooms, smiling in welcome, several even shake my hand, and someone I've never seen before comes up and introduces himself, politely, giving both first and last name. Everyone says hello. They are proud of their cottage and like having visitors. It is a Friday afternoon at the beginning of September. The school term has started and this is the first rehearsal after the summer break. I have only been here once before at the start of the summer, in June.

They all look well – healthy, suntanned, and young, even for 15–16 year olds. They are trim and lively and have obviously been to the hairdresser recently. Their clothes are more 'grown-up', almost as if taken directly from advertising posters: generally light-coloured, fresh and clean and not patchy – almost impersonal. No one stands out with any deviating style: the boys at least at first seem identical. However, after a while one notices a

Björn: There's not really been any problem with the cottage. Dad thought we should take away those crosses [laughter] in the garden there. I think they're still there. But otherwise there's no big problem between . . . We pay our bills on time and that [. . .] I think the cottage's a good thing now. It's good to have all the gear there, you can go in and play and Talle can have his drums there and go in and practise when he wants. And we don't bother anybody either, really. You hear it outside but I don't think it disturbs anybody, I hope not anyway [laughter].

Björn: I think we're really lucky. A lot of groups complain that 'Nah, there's no place to practise, you never get to practise, it's too hard to pay for instruments and . . .'
Gösta: We've got such a good thing going, we don't know how lucky we are . . .
Gustav: Right, it's only a few meters to our place.
Olof: We only need three things: echo, running water and a toilet.

Gösta: Like we're a gang and we've been together a long time. Most of us have been classmates since the first class and we play about once a week. We try to mix all the music we think's fun so we won't be . . . We don't want to have any special style that we *only* do, no, we want a little variety . . . It's a little more fun to listen to us then, I think. And we do a lot more than just play – in our free time. We travel together and that too.

B-A: There's eight of us. Two of us are girls [. . .] We play music. Sometimes it can sound like Dire Straits, sometimes like Simple Minds, sometimes like Talk Talk, sometimes like Talking Heads and sometimes it can sound a little rasta-like. 'A garage band' you can say, so people understand what it is, so they don't think we're a dance band. 'And we play rock,' I always say. 'Musical music, rather commercial but not schlager, but commercial rock.'

From *Chans Mag* no. 9 (March 1983): DO YOU KNOW THAT: – Håkan can't stick out his tongue. – Gran is drowning in tables and lists. – Bergman often has a cold. – Valle always reads comics. – Talle is good at balloon dancing. – Olof is a computer genius. – Frasse wants to be in the movies, G.

few variations. Björn is rather elegant – loafers, wide, light grey modish trousers, a white shirt and a short, bulky jacket in the Italian style. Most of the other boys have white trainers, moccasins or sandals, white or blue jeans without patches or slits, thin cotton T-shirts in light shades, one or two in somewhat darker pastels with a geometric pattern. All of them wear short, thin, light-coloured jackets. The group's 'manager', Karl, has a wrinkled trenchcoat and is today less well groomed than the others. He has just returned from practising for a sports event to be held at the weekend and still has on his light grey training suit with the trouserlegs stuck into a pair of long white socks. The guitarist, Håkan, is also more casually dressed, and has a badge with the name of a Stockholm football team on his blue denim jacket. Björn is wearing a silver cross around his neck and later reveals an M badge (the symbol of the Swedish Conservative Party) turned upside down, on the inside of his collar, but otherwise I see no insignia other than the crocodiles and other labels from clothing manufacturers.

All the boys have the same basic haircut: fairly short behind, brushed up with the help of gel, sometimes a fringe. Betty has the same hairstyle, though she has bleached and coloured her hair (in shades that change quarterly). The other girl, B-A, however, has long black curly hair. She is wearing a red Lacoste shirt and dark blue, elephant cord trousers. Betty is more made-up and seems more tense, highly-strung or energetic. She is wearing a turquoise sweatshirt with a label I've never seen before and a pair of black, tricot-type slacks. In her ears she has a series of rings, the smallest highest up, in good quality metal. She wears glasses and is eating an apple. Björn has recently acquired a pair of contact lenses and Betty is thinking about doing the same.

The girls arrived together, on the train before mine. B-A lives in the city and Betty lives in an inner bungalow suburb, near the old customs gates. They go to the same school and have only been with Chans for six months. They are fascinated by the boys, by singing in a rock band – especially Betty – and by being the object of a researcher's attention: 'Are you going to write a book about us?'

Music pours out of one room. A barely functioning

stereo stands on what had been a sink (the room was once the kitchen). The boys speedily alternate between the local radio's Big City Pulse programme, a record with a collection of recent British punk, and a record of the American cult rock group Talking Heads' better-known songs, which Björn loves. A few listen with concentration, others stand and chat. Across from the stereo, someone is sitting in a tattered old sofa, stringing a guitar. Someone else is sitting in an armchair, leafing through a comic. The remains of a Christmas tree have today been finally swept up and thrown out. Old, pastel nursery curtains hang in both windows, and on the floor is a worn, dark blue wall-to-wall carpet, doubtless a comfort on cold winter days. The room is hardly neat or cosy – rather, somewhat messy.

Some of the boys are doing acrobatics and shadow boxing, possibly a demonstration for the girls, and/or me. The atmosphere is casual and relaxed; there is no question of any open aggression. Neither is there much more than the most innocent of sexual manoeuvres between the sexes. Only the bass player, Olof, plays about with obscene gestures and jokes, which the girls respond to with a mixture of fascination and indignation. I see no alcohol consumed – either now or later, not even beer. They do drink, but always with their parents or with mates at parties, never together at the cottage. I see no smoking either, and the absence of ashtrays suggests that no one smokes. Very rightly, they are considered conscientious and reliable young people by their parents and their teachers.

I go into the other room where Olof and the drummer Gösta have begun to warm up. The rest trail in and try to find their ends in the tangle of flexes on the floor. The room is crowded with instruments: a drumset, a small voice amp with a band echo and large black speakers, two guitars and a bass amp, a fairly dilapidated Siel synth on a stand and three microphones. Someone has brought in a Highway Department signal lamp, given it a cap and eyes so it looks like some sort of robot. There are also ear shields, which are sometimes used during rehearsals, especially by Gösta. The single unbroken wall is covered by a huge poster filled with light green foliage, confusingly similar to the view through the window. Over the window is a curtain which blocks the view from the parents' house, and on which is written something about a party. Other-

Betty: [Music] is certainly one of my main interests. Theatre and anything to do with style, fussing about with hair . . . [. . .] use several cans of hair spray every day . . .

Betty: Oh yes, Olof [laughter]: Well, he's got two sides. Sometimes he's really perverse and really strange and really yukky and dirty all at the same time. Boy! And then he can be really difficult in rehearsals. But also he can be incredibly nice, you know, and incredibly pleasant. But most of the time he's weird! [laughter] He's the weirdest in the band, you could say.

Björn: Sometimes there's *too* many people.
Karl: Yeah but, that's what we want, a little . . .
Björn: My . . . my dad doesn't think it's so good with a lot of people coming and going, sort of . . . he doesn't want it to be like some youth club where everybody comes to . . . [. . .]
Håkan: But you can't just chuck them out, drive them away, that doesn't feel right.
Gustav: Yeah, but you don't need to invite them here either.

Karl: I've thought sometimes that it was so lucky . . . 'cause there's other people, other kids in class who live here too who didn't get to be in Chans, and they're outside, separate from us now. There's such a bloody difference [. . .] I think it's only natural to do things for those airheads, 'cause [laughter], I mean I'm the one who keeps things in order a little more.

Frasse: In the last class I was in – I went in the ninth class then – it was, how can I put it, a snob class. It was attaché cases and loafers and . . . [. . .] Ever since I was little my mother has said, 'Per, now he's going to be proper!' [. . .] I think you can look nice, I do. I don't think it's . . . But I think it's bad when people think, like they connect the person you are with clothes, that's dangerous. [. . .] Lots of people think I'm stiff, boring . . . that kid with his nose in a book who only sits at home with his mum. But I think everybody who knows me knows that's not true. But lots of people think that when they see how I look and that [. . .] I think clothes are fun. I think it's cool to have hairstyles and all that. Then it's always been like 'Clothes and cars, that's Per's thing' [laughter].' [. . .]
Johan: You've got a certain group style anyway? [in Frasse's class]
Frasse: Yeah . . . a little . . . like brand names and . . .

wise, the walls are decorated with an incredible mess of pictures and things, mostly music posters: Carola, with a breast carefully drawn on her blouse, Rockfolket, Clash, Echo & the Bunnymen, Simple Minds, Strindbergs, KSMB, Talking Heads, Elvis Costello, Billy Bragg, Uriah Heep, Yngwie Malmsten, Dead Kennedys. The girls have not yet set up any of their idols – David Bowie, Annie Lennox or J-M Jarre. The mixture on the walls is perplexing; it is difficult to decide what is serious and what ironic – perhaps it is all one big joke – even though all the boys like punk. There is also a variety of other signs or posters, sometimes humourously modified, and a condom, photos, bits of paper with cryptic messages for the initiated. Trophies and memorabilia everywhere: posters from school concerts in which Chans have performed; a sheet with the special CHANS logo printed on silk screen by Håkan's aunt. On the floor in the midst of all the mess are sheets of paper with lyrics written on them, but no one has systematically organised either lyric sheets or notes.

The room is crowded when everyone has taken up their instruments and found their places. The girls crowd together in the window, opposite the door. They keep fairly much together, even though B-A has been going with Frasse for a few months (a relationship that now seems to be fizzling out). Sometimes the girls joke around affectionately with the synth player, Gustav, who is shy and embarrassed. He is sitting on a stool, playing. I crouch in a corner together with two, somewhat younger, long-haired boys who have also come to listen. They have coats on and sit quietly, like me. One of them is Håkan's cousin, a few years younger than the band members, but on one occasion he said 'we' when talking about Chans. The boundaries between the group and their mates outside seem fairly fluid, but when you have been around the band a while, you understand that they exist. Chans consists of nine people, of whom the seven boys comprise the original and existing core. Aside from the girls, no one has either joined or left the band since it was formed five years ago.

The younger listeners leave after a while together with the ninth band member, Karl, the manager, who does not play in the band but manages bookings, etc., and who has just put together the final number of the group's fanzine, *Chans Mag*. Before he leaves, he promises to give me a few old copies, some material on the group's history, and a cassette with recordings of their songs. I shall also be able to see two 3-minute videos of Chans at his house. At this point the guitarist Frasse arrives, late as usual. He is notorious for forgetting things and also for being a snob. Today he is razzed by the others for his white linen suit. He is particularly well-dressed today since after the rehearsal, he and a few others are going to the TV studio to be in the audience during a live discussion programme about food, at which Astrid Lindgren is to be present. The boys joke about this, they are excited and a bit proud about this adventure, even though they won't be able to say a word in the programme.

The girls relate, equally proudly, that they have been extras in a video with the band +1, a passing star in the synth-based pop heaven. They want to sing Alphaville's *Forever Young*, but Håkan and Björn show little interest and steer the group carefully but firmly towards the band's own songs. The rehearsal lasts one-and-a-half hours, half of which is spent fussing, waiting, tuning instruments, adjusting the echo and volume, joking and nattering. Nevertheless, no one gets irritated, even though Håkan's patience is sometimes very strained. The band goes back and forth between different songs; some, started, simply peter out, but some are worked on more systematically. This is the first rehearsal of the autumn, so they all are very enthusiastic. There is no virtuoso and the playing is hardly tight, but the atmosphere is good and playful and everyone actively participates. Now and then bits from signature melodies on the radio are improvised, and suddenly *Helan Går* (a traditional Swedish drinking song) emerges, in a spontaneously innovated rock version, but is abandoned equally quickly. Then they rip into one of their old punk-style songs, only to hop back into a new song that sounds like a blend of synth pop and new-wave rock.

Suddenly, a new Mercedes honks outside – Frasse's father come to drive his son, Gösta and Olof to the TV studios. B-A plays around with the drums. Gustav and Håkan talk about the gig that Karl is planning for them later in the autumn. Betty knows a journalist who will write it up.

Beaming, Björn shows me some of the gang's 'secret' trophies: a bottle with indefinable, malodorous contents, a

Johan: How would you define the music you do?
Gustav and Björn: As Oasis rock!
Johan: Oasis – that's a special genre you've created?
Håkan: Yes.
Björn: We play such different music.
Gustav: Yeah, I don't know what kind of music we play really.
Johan: What's important then in the music you play? What's it supposed to be like?
Gustav: Fun.
Olof: I also think it should be fun. It should be cool to listen to.

Gösta: We call it Oasis and it's generally based on mixing [different kinds of music].

Håkan: We want to create our own thing. We don't want to grab, like jump into anything, like hop on a trend. So we just took the first, best hip word – hip and hip, but anyway . . . . Oasis, yeah well . . . It's not any special music style, but . . . It's nothing serious [. . .] Funk, punk, those kinds of styles . . . we wanted a short name [. . .] Cult, like, so it was Oasis [laughter]. I don't know why, but I don't think it's got anything to do with the desert.

Björn: Ebba [the band, Ebba Grön] came from Rågsved. I think that meant a lot. Then when *Ebba the Movie* came out, well, they come from 'The Oasis' in Rågsved and we had a tune called *Rock in the Oasis*. So it was Oasis.

Karl: They go to Storby [school] and we go to Villis.
Håkan: Storby's best!
Gustav: Shit school! [giggle]
Björn: See what happens when you go to Storby: break lamps, kick in doors, raise hell, right? [. . .]
Håkan: Too true, it's more fun in Storby, there's more people there.
Björn: No class then!
Gustav: New people . . .
Håkan: At Villis, everyone's sort of . . .
Gösta: Yeah, you get to see a bit more . . . of the world, so to speak [. . .] In Villis you only see *those* people . . .
Gustav: Everybody knows everybody else, like everybody knows who everybody is . . .
Olof: 'Everyone knows the ape but the ape knows no one.' [Swedish proverb, like living in a fishbowl.]
Björn: I think that's great!
Gustav: I don't.

bag of exceedingly mouldy bread and several other plastic bags with evil-smelling, decomposing contents. He tells me that they have their own 'god' called Hu and a special hill that they dig up during rituals at certain times of the year. They also have a party with music late in the summer called the Oasis Party after the name of their own music style, Oasis Rock. This year there was no party, however – perhaps they are growing out of it? Instead, there are more and more ordinary parties to attend, given by mates in Villaholmen.

Björn also relates that the band performs in various guises in addition to Chans. They may flip out as 'cult' punk bands, or don hoods and perform anonymously as a strange African percussion group – always balancing on the borders between children's games and youth culture.

Björn is called to dinner by his nine-year-old brother and I take the train back to the city with the girls.

VILLAHOLMEN

Villaholmen dates from the turn of the century and at present has about 10,000 inhabitants.[2] Blocks of flats were built in the 1950s; today, they are mainly occupied by elderly people who have given over their houses to their children or grandchildren. Every other resident lives in a single-family house and more or less the same number own their dwellings. The population of Boviken is about 1,000 and their houses are not quite as luxurious as those in the rest of Villaholmen. However, Boviken is a green and settled district and most of its houses have been individually produced in the course of the century.

The city lies only half an hour's train journey from Boviken (even quicker by car), and a modern high-rise area, Storby, is within walking distance. However, Boviken feels much further away, with its hills, luxuriant vegetation, idyllic small houses, and relatively homogeneous middle- and upper-class population. It feels cosy and protected – in a way, rather old-fashioned.

Large workplaces have always been few and far between in Villaholmen: people commute to the city to work. In the early twentieth century, a few railway workers lived in Boviken and Villaholmen had a waterworks, power station, joinery shop, small shipyards and various craftsmen, but neither agriculture nor fishing. Near Villa School (upper level comprehensive and gymnasium) a modern shopping centre was built in the 1970s, but otherwise Villaholmen lacks any sort of urban centre. The lower and middle school is situated in Boviken. Certain gymnasium courses, among them the technical, exist only in Storby, so half the boys in Chans are forced to commute there to study. Everyone commutes from these idyllic residential neighbourhoods – to the workplaces, shops or amusements of Storby or Stockholm. And so Villaholmen can remain clean, quiet and beautiful. 'Closeness to nature' is considered one of the area's major attractions, the 'nature' in this case being neither vast stretches of wild countryside nor fields and farms, but rather a recreational area.

Emigration frequency in the area is only 10% (as against 13% for greater Stockholm). About 4% of the inhabitants are foreign nationals (10% for the county), and 9% (14%) were born outside Sweden, in 24 different countries. Two-thirds of the adult residents of Villaholmen are married. Boviken contains just under 500 households, of which one third are families with children. Only 13% of the families in Boviken are single-parent families, which means that about 10% of the children live with one parent, usually the mother (17% for the county). The population of the area is quite young: 30% are under 20 years of age.

The supplementary benefit index for the whole of Villaholmen lies around one fourth of the average for Stockholm, early retirement, just over half. Villaholmen residents tend to be native to the area, healthy, married and anything but crowded: only 25% of the flats are one- or two-bedroom, almost half are at least four-bedroom.

Nor are the residents poor. Twenty percent are workers (35% for the county) and 30% in the higher echelons of white collar professions (14%). Just over 10% are low wage-earners and almost 50% high income earners (both 20% in the county). Boviken residents have high incomes but not as high as those in the better neighbourhoods of Villaholmen (index 120 against 100 for the county). Sixty percent of the women work, about half of these part-time, whereas nearly all of the 70% of employed men work full-time. Half of the employed women work in the public sector as against only

Gösta: There's like a sort of real control here. And everybody knows everything about everybody, what you do weekends, who your mates are and all the gossip and that. [. . .] I think there's good in that too and that there's a communal feeling as everybody knows everybody else in one way or another. You can be more anonymous in Storby and that's pretty nice actually.

Female teacher: A few years ago, it was rather bad. They beat each other up and there were raids too. Especially, so I've heard, from Storby. But as a teacher, I know that our students have been terrible to the students from Storby school, making derogatory statements and acting like snobs.

Björn: Residential area with houses, if you've got kids anyway, I think that's bloody important. [. . .]
Olof: You can get out into nature and relax and you can get into town if you want. [. . .]
Björn: It's like, you're not in town a whole lot anyway, but I think you'd miss a hell of a lot if you lived in one of those . . . somewhere where there wasn't anything. Here you can, like say 'I'm going into town to check out the movies' or go in and window-shop or buy something – you've got everything . . .

20% of the men. Forty percent (mostly women) work in service industries. Very few in Boviken are unemployed (only one fourth of the national average); the unemployed can actually be counted on the fingers of one hand. In comparison with Villaholmen as a whole, Boviken is rather mediocre, but compared with the whole county of Stockholm, it is an extremely well-off middle-class area, in which wives still, to a greater degree than usual, devote much of their time to their homes and family.

Voting figures from the last election confirm this picture: almost half of Boviken voted Tory, two-thirds voted for some party in the bourgeois bloc, less than 30% voted Social Democratic and the Communist Party received only a few percent. The local council is also bourgeois, but perhaps these figures should also be compared with those of the 'posher' parts of Villaholmen, in which three-quarters of the votes went to the Tories and 90% to the bourgeois bloc. In the nearby high-rise area in Storby, the figures were totally different: the Social Democrats and Communists together received 60% of the votes, the Tories, only 20%.

All the boys in Chans, except Frasse, have gone to the same class in comprehensive school, first in Boviken School, then in Villa School. Several of them had the same childminder and have been neighbours, so they have known each other a long time. Now in gymnasium, four of them have landed in Storby, which is large and socially much more heterogeneous. They are all aware of this difference and generally welcome the change – from the social insularity and strong social control of Villaholmen. All of them have done well in school (B+ average in their last year) and they set great store by good marks. The girls were in the same upper level class in Adolf Fredrik in central Stockholm, a school specialising in music, but have gone to different gymnasiums. Not even Betty or Håkan, perhaps the two most seriously interested in music, have dared specialise in artistic subjects: they all opt for safer options, following their teachers' and parents' advice about securing entrance to the labour market.

With the exception of B-A's parents, who live in a flat in central Stockholm, all the band's families live in their own houses. Most of the band members have sisters and brothers. Nearly all the parents have middle-class or white collar

Håkan: Here in Villis, there's not a lot . . . you live pretty cut off [. . .] Of course, you've got Storby here close. It's a little more typically Swedish, sort of [. . .] It can be hard later when you enter life, like, if you think this is the *whole* of Sweden, protected like this – it's very protected here. [. . .] It's great in a way too. And then it's very near town. You only have to take the train. It's really terrific how [we] live!

Håkan's father: Håkan [. . .] was about a year old when we moved here [. . .] He doesn't have any memories of anything other than this house, this home. [. . .] I think it's a pretty undramatic life, without any great dramatic turns . . . Time passes in peace and quiet. Very likely a fairly good childhood background. Today, professions – small businessmen, teachers, etc. They are not aristocratic or upper class, neither have they particularly impressive academic educations. Over one or two generations, several of the families have worked themselves up from working-class or agrarian backgrounds. They are more oriented towards technical and economic professions than towards the academic or cultural, but sometimes cultivate the odd cultural interest in their free time, which of course may have encouraged the formation of the band.[3]

There are a great deal of recreational activities to choose from in Villaholmen, not to speak of Storby or Stockholm – old-established sports clubs, primarily for individual sports such as tennis, golf, sailing, etc. There is a football club, in which several of the boys have been active. The school also offers extracurricular activities, for instance concerts, in which Chans has played. However, the area offers little in the way of extensive state, municipal or commercial cultural events or entertainment aimed at the local youth. Social workers, youth leaders, theatre producers or disco owners contribute little to the Villaholmen milieu. Parties are arranged privately – in school or in the home – and peer groups obtain the resources they need for their activities from parents or teachers. Recreational activities are thus steered more by individual initiative than by voluntary organisations or the public sector. Chans members are only marginally involved in religion and politics. A few of the band members are avowed Christians, but only the drummer is active in the church. A few are members of different bourgois party youth organisations, but mostly for social reasons (parties) than because of any active political engagement. The most organised events the band participates in are youth festivals arranged by an educational association, where they meet other young people under almost boy scout-like circumstances.

HISTORY

The group's history stretches far back into the boys' early childhood, a melding of neighbours, playmates and classmates. Being neighbours and going to the same schools contributed to the spontaneous formation of a gang of mates. When the boys were 10–11 years old they started

probably just the parents keeping together has great importance. You only have to look around here – we know about how many break-ups there've been. It's the times we live in in a way. For my part, I've found it a bit hard to understand.

Håkan: We've been together since the first class, since playschool really, we've known each other. And we've sort of built up all this together, a special humour or whatever you call it.
Gösta: Olof and I started [. . .] We were in the same class and we'd started the same gymnastics I think it was. So we got to know each other well. And Olof played trumpet and so we thought we could do something, and so we tried. We carried on and practised and practised and we did a few other things. He and I thought we'd open a little amusement park – as a joke [laughter]. You know, little dreams [. . .] Then Wallin and I made recordings, vocals and drums. It was very good [laughter]. No instruments otherwise, only drums and voice [laughter]. We had a few hit tunes like *Ba Ba Blacksheep* and such-like [laughter] [. . .] Håkan could play one of those gourds, and we had one of

those soap dishes that was grooved so he played on that [laughter] [. . .] Then it was the summer after the fifth year, before the sixth I think, then he bought an electric guitar and then it all *began*.

Karl: We probably know each other even better than we know our parents. We've been with each other more than we've been with our parents . . . playing [. . .]
Björn: I think everybody has a dream of playing in a band. We realised it.
Gösta: And then it was so perfect; everybody lives so near each other [. . .]
Johan: Why did you start to play just the sort of music you began with?
Gösta: It was the simplest, it was the closest to hand.
Håkan: We listened to it, Clash for instance.
Johan: Punk and that?
Håkan: Yeah.
Gustav: Yeah, it was punk.
Håkan: KSMB.
Gösta: It was the easiest to play.
Gustav: Ebba Grön.
Håkan: Mostly why we started to play punk, was probably not because we wanted to shock *directly*, I think. It was because it was easy, like an easy style to play . . . [. . .] The lyrics, they were a bit rough [. . .] but we really didn't believe in them I don't think.

Håkan: I felt, when I heard sharp, rasping chords and, you know, punk and noisy drums, you know, I felt like . . . it felt cosy, sort of. You thought like that was it. [. . .] It was the first thing that meant anything. Before there'd been Gyllene Tider [mainstream pop band where Per Gessle of the now famous Roxettes started] and such-like. But then . . . it said more – punk did. It was more . . . Gyllene Tider and Freestyle and those bands . . . had nothing to say, nothing personal at all in it. Like . . . When I listened to those old tapes I recorded – maybe you

in the municipal music school; they listened to and were interested in music. A few had older sisters or brothers who played, not least Gösta's big brother who provided the group with many musical ideas over the years.

To the influence of parents and school must be added that of the media. Punk reached its zenith in Sweden in the early 1980s and bands such as KSMB and Ebba Grön, the Clash and Dead Kennedys inspired the boys via radio programmes and the records of older mates and brothers and sisters. Also, a new wave of young amateur rock bands attracted a great deal of attention and stimulated other young people, including Chans.

The families and the school brought the boys together and inspired music-making; the media stimulated the idea of a rock band. In 1980 Gösta, Olof and Björn played around with drums, trumpet, singing and acrobatics. In 1981, the year the boys became 12, a group gradually took shape, gathering around Gösta as the informal social hub. The band as such was formed that summer when Håkan got an electric guitar. 'Chans', Gösta's proposal for a name, was accepted and his parents' cellar turned into a rehearsal room. During the first year, until spring 1982, their music was basically a weakly structured form of play, in which their own versions of folksongs and children's songs were mixed with punk and their own, very original lyrics. During this playful *first phase*, the group became close-knit and more clearly separate from their peers. The 'we' feeling was strengthened and richly varied texts were quickly and freely composed – a repertoire. The decision to form a rock band emerged gradually through playing games together, and through a common need to amuse themselves. During this first year Chans performed a few times for their parents and in school, in safe environments and playfully – not yet with any great seriousness.

Playfulness was of course an important ingredient in their choice of musical style. Punk put few demands on performance or perfection and suited original, somewhat naive lyrics. But did punk's anarchistic uproar actually mean nothing – which is what the boys later claimed? Although issues such as failure in school (there was none), opposition to parents (I saw no traces of revolt – the parents supported the band from the start and the boys

were very aware of that) were hardly immediate or relevant, the boys would nevertheless act-out wild, shrieking
songs with lyrics like the following (all are translated from
the Swedish unless otherwise indicated):

> I dig sabotaging all kinds of politics.
> With all the shit you pour over us,
> how can you think we'll get up and fight?
> When you ruin forests, tear our houses down,
> destroy playgrounds – we have sit-ins, but you shit on us.

or

> The day the bomb falls, we'll all be there,
> and Adolf in his heaven can shriek, can swear:
> Let it all burn, let it all burn up!
> They blow up all the people, blow up you and me,
> they blow up all the rotten shit that's loaded on to you.

besides calmer and more childishly naive lyrics like

> Aooo, aooo, aooo, aooo
> The leaves are falling for me and for you
> for everyone living on this planet [. . .]
> for everyone living and the ants too.

It is interesting that the boys today are so unaware of the
motives behind their early music-making. Possibly there
were several motive forces. On the one hand, in recordings
of Chans' early songs one can trace the acting-out of feelings and instincts, of both an aggressive and sexual nature,
which quite naturally go together with development
processes in early puberty, and which presumably also
contributed to the formation of this gang of boys. On the
other, these expressions seem primarily to be directed
against feelings of being cooped-up, of being failed by
adult authorities and threatened by an uncertain future,
etc. These themes permeated the period's teenage music
life and thus were determined and formed by the stylistic
field comprised by punk. But Chans' choice of just this
field and no other (hard rock, synth pop, reggae, mainstream pop, etc.) and the band's specific way of utilising
the raw material of punk nonetheless suggest an area of
conflict in the band which largely remained unconscious.
It is not difficult to imagine that the formation of the band
as well as the choice of punk was a sort of half-hearted
attempt at separation from parental and school milieus

know that [punk and new wave] programme, *Ny Våg* [New Wave] that was on? I recorded some of that [. . .] They had such incredibly creative music on that pro-gramme.

Gustav: You could say it was a game until we had to do a soirée. [. . .] And then, like we started to rehearse for that, get all the tunes together we were going to do and that. And it was then, you might say, it started to get serious.

From *Chans Mag* no. 10 (April 1983): We in Chans listen to a certain kind of music – 'punk music', like KSMB, Ebba Grön, Dead Kennedys, Clash, AC/DC. That's the music we dig. So it's not so strange that we play as we do, every one of us plays what he likes??????? 'Håkan'

From *Chans Mag* no. 9, vol. 2 (April 1984): Håkan Bengtsson: – How do you get inspiration for your songs? – At bottom I'm a hard rocker so I prefer playing rather harder songs with a real beat. But we also have other songs with a little reggae in the rhythm.

and a reaction against the demands for adaptation which so heavily pervaded these social environments.

Spring 1982 saw the beginning of the group's *second phase* in which the band was institutionalised, a process which was at first expansive and productive but later began to stagnate. In the spring of 1983 the band played at a *soirée* at school in which their performance was more serious – they realised they actually had a public. Towards summer this awareness became confirmed when the fan club and *Chans Mag* were initiated by their manager, Karl Gran. The band began to be more self-aware, objective about itself as a group, to regard itself and its music as an independent product to be described and marketed – not merely as a process. Consequently, recordings of songs became more important and a super-8 film was even made – influenced by rock videos. In short, the band acquired all the accoutrements of a 'real' rock group – portrait photos, decals, etc.

During this phase the band played a fair amount of gigs – in school, in the neighbourhood (in garages and cellars), but also in less 'safe' venues such as talent contests, youth clubs, festivals arranged by the youth section of the educational association Chans is connected with. Solidarity and communality were mythologised in the word 'Oasis' to denote the band's own (and hardly well-defined) music style. The boys performed in other, more or less transitory combinations under other names and other styles – rhythmic percussion, synth pop, underground avantgarde, etc. – parodies of styles which the group as a whole did not stand for but which were part of what could be called a youthful search for identity. Through Håkan especially (and his somewhat younger cousin) punk was complemented by strains of hard rock. But hard rock never became the group's genre – despite Håkan's musical dominance; possibly hard rock was too alien to the prevailing culture in Boviken and Villa School. However, Håkan incorporated hard-rock elements into certain songs and played more of his 'own' music together with his cousin in another 'Oasis' band, the Pimple.

Gradually problems began to arise. The group encountered dead ends and ceased to expand. The second phase ended in stagnation, especially during 1984. Several recordings were cancelled, to the great disappointment of

Håkan: Well, then I started to like hard rock more. It was a pretty obvious progression from punk I think, I mean they're closely related, musically and that. Not in lyrics or message [. . .] Only it was hard rock, it was good, I thought. But towards the end, then I wanted a little more melodious stuff – Deep Purple and Yngwie [Malmsten]. [. . .] It was then I started to like this . . . like more symphonic rock [. . .]. Yeah, that was the next, symphonic rock [. . .] That was this summer [. . .] And now I can't understand why I liked hard rock [. . .] [U2, the Cure, the Cult, Lloyd Cole etc.] are the latest I'm into – they're more . . . I don't know if you can say 'cult rock' or what [. . .] What I think's so good with such bands is that they're a bit mystical, like there's a bit of distance with them. There's a sort of mist around them in a way.

the manager, Karl (who later on began to withdraw somewhat, closed down the fan club and *Chans Mag* in 1985
in order to devote himself to a more successful career in
athletics). The 'crisis' was caused by several factors.
Possibly the band realised a turning-point had arrived as
regards competence: a few unsuccessful concerts and
criticism from friends and audiences shattered any hopes
of a rising career. At the same time, ambitions expanded
through listening to increasingly differentiated and complex music. The band became stuck between greater
insights into its own technical and artistic incompetence
and higher demands on their own music. The criticism
focused largely on the singer – central to the audience in
most vocal music (Björn could very well have had problems with a breaking voice). All this fed internal disputes
in the band, which, however, never resulted in open confrontation or actions.

During the same period, band members were confirmed
and Gösta became involved in the church, which aggra-
vated the wavering group cohesion and security since he
played a pivotal role socially. At the same time he also
started to breakdance and played on the side with two
older mates in a synth group. And he got a girlfriend.
Another cause of the group's stagnation was that school
demands, mediated by parents, were heavily increased in
the 8th and 9th class. The parents even intervened, wanting to reduce the number of concerts so that school work
would not lag – a demand that the boys reluctantly
accepted. The band also grew out of Gösta's cellar and
contemplated moving into studios in Cold Storage, a large
youth project in central Stockholm. This was emphatically
opposed by their parents as the journey would take too
much time from school work (and diminish social control). So instead, Chans landed in the cottage in Björn's
parents' garden, a solution which pleased everyone.

In summary, Chans' problems may be related to three
areas of conflict. The expansive group dynamic clashed
with demands issuing from the social environment, particularly as represented by parents and school. Intractable
tensions arose between playfulness and seriousness,
between desire and demand in that the band's limited
musical abilities collided with increasing demands from
the public, from music life in general, and from the boys

Betty: Before we were like two
people, a pair. Now it's like I
run around a little with
whoever. Lots of my friends
don't have just one, but we all
meet, we're a big gang.

Betty's mother: I think she
wants to keep in contact with
these boys anyway. It must give
her something somehow.
Anyway, I think she gets a kick
out of it. And then I think
there's a bit of vanity in it too,
don't you? To be *in* a group
and make a record . . .

themselves. And finally, one suspects that the group was no longer enough for individual development requirements; it needed to be complemented by other contexts, which is why the members became engaged in other activities and situations, without, however, disbanding the group and losing its security.

A reappraising *third phase* was initiated when the band members met the girls in the spring of 1985. Betty and B-A were not part of an equally clear-cut group; rather, they were involved in shifting female groupings – fairly typical for young girls. Initially there was also a third girl, sometimes friend, sometimes foe, who occasionally sang with the band. B-A and Betty's relationship with Chans was not all that smooth, either, in the beginning, but it held, reinforced by a common commitment in the band. Although the girls did not live in the same place, they were friends from school and, as has been mentioned, met the boys on a skiing holiday. Both girls played piano in music school, they both sang and had indulged a little in a barbershop quartet with two girl friends. Inspired by a jazz-loving former step-father, Betty had tried playing in a big band for a short time. Otherwise, the girls' social backgrounds were fairly similar to the boys'. The girls lived in a somewhat less insular environment, closer to the city centre with divorced mothers, and at least Betty's background was a little more 'cultural' than 'economic' (her mother was a journalist). But in neither case were there any considerable class barriers to cross to Boviken.

The girls' meeting Chans satisfied many needs. Getting to know boys close up, in their own gang, was exciting. For a few months during the summer Betty got involved with one of the boys, Frasse. The girls also thought it was fun to participate in the group's slightly unconventional social life which was boisterous and playful. And above all, it was fascinating to suddenly be part of a rock group, to stand on stage and be part of the band's image and reputation. For the girls it was a large step – away from school and their home environment, from other mates and from their own sex.

For the boys, the experiment with including girls can be viewed as an attempt to solve the problem of stagnation by taking on new sources of energy – social as well as musical. To allow 'outsiders' into their hitherto clearly delimited

Karl: That was when these Chans parties started – on our birthdays [. . .] and it was just us guys. [. . .] It was then we started getting called gay [everyone laughs]. And that sort of kept on till the ninth class.
Gustav: But I think it was . . . I think because they found out we ran about naked in the field there.

Frasse: It was probably part of the process, I don't know . . . [. . .] The day after everybody started to wonder like 'What are we doing?' That's what I think anyhow. *I* thought so anyway [. . .] It was probably good that we met the girls . . . yeah I think so. Otherwise we'd been a bit out of it, just stuck in the same groove.

Olof's mother: Well, first, it's good they socialise with girls in a natural way, do the same things, so to speak. And then I think they [the girls] give the band a lot, in that they go to a music school, they know and can do a lot. And then there's usually a bit of a different atmosphere when girls are around – a bit lighter and softer and that. And they behave a bit differently perhaps.

group was also a big step for them. The girls opened up the group for new impulses, which gave a different dynamic to the oppositions and reshaped the areas of conflict. The entry of the girls answered a need for social regeneration, for relieving the sense of being shut in, which in the long term would be stifling. And Chans broke up their single-sexed insularity during a period when the boys were becoming more interested in the opposite sex. At parties and in unpublished lyrics they had acted out taboo-laden feelings in the 'social womb' provided by a safe peer group. However, this protective incubator could also be experienced as altogether too homogeneous and uniform. The group's collectivised longing, desires and memories needed new outside impulses in order to satisfy the boys' current development needs.

Thus the two girls effectively fulfilled many important needs of the group as a whole. Even if Chans also occasionally let in other boys from Boviken to play different instruments (especially saxophone), it may be presumed that the girls would be permanent members precisely because of their social distance. It was this separateness (different gender, school, residence, age – one year younger – circle of friends) the boys needed, not consanguinity. And it provided a guarantee that the original gang would somehow be able to remain intact as the core of the new Chans. The girls became backing vocalists (dua dua girls), that is, they were placed on the musical periphery, and were 'allowed' neither to play instruments nor to sing solos (either they did not want to or did not dare). It was always possible to ditch them and even if they became integrated into the group, it was easy to separate out the boys as a distinct subgroup.

The girls' entrance into the group was only one of many revitalising elements in this phase. I [Fornäs] happened on the scene during that summer and was welcomed by a group of youth greatly needing to think about themselves and their history. The boys had begun gymnasium and were split up by different courses of study and schools (Storby and Villa School). The girls faced the same the following autumn when they too went to separate schools. Instead of devoting themselves to rather more 'childish' and punk-inspired activities (including the fan club and fanzine), the band recorded a single, produced in 500

Johan: Do you think it's common for girls to have boys as mates?
Betty: I think that at our age there's lots of girls that think boys are . . . Before, boys the same age were a bit younger and then it was only interesting with boys who were older. Now it's still – with boys around, it's still fun if they're a little older, but you've started to go around more with boys your own age.

Johan: Have you ever thought about whether to have a mixed or single-sex band, where there are only girls?
Betty: Mixed.
B-A: Me too [. . .]. As there's such a big difference between boys and girls, it's like they've got to balance each other.
Betty: Otherwise it's boring, if it was a band with girls – it's easier for girls to be enemies, easier than for boys. Boys go and have a fight and make it up that way, but girls, they go and talk rubbish and it's easy to make splits that way. Then, if there's boys there who keep it together, then maybe . . . .you become friends with the girl for their sake, to like keep it all together. [. . .]
Betty: Girls certainly talk more shit – about each other.
B-A: Yeah, I think so too.
Betty: Behind your back.
B-A: Yeah, and boys maybe think it but they don't say it.

copies during the winter 1985/86. During a winter break holiday in Austria in 1986 they thought up a new name: Kirschberg after the Alpine resort where the Swedish comedy *Sällskapsresan* (Group Holiday) was filmed – the name reflects their own experiences as well as media material.

An important change occurred when Björn went to the USA as an exchange student for one year in summer 1986. Frasse took over as lead singer, but despite his hopes to the contrary, he did not become a permanent replacement. The band experimented with an increasingly wide range of musical styles and their technical skills improved, albeit not by leaps and bounds. Only Björn, Håkan and Betty seemed to have any serious dreams of a musical career, so Chans remained a 'hobby band' – with no illusions of a career in rock. At this point in time, the character of the group definitely changed. Reminiscence, playfulness, and the social circumstances remained, but the individuals were maturing and the gang had lost some of its symbiotic character. Instead of *being* Chans, the nine members of Kirschberg *used* the group for specific, limited purposes while they invested their energy and engagement elsewhere.

THE CHANS CULTURE

Chans originated in a close-knit gang of boys but later incorporated two girls. In addition to their being middle class, it is this which primarily differentiates Chans from OH and Lam Gam. The girls are not in the band on equal terms with the boys. Being a singer is a typical female role in music, and even though rock has had more female instrumentalists since the advent of punk around 1976, they are still a small minority. To 'only' sing backing is a marginal position in a band. The girls in Chans do not attend all rehearsals and the boys may sometimes even do gigs without them. Neither do the girls participate in other group activities in Villaholmen (parties, going to films etc.). However, they *are* in the group, which means that the group is not single-sexed. The girls' wishes and their actions are part of the group dynamic.

This makes it difficult clearly to delineate the Chans culture. On the one hand, it is still primarily formed by boys and its roots are buried deep in their shared child-hood experiences; on the other, girls are present with their different backgrounds. In the interplay between the sexes, many different tendencies coincide. The boys are at once attracted to and reject certain characteristics of the girls: their greater and more 'female' awareness of style as regards image, fashion and popular music; their musical competence (being pupils in a music school, involved in many musical activities, their previous performance experi-ence); and not least, their – especially B-A's – ability to handle social relations sensitively. As former outsiders, the girls were capable of detached insights into the boys' relationships and were therefore able to act as dialogue partners and conflict mediators. B-A spent a great deal of time on the telephone, talking to girlfriends, classmates and the boys in Chans – behaviour associated with particu-lar female qualities and traditional female socialisation. The girls noticed relationship problems and functioned as lightning-conductors. Internal conflicts, for example between Frasse and Björn or Frasse and Gösta could in part be deflected in the girl–boy polarities, but they were also worked on in conversations with the girls, who were concerned and interested in dealing with such questions.

For the girls, this is a continuation of and a socialisation in the pattern our society prescribes for women. There are maternal elements in B-A's relations with the boys: her role in the group has qualities of caring concern. Typically too, this socialisation proceeds into adapting to subordi-nation: the girls do not have an equal say in the group's activities – musical or social. In order to be included at all, they must put up with a subordinate, marginal position.

Such is doubtless the case with most if not all of the few mixed-gender bands in this age group. There are many reasons why girls seldom play rock music and why young bands often tend to be single-sex. It seems probable that the girls involved in rock music begin to play and form groups at a somewhat older age, in their late teenage years. Among younger girls, there are female pop singers – in typical subordinate positions, and single-sex female groups involved with other music than rock (barbershop). In the middle or later teenage years, girls may form rock bands in order to avoid conflicts with boys and to have a chance to make their own decisions. 'Equal' mixed-gender

Håkan: I think the sexes are so different that there'll always be different purposes for them in life. OK, you don't need to go to extremes, but I don't think you'll ever get away from it so there'll be total equality. Then I think you'll lose a bit of the tension [. . .] There's a clear tendency that if there's girls in the band, then they usually sing and the boys accompany. Maybe boys are more interested in technique and equipment while girls are more into the music itself and singing.
Johan: Why aren't there more girls playing instruments in rock? [. . .]
Gösta: I don't know. There's still a lot of girls who sing. But maybe that's got to do with it being really tough in a way, a little raw, no not raw, but it's tough, raunchy to stand there with a distorted guitar or drums or bass with the volume turned up . . . It's boys who want to stand there and be hip in a way. [. . .] They [the girls] have other ideas, they often have another way of seeing things – and other tastes in music, of course.

B-A: I think that when boys get into something, they really commit themselves and think, 'Now I'm going to be good at this.' Girls maybe think, 'OK, this is cool, so we'll do it,' but then they think: [...] 'Yeah, well I can do this a while but then I want kids and a family' – more or less. But boys say 'I'm going to do this my whole life, and I'm really going to be *good*'. [...] I think more like 'This is cool for a while' – it's nothing I'm going to commit myself to.

B-A: Mother, now she's had a great time, and so you think, 'Now I'm going to try that as it looks really cool.' Yeah, I think my mother and I are very alike actually [...] It was hard for her when she was pregnant and that and so she needed my support, she thought it was difficult then, to get married and have a lot of kids hanging around her skirts [...] *I think I became independent because of that*. I learned to take care of myself and help my mother *too*. And then my sisters and brothers ...

B-A: I think most women *don't* accept men lording it over them in a way. But *I've* never ... Well, maybe I've been discriminated against because I'm a girl, but *somehow* I've always turned it around so I've got what I wanted anyway.

bands, with both sexes having achieved sufficient musical competence and experience to warrant mutual respect, usually only arise when the members are in their early twenties.

In Chans, the girls seem to illustrate different possibilities, which I shall try to outline. Of the two girls B-A is least critical of traditional female roles both in life (with her mother, who works in her step-father's company, as a role model) and in the group (as problem-solver, without any particular claims on occupying a more central position musically in the band). She most clearly illustrates the fact that the group role also contributes to socialisation in the sexual role. In her close relations with the boys B-A manoeuvres and nurtures. Betty gives more resistance, her role sits less comfortably – in life (inspired by her independent mother, who is very concerned about professional pride, solidarity among women, and about keeping men at some distance), as well as in the band. Betty expresses dissatisfaction with her peripheral position and 'disturbs' the boys sometimes by recklessly flirting with all of them instead of following B-A and going with one, if only for a short time. Both girls developed different forms of defence and protest against the boys' dominance, primarily a retreating and passive defence, such as avoiding engagement in or responsibility for gigs, and retaining certain interests, female friends and activities apart from Chans.

The reasons why Chans, despite everything, allowed girls in the band, whereas OH and Lam Gam would not even entertain the idea, have to do with a less expressed 'male' quality in the original gang. Testing out a common masculine identity seems less problematic for the boys in Chans than for the members of the other two bands; or at least the Chans boys have other methods of dealing with sexual identity than acting out in a single-sex band.

In summary, the girls were allowed into Chans on the boys' terms because they could fulfil certain functions for the boys and for the group during a particular (individual and collective) phase of development. The relations between the sexes in the group exemplify sexual role socialisation within the same age group, where social expectations and parental norms are pronounced. The girls occupy a marginalised and subordinate position largely because of the lack of possibilities for alternative action. However, there are also gestures of at least passive defence and resistance from the girls. They are held at arm's-length, because Chans was from the start a boys' band, because rock is still male-dominated and because they do not belong in Villaholmen. Gender relations can thus be interpreted as an expression of male dominance and the reproduction of traditional patterns in the peer group. Yet, at the same time, a nascent opening may be discerned, for example, in the fact that the girls are actually permitted as partners in a somewhat democratically functioning collective.

Consequently, Chans is not representative of a 'boys' culture in the same way that OH and Lam Gam are. In terms of class, however, the Chans culture is strongly marked by its members' social position – a totally middle-class culture, cultivated in an environment in which money means more than education. Chans' (male) members live in almost identical circumstances in the same neighbourhood, they are the same age, have gone to the same comprehensive, are affiliated with the same class. All this naturally renders the group very homogeneous. However, two factors make it slightly difficult clearly to determine the group's culture. First, the culture does not encompass any common ideological project or message such as those borne by the Lam Gam and OH cultures. Secondly, the Chans culture is situated in the midst of a complex crossfire of demands from the boys' surroundings, which, internally recreated in the individuals, creates a particularly contentious, unharmonious pattern.

Chans' socio-cultural milieu is intersected by a series of disparate demands: to perform, to make money, to have many contacts and many recreational activities, to have a wealth of experiences, to control life, to have fun, etc. The individuals in Chans have internalised these demands; they have by no means broken with their parents' or school milieus. By means of various group activities they attempt to deal with these external and internal demands and to cope with the antagonisms between and among them. They wish to take advantage of as many of life's promises as possible and not miss any opportunities for a good life. Consequently, they must be achievers in many areas simultaneously – their parents', school, among their

Betty: Anyway it's *them* who do everything. It'd be cool with a band where I was in more with creating things. But then I can't write songs [. . .] I'm not usually nervous that it won't sound good, 'cause I know if it sounds bad it won't matter . . .
B-A: Yeah, then we blame them! [laughter]
Betty: It's up to them, right? we have so little to do [. . .] Since we're just background, we can say 'Wasn't us, was somebody else,' more or less.

Gösta: You want contact with people.
Håkan: Exactly. The most important thing is not making a hell of a wad.
Gösta: No [. . .]
Olof: It's not just that, like there's a lot of other more important things.
Johan: All this about having your own business, why . . . what's so good about it?
Olof: It's freer. [. . .]
Karl: You should be able to advance . . . in many different professions.
Gustav: I think so too. You could chop and change a bit.
Karl: OK, when you're about 40, then maybe you can have a steady profession you keep with later, that you really like.

mates, in recreational activities, and *vis à vis* media ideals. This makes the Chans culture somewhat stressed and nervous – a sort of restless striving to manage to do everything and not get stuck anywhere.

One means of living up to many different internal and external demands is to seek some sort of dynamic balance between the different sides of life: not a static 'middle way', but rather a mobile equilibrium in which every movement in one direction must be balanced by one in the opposite. In this way work and leisure, home and school, discipline and letting go, are balanced. This attempt to achieve equilibrium between extremes is obtained through continual flexibility, which seems to be the substance of the freedom that Chans strive after. Their lives are chameleon-like and capricious: they do not wish to stay long in any field, they do not want to work too long with anything, or to bind themselves to any particular style. Their striving for constant change also contains a fear of bonds and continuity, which pervades and complicates intimicy and depth of experience. Flexibility is an invaluable resource and source of pleasure, but it is also sometimes a torment and an almost neurotic compulsion: one has constantly to be prepared to alter or change in the face of new situations and to have various alternative moves at hand. It is also difficult to make any real choices, and such restlessness paradoxically seems finally to dissipate into inertia and become entrenched in just the sort of life that Chans' parents lead in which no one (so far at least) seeks to realise a great dream or bring about any sort of radical change. Flexibility is compatible with an obvious conformity. It is a way of handling a position between a kind of insularity and traditionalism in the socio-cultural environment and the sort of modern openings that also exist there, *inter alia*, via the media. Flexibility and oscillation provide an opportunity actively to confront and manage a future full of rapid changes without losing those resources which the parental culture has bequeathed. A few somewhat anachronistic alternatives exist in the parents' generation; and the alternatives in the media world are much too abstract. Chans' immediate environment contains hardly any visible and concretely different alternatives – no Ark, no clearly deviant subcultures – only a strong homogeneity and conformism

Gosta: I think you work best if you have a mixture. A balance like, not too much, not too little, but so you know that *if* it should go wrong in one area you've got *something* that makes you happy.

B-A: I want to work, I don't want to be any housewife – I'd never manage that.
Betty: No, never! But before, I think I'll try a lot of things but then, like around 40, then have something permanent you like and want to go on with.

among both their peers and adults in Villaholmen. On another level, flexibility, restlessness, help to keep the group together by satisfying each member's special interests: having songs in a wide variety of styles, allowing the group to flit from one activity to another. Clearly, balance and flexibility also require and create *distance* or detachment – for better or worse. Social relations in the group are marked by detachment, as are the individual members' relations to everything from music styles to politics and choices of profession. Detachment is both an ideal and an actual characteristic of Chans.

Detachment has various aspects: a sort of impersonal friendliness towards outsiders, a way of always showing an impeccable facade and ostensibly accommodating everyone – but this at the expense of being able to establish real intimacy and depth in relationships. Another aspect has to do with individual subjectivity: a tight control over instincts – self-restraint in other words. These two aspects complement each other and are directly connected to the predominant parental culture. They are prerequisites for melding into the upward-striving middle class with some economic capital from which Chans emerged. One must be poised, have moderate tastes and styles, be attractive and not be pushy. A third aspect of this detachment has more to do with modernity and youth culture: it is about a sort of transitory preparedness, a protean attention to all (symbolic) objects and styles. It is a modern, urban way of modelling or presenting oneself, of attaining a continually variable surface in order to be able to be accepted anywhere.

The boys in Chans do not seek closeness, intimacy, authenticity or truth at any price. Like images in a rock video, they cast themselves back and forth between opposites in order to achieve balance and distance in each individual sphere. It may seem reasonable to assume a gap between appearance and reality, surface and depth, style and identity, inner and outer, but that would be misleading. The youths in Chans are in fact not other than what they appear to be in different situations. Roles, style shifts and detachment are not the effects of the search for a firm centre. Internally as well as stylistically, the boys express conflicts and fissures between the different demands and impulses they try to cope with.

Betty: I want to have a profession . . . I want several. I don't know what I want to do. I could imagine being an economist. I want to travel abroad. [. . .] I don't know yet, I don't know . . . I have to see what seems cool first. And then . . . I'll do something else. Then if I want to study, then I'll do that instead. Since I don't know . . . [. . .] You can always get hold of money, I think. I'm not worried about that . . . Something will come along . . . I don't think I'll be rich, but I'm not worried about money 'cause I believe I'll always manage, and I'll never sit around getting grey on some sofa, being unemployed. OK, it's possible I'll be unemployed, but I'm not worried about the future.

Male teacher: Rock and that type of music still has low status around here. [. . .] I think, for instance, that a very common dream is to be a director of some sort, to land in some sort of managerial position and be active in business and industry in some way. [. . .] They [Chans boys] are a little phlegmatic. Possibly at bottom they aren't that engaged in *anything* actually. But then they're so young [. . .] They think 'It will turn out alright somehow.' That's one side of their security . . . a little false too – a security they must break out of. Then there's the security in the band . . . I think anyway they're secure in themselves too. But then, that has a reverse side – that they're not really 100 per cent engaged in anything.

Håkan: I think we can let loose a little at any time. We are almost never bored. We can never be bored, we always find something to do. You know, we have a very special humour too. If we really get going, we can think everything is fun and that's just great. But it can be difficult sometimes too . . . It can be awkward too – to never be able to be serious.

Gösta: To have fun is having a mate to joke with, to enjoy yourself with – I think dancing's great fun. To just dance your heart out. Forget about the sweat and that and just dance.
Johan: To throw yourself into it, to act-out?
Gösta: Yeah, that's it, that's what it's about. Act-out and . . . say what you think.
Johan: What's the opposite to having fun?[. . .]
Gösta: It's . . . yeah . . . just doing one thing, or . . . to have friends you can't talk to, say what you think, or joke with . . . can't be natural with. *That's* truly dull, I think!

The Chans culture may be summarised in a diagram. In the middle are the central characteristics; above are positive ideals and below, negative, threatening elements. On the left are placed those elements having to do with tradition, stability, the adult world and what is 'Swedish': security and order, routine and coercion. On the right are the modern, mobile, youthful and 'foreign' elements: fun and cool, affectation and the dangers of competition.

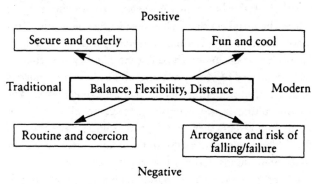

Figure 5 The Chans culture

One of the band's central values is 'having fun'. Music should be fun, people should be fun, life ditto. The members of Chans do not talk as much about communality/ solidarity ('G') in terms of having an intrinsic ideological value as do the members of OH; it is valued instrumentally – as providing an opportunity to have fun. The group heightens the feeling of life and through farce and physical as well as verbal acting-out, the group increases intensity in different life situations. When 'boring' demands are expected or placed on you, you brighten up the time together through jokes and acrobatic games. Farce, with its strong elements of ironic detachment, possesses several sides. It may be seen as a defence against the demands of the world and against a too emotional engagement in people or issues. Jokes and detachment enable you to avoid conflicts in and around the group and to manoeuvre boring situations and demands. Numerous activities are resorted to to fill empty hours and make boredom tolerable or to repress it. Perhaps fun is also a defence against a colonialised future, a future life which already feels circumscribed by demands from school and parents – demands that the young feel obliged to accept since the promised future has too many attractive privileges to be rejected but still not sufficiently attractive to commit oneself to. We shall return to this hypothesis later.

At the same time, fun is a constructive and symbolic way to produce pleasure and desire, to raise the quality of life, to live intensely and transform gloom to gaiety, greyness to colourfulness. The hedonism of 'display', of letting go, gives an aura of pleasure to the surroundings. Joking together establishes a private space around the gang in which the members themselves decide the conditions. This whole manner of handling time has parallels with Lam Gam's 'doing nothing'. The difference, however, is characteristic: instead of 'doing nothing' Chans burst into flurries of activity, engendering thereby a collective euphoria. The Chans culture is not defensive enough to allow time to stand still; rather, there is a fear of stillness paired with a fear of binding engagements and intimacy. They do masses of different things in order not to get stuck in any.

Chans' language is also loaded with very diverse associations – keeping abreast of idioms, word-play and references to TV and radio programmes, artists, current events and drawing on their own shared experiences and memories. In the total interview material, Chans mentioned 170 different artists (90 per cent of whom were in rock and pop music), some 90 different genre terms for music styles, and used around 160 different value judgements on music. This versatility may be very disarming for an outsider who lags behind; and it contains a youthful variant of a sort of upper-class-oriented exclusivity in tastes and style. However, there is an equality to the language: everyone participates in it more or less equally, no one dominates (in contrast to OH).[4]

The Chans culture can sometimes seem paradoxical. It celebrates fun and intensity, but rejects deep and binding engagement in experiences. It condones freaking out, but only under orderly forms, only intentionally and temporarily (for example, at parties) – not more daring escapades into the unknown. That the triad of security, order and control comprises a strong ideal is obvious in Chans' vision of the threats and attractions of the future. It is also present in some of their song material, which describes the risks of 'flipping out' (drugs, etc.). Whereas fun is pitted against the boredom of routine and being

Betty's mother: To me, just the fact that they're involved with music makes them a little more flexible and perhaps more fun as people [laughter]. I think people that do music are sympathetic. And I think they'll retain some of it. They'll certainly *not* become any standardised, stuffed-shirt bank clerks. [. . .] It's good for them to devote themselves to music because I think it makes them more open. You become a more open person.

Johan: What are you most afraid of when it comes to your own future?
Karl: To be injured, or sick in some way [. . .] so that you can't live life to the full.
Gustav: You've got to be healthy!

Björn: I don't usually worry, I don't think it's worth it. Either it happens or it doesn't – there's nothing you can do about it.

Gustav: I'm quite worried about the future. With wars and all that. And . . . Yeah, like the unknown – you don't know *what* will happen. And then, there's how it'll be for us in the future. [. . .] You don't want to get sick, no accidents and such. And not to be hated.

Johan: What kind of life would you least like to have?
Betty: To be a junkie, prostitute in Stockholm's slums. I think that'd be the worst as I have such high ambitions, that'd be a real failure, to get so far down that . . . Maybe to have to go on the social, not have a real job [. . .] I know I have possibilities and I want to use them. I don't want to waste my life.
Håkan: If you take housing, I'd rather live in a house, maybe preferably in Villis – I've grown up here and there's something in that. But life – rather not be one of these geezers with a briefcase, who goes with his briefcase by *train* to the city, works and then goes home last, late like. [. . .] Sort of a 'Svensson' type.

hemmed in, security and control are contrasted with the risk (with a life of freaking out) of 'falling' socially or psychologically, and through pride or foolhardiness, losing control and gliding out of the parental culture's protective arms. Thus Chans strive upwards along both sides of the tracks. The conundrum is that the two sides contradict each other since security is inseparably connected to boredom, and fun entails a certain, if containable, risk of losing control. These contradictions are inscribed in Chans' social environment; they are expressed in certain conflicts within the group and are deeply etched in each individual.

These polarities may now be connected to other dimensions. To Chans fun tends to be geographically associated with abroad, particularly the United States, England and France, while boredom is linked to the Sweden outside Villaholmen. Chans do not lack neighbourhood or territorial pride, but this pride is not as unambivalent as it is with our other two bands. The cottage and Villaholmen are perceived with mixed feelings which are surprisingly realistic and objective.

The boys have a clear bond to a social space – a high degree of awareness about their own class affiliation. Through the media (for example, listening to music) and activities outside Boviken (via school, sports, entertainment, etc.), they obtain knowledge of the outside world. Class differences are palpable in comparisons with nearby Storby. Threatening images are very closely linked with class: on the one hand, a grey 'Svensson' existence, perhaps especially embodied in monotonous lower-middle-class white-collar occupations; on the other, a tasteless assertiveness, a too-rapid ascent up the ladder, which is expressed in affectation and insecurity. Chans' hostility and wariness towards affectation and arrogance have less to do with resistance against their own nature than with a distaste for the vanity of the social climber. The world of Villaholmen consists of many *nouveau riche* careerists, but even though ambitions are certainly allowed, there is a sort of parsimonious, parochial contempt for those who do not manage the climb elegantly enough. One should not study too much – marks should simply come out of the blue more or less. In several songs Chans criticise various figures for having dissembled in one way or another. Total 'naturalness' is never praised; on the contrary, one should fully and attractively employ the montage of styles from which one moulds one's personal image.

This is not without conflict, however. Certain members of Chans were secretly very critical of the vocalist Björn the year before he went to the United States (although we researchers thought the singing in Chans to be relatively good). Various elements came together in this criticism: the relief singer's struggle for a stronger position in the band, the group's shame and embarrassment over its technical inadequacies, which tended to be focused on the singer (usually the target for audience criticism); individual feelings of shame having to do with puberty (Björn's problems with a breaking voice); and, last but not least, social conflicts. Björn was accused of being a poser, of making himself out to be better than he was, for instance, by always asserting his interesting experiences, by making out that his parents had 'posher' jobs than they actually had, etc. During one period these bad feelings in the group weighed very heavily; however, especially after Björn had left for the United States, the tensions were defused as the group members found they missed him, and also his status seemed to rise because of the trip.

In any case, Chans detest fragility, and this can be seen as an exaggerated and therefore revealing form of the refinement that they aspire to. Their style consciousness is balanced and cautious, almost conventional and conformist. No one departs from the rest through boldness of style – in life-style, personal appearance or furnishings in his room. Each of the boys' rooms seems to contain more or less the same fixtures: a single bed, an untidy desk, a small bookcase with one or two shelf-feet of books, a good stereo with more cassettes than records, music posters on the walls – all in light colours – and a few personal effects and photos. There is a good deal of fear of deviation – their own and others'.

The conflict between acting-out and order is interwoven with contradictory demands and promises from the institutions and milieus surrounding the band and against which the group's relative autonomy is established. To detach themselves from performance demands, group activities must remain a game, playful. When playing music the boys avoid seriousness and effort and therefore they entertain no common dream of stardom (instead

Gösta's father: I think in general that group activities, with everyone the same age, they're a way of growing up. To gather around an obviously engaging activity like playing music together is a way of cutting the umbilical cord, so to speak. They're doing something, bringing each other up and stimulating spiritual growth in each other in a way.[...] It's a way of getting involved with something outside the home, independent of their parents.

Frasse: No, it wasn't to challenge them, no not like that. No, not revolting against parents, no, no. [...] Then, these rather more right-wing words ... that wasn't good either for our parents don't like them either. [...] We've decided not to deal with politics so to speak much longer, but write, yeah – like more varied things.

Håkan's father: First of all, he's a calm kid [...] Decent, in a good way I think. All this stuff about puberty, haven't noticed it actually. No upheavals, contrariness, no crises, nothing.

Betty's mother: Only that she doesn't marry the first best man, that's the only thing I ask. But I don't think she will. Equality, now that's bloody crucial. Not to be dependent but live on the same terms.

Frasse: I'll probably have a family . . .
Johan: Something like your parents – same kind of life?
Frasse: Hard to say . . . yeah . . . no, no, not the same kind of life. [. . .] I want to live more. [. . .] We have it good, can't deny that, but . . . I think I'd maybe rather not spend so much time on a house, you know, always fixing, touching up here and there. I'd rather . . . yeah, my little thing with cars – a really super car [. . .]. Very probably, I'll just go like all the others. Everybody, when they're young, I think has dreams of living it up . . . [. . .] Just the house, I don't know . . . It's sort of like a monument saying 'I've succeeded.' [. . .] You don't get anything out of it, it's just there, a house there, that you might get a couple of million for when you die like, but who thanks you for it? [. . .] It's easy to say all this, but . . . when you get the money, you begin to think, 'Oh yeah, I'd like that too' 'cause it like fits the pattern.

Johan: Who do you take after most?
Håkan: Yeah, that's really funny. Sometimes, you know, with certain gestures I make, it feels like it's dad there [. . .] It's no good being like him, it's not cool! [laughter] I think I see myself in both my mother and dad as if it were them standing in my clothes. [. . .] I don't want to resemble them. You want to be yourself.

such dreams are entertained by a couple of individuals). However, their little oasis is established partly in alliance with and as a complement to the world outside and is pervaded and formed by forces in and around the individuals. The group provides a recreational haven, but, in contrast to OH, it provides no role models for the world. The group requires constant compromising and negotiating with the world at large, especially with parents. On occasion their parents have intervened to cut down on band activities for the sake of studies and they were emphatically against the idea of obtaining rehearsal quarters in the city in the spring of 1984. The garden cottage in Boviken presents the parents with no anxieties about their childrens' activities and the girls' mothers took care to inform themselves of the boys' characters, homes and families before allowing their daughters to be in the band.

The parents are closely allied with school. They have great respect for the school's norms and demands, which they endorse and mediate to their children. Their educational plans for their children are fairly formal and narrow; in several of the families the fathers are keen that their sons have the same education they had – to be acquired as rapidly and directly as possible in order to qualify for a well-paid profession. Chans parents do not encourage optional courses: they prioritise certainties over uncertainties. Not even Betty or Håkan, the two most musically interested, dared to concentrate on artistic subjects in gymnasium.

The members of Chans do not foment any sort of open conflict with either school or parents. They do not 'revolt' against their parents' culture – rather the contrary. Most of them do not long to leave home; they are rather afraid of breaking parental bonds, of standing on their own two feet. They accept the norms and demands of school and parents. However, this is not without problems since the demands are hard and sometimes contradictory – independence and obedience, self-realisation and conformity. Their life situations are firmly structured through a closely woven net of activities, control and other mechanisms in and around the youths. They go along with certain of the parental and school demands (high marks, keeping to the neighbourhood, avoiding political messages in their lyrics, etc.) in return for certain favours (being chauffeured, helped with equipment, rehearsal quarters, etc.). Chans see school as necessary for a good and secure future. They want to keep up good marks in school to ensure that they do not give in to laziness. Moreover, it was in school that they all met – and the band has been very much a 'school band'. School provides a gathering-point and strong bonds while at the same time the group also seeks to establish distance and autonomy. For the parental culture also contains other hidden and unhidden aspirations that point in another direction: the desire for a good and easy life, for career advancement, pleasure and, with some, for education and/or artistic freedom. These aspirations are nourished by the mass media, not least the music media.

In this way Chans stand in a cross-fire: on the one side, everyday dreams, pervaded by the pleasure-oriented, consumer morality in their intimate spheres – in the gang and to an extent in their families – and which is fed by the culture industry; and on the other, the obligations of school and working life, with their competition and sacrifice-oriented production morality that requires the deferment of needs and investment in the future. Chans copes with these contradictions largely through their skills in changing perspective at the expense of integrating the conflicts physically and psychologically.

Chans' views of work are in many ways extremely negative. Regrettably, it is necessary to work to live – and to live is to let go, party, be with mates and have fun. Several band members would like to avoid waged work in order to escape long working hours, lack of freedom, monotony. Those whose fathers are small businessmen, especially, would prefer to set up their own businesses – an idealised alternative.

The band members' need for activity, their desire for contacts with others and for freedom are pursued via small enterprises rather than participation in voluntary organisations. Money was involved at an early stage in their activities via their fanzine and fan club, study circles and the deals that Frasse and Olof especially occupied themselves with when they bought and sold through advertisements – everything from mopeds to furniture and amateur paintings. Thus their own group activities were shaped by the same contradictory forces that penetrated

B-A: When I'm in a bad mood my mother thinks I'm just like my dad [laughter]. I don't know, I don't really know him. I think it's more fifty-fifty actually. But moods, now I don't know what my dad's are like, but sometimes I see myself like my mother and then I get even angrier. When I see how the two of us stand there quarrelling and I know we both argue about things that are wrong [. . .]. Yeah, mother and I are very alike, we are. But that's the way it is if you grow up together.

Johan: What sort of life do you want to avoid in the future, when you're grown up?
Olof: . . . Working day and night [laughter]. [I want] free time. To do what you want and not work from morning to night.
Johan: What do you want out of life?
B-A and Betty: A good life.
B-A: I don't want, like what some people say, 'I'm going to do something enormous, tremendous, so everybody will remember me' [. . .]
Betty: Yeah, have a great time – without going to extremes. [. . .] Meet people.
B-A: You should take advantage, like when you have the chance, I think, and do a lot. But, like you shouldn't try everything just to try it.

B-A: Actually – to live really spontaneously and take one day at a time and do whatever you feel like and that, that can be wonderful, but I get really stressed. I like to have order around me. I want to know where I am. [. . .] I think if you complicate things around you, then I think you make things complicated for yourself in some way. Because then you can't keep track of yourself either. Make a mess of relationships and that.

the group's social milieu: competition and demands for efficiency versus the need to act-out and play. But at that age, no one dares to consider more risky occupations as realistic possibilities and they are too anxious to retain security and a good financial situation. Many are tired of studying and are not keen to continue their studies for any length of time. They identify with their own parents' professions and seldom trespass outside their families' frames of reference. Their aspirations still largely correlate with those of their parents.

Olof: I think it's difficult not to have money.

Karl: Relationships are always the best thing.

Johan: What do you personally think is the most important in life?

Håkan's father: [. . .] There should be a good mixture of decent work, decent housing and enjoyable leisure time. Those are good cornerstones. [. . .] To live in fairly orderly conditions . . . that I think is important.

Olof's mother: I want to have a reasonably well-ordered life with a certain amount of comfort and . . . yes, well . . . do things one likes to do – read a little and that sort of thing. Maybe learn a few new things.

Gustav: I think leaders are needed . . . otherwise it doesn't work. Somebody has to decide on the job, like distribute the work, tell you what to do and that. [. . .] If it's over the top then you've got to protest. That you have to do: if you're not satisfied, then you have to say so.

Johan: Who are suitable leaders?

Gustav: Those who understand . . . They shouldn't only think of themselves, they have to think of everyone in their area, like. Listen to what they think, suggestions and that.

Chans members' views of authority tend to be somewhat ambivalent. They are not blindly loyal or submissive to given leaders, neither do they harbour any utopian passion for total equality. Instead, they have a realistic and pragmatic view of relationships. Authorities are needed in some situations but not in others, and leaders ought to listen to their subordinates, who in turn have the right to protest when things do not function.

All these relations and attitudes are connected with becoming adults. Chans know that they will embark upon the future staked out for them by school and parents and this entails both security and a certain amount of anguish. Many of their group activities demonstrate this: fear of separation from their parents and from the group, their thoughts about their future, etc.

These mixed feelings are also illustrated in their view of drugs – and of falling through the safety net comprised by their friends, family, school, etc. Drugs are at once tempting – in controlled and circumscribed forms such as drinking at parties – and threatening. Chans have written a couple of songs about drug misuse which contain warnings about the devastation irrevocably caused by narcotics (original lyrics, this page, in English):

> Stop tripping, stop getting stoned
> you can overdose in a toilet in town . . .

Drugs threaten the ego, one's control and discipline and consequently clearly illustrate the risks of 'excess' when having 'fun'. In other songs, 'falling' is described more symbolically, in terms which socio-culturally can be associated class-wise with degradation and, psychologically, with lost self-control.

Anxiety about impending adulthood also includes a fear of separation from the group itself. The group is experienced as both insular – some members try to open it up a bit or to find outside activities – and as an earthly paradise.

> Scream on, scream on
> your time has gone.
> You're over eighteen now, too old to cry,
> you're over eighteen now, too young to die.
> Scream on, scream on tonight!

The group's preoccupation with its own history, their constant self-references, should also be seen in light of this separation anxiety. Through their fan club, their own magazine, films, band recordings and continual reminiscing, childhood or youthful memories are kept alive.

Occupying themselves with their own long, shared history is a way for the band to extend an older collective identity, presently threatened by adulthood – childish, innocent, free play. This also contains a tragic awareness that the good old days are soon over. From a development perspective, the group has functioned as a station on the road from parental symbiosis to an independent adult life – as a transitional object. Through, among other things, incorporating the girls and making recordings in 1986, Chans have tried to preserve the advantages of the group while getting away from its insularity and naiveté.

CULTURAL TASTES

With the exception of Betty, who has been involved in amateur theatre and is interested in style, fashion and interior decoration, the members of Chans seldom go to the theatre or art exhibitions. They accompany their parents or their school class to cultural events occasionally, but not often, as most of the parents are not very interested in such things and Villaholmen has little to offer in the way of 'culture'. 'Culture' is something one should know a bit about – otherwise one would be an embarrassment in Villaholmen – but it is always difficult to find time . . .

Sports are interesting, of course, but mostly as an individual activity. Sports events do not draw Chans to either

B-A: I think it's nice not having to decide everything. Maybe you only hear: 'It *is* like that'. [. . .] Yeah, there's a few signposts here and there you can like hold on to. [. . .] It's good that *somebody* decides, but then you should get on their good side.

Karl: I've thought like this: 'Shit, what a boring old fart I am . . . like I'm soon twenty.' It seems completely . . . I'd rather stay here, where I am, I mean time goes so bloody fast. [. . .] It's now that's so bloody cool!

Björn: But you can have fun when you're twenty.

Olof: You don't want to stop here either.

Karl: No, not really . . . but then you think, 'Soon you're . . . shit . . .'

Johan: What are you afraid of then, what's going to happen when you are twenty that doesn't feel good?

Karl: That you're not, you're not, that you lose all this . . . that it's not as much fun any more.

Gustav: Yeah, we can lose each other and all this, we can lose each other.

Olof: But everybody else grows up too, so you've still got your mates.

Gustav: You move somewhere else and that.

Gösta: But I think, like . . . everything has its time, like, and you'll still have fun later . . .

Björn: Imagine, when you're twenty-two you can get into Café Opera!

Gösta: Yes indeed, like it's fun in different ways.

Håkan: I might just manage without Café Opera [laughter].

the television screen or the stadium. A few members play football in the local team, Chans' manager is good at orienteering, and the whole band likes to ski (not in competitions, but always on winter holidays) and a few windsurf in summer. But generally sports have to do with leisure activities rather than with any sort of serious commitment.

Neither are Chans avid readers of books or magazines. Some hardly read at all while others have mixed reading tastes, from comics to novels and non-fiction. They all have have bookcases in their rooms, but the shelves are dominated by stereo equipment, not books.

For it is music that pervades their lives. They are large-scale consumers, mostly of media-conveyed music – radio, cassettes, records, and to some extent, TV and films. They listen to music for over 30 hours a week, sometimes even 60 hours, and actively listen about 15 hours a week.[5] However, they rarely listen to live music. Occasionally they go to big concerts with internationally famous rock and pop artists and to local concerts, for instance, in school (where they also perform) where they can hear other local bands. The musical venues in between – clubs, small and medium-size places in Stockholm – are relatively unknown to Chans and relatively inaccessible as well because of age limits (often due to alchohol being available on the premises). Villaholmen contains no music clubs for the young and those that exist in nearby districts have not yet been discovered by Chans.

According to their own statements, Chans seldom watch TV – one programme a week, or at most an average of an hour a day, and weeks can go by without watching any TV at all. They are fans of zany comedy series, some children's programmes and youth programmes with rock videos, etc. Nonetheless, they seem quite familiar with the TV menus – possibly the TV is on more than they admit, or they watch bits and pieces, or hear of programmes from members of their families.

Chans listen a great deal to the radio – several hours a day – mostly to the popular music station and the local (Stockholm) station. They spend equal time listening to records and cassettes – in the morning, on the way to and from school, at mealtimes and when doing homework and before they go to sleep. B-A relates that she has never

Björn: Each age has its own charm, sort of. I don't know – I'm very happy as it is now, I think it's really cool. But it's probably cool being a bit older too. Just so you don't get *too* old [laughter]. [...] Of course, you long to be like twenty, twenty-two, then you can go to places a little bigger, get into places, like, yeah ... Café Opera, and discos and that. [...] Even if it's cool now, all the parties ... They don't disappear before you're maybe, like twenty-five – then they begin to thin out a bit ...
Betty: Think if somebody took a picture of me that showed: 'Now you look like this, and now you look awful, and now you look ... ' I don't know but it fascinates me incredibly. [...]
B-A: When you stand in front of a mirror, you don't put on a pose and be sad in front of the mirror to see how you look when you're sad like. [...] I don't know how I look when I cry.

B-A: I think it's too bad every time you have a birthday, 'cause like you'll never be fourteen again. Some people go around longing: 'Oh, how I long to be twenty, I long to have a driving licence when I'm eighteen.' But I think, OK, then you'll never be able to be a child. I think time goes much too fast!
Betty: But at the same time, you want to be ... It's good for us that you can get in anyway when there's age limits – so you live on being eighteen in three years time ...

skied down a slope without either listening to her Walkman or singing a song herself and could not imagine a ski slope without music! They surround themselves, more or less constantly, with music of two kinds: music they choose themselves or borrow from mates (cassettes, record-player) or music that becomes a media channel to the outside world, a 'window on the world' (radio).

The music they hear on the radio or that recommended by mates in school or others (particularly Gösta's older brother) is first distributed among band members and then discussed and evaluated. The same is true of the films they see on TV or at the cinema. Sometimes the band (at least the boys) go to the cinema together, sometimes with others. Villaholmen does have a cinema, managed by a local association, which shows films every other week. The boys go there fairly often, and possibly once a month to an ordinary commercial cinema in Stockholm. They prefer more or less 'cult' music films such as Talking Heads' *Stop Making Sense* and *True Stories*, but also enjoy hit films like *Ronja Rövardotter* and James Bond.

Chans use music in an amazing number of different ways. Music creates lovely atmospheres, calm and peaceful, but it also expresses and dissipates aggressions and dissatisfaction. Music fills dead time – like 'having fun' mentioned earlier. Music is used as a means of communication in the interaction within and between gangs in order to create togetherness and demarcate differences between the individuals and the groups. And on several levels, music provides knowledge of the state of the world.

The significance of the radio as a 'window on the world' cannot be underestimated. For instance, around 1980 a programme called *New Wave* was instrumental in giving the band access to punk. Media such as the radio and the record player function as raw material from which you pick and choose, according to interest. Chans are selective: they despise a great deal of radio music, for instance, much of the mechanical disco music, and many of them are not very keen on traditional, '60s-based rock, *à la* Rolling Stones. Nevertheless, radio music's raw material offers new and different experiences which are absent from or alien to home and school.

Members of Chans do not always agree about the music they hear on the radio or get to know through mates.

B-A: But you can still go home and be a child and a girl, like a little girl.

Gösta: We've got so many fun things you can remember. [. . .] Especially the parties and that. Our own, what we've had together.

B-A: The best thing is skiing. Satin-smooth slopes, wonderful weather and Jean-Michel Jarre in the headphones.

Betty: Sometimes I can sit and listen, but just as often I have music in the background because I think, like 'How quiet it is, there must be something.' Then, when you're really listening, then you can't do anything else.

Håkan [on punk]: Oh, that lovely feeling when I heard a really terrible chord.

Several (particularly Håkan) like hard rock better than the others; several have more sympathy with disco and synth pop (for example, Gran, Olof, Frasse and B-A). Not all of them listen with interest to newer, more avant-garde 'cult' rock (such as certain British groups and Talking Heads). In fact, the individuals in the band have rather heterogeneous tastes. When I played ten different rock and pop songs to the whole group, for each song (and genre) there were always positive and negative opinions. Neither did the individuals form themselves into clear subgroups – each one had his or her individual preferences.

Of course, despite the divergent opinions, a great deal of music is cultivated by the band as a whole. During autumn 1985, they worked with two new songs, one with elements from classical music (inspired by records of the Dutch band, Ekseption, from the early 1970s), the other, a musical pastiche of Dire Straits. Especially in connection with the latter (and partly inspired by hearing a live concert in Stockholm), all the band members listened systematically to Dire Straits' music. This is a normal routine: before going to a concert or a film, Chans members prepare themselves by borrowing records, reading newspapers and getting information from mates. Similar shared interests have been cultivated as regards the Clash, U2 and other bands that have been important for Chans' development.

Chans are clearly more oriented towards foreign (English and American) rock than Swedish. They can appreciate local Villaholmen bands while at the same time censuring Swedish groups in general for being provincial and dull. In Chans' vocabulary, 'Swedish' is more or less synonymous with 'dullness' and 'primness'. Naturally, they enjoy certain Swedish rock and pop, but the Anglo-Saxon music scene has much more luminescence and charm. An example of this prejudice is that no one in Chans was fascinated by perhaps the most famous Swedish rock group of the day, Imperiet, neither was anyone that taken with Imperiet's predecessor, Ebba Grön during the punk era. Instead, they all preferred the other well-known Stockholm punk band, KSMB. Ebba Grön and Imperiet developed just the sort of 'Swedish' sound that Chans did not much like, possibly because Ebba Grön and Imperiet possessed a sort of engagement that could be somewhat uncharitably described as pathetic or sentimental, whereas KSMB (like the comparable American punk group, Dead Kennedys) were more congenial to Chans' attitude of detachment.

Chans' musical tastes lack a common sub-cultural profile. Several years earlier, as early as 1983, when punk provided a common identity, it was different. Since then members have explored different directions: some from hard rock (1983–1984) to new British 'cult' rock, some towards detached, bohemian 'camp' rock, others towards mainstream genres such as synth pop (which began to crop up in the *Chans Mag* in 1984) and disco-funk. The variety has increased and no one in the band identifies him or herself with any sub-cultural style or genre, preferring versatility and detachment. Thus this preference is true for the band as a unit, in which different wills have to combine under the aegis of a sort of 'minimum programme'. Being versatile is a way of living up to the dominant norms (flexibility, omnivory) in the band's social environment and of balancing differences among individuals. Detachment, variety and balance are socially appropriate attitudes, individually as well as collectively. Detachment entails control, mastery, having a general view, and flexibility, but it also allows acting out and intensity in a number of different ways – similar to the way a rock video rapidly flits between diverse forms of experience. Detachment is also a defence against conflicts, a way of avoiding threatening confrontations between in principle contradictory views in the group.

B-A: Yeah, it's mostly boys who like hard rock, but I think there's as many boys as girls who like synth. It's mostly girls that like that buttery stuff, Carola and that . . . [Swedish pop mainstream]

B-A: I wouldn't have continued for the music – never! Except now – it's mostly, nearly all, for the sake of the mates. Like, they're so cool, so great to be with. They're great boys, all of them.

Håkan: Yeah, it's Gösta who's like the leader – well, not the leader, but *if* you had to name a leader it'd be him.

Gustav: When he [Håkan] comes along with the opening like this, it's hard for us to add to it, together, all of us. All together it's hard to build together – have different ideas. But it's better if he like has a base, then we can change it a bit.

CHANS' OWN MUSIC

To a great extent, Chans function as a gang of mates. Arranging their own parties and going together to others, going to films and so on are as important as making music for some members. These activities also make the group more open. But playing rock under a band name still delimits and distinguishes – a sign of exclusivity, giving status in the immediate environment and strengthening identities *vis à vis* the outside world (the girls were very impressed by the boys when they met them in the winter break in Austria).

Betty: After a while, when you just fool around, it gets louder and louder and then everybody sits and plays their own melody, then it's one of those messy kinds of rehearsals, it gets louder and louder, and in the

end, you can't be in there any
longer. [. . .]
B-A: Håkan maybe doesn't
know what they're able to do,
so he says like, 'I've got a tune
here. Olof can you do a
raunchy bass?' you know,
maybe he just can't cope with
sitting and figuring out a bass
line. So they sit around the
cottage and it's like 'du-du-du-
duu – that sound good?' 'No!'
everybody shouts. - 'du-du-du-
du-du-du-du' like. 'Well, this
then?' 'Yeah that's good', and
then Talle comes in: 'I've got to
have something like 'digediged-
ing-ding-punk', like 'to go with
it'. And then they think, 'Boy
that's sounds good' and then
they play. And so Valle says,
'Yeah and how'm I supposed to
sing then?', 'Begin about there,'
says Håkan. Right, then they
sing something. 'No way, it
sounds like hell' and then, 'no,
let's quit now' and then they
start all over again. Then they
play the same thing again, and
develop it like that, so nothing's
written down or anything.

B-A: You get into fantastic
contact . . . like 'Now we're on
stage' not 'Here I am and
there's the others', no it's like
we – like, the masses sort of.
[. . .] If anybody in the band
makes a fool of himself then
everybody's embarrassed, and
if somebody does something
great . . . then we're all proud.

To all appearances, the group functions very chaotically.
It is difficult to see how common decisions are made since
everyone talks at once, goes in and out and is busy with
different things. However, despite this apparent leaderless
anarchy, under the surface there is a network-like structure
of roles and relationships. The boys, especially, meet
frequently and regularly – in school, in the neighbourhood,
at each other's homes and in the cottage. They sometimes
ring each other (this includes the girls, especially B-A). In
these ways, important information is spread – seldom in
writing. They rarely write letters and have no noticeboard
in the cottage. Members have particular key roles or duties,
for instance, communication with the girls usually goes via
Frasse/B-A.

The band's rehearsals provide many examples of this
special, organised chaos. It is typical of rehearsals that
people come and go all the time. Rehearsals have an
agreed starting-time, but usually someone is late (regardless of whether the others have been told) and someone
always has to leave early – to eat dinner, go to a party etc.
Håkan, Olof and Gustav are the most 'conscientious'; they
are almost always there the whole time, working more or
less systematically with lyrics. Björn is also dutiful, but he
can disappear for a half-hour to eat dinner without disturbing the others' work. Gösta is extremely important in
rehearsals. Songs can only be run through in their entirety
when he is present, and shouting with his loud voice and
rattling the drums, he seems to be the only one who can
gather all the members together to work. The girls are
present only at certain rehearsals when songs are to be
worked on, but then they are there from start to finish and
actively contribute ideas. The most undisciplined Chans
member is Frasse, who always seems to come and go as he
pleases.

Rehearsals usually occur on Friday afternoons, after
school; they can be more frequent, especially before gigs.
The band rehearses only a few hours a week. The time is
divided between going through the songs and conversations
about completely different things. Some members can be
practising figures while others talk about school or what is
going on at the weekend. Håkan is the hub of the music
discussion in that the others go to him with suggestions
and questions. But he does not direct or give orders; he is

actually rather taciturn. Musically there seems to be a quiet but well-functioning cooperation between Håkan and Olof on the bass, Gustav on the synth and Gösta on the drums. Björn seems to be largely responsible for his own singing. He is also responsible for the echo and voice gear and he often comes up with lyrics and melodies after Håkan and others have worked out at least parts of the music.

The playing is seldom very concentrated or disciplined, even when the band is practising new songs. Gösta often starts up with the drums, but musically, the greatest confidence seems to be placed in Håkan, who is not an authoritarian leader, but controls the playing with sensitivity and without fuss. Gustav and Olof often seem to have problems concentrating (as do the others) and fool around, making mistakes, which increases the chaos. Solo playing is not predominant – everyone in the band contributes. Sometimes Björn hands the microphone over to Frasse in exchange for his guitar.

Now and then during rehearsal times other things are discussed: people's absence, arrival and disappearance are always commented on. There is often a guest who has come to listen a while, and if there is an instrument free, the guest might try it, sing backing with Björn or offer suggestions. Rehearsals are disorderly but also by their nature, wearing and demanding. Relaxed playfulness creeps in, sometimes when a song comes off right the first time and the band realises that the agony has gone, that playing has become a collective act. Then the group can euphorically erupt into spontaneous variations on passages in the song and in this way develop it collectively. Sometimes exhuberance spontaneously spills into other songs not on the rehearsal schedule – something punkish, a signature melody from the radio, a disco hit, a Mozart theme or an old Chans song. If someone starts this up the others very quickly fall into it and keep it up for seconds – or minutes at a time. These spontaneous outbursts reinforce the 'we' feeling and the players find an outlet for an emotional release that breaks the demanding tedium of practising passages of songs they are learning. This happens only a few times per rehearsal, but it comprises an important breathing-space, awakening positive memories of the group's origins in musical games: it is a way of retaining sponaneity and liveliness in the group.

Olof: I think it's really cool to play music . . . like when you see it's starting to get good, like when you build up a tune. You see it sounds better and better, that's bloody magic. Then we're getting better all the time, that's great. Then, 'course it's amazing to play with an audience too.

Gigs vary a good deal depending on the audience and the venue. In shopping centres and similar places, more adult, controlled and less secure, the band's performances are more cautious and controlled. Songs are played in an orderly way, as if at an end-of-term assembly at music school or a concert on the radio or TV. In more domestic, youthful venues, not to mention neighbourhood parties, with an actively supportive audience, the situation is totally different.

The individual band members function differently in such a situation: some continue to be quite controlled and purposeful, while others let it all go, sometimes pouring it out over the public. Björn presents the songs and has learned a great deal from his role models in the music industry. Humourous asides occur, jokes are made (Björn, Håkan or Olof), sometimes another 'Oasis' band comes into it with pastiches of different styles, Gösta break-dances, and so on. Despite set boundaries, to the band the public is 'we', the feeling is one of community – even when parents and classmates are present. Chans perform as a band, as a group, both in opposition to the listeners and in such a way that there is no question of one or more soloists with an accompanying group, or of a gathering of individuals. Solidarity or affinity within the band is stressed even though the playing in concert is sloppy and uneven.

It is very difficult to give an overall description of Chans' own song repertoire: diverse and constantly vary-ing, with humorous and playfully detached elements. In autumn 1985 the band had 18 songs in its active reper-toire. There were no covers from any other group; all the songs were Chans' own, even if they contained borrowings, stylistic and musical, from various sources. Occasionally, older songs were revived, with some nostal-gic and self-deprecatory flourishes. However, even the new songs contained great diversity – the aim was that each new song should have its own (new) style.

An early song (from 1982), which was still being played in 1985, is the reggae-inspired *Totte*. The music is easy to sing as the same melodic pattern is repeated over and over again. The melody is the same in verse and chorus and the accompaniment corresponds with the same repeated four beats (A minor—E minor—G major—A minor). The effect

Björn: We don't want to get pigeon-holed. Not before we've tried everything. [...] But I think when we've tried everything, then we'll go for *something*. [...] It also helps to keep the band together in a way. I definitely think that it satisfies everybody, and everybody gets to play the music they like. And then we can go on.

Håkan: One thing I've thought about is ... some bands, they change style on every record. I think that's cool. [...]
Olof: I think you should mix. [...]

Figure 6 Chans: *Teheran*

Teheran

verse 1   I got my money from my daddy in Teheran.
(I got my money, Lord I got my money)
He is so funny there, funny funny in Teheran.
(He is so funny, Lord so very funny)
Chorus: My father is born
My father is born,
My father is born in Teheran.
[Break:1]
[2 as 1, same chorus] [3rd verse musically the same as 1 and
2 but talked not sung]

verse 3   My father, he lives down in Teheran.
           They're fighting every day, they're fighting
           for Allah
           My father he's very poor, he lives down in
           Teheran.
           He sends me money home to Sweden,
           poor father
           [Break and guitar solo]
           [. . .] [Chorus as above. Break.]
           [. . .] [Chorus as above. Break.]
           [Same break as coda but with voices in harmony]
           Allah Khadaffi Khomeini Allah-la-la Ils sont tous là
           Khomeini Khadaffi.

Gustav: Yeah, I don't think we should specialise in one style especially. We should play a variety. [. . .]
Björn: I think it's really important to mix music. I think it'd be super boring to only play the same kinds of music the whole time as we listen to lots of different music styles in the group.

Björn: We play to have fun ourselves. We don't do tunes here to get to the broad masses – we're almost critical towards that [laughter]. Real opponents of hits. Though we don't think there's anything wrong with hits as such actually.

is monotonous, almost hallucinatory. The song is a somewhat improvised rap song. It is about Totte, who is lured into buying drugs ('a tablet') by a street gang and goes under as a result: 'Totte's got the habit now/he'll die in the end' – so goes the chorus, almost maliciously. The music and lyrics meld cunningly together: reggae and rasta, which were very popular in Sweden and in Storby when the song was composed, are generally associated with smoking marijuana, and so the song's warning about drugs becomes ironic when set to this music (which is hardly Chans' most common genre).

Totte also expresses an ambivalence. It preaches against drugs – which the boys do as well, receiving praise from parents and teachers. At the same time, when performing the song, the band are totally absorbed, living in the song in just the sort of inverted, trance-like, monotonous high (albeit without drugs) which has such an attraction for Chans. The same is also true of another, older song on drugs, in which the injunction to 'quit . . . . you can overdose' etc., can be alternated with 'start sniffing', ironically meant, of course, but the irony is so total that it renders the message nonsensical.

In another, newer song, *Teheran*, an immigrant relates in broken English how he is supported by his cheerful foolish father in Teheran, where they are poor but have fun and worship Allah. The music is a mix of different ingredients – a trace of Talking Heads in the overall sound, a little Arabic in the singing style, melody and harmony. Frasse and Björn alternate singing and Betty and B-A sing in harmony in the chorus. Instrumentally, the song is equally diverse: Olof plays a *Goldfinger*-like riff on the bass, overlaid by sweeping sounds on the synth and a guitar riff (Håkan). The bass is borrowed from the bands,

Bauhaus and Lustans Lakejer (The Lackeys of Lust). The song ends with a hymn to Mohammed and Allah played in an exhilarating calypso rhythm. Again, there is total irony, and the aim of the satire, if anything, more difficult to establish. Chans contend that the song does not satirise immigrants or Arabs. They admit that the song contains some criticism of Muslim fanaticism, but otherwise, the song contains wordplay and nonsense with no intended meaning.

Longing for Peace, strongly influenced by Dire Straits, was composed in autumn 1985. The lyrics, written in rather awkward school English, depict the miseries of a soldier in war and his desire to flee:

> In the nights I try to sleep
> but the feelings won't leave me.
> The disgusting things I do,
> my hate and my grief.
> Instead of giving love and joy
> to the human race
> I just kill and destroy
> Is it for this I was born
> . . . Forgive me, my brother
> We're fighting for the same cause:
> For what's wrong and what is right.
> I better leave this place tonight
> to a land where there's peace.

However, neither text nor music seems truly felt. Chans has difficulties with the sense of intensive presence that such a song requires. The song's message is general and loose, with plenty of stereotyped phrases. The music to the verses cited above is lively and ebullient, but elsewhere – in the introduction, breaks, and a long guitar solo – the music is much sadder, calmer and more beautiful, very much in the spirit of Dire Straits. *Longing for Peace* is also a montage, scarcely unified or consistent. It is a beautiful and occasionally skillful pastiche, but the sense of detachment has not disappeared.

The three songs discussed above are fairly representative. Of the 18 songs in Chans' active repertoire, 4 may be roughly described as synth pop, 4 punk, 3 hard rock, 2 ballads, 1 reggae, 1 classic rock, and the others as various sorts of pop, some with traces of ska. The songs' atmosphere also varies, from anguish and sorrow, to aggression, frantic craziness, to exuberance, joy. The length of the songs is equally diverse, from 2 to 8 minutes.

Johan: Is it important to have a good chorus, one that sticks in the memory?
Karl: Yes, exactly, something that sticks. Yeah, something that you can associate with something. If you're on a trip or something and you hear this song, you can remember it when you hear it again.

Formally, the songs consist of 4-bar periods – what the band calls 'Chans bars'. There are no time or rhythm shifts, except for certain triplet passages and syncopation. The melodies are sometimes irregular and surprising, but most often they are polished, easy to sing and conventional. Half the songs contain clearly distinguishable instrumental solos, a few two solos (usually Håkan on guitar, but sometimes synth or trumpet solos). Straight major/minor scales dominate, even though about a third of the songs used the aeolian mode and several different types of cadence and harmony occur. Talking, speech song and shouting occur in every other song, and Björn's singing has developed from a wild shrieking to an assured, slightly tense style, obviously inspired by David Byrne of Talking Heads. The tempo is driving, usually from 120 up to 160 beats per minute. The bass is often quite melodic and prominant, sometimes punk-inspired. The synth also has a prominant role, with fairly straight and simple but squeaky and clearly melodic figures. Otherwise, the guitar is the group's anchor, very assured stylistically and given to inserting an assortment of different rock stereotypes of a modern 'white' variety – far from the 'black' blues-based tradition. The percussion is even more 'white'; it lacks the stable beat required by the heavier rock tradition. Instead Gösta clearly has been affected by his lessons in the municipal music school; he tends to blend march rhythms and calpso impulses in a sort of loose, playful, undisciplined jumble. In general, the music is far from tight, but seems charming and spontaneous.

The lyrics are equally heterogeneous. Several are clearly influenced by the media, for example, pastiches of songs from films. About one third are 'love songs', of a sometimes happy, sometimes unhappy jejune sort (either romantic infatuation or curiosity about sexuality). Another third are satires, and others are narratives, or have elements of horror or craziness. One third of the lyrics are in English. Two-thirds are monologues by a fictitious first-person narrator who can sometimes be identified with the singer/band, sometimes indirectly satirical.

Most of the lyrics are fairly abstract, but a few contain more realistic references to places or events. Rhyme is not common – only one song in three has many noticeable rhymes. However, repetition is present in almost every

Håkan: I think, like, music gets better if you say something with it. [. . .] I don't have that much experience of life. [. . .] I haven't got so much to protest against either as I live pretty well I think. That's a lot to do with it. But it's true that when you listen to lyrics from these bands [Clash, U2], like you can live right in it. And like you'd

song – words and phrases are repeated several times, occasionally with variations. Antitheses are relatively rare: the songs are not constructed on patterns of conflict as are those of OH and Lam Gam with their constant references to we/them or up there/down there polarities. But Chans is very adept at finding clever connections between text and music, as we have seen in *Totte* and *Teheran*. The content of the lyrics often refers to youth or even childhood; class and geographical references are much less common. Several songs obviously have male narrators, although Chans also have written songs, even love songs, in which the singer's gender is not clearly indicated by the text.

Looked at from a historical perspective, there are perceptible pattern-changes in Chans' songs. In the first phase, from 1980 to 1982, two main types are roughly distinguishable: first, songs with music inspired by children's songs and nonsense or playful texts, with vaguely autobiographical or sexual undertones. Examples include the wonderful *Whata Dream* ('We dance the waltz in the devil's house/look at mum, tipsy as a plum/oh! whata dream whata dream/oh! whata dream whata dream./Over wide fields we shall row/till we come to jappato!/Jappato, jappato, jappato, jappato'), and *Summerland* ('You ride around in a green summer meadow/but it's dark and damp/ in the land of my dreams no one comes in/ only you/ But when you wake/it's not there/it's far away/from my dreamland'.) Second, there are raw, raucous punk songs, often with left-wing or anarchistic lyrics, inspired by KSMB especially. Some of these are quoted at the beginning of this section.

During the second phase, Chans underwent a complicated development. New musical influences crept in – hard rock, new wave, various types of post-punk. The band's musical spectrum broadened. A rift began to show itself between the more actively musically interested members (e.g. Håkan, Björn, Gösta, and later, Betty) and those with less interest, who in any case preferred more mainstream genres and tended to use music as a background for other activities (Frasse, Karl and, later perhaps B-A). No clear lines of demarcation or conflicts arose. However, since Chans as a group felt obliged to satisfy everyone's needs, the more extreme interests were channelled into outside

fight for them . . . even though you've got it good yourself. [. . .] When they've got something to say, something to scream and shout about, they're on fire and then they can get out more aggression in the music [laughter], or whatever. [. . .] It's a little hard to get that spark. It'd feel more right to sing socially critical songs – now we don't do that so much, practically nothing, absolutely nothing, no! Not now anyway . . . [. . .] We haven't got the incentive – of not having such a good life.

Olof: I think almost *all* music that exists is against . . . like against capitalism. [. . .] Most people that play music are socialists [. . .] It's like music started from the poor . . .
Håkan: Yeah, but it's almost the *best* music. They've got something to say. [. . .] They like get their aggressions out. [. . .]
Olof: There aren't any real snobs that play music . . . that don't like the workers.

Olof: Lots of lyrics are about . . . well, they complain about something, or have it bad, or . . . People wanting things better . . . It's that music that's something . . . revolt like. [. . .] It's easier to do lyrics if you've got something special you want to write about.

Gustav: Our lyrics are, like . . . We don't take anything seriously, while those in the working class, they take lyrics like serious. They probably have more empathy with their lyrics.

Betty: I think that, like England – there's a lot of unemployment there. Maybe they just don't have so much to do, maybe it's all they have to do – to play, and they do that incredibly intensively, and they come up with new things as a result. It's their only interest, there's nothing around they can get interested in. [. . .] The people from the working class – maybe, I don't know – maybe they want to escape a little, while the person who has it good doesn't have so much to get away from, and is probably quite happy.

B-A: I think the ones who are better off will probably put more into studying and really achieving something, 'cause I think they've got more pressure, much more pressure on them. [. . .] I don't think [becoming a musician] is regarded as anything *special* [by the upper classes] unless it's something classical.

Female teacher: They can't really say why, it's forbidden because everything is supposed to be so terrifically *good*, everything. Everything's to be *bright* and they're going to *succeed*. And the parents are supportive and drive them here and there and give them places to be and equipment.[. . .] How could they get words to work? They can't and won't . . . It blocks them, everything's *so good*. [. . .] They can't come up with it, what in the hell should they say? What words should they choose? The rest of the world doesn't understand – why should they protest when they have it so good? OK, there's protest, but it's always *another* group's protest they copy. It's legitimate to copy. But to say 'It's mine too' – how in the hell is that to be expressed? And they don't express it either.
Male teacher: It could be another side to lack of engagement too – that they also detach themselves from protest.

Johan: Are there any of you who see music . . . who could think of working with music

activities, playing in other bands or other informed groups. During this phase, the band became increasingly alienated from their previous political lyrics. Under pressure from parents, mates, and also their own views, the group dissociated itself from these rebellious song words and turned to more a 'bourgeois' content that better suited their own social situation and political stance. However, this proved problematic: more rightwing-oriented texts could overstep the mark and the group was not politically united around any social message. Not even the theme of peace found any sort of real or serious expression in Chans' repertoire, with the possible exception of the above-mentioned *Longing for Peace*. The group is also aware of how difficult it is to compose good music and lyrics if one 'has it too good'; real rock music comes from poor and oppressed people who are driven to resist. All this makes for an uncertainty that compels examination, review, the search for new themes and forms of expression.

Consequently, a change occurred in the two main types of Chans songs. The first type (naive lyrics with sexual associations or obvious nonsense words) was altered in two ways. The sexual/relationship aspect was refined into a sort of rather abstract love song accompanied by schlager or synth pop-type music, for example, the strongly melodious, synth-based song containing repeated synth riffs and the following lyrics: 'I must stand strong as a castle/ for if I fall I lose all/lose all I ever dreamt of/I lose all of you/I want you, want you, want you with all my heart/Never never love anyone but you/never never make love to anyone but you . . . ' Then, a zany genre was cultivated, with imaginative musical forms and mildly crazy lyrics which sometimes symbolically expressed the agonies of their impending adulthood: 'I'm sitting up here in my climbing tree/I look down and what do I see?/I see people who fight, I see people who run/but they don't mind – I'm falling! . . .' These songs lend themselves to a spectrum of psychodynamic and socio-cultural interpretations, in keys alternating between F minor and E flat major, overlaid with a frantically stressed voice.

The other political–punk line was developed via hard rock-influenced horror and fantasy songs into a great variety of ironic and loosely satirical songs in motley musical styles and subjects. These included the war song (as a serious exception), and a number of humourous, satirical songs such as those above. For a while, the political colour was very nearly Tory, but this was purged and henceforth politics, in any sort of narrow sense, were consciously avoided. Chans have obvious problems with 'message' in their songs, and to offset these difficulties, they stress having fun, detachment and variety, both in musical forms and lyrical content. Håkan has transferred most serious experimentation to working with his cousin in the band, the Pimple.

Chans' musical development has, of course, led to increasing technical competence, if not to virtuosity. Even though they have played together for a long time and most have also studied their respective instruments at the municipal music school, they still sound quite chaotic. One suspects this is the consequence of demands for playfulness and diversity, which hinder serious practice and consistant repetition of any one of the many styles they test out, and of uncertainty about their own common identity – fear of conflict and self-criticism – all of which thwart the possibility of standing 100 per cent behind a style or a song.

professionally?
Björn: It would be amazing, really cool.
Gösta: In that case, on the side.
Håkan: Black.
Gustav: It's not something to commit yourself to.
Gösta: I think it'd be more fun if you played like at weekends and had it, like . . . on the side. Otherwise, it wouldn't be fun if you had it as an occupation. Then it'd often be boring – it gets so intensive . . .

Håkan: I think listeners should really have to exert themselves a little and try to listen properly to the music and the lyrics. Of course, that's not what we in Kirschberg do. We just play straight out, but I think we suit that type of music best. I don't think we can reach deep into people.

Figure 7   Illustration from *Chans Mag*, autumn 1982.

A well-known cartoon character yells 'Open up!' and demands entry to the 'concert house'. The handwritten caption reads: 'This is what it looks like now in our practice room, or concerthouse as it's sometimes called. The egg cartons are to cut the sound. There's no point in coming here and knocking on the door – we won't answer anyway, as you see in the picture.'

OBJECTIVE LIFE
CONDITIONS

LIVING IN THE LATE
MODERN PERIOD

In this chapter we shall begin by examining our bands' objective life conditions in modern society. We go on to explore deep subjective structures and finally arrive at how our groups' collective creation of symbols functions *vis-à-vis* their internal and external backgrounds, and what learning processes take place.

Common to most of the individuals in all three bands is their year of birth (1969), and consequently they were all in their mid-teenage years in the mid-1980s. What their age means on an individual psychological level will be discussed in the next chapter; here we will only touch upon the socio-cultural framework of this phase of life. However, first we shall look at the significance of the other two dimensions: Swedish nationality and, particularly, the late modern decade of the 1980s.

PREHISTORY

Several historical periods were present in the background when OH, Lam Gam and Chans began to play rock music. On one level, of course, all history contributes: various forms of cultural commerce, including the media, school and indirect effects of early processes, all have repercussions on the long prehistory of young people's lives. Hence it is impossible to isolate one starting point and clearly delimit one historical period as the valid framework for present-day youth cultures – their roots and predecessors go far back in time. Having said this, however, it seems reasonable to place somewhat greater weight on the course of events that began in Sweden during the nineteenth century: industrialisation, the penetration of the bourgeoisie into state power, the expansion of education, the dismantling of the guilds and other feudal structures, and the development of a modern capitalist society. In a novel way, youth gradually became a separate and general social category, determined by modern society's new, contending forces.

Thus, in the nineteenth century, a societal structure was formed which still functions as a framework for our three groups (as well as for the authors). Through a series of transformations, capitalist social forms and institutions grew out of the feudal. Even if these institutions often still retain the same names (the state, parliament, school, family), their roles and internal relationships have changed. A new social differentiation has arisen, a clearer division of labour among different spheres. The productive sphere has been industrialised and productive work become waged. The state has been separated from this privatised production, and the intimate sphere of the modern family crystallised out as the third pole. In the bourgeois public sphere, with its political and cultural offshoots, in the media, and in associations and other forums, individual and group interests are mediated, among themselves and in relation to the state.

Against an increasingly individualised and secularised everyday life stand two systems: the state and the market, each with its own means of control (power and money).[1] Various agencies and institutions mediate between and within these three polarities, cooperatively or in opposition. As regards the young, the pattern might look something like the following:

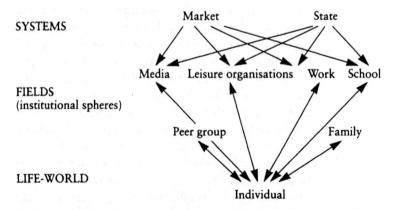

SYSTEMS

FIELDS
(institutional spheres)

LIFE-WORLD

Figure 8   Daily life, the state and the market

In the field between the state and the market on the one hand and people's daily lives on the other, operate (from above) a number of institutions that intervene structurally in the life-world. From below, that is from the perspective of individuals and their immediate relations, a number of fields of action are formed, each with its own rules and forms, limits and possibilities, demands and resources.[2] It is not difficult to see such fields in action in our three groups.

In modern society, another differentiation cuts across these types of institutions. The communicative activities which occur in large and small public contexts can be divided into three or four main aspects. One aspect comprises questions having to do with truth, with the external, objective world, whose most specific form is science. A second has to do with normative propriety and justice, in other words, the inter-subjectively divided social world, and it is cultivated in the judicial system. Another inter-subjective sub-aspect is the cultural world of symbols existing in the sphere of art. A third aspect involves honesty and authenticity and thus concerns the inner, subjective world, and is expressed *inter alia* in the intimate sphere.

One modern set of problems arising from this new dynamic has to do with the systems, that is, the all too great influence of the state and capital over other areas. The capitalist form of modernity encourages technocratic and unilateral goal rationality – efficiency at any price. The communicative actions necessary for the continuation of culture, society and the individual are threatened by the dominance of instrumental rationality. The state generates demands and tendencies that threaten to bureaucratise various fields of action and areas of life: the institutionalisation and integration of high bourgeois culture (for instance, 'classical' music) comprise an example of this process in the area of aesthetics (including music). The market generates tendencies towards commercialisation, exemplified by modern popular culture (and popular music). Friction and conflict arise between these two tendencies, but primarily they interact with and oppose the communicative needs and abilities that exist in people's daily lives.

A few of these general features of modern society have particular attributes in Sweden. An unusually strong and centralised state power and extensive (mainly Social

Democratic) popular movements are part of our national characteristics as are life patterns anchored in the climate and deep cultural traditions, which are harder to formulate concisely.

Prior to the nineteenth century, there were definite structures for socialisation in which young people had their places and roles – in journeyman organisations for instance.[3] These structures fell apart during the nineteenth century, to be replaced only after a long process in which the school played a central role. Right from the start, at the introduction of the Swedish elementary school in 1842, the school was given the responsibility of sorting, controlling, disciplining and adapting children, especially from the working and agrarian classes.[4] Cities grew enormously during the rapid industrialisation in the 1870s, an urbanisation which continued in waves throughout the twentieth century. These new conditions also led to new 'problems' with young people. In the decades around the turn of the century there was a great deal of anxiety on the part of adults and authorities about the lack of order among the young (the commercial wave of Nick Carter literature was attacked for brutalising Swedish youth).[5] During the same period, psychological concepts for youth development phases were formulated – for example, the concept of adolescence to denote the psychological counterpart of puberty (a concept introduced by Stanley Hall in 1904).[6] During the twentieth century the age of puberty has dropped considerably – a fall calculated at about three months per decade.

From 1910 onwards, the educational authorities carried out reforms with the purpose of reaching greater unity. In the 1930s the word 'teenager' came into general use, imported from the United States.[7] As the period of youth was thus prolonged regardless of social strata, important qualitative changes also occurred. The economic policy of the welfare state gave more and more resources and leisure time to the new and growing youth cohorts. A new phase of social and cultural modernisation was beginning to take shape, even though the Second World War temporarily curbed its development. A few new types of youth culture arose, revolving around swing and jazz clubs. Avid consumers of the media – jazz and swing on records and radio, and popular magazines – and with provocative, sensual and gendered body language in dance and general style, these youth cultures heralded tendencies that came to fruition by the end of the 1950s. They were met by new surges of moral panic that can be read as misguided reactions to feelings of insecurity and fear in the face of the impending late modernity.

THE CHILDREN OF THE BOOM

We are now into the second historical level, which not only lives on through its historical effects or in media-conducted discourse, but has also etched itself on the subjectivity of our youths' parents' generation. They were children in the 1940s and youth in the 1960s. It is the conditions and events, promises and betrayals, hopes and problems of these decades which have coloured this generation's mentality – variegated, of course, by the prism of gender, class and geography.

By the 1950s, traces of this long period of expansion were noticeable in Sweden; modelled on America, the boom peaked in 1960. Structural rationalisation brought about increasing urbanisation and thus a depopulation of the countryside. New demands were placed on workforce mobility, which helped to weaken local traditional family bonds. Parents of today have experienced being cut off from their own childhoods' relatively (and in the rosy light of memory) stable and traditional environments and thrown into new modes of living in large cities and suburbs, in a society undergoing an accelerated modernisation. During the 1960s, the old city centres were razed and replaced by more or less identical shopping centres at the same time as 'Million Dwelling Programme' new suburbs mushroomed.[8] From the start of the boom, labour was steadily intensified and rationalised. Expansion required and obtained much increased immigration, which augmented the multi-cultural aspects of many Swedish cities and communities, and in the long term contributed to breaking up the rather insular routines of local tradition. In industries, a great deal of the work was determined by measured time management (MTM) and the assembly line, which, in principle at least, rendered many industrial workers easily replaceable by machines and deprived them of their traditional professional pride. The number of routine tasks carried out by white-collar workers multiplied, which meant, in part, that a new and modern type of middle strata was established.

All this also contributed to an explosion in education. Elementary school was extended, gymnasium was rationalised and expanded and the universities overflowed. In 1936, compulsory education had been extended to seven years, and in 1962 the nine-year comprehensive was introduced. In 1950, three-quarters of all 14–19-year old boys were working – two decades later, the proportion had dropped to one quarter. The number of students beginning gymnasium increased more than four-fold. From 1940 to 1970 the number studying at colleges and universities increased from 10,621 to 124,440 – an eleven-fold increase in only 30 years. School became an increasingly dominant life sphere for youth during an increasingly prolonged phase of life. A long education became normal for youth of all classes and entry into working life, ever more delayed.

Our band members' parents and teachers belong to that fortunate generation which, at least in principle, reaped the benefits of this development. They took advantage of opportunities that their own parents could have hardly conceived of – in the labour market, housing market, the educational and consumer sectors. There were, of course, 'losers' too, but the 1950s and 1960s were suffused with an optimism and belief in progress which in retrospect may seem very remarkable if not alien.

The absolute and relative growth of the middle strata was also connected to the heavy growth of the public sector in the Swedish welfare state. To work in state or local authority agencies was no longer the privelege of dutiful bureaucrats but one means of earning a living among others. At the same time, the state intervened in more and more areas of life. Women were again in demand on the labour market and families with both parents working became more common (at present, 47 per cent of the workforce are women, although more women than men work part-time). This in turn required expanded public (state) childcare. The family structure in all social strata changed and collective upbringing of children by employed staff altered the conditions of childhood. The nuclear family's autonomy was at least partially broken, while the presence of paid staff in childcare sometimes gave rise to secondary problems such as insecurity and a split existence for small children.

Expanding welfare also gave families more money, while at the same time, the rapid socio-cultural changes and intensification of work increased needs for warmth and communality in intimate spheres. What remained of the family's productive functions was undermined in favour of the reproductive. The family's emotional security had to compensate for the hard, fluctuating social climate, for stress and frangibility. The intimate sphere thus also became more consumption-oriented and formed the basis for the rampantly expanding consumption and leisure industries – more and more people went on holidays abroad, acquired summer cottages, caravans, boats, TVs, stereos. And not least, the media expanded enormously. Television arrived in Sweden in 1957, and was followed by FM radio, the transistor radio and stereo LPs. By 1961 three radio stations were established, largely due to pressure from various pirate stations that responded to demands from the new teenage music-loving public. The information and entertainment industries brought the outside world closer and media-conveyed experiences began to acquire a greater significance alongside the private ones. The media also brought particularly intensive cultural currents from the United States to Sweden.

All these rapid changes widened the generation gap. Our band members' parents grew up with these developments and both enjoyed and suffered from them, whereas their elders recalled much poorer and more traditional childhood conditions. The 1950s also introduced the first of a series of new youth cultures centring on rock music: from about 1956 onwards rock 'n' roll stood out as exclusive youth music.[9] The *raggare* (gangs driving big American cars and listening to rock 'n' roll), a special Swedish youth culture, expressed the Americanised dream of rising careers and the 'good life'. Teenagers again clearly appeared as a special sort of people, united by their openness to new cultural expressions, and they formed the basis for an enormous expansion of the culture industry focused on music and fashion. In the 1960s class boundaries in youth culture were further softened by the advent of the mods, modelled after their British predecessors (but more socially mixed), and by various youthful movements like the anti-Vietnam war movement and later music and environmental movements. Generation gaps and style differences were not only extended expressions of class cleavages (as they were in previous class-dichotomous youth cultures in the 1920s and 1930s or in the polarity between the 'bikers' and the 'dixies', a Swedish middle-class youth style revolving around dixieland music). Class conflicts did not disappear but they were complicated by other kinds of oppositions and style demarcations that went in other directions.

In many ways, the late 1950s witnessed a breakthrough of tendencies which were heralded in the late 1920s and 1930s. Modernization processes restructured everyday life and popular culture on a new level. Social relations, cultural forms and personal identities gradually changed. The 1960s brought about a new phase of modernity, a radicalised, extended and deepened *late modernity* that penetrated ever deeper into the everyday life of more and more people.[10] We use the concept of late modernity to be able to discuss recent cultural tendencies without falling into the postmodernist trap of making a categorical break with the long-term processes of modern society. Like Habermas and Ziehe, we perceive today's cultural life as the radical continuation of the forces of modernity, but unlike them, we find it useful to work with a term for the most recent stages of the modernization process, where tendencies inherent in the modern era fully flower rather than disappear. We might be living in a phase where the modern epoch is in transition to a new and still unknown future, but the phenomena discussed in our times are better conceptualised as a heightened, radicalised 'super' or 'hyper' modernity. We think our concept 'late modernity' avoids many of the contradictions and fallacies produced by postmodernist formulations while retaining the possibility of being inspired by their acute sensitivity to the phenomenology of the present.

THE LATE MODERN CRISES

Already in the middle of the 1960s, the reverse side of the welfare state began to be marked. Various social movements (and they were not alone in this) called attention to problems of alienation and psychological suffering in the new cities, exploitation and war in the third world (indelibly stamped on the minds and hearts of the nuclear family through television), environmental damage in the wake of industrialisation, the eradication of traditional continuities and norms which were previously considered self-evident, but which were replaced by an enormous muddle of contradictory life forms. Many youth cultures may be seen as attempts to handle symbolically such crises in the parental culture.[11] However, initially optimistic and aspiring attitudes dominated, in Sweden exemplified by the *raggare*. The British skinhead culture at the end of the 1960s brought the first clear example of the opposite: a youth culture that exaggerated – almost travestied – the (lumpen) proletarian and derided all middle-class snobbery. It was, however, not really introduced in Sweden until its revival at the end of the 1970s, contemporary with the advent of punk. The hippy culture also levelled broad and sharp criticism against the middle class when it questioned the values of the economic boom and sought alternative solutions.

Our band members were born during this phase. They have experienced neither the secure, traditional plod that preceeded the boom nor the euphoria and expansion that their parents grew up in. Instead, from the start their lives were stamped by a new kind of uncertainty and a burgeoning and irremediably chronic awareness of crisis. They belong to a late-modern crisis generation. Particularly from the 1960s onwards, the continuous social modernisation led to a new degree of cultural change which bores deeply into people's everyday lives. Whereas modernisation had previously augmented conflict between generations, it later came to do the opposite through directly affecting parents as well as youth, and thereby it created possibilities for a new dialogue between generations.

Modernisation has positive as well as negative sides, but both cause adjustment problems.[12] Thus many youth cultures may be seen as attempts to handle the break with norms and traditions caused by modernisation, for example, when the traditions and communality of workers are split up or reshaped by the individualised life forms of urbanisation and the welfare state. However, other youth cultures, not least punk from the mid-1970s, express experiences of the negative sides of modernisation: unemployment, economic crises, environmental destruction and threats of war. Modernisation shatters local and social traditions through the rapid cultural transformations accompanying it. This engenders a localised crisis aware-ness – within particular geographic and class-defined areas (for example, working-class neighbourhoods in England or small towns in Sweden) – as well as one which is broader and more generalised (especially during the 1970s and 1980s). Modernisation is the driving force behind youth cultures that express different ways of managing crisis experiences along with, *inter alia* class, gender, race and geographic lines.

Of course, a more differentiated and detailed analysis of the late modern condition should be given, specified accord-ing to the particular social forms it adopts in different classes. However, first a few general tendencies may be out-lined.[13] Transformations require and make possible greater flexibility in the conduct of one's life, a preparedness for changing residence, work and friends. Fixed spatial borders become moveable and the living environment is exposed to greater differentiation. Diverse opportunities throng, point-ing in different directions. This differentiation creates more complex oppositions, for example, between different educative norms or between different ethnic traditions in the same housing area. This also means a greater variety for the individual. Numerous choices seem to lie within reach, different actions seem feasible, all of which give a sense of freedom, but also greater individual responsibility for one's actions in more and more areas. The 'expectation gap' between culturally instilled hopes and promises and the actual ability to realise them (at least all at once) deepens – as does frustration.[14]

The process of traditions being de-mystified and rendered less self-evident leads to a cultural release for individuals who can no longer clearly lean on time-honoured manners and customs, but instead are allowed, if not compelled, to choose from among a growing number of proposed lives in areas hitherto more tradition-bound (work, family formation, housing, style). This tendency towards individu-alisation means that, more than before, each individual perceives more opportunities, more choices and more individual responsibility. One may choose traditional modes of living, but they are no longer 'given' or inherited.

Late modernity also furnishes individuals with a rich

choice of opportunities to reflect upon their identities in order to confront the openness brought about by the dismantling of tradition. The partial erosion of the walls of tradition does not reveal a totally free space; it opens onto intersecting signs and images which in the media and social interaction give divergent proposals for how to live. Consciousness is 'colonised' by media-conveyed images and symbols that equip people with a language for experiences which had often been taboo (for example, sexuality or aggression), but these images and symbols also make it more difficult to distinguish one's own, authentic experiences from what is indirect, media-conveyed.[15]

On the third historical level, the period our youths themselves have experienced, these late modern elements have been present right from the start. Our band members have no older fund of memories to compare with. How these late modern conditions may have formed their inner subjectivity will be discussed in the next chapter.[16] Here we will concern ourselves with the 'outer', objective conditions of life.

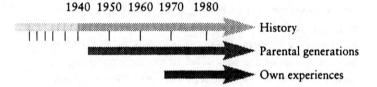

Figure 9 Experience of youth and parents

On the public and social levels, the 1970s in Sweden were deeply affected by renewed signs of crisis: the oil crisis, growing unemployment, slow growth and cultural signals of a change towards a pessimistic world view. The boom had come to a halt, but changes continued at an undiminished rate. The young were greatly affected by all this. The boom's educational explosion had come to an end and was replaced by restraints. The end of the 1970s saw extensive threats to the future of mankind in the environment, war and real threats of chronic mass unemployment in the economic crisis. The punk culture of 1976 and the squatters' movement of 1980 expressed these apprehensions in a new way, with paradoxical slogans (typical for the decade) such as 'You haven't got a chance – take it!'

To our three bands, punk was a significant experience and stimulated their own music-making and search for culture.[17]

Hence, the youths in our bands were born at a turning-point between two main tendencies in late modernity. On the one hand, the 1950s and the 1960s were pervaded by a comprehensive socialisation in which increasing areas of life were drawn into an instrumental rationality in state or private capitalist control and efficiency of the sort that had long dominated bureaucracy and industrial production. Childcare, education and immediate social environments became the objects of a technological rationalisation which shattered older forms of communal living. Life patterns were de-traditionalised, a process that was expressed in a more pragmatic relation to work, in Christianity's diminished importance as a source of guidelines to live by, in less respect for and belief in authority, and in changed forms of sexuality and social life.

On the other hand, in the 1970s there was a growth in the occasionally critical reflections over the 'achievements of civilisation': 'progress' was seen as problematical, official language was increasingly filled with attempts to work out and take a stand as regards its own, individual and collective identity. These tendencies work in tandem, both arise out of the new level of de-traditionalising in society and infuse late modern everyday life, in which demands for qualification and performance, dreams and expectations look very different from what they did only a few decades earlier.

THREE SPHERES

Ronny [Bergslunden social worker]: Most of the Ark kids live round the square in Bergslunden [. . .] They are fairly regular working-class kids, you could say. Most of them haven't done very well at school, some really really badly. If the working class can be divided into two halves, they belong to the lower half – they've got no terrace houses or cooperative flats, their parents don't have supervising jobs as foremen, nurses and so on, they're just ordinary workers. They work at Volvo [or] in nearby small industry.

Female teacher of Chans: This community is an old area with detached houses, where the elite of the economy is well settled. But there is some social movement. The sad thing now, I think, are the *nouveaux riches*, whose kids may be sort of left to fend for themselves – the parents go abroad or leave them on their own. They ask a lot of the kids, without love, or so it seems. But it's a mixed picture. As in the rest of society, there are [also] islands of enormous harmony and happiness, peace and quietness.

Among our three bands Lam Gam and Chans comprise the outer poles: the two environments they live in are tantamount to two separate worlds. Although OH certainly occupies a middle position in some respects, the OH culture should not be reduced to some sort of average; nor are the band members to be classified as 'mainstream youths' on account of socio-economic criteria. In some ways Chans and Lam Gam have things in common not shared by OH.[1]

At first glance, the differences between the worlds of Lam Gam and Chans are very striking. Bergslunden and Villaholmen lie at about the same distance from their respective cities, but there the resemblance stops. (Since OH members reside in two quite different residential areas, it has not been possible to present their living environment in the same way.) Bergslunden appears to be a newly built, open melting-pot for a number of divergent cultural currents, whereas Villaholmen seems rather like an old-fashioned, closed reservation for traditional values and patterns of living (see Figure 10).

Differences in the size of flats, income, unemployment and political sympathy of course primarily express fundamental class polarities in the two areas, regardless of the degree of modernity. Bergslunden is a poor, low-status area with a working-class population; Villaholmen is a fairly wealthy, high-status area, with a middle- and upper-class population. In the present case, the working-class area happens to be modern; presumably it could just as well be the opposite. Bergslunden was built later than Villaholmen, in a great building wave during the 1960s boom; Villaholmen has a longer history, which lives on in the residents' memories as well as in its planning and kinds of housing. Migration frequency, immigration and family type show that Bergslunden has a significantly higher

	Bergslunden	Villaholmen
Number of inhabitants	12,000	10,000
Year built	1960s	Throughout twentieth century
Dominant building type	High-rise flats	One-family house
Accommodation	70%, 1–2 bedrooms	50%, 4 bedrooms
Out-migration frequency	30% (central area)	10%
Resident immigrants	9%, from 37 countries	4%, from 24 countries
Residents under 20 yrs	25%	30%
Single parents	40% (central area)	13%
Income index	85	120
Unemployment	10%	1%
Social Democratic voters	60%	30%

Figure 10   Bands' home districts compared

mobility (or instability). To a much greater degree than Villaholmen, Bergslunden seems to offer a multi-cultural openness and blend of modes of living.

However, when we examine the individuals in our bands, the picture becomes somewhat less clear. Lam Gam does not have the largest proportion of members with immigrant or ethnically/nationally mixed family backgrounds – perhaps surprisingly, OH does. Two members of Lam Gam have single parents, but – mainly because of the girls – three members of Chans have divorced mothers. This suggests perhaps that we must probe a little deeper into the two (three) group cultures in order to make any precise statements about the possible degree and kind of late modern impact in the respective groups.

The 'micro-cultures' comprised by the bands are part of their radically different respective local cultures (life forms, customs and habits). In addition, by a conscious choice of style and music, these micro-cultures relate to partly similar, partly different subcultures within the youth culture spectrum which form the immediate frames of reference for their identities as teenagers.

The groups and individuals live in social environments structured according to similar general principles and frames of reference. We shall distinguish three primary *spheres*, types of institutions or social units: families and their ways of raising their children; schools and working life; and the media and leisure organisations. Needless to say, there are differences within each sphere, but they have enough in common to compose three main types.[2] The peer groups that comprise the main subjects of our investigation form a fourth sphere, which we will examine later on. Each individual in all three groups moves between and among the three (other) spheres during the course of a year, week or day. Each sphere contains particular material and social boundaries indicating demands or rules for the individuals and groups, to be used as resources and opportunities for them and the satisfaction of their needs. The spheres encompass different *fields of action*[3] which individuals and groups can and must enter and leave. In certain respects, the spheres stand in opposition to each other since their promises and demands can be in conflict. Internal and external problems can arise in both groups and individuals at the same time as these conflicts involve openings and opportunities for them to play with and manipulate the different spheres. We have seen how each group places itself in its own complex pattern. Here we shall concentrate on two things: a comprehensive analysis and comparison of each sphere for all three groups (focusing on Lam Gam and Chans as the outer poles); and a study of the relations between and among the three spheres – how the triad of relationships family–school/work–media/leisure is determined for each group.

These spheres also comprise *socialisation units*: they help to shape individual identities. This is not a matter of simple moulding or reproduction mechanisms but of a complex interaction between reproductive demands from each unit – sometimes in mutual internal conflict – and the groups' and individuals' own unique history and experience, motives and abilities, problems and dreams.

THE FAMILY

In our society, the family is the arena in which the basic formation of the individual occurs, in which the psychic constitution and social competence of the individual are established and developed. Over recent decades the family has undergone considerable changes, but it is still organised according to the same monogamous, patriarchal principles that have long dominated Western societies. The present-day family consists of parents and children who are minors according to law (legally incapacitated). The old type of 'extended' family which was based on its capacity as a production unit has totally dissolved. However, although the relations between and among family members are no longer determined by production and many of the functions previously ascribed to the family are disappearing, the family remains as an institution. Equally, the ideal of family togetherness and intimacy lives on. The family's function as a unit of consumption has been strengthened, and the family has acquired a stronger affective compensatory function. Intimacy and 'warmth' in family relations function as a defence against and antithesis to the 'cold' conditions prevailing in society, especially in the productive sphere.[4]

At the same time, it is incumbent on the family to shape an individual who assimilates the requisite fundamental psychic disposition to function in a society based on waged work. The prerequisites for this are security and the utility-oriented satisfaction of needs of the mother-child relationship. This relationship is initially the child's entire world. Gradually, in parallel with physical development and maturing, the child develops independence and becomes an individual. The birth of the human organism is biological, but the birth of the human individual is social – the result of the encounter between the child's 'inner nature' and the conditions of society. This birth occurs in the family through society indicating via parents the boundaries for the child's relation to the surrounding world and his/her identity development.

The primary socialisation taking place within the family occurs during the child's first three to six years. Thereafter, the other institutions of society penetrate more directly.

Ulf: How have you tried to bring up Micke ?
Micke's father (born in Yugoslavia): Well, I want him to obey. Like I've been brought up. You did what you were told, right?
Ulf: And you still think that's right?
Father: Yes I do.

Lollo: I've worked a lot with the old man, like when we bought the summer house [. . .] We did a lot of building work on it and I was with my dad a lot then – my uncle and grandad were smiths then, you know. So I started fuckin' early burning my hands with hot iron and such. Learned to forge, made tools and that.

Ove: Your dad, does he live with you?
Jonna: No, he lives in Halland [south of Gothenburg] and I don't give a shit about him.
Ove: Was it long ago you met him?
Jonna: Yeah, about a year. That was the first time I seen him for eight years. I don't give a damn, and then he goes and rings up and wants to know if I couldn't come. Yeah, so I say I'll come.
Ove: How did it feel to meet him?
Jonna: Na, it felt like meeting a whole new person, but I don't give a damn about him.

Johan: Have you participated equally in your children's upbringing, both of you? [. . .]
Gösta's mother: Yes, I should think so. Often mothers used to feel it the most [responsibility], but I should think that with us it's been exactly equal.

Johan: You've been very important for the band. You've supported them from the beginning and encouraged their playing, haven't you?
Håkan's father: Yes indeed. Because I like music myself. So it's been natural. I know how much fun music is.
Johan: You play yourself too?
Father Yes indeed. I play the fiddle.
Johan: In a folk group?
Father: Exactly. The folk group is *one* part of it [. . .] Earlier I played in another way, in more serious contexts. Classical music.
Johan: In an orchestra?
Father: Yes.

Jonna's mother: But those gigs were such fun I think, I even dressed up, I think so . . . yeah well, it was for Jonna too, for his sake. Because there never were any other parents that came and watched and then I dragged along my mother and friends who are around 40 or 50. They just sat there and maybe didn't think it was so good all the time. But Jonna, I could just see how his self-confidence grew when he played and I stood there snapping my fingers and digging it even though the music isn't really my sort of music.

Both the demand and the ability to relate independently to society intensify, but the individual, in the view of society, does not become an autonomous subject, that is, a full member, until he or she has reached 18 years old. The socialisation occurring in the family today is anything but uniform. Yet, despite class, cultural and geographical differences, there are still tendencies which in principle affect everyone. Generally it may be said that in several respects, the family remains a cornerstone of social organisation; but as a biographical project, the family in our late modern society has acquired serious competition from other cell formations.

One modernising tendency is the mixing of nationalities. Two of the six youths in Lam Gam have immigrant parents – from Norway and Finland. Among the nine Stockholm youths, one has immigrant parents (from Finland). However, the original group in OH contained only one wholly Swedish family, a fact that contradicts the assumption that through its position in the working-class aristocracy of a middle-size town, OH should reflect more traditional patterns. In all three bands the proportion of members with at least one non-Swedish parent is one third. Growing up in a multicultural family naturally involves a fair amount of types of problems and demands other than those presumably present in a wholly Swedish family. In our interviews we detected certain contentions between the freer and more slack child-rearing praxis of Swedish society and more traditional and authoritarian attitudes. Also it seems as if the youth in our bands with multi-cultural backgrounds are the most eager to talk about and maintain family and kinship bonds: they have the most regular and frequent contact with their grandparents, for instance. As regards family ties, it is difficult to detect any class-influenced differences in our groups, and in this one may well suspect a departure from their parents' generation. Our youths are oriented towards class-determined professions, but not towards the same professions as their parents.

Another tendency concerns the splitting of the nuclear family and the division of roles in the home. Two of the members of Lam Gam, Jonna and Lollo, have grown up with one biological parent – the mother. Jonna has had several fathers, but neither he nor Lollo have had any real contact with their biological fathers. Since he was 16 and moved away from home, Lollo has had no contact with his mother. The other four in Lam Gam have lived and still live in traditional nuclear families, most often with sisters and brothers. In Chans the divorce frequency is the same as in Lam Gam, with three of nine parents divorced or remarried. Only one parent in OH is a single parent and there are no non-biological parents.

All the parents of the members of Chans have qualified occupations (this is also true of OH fathers, although they have manual jobs). In Lam Gam, two of the single mothers are unemployed and dependent upon social welfare; the other parents have unqualified and low-status jobs, with the exception of Conny's father, who heads a department in a small company. It would seem that there are some differences among the bands as regards division of work and responsibility in the home. OH and Lam Gam's family pattern is fairly traditional, whereas the fathers of Chans seem to participate more actively in the household. (This is the picture given in the interviews, which does not necessarily reflect the real situation.)

There are also differences in the parents' activities and engagements outside work. Lam Gam's parents appear to be rather passive socially, they mostly stay home and watch TV; no particular political, cultural or sports interests appear to compete with home life. They occasionally go to a restaurant, or away for the weekend ('mini-holiday'), but seem not to cultivate any interests. Some of the OH parents are criticised by their offspring for passivity and lack of social intercourse. The parents of Chans demonstrate a more active and varied social life. They socialise outside the family and are generally interested in the culture on offer – theatre, concerts, literature, and so on. They also spend more time with their children and are involved in what their children do much more than the parents of Lam Gam. Some OH parents take part in their sons' activities (they especially support music-making), while others do not. The members of Chans get help and support with their school work, they are driven to and from gigs and parties, and their parents are often present when they play. In Lam Gam, only Jonna's mother has ever turned up on such occasions and she is also the only parent showing any real interest in the band. As regards economic resources, the differences are even more striking. In Chans' parents' houses the children have their

Jonna's mother: And my greatest dream, is that one day I'll have the money to buy Jonna a bass. So now, you know, I've applied for a grant, I just thought either it works or it doesn't. I went to the library one day and looked up everything there was to apply to, but it was mostly for old railway workers and God knows what. [. . .] But finally I found a grant [. . .] So I simply wrote about the situation, that I have a boy who plays, that I support us on my own and that I don't have any way of saving any money. But it's Jonna's greatest wish to have a bass and not just any old bass either – something that costs like 4000 kronor. [. . .] You know, they talked about a robbery here on the radio this morning. There's so much robbery in Gothenburg nowadays, and I thought, 'Well hell, if worse comes to worse, I'll have to do a robbery then.' You know, I was down in that music store in town and looked [. . .]. I bought a few pluc-trems [*sic*] or whatever they're called and I must say that [the sales clerk] seemed a little absent-minded . . . It's amazing more instruments don't disappear when they hang like that, so unguarded. But I'm going to get a bass, because I want to see Jonna's eyes light up on Christmas Eve [. . .].

Gösta's father: We read a lot, yes.
Johan: Have you tried to get Gösta interested in different kinds of culture – music, books, theatre? You read yourselves, have you tried to get him . . . ?
Gösta's mother: We have tried . . .
Gösta's father: He's not been all that interested. I think the last few years we've tried to get a discussion going at the dinner table, you know, on a little more cultural and intellectual matters and I think that's turned out well. And also in connection with what he reads in school, to give an all-round education, which we probably neglected to do earlier, to talk about things like that . . .

Kurre: Yeah, I've got big feelings for her. I like her. I love my mum, I do absolutely. Because she . . . she always helps me if there's any problem [. . .] She's just there. Without her everything would be a lot more difficult. [. . .] Sometimes I think I know my dad and sometimes I don't.

own rooms, the parents' financial position allows the families to travel together, the children to have skiing holidays and go to camp, to buy instruments and furnish rehearsal quarters. OH member, Micke, was assisted by his mother when he needed new drums – an exception to the rule that members pay for their own instruments by working holidays and eventually working full time. In Lam Gam, only Sigge has his own instrument, an electric guitar, which he has saved for by working summers. Several of the Lam Gam boys spend their summers at home in Bergslunden. A few of them have also been on skiing holidays, but not in the Austrian Alps – on Swedish slopes, the trips organised by the Ark and financed by the social services. And only because of local authority support for the music project at the Ark do Lam Gam have somewhere to practise and instruments to use. Only Conny has music-making at home – his father plays piano; otherwise none of the Lam Gam parents has demonstrated much interest in music. Most of them have record players and occasionally play Elvis or popular dance band records. It is very different in Chans' families. Several parents or siblings play music and most of the parents consciously wish to make their children cultivated. Two of the OH parents have played an instrument at some point in their lives, but that is all. In short, the Chans parents' cultural capital is of another colour from that of Lam Gam's parents – without being remarkable in any way.

A modern – if not specifically late modern – element which seems to be shared by all three groups is the position of the mother in the family. It is probably not so remarkable that the mothers are generally the emotional centres of the family; however, they also have a strong position of power.[5] The mothers are not only the hub around which the family's emotional life revolves, they also seem to take greatest responsibility for rearing the children. The fathers tend to be 'estranged' in those cases where they are not physically absent. To a degree, this 'estranged father' pattern is not as obvious in Chans' families.[6] One of the OH families is markedly different from the others – a family with a very strong traditional patriarchal structure, in which the mother is demanding and penalising.

A comparison between the Chans parents and those of OH and Lam Gam reveals that the former are much more controlling in their child-rearing practices. This need for control is clearly based on an anxiety about their children making the wrong moves: for example, it is considered essential that the children's free time is occupied by organized activities. The girls are on a tighter rein than the boys. Although this is doubtless anchored in traditional patterns, it might also be because the girls do not live in Villaholmen but in the city and therefore cannot enjoy the Villaholmen home life, or because the girls are actually more socially curious, more mature and restless even though they are a year younger than the boys. The Chans parents place more or less expressed demands on their children to perform and 'succeed' in life. But they also stress the importance of developing individuality and uniqueness and the ability to act independently and rationally in relation to one's surroundings. As regards pressure to achieve, it is the fathers who are the most active.

Parental demands for social advancement are more outspoken in OH families. Several of the fathers, especially, refuse to accept their children's relative educational shortcomings and the low levels of ambition. As is the case with Bamse's parents, criticism may involve a condemnation of the son's behaviour in general. At the same time, basic faith in the educational system is lacking: only Finn attempts a three-year, non-vocational upper secondary course (but leaves during the first year). Instead, hope is successively attached to educational alternatives such as folk high schools or work place courses in order to complete vocational training. The result involves a fairly modest social promotion – from the upper working-class to the lower strata of the middle class.

In the same way that Chans families illustrate a pattern of child-rearing which is typical for a middle class with primarily economic capital, Lam Gam families represent conditions prevailing in the lower strata of the working-class. However, in both environments it is common that children are an opening to society, a channel through which it is possible to keep abreast of what is happening around them.[7] In Lam Gam, the families' capital entails a constriction of the children's possibilities to act, but direct demands are fewer. In Chans, however, there are grounds for dispute between parental demands and the band's needs – for example, time to rehearse. Most surprising in

Micke: But my old man wants [sigh] me to start my own business, like lots of people do when they're around my age. It's true, he's makes impossible demands, you could say.

Björn: My parents think it's difficult sometimes when we go and practise, don't keep mealtimes or anything you can keep to.
[...]
Olof: It was maybe some time around the ninth year that they didn't want us to play anything.
Gustav: *Anything*, they didn't say ... [...]
Björn: Yeah, but we had a parents' meeting here and they went on about 'Yes, yes, you can't have more than two gigs this year 'cause now you've got to study' and all that. [...]
Karl: We actually had a parents' meeting. [...]
Olof: It's a bit boring to rehearse all autumn if then you can't play anywhere.

Jonna's mother: Jonna, he goes to gymnasium, the second year ... and it surprises me that my children have got so ... what shall I say, purposeful, it really amazes me. Because, as I said, I've been really sloppy. [...] Yeah, I still can't really grasp that he's getting an education and that he'll be a cook, he who has never even cooked an egg his whole life! You know, I didn't even know he'd applied. [...] And then he says he didn't know either he'd applied but that it was a teacher in school who'd filled it in as a second choice or something.

Johan: Is there music in the family?
Gösta's mother: Yes. We had an *enormous* amount of music. My

father is very musical, and my brother is. He played the piano, my dad, but no other instrument. But he's sung in choirs and there's always been a lot of music and singing – always.

this regard is the young people's inclination to adjust themselves to their parents' wishes – without protest. Even so, the Chans parents are aware that they cannot pressure their children too hard, that there has to be a balance – they must be allowed outlets for their needs. In this there is an ambivalence about upbringing strategies: to what extent should one stick to a time-honoured pattern and to what extent is freer upbringing justified? This ambivalence is rooted in the type of norm conflicts engendered by our late modern, de-traditionalised society.

THE SCHOOL

Sigge: ... It would never occur to me to go on a three- or four-year gymnasium course . . . shit . . . the people going on the four year technical think they'll be engineers direct, but they've gotta go on – if they're not good enough already of course.
Ove: Yeah, but if they're going to be full civil engineers, they have to go for four or five years to Chalmers [Institute of Technology in Gothenburg] after gymnasium.
Sigge: Yeah, yeah . . . and then you've already earned a wad if you go two years . . . let them come then . . . it'd never occur to me to go so long . . . like finish school when you're around 25 or so . . . get a doctorate and that.
Ove: You'd never consider being anything like that?
Sigge: No, I'd never be able to work so hard, it's too much work . . . but it's good that there are slobs like that – otherwise we'd never have any medicos or doctors.

Gösta's mother: They *never* said anything about parents interfering, but we did sometimes. We had little meetings sometimes, the parents and them, to decide certain things, like, for example, they should practise at particular times.

The functions of the school in a modern society reflect prevailing oppositions and complexities. At the same time, school and the world it represents are of crucial importance in our type of society: it is here that an important part of secondary socialisation occurs.[8]

One of the most important functions of school is linked with social organisation's need for common values and basic knowledge; it is up to school to maintain an educational level necessary for society. This involves coercion as well as opportunities for growth. Another important responsibility is the disciplinary function: society demands individual self-control and an ability to subordinate and adapt to various forms of organisations or social structures based on division of labour. The school socialises – for better or worse. Moreover, it functions as an instrument of selection, that is, via the system of performance and demand which is controlled by marks, the school selects and sorts pupils according to the needs and demands of the labour market. All in all, the school both opens and closes doors to the future, and is contradictory since it is at once an institution, peer group environment and individual educational instrument.

Entry into the compulsory comprehensive school involves a decisive change in the child's life conditions. The personality growth and learning rhythm that the child has previously experienced have largely followed patterns of play. Upon entering school, formalised and controlled learning processes in large groups take over the search for knowledge. The school's demands for discipline, concentration, performance, self-control, etc. contrast with the freedom and intimacy of the home environment.

For the youth in Chans, school and parents support and confirm each other to a large degree. The type of performance and behaviour demands placed by the parental culture are largely in accord with the 'culture' dominating in the school, a culture which is of course upheld by middle-class teachers. Lam Gam and OH do not experience the same congruity between home and school. In this respect, there is an inequality in the basic preconditions for making use of school instruction. Even if, as with Chans, there is accord between school and the home environment, entry into school is a painful break with the child's previous life contexts. Starting school may almost be compared with splitting the identity: individuals learn to divide their identity between the 'real me' and their role as pupils.[9] Even if the young people in Chans find it easier to adjust themselves to school, subordinate themselves and take advantage of the teaching, the school's identity-cleaving also affects them – school is also for them an enforced environment.

However alienating the school environment, and however difficult the collision between the home environment and the school may be, school does open the world. When starting school the child goes beyond his or her domestic horizon, and commences a journey that starts off with the acquisition of our cultural techniques – reading, writing and arithmetic.

Regardless of class background, for the child, school is an important meeting-place and peer-group arena. For our band members, school is the place where all their mates are. In the social interplay between pupils inside and outside the classroom, they can test relations and learn important social lessons. The social opening to the world may conflict with knowledge, with the educational function. For the members of Lam Gam, peer group relations are prioritised: demands placed on them by the school are secondary. From their home environments, they have not internalised the performance demands required for success in school. The same may be said for the boys in OH.

Mates are important to Chans as well, but Chans members have adapted to school in another way. There is a latent conflict between getting good marks, demands for

Johan: What have your child-rearing principles been?
Gösta's father: We haven't had any principles, we've ... well, we've tried to keep to a middle course ... not to be too indulgent as they were in the 1920s.
Gösta's mother: The twenties?
Gösta's father: Yes, the twenties and thirties it was, when Freud began to be misunderstood – that one shouldn't ... that one should let go ...
Gösta's mother: Well, it was a bit different in different families ...
Gösta's father: Yes, it probably was, yes ... But we've tried to hold to a sort of middle course.
Gösta's mother: Yes, and we've thought it very important to explain why we think and do certain things. To motivate, not just say no, but also why.
Johan: Have you two behaved the same way towards him?
Both: Yes, I think so.

Conny: I want to be seven again, sit in a sandbox and play with cars. It was such fucking freedom, sort of.
Ola: Then you could put up with everything.
Conny: Yeah, didn't give a shit if you had sand up your ass, you just went around laughing with your snotty nose – it was shit cool. Now everything's supposed to be so fucking perfect.

Johan: Do you go to parents' meetings in the school and that?
Håkan's father: Always.
Johan: You are interested in school work too?
Håkan's father: Yes, it's a way to show your interest – to go to *all* the meetings at school. [...]
Johan: Do you think they've had good teachers?
Håkan's father: Absolutely, all through. Perfect teachers!

Frasse: For me personally, it's been very good having marks. I can imagine that for some it's been lousy, just crap. But I mean, when it comes to that question, you've still got to think of yourself, haven't you, I think – even if you should always be thinking of your fellow beings.

Karl: Sometimes, you think: school, like . . . what the hell, why the hell should you go there?
Håkan: What the hell am I doing here? [. . .]
Gösta: It varies. I mean, it's really a benefit.
Olof: But if you stay home for a day, you notice the difference. It's not so fun to be there either. [. . .] I mean, everybody else goes to school, so what do you do there [at home]?
Björn: It's not a pain to *go* to school or to be [there].
Gustav: The pain's waking up!

Ove: Why did you go there [to school] at all?
Jonna: Meet mates.
Ove: You didn't bother going to class?
Jonna: Yeah, I didn't. I didn't go just because they'd decided all kids should go to school. I had no books with me, didn't give a damn about them.

Frasse: OK, like you're in Sunday and Saturday lunch maybe, but you don't need to be in evenings – so much studying you don't need, I think [. . .] Marks aren't everything. You should be able to live too at the same time.

Johan: Do you think they worked hard – on homework? [. . .]
Chans' teacher: I've an impression that the boys in Chans worked fairly hard. [. . .]
Johan: Did they like school in general? [. . .]
Teacher: They didn't talk about it right out, but other pupils in their class did.
Johan: Negative? They complained . . . ?
Teacher: Yes, exactly.

discipline and self-control, and reducing free time on the one hand and life with their mates on the other. They manage to hold this conflict in check partly by being efficient and fully utilising their time together with their mates. The Chans culture contains a very different intensity and industriousness from that of the Ark culture. In an entirely different way from Lam Gam, Chans are also prepared to give up and take the consequences of the knowledge that achievement in school is crucial as regards opportunities for future interesting and well-paid work. There is no doubt that the young people in Chans have taken better advantage of the resources offered by the school – knowledge and proficiency in solid subjects, social contacts, perspective and the ability to orient themselves towards advancement in society. But the peer-group environment can also contribute to educating the individual, and through this all our bands have come into contact with ideas, political ideologies, lifestyles and youth cultural expressions, which they would never have encountered in their homes or parental milieus. And it has provided not merely a secondary but a broadened knowledge of the world and extended possibilities as regards modes of living, identities, etc.

The school as an institution has to satisfy the continually changing needs of the labour market. The system of marks is the school's decisive instrument for setting demands, and testing and sorting pupils, and thus marks are nothing less than a socially approved declaration of contents. Contrary to the national curriculum goals of equality, justice, education and all-round personality development, the school actually contributes to the reproduction of class society. The opposition between culture and education, between humanist ideals and the sorting function of the school is expressed in the criticism that school is not a preparation for life but for obtaining marks.[10]

Thus three different forces interact in school. The school as an institution is directed towards the goal-oriented education of pupils to satisfy labour market demands, which leads to prioritising performance and instrumental learning. The school as a peer arena, in which children and youth meet in large and relatively heterogenous groups, exposes the individual socially to new areas of experience and allows testing social relations, group solidarity and acting-out. The school as an educational centre systematically organises the search for knowledge and alerts its pupils' thoughts to the outside world. Sometimes these three forces cooperate, sometimes they are pitted against each other.

This whole complex of oppositions is accentuated by late modern tendencies. Generally, the struggle for jobs is intensified and the labour market's demands for flexibility and mobility increased. Today, during one's working life, one must be prepared to change professions, re-train oneself, and move more than once. Nor is one's identity any longer as closely linked to one's professional role, which is a prerequisite of flexibility. Moreover, the workforce places different demands on work, and the trade union movement as well as industry places increasingly clear demands on school to help motivate youth towards occupations they are not interested in – factory work, for instance. This development, which has its roots in the revolutionary social changes of the last two decades, has intensified the incompatibility of the school's functions. Educational ideals have been weakened in favour of instrumental competence; the school has become technocratic. Modern, technologically advanced industrial society places high demands on general social competence and maturity among its workforce, and in consequence, education is prolonged and entry into working life delayed. In practice, compulsory schooling at present ends at the age of 18; however, only an extremely marginal group of school leavers start work straight after school (during the 1980s, 5–10 per cent). For the pupils, this means school can resemble a reservation or quarantine. When working life is made uncertain by a fitful labour market, school tends to offer security, to be a place where one can temporarily avoid the demanding aspects of adult life and work. This renders the period in school independent and peer-group relationships more important, but it also means an erosion of content. Gymnasium education has today become mandatory.[11] To get a job, it is more important than ever to have graduated from gymnasium; what one has read there is of less importance. The present value of a gymnasium diploma on the labour market is not comparable to what it was before or to previous vocational diplomas; the value of education has been inflated. Flexibility, the ability to acquire as broad an education as

Johan: But the Chans boys didn't?
Teacher: Not as much, I think. They [. . .] came from a more established background and so on – it was more self-evident that one should go to school. They were sort of distinctly secure in themselves and maybe that's also one reason why they didn't have the same mad scramble for marks and the same pressure that I noticed some of the others in the class did. Of course it's always there, but in comparison, it wasn't as great [with Chans] . . .

Lollo: Well, when the old man was working and that, I had to go to a summer camp [his mother couldn't look after him] . . . every bloody summer break, so I got to know lots of people and started to think like 'what the shit is this'. Yeah, I've had to get into a lot of different lifestyles, how people live, and that's like made me start thinking . . . like, this isn't at all like with mum and dad . . . how they have it. So you learn a helluva lot that way.

Sigge: It was us that had bad marks, we wanted to have fun, not just keep our noses in the books like . . . wanted to do things that were fun, not do so much . . . lots of lessons and that. It takes so much time . . . your free time is the most important isn't it?

Gustav: But like we had fun in school, met new people . . .
Björn It's *safe* to go to school. I'm a little scared about what's going to happen after, when we get out and have to get jobs and that.
Olof: You don't make friends, it seems sort of, a little like . . . empty.

Jonna: . . . You have to have an education, it doesn't matter if you don't work and that, if you've got an education it'll always be easier. Cooks there's some jobs for.

Ove: Do you think you learned anything in school?
Ola: I hardly remember anything. I remember a few like basic things, the alphabet, plus and minus and that. But then I don't remember much more.
Ove: Didn't you learn any English?
Ola: Oh yeah, I know a little English. Know that [the 16th-century Swedish King] Gustav Vasa built ships and that, but what the hell – don't remember much more.
Ove: Gustav Vasa – did he build ships?
Ola: Yeah, the ship Vasa.
Ove: Did he build that?
Ola: Yeah, him and his wife, I dunno.
Ove: But it was built a hundred years after his death, it was built in the 1600s.
Ola: What?
Ove: It was a hundred years later. Gustav Vasa lived in the sixteenth century.
Ola: Yeah? I don't remember, I forget everything.

possible, is a prerequisite for success – for being able to choose among alternatives depending on the current labour market.

Making the period in school an independent entity and making peer-group relations more central, prolonging education and school as an obligatory stage in life, eroding its content, an unstable labour market, all make the pupils feel ambivalent and provoke motivation crises. On the societal plane, the school is increasingly losing its function of bearer and mediator of a superior cultural and symbolic reality, thus contributing to the crisis.[12] The 'atmospheric density' of the school, which made it possible for weak teachers to carry out their work with authority, is disappearing; the school's 'aura' is undermined. In the classroom, teachers can no longer profit by the traditional relationships that gave the older generation unquestioned precedence and authority. If school has increased its importance for young people by prolonging the time they spend there, it has also lost ground though the increasingly significant influence of the culture industry imposes on young people's identities, language and cultural symbols. The loss of the school's aura is palpable in each of our three bands.

LEISURE

Johan: Are you in any clubs or anything?
Betty: Well, Our Theatre [amateur youth theatre club]. And the municipal music school.
Johan: And you're in some sort of sports . . .
B-A: Yeah, Friskis and Svettis [workout gyms] and a slalom club, and a bit more here and there.
Johan: No religious, political or other . . . ?
B-A: Yes, well, I'm a Tory [laughter]. No, I don't know, but I joined 'cause I think . . . well . . . like I wanted to see how the Conservatives advanced, as they say. And then . . . I don't know, I haven't formed any opinion.

Not all activities outside school or work should be regarded as leisure or recreational. For Lam Gam and Chans, school indicates the outer limits of free time: school sets boundaries for how much 'free time' you have, and in addition school helps to create needs which influence the content of free time. Leisure can obtain a compensatory function in that you do very different things from what one does in school. However, it can also function as an extension of school – doing homework, for example. Other, in principle obligatory, activities on the side of school and work include sleeping and getting yourself to and from school or work. Since their parents work, both Lam Gam and Chans spend some time doing housework – mainly cooking (or warming up) food after school. There is a great deal to suggest that girls have less free time than boys – in our groups and in Sweden in general: girls are more diligent with homework and help more in the home. Also, students in three- and four-year gymnasium courses have less free time than other students.[13] The youths in Chans each spend on average eight hours a week on homework. Homework never impinged on the free time of the boys in Lam Gam while they were in comprehensive school; in gymnasium they have spent an average of one hour a week on homework. Generally, working-class children do not study as much as do those from the middle class. Working-class children also tend to have fewer adult-steered leisure activities.[14] For most of the boys in Lam Gam, their autonomous rock-playing is their only organised free time activity; only Conny and Seppo do any sort of sports. The members of Chans have the most adult-directed activities other than playing in the band. The increase in the amount of leisure activities and their degree of organisation is an historical tendency, which means that a lifestyle from the upper levels of society is spreading down to the lower.[15] Examples of this from our bands include the church youth group (OH), the educational association, We Youth (Chans) and the music club, the Ark (Lam Gam), plus – particularly with Chans – theatre circles, sports clubs, the municipal music school and choirs. A clear pattern emerges if we compare Lam Gam and OH on the one hand, and Chans on the other: Chans have a much greater degree of scheduled leisure time, in which the activities are planned and determined by adults.

Alongside these sorts of organised leisure pursuits, there are of course free, spontaneous activities – parties, socialising with family and friends, hobbies, individual music-making, play and physical exercise, dancing and entertainment, media-consumption (for example, listening to music), reading, TV, films and theatre. Also in this category are resting, day-dreaming, musing – ways of spending time that are diminishing. However, collective daydreaming and voluntary, unorganised socialising with mates comprise an important part of OH and Lam Gam's free time. As regards self-organised music projects, they differ greatly. Whereas OH rehearsals approach organised work, chaos, jamming and playfulness threaten to take over both Chans and Lam Gam rehearsals. Chans are rather negative to too much organised leisure. If they nevertheless organise their music-making through an edu-

Gösta: And so we had a party in his guest house, the whole night . . .
Håkan: Yeah, didn't sleep a bit . . .
Gösta: . . . ran around the whole night, in . . .
Håkan: Yeah, we've got to tell you, when we ran naked in the meadow there . . . [. . .]
Karl: And met the paper boy at three o'clock. [. . .]
Håkan: Can't we talk about the parties we've had?
Björn: Rave-ups . . .
Håkan: Yeah, Gustav's party was a ball . . . [humming and buzzing]
Olof: Gösta shat in the woods!

Lollo: No, I don't read books, I can't read books. Films . . . yeah, if they're good . . . I don't much like that crap, like James Bond stuff. But there's lots of those novels and such shit in films that're about people – like penal islands and that shit, that I like . . . you know, like those films that are about how people live, how it is for people . . .
Ola: I only know that I just get off/lost listening to music . . . like when you sit at home and put on a cool record and you sit and mime playing, or drum with it like . . . and then you dream about getting as good as the people playing on the record . . . or that some time you'll be as famous as them . . . but you'll never be, ha ha ha.

cational association, it is because it is profitable, and through this and Olof and Frasse's moped deals, their free time is used for putting middle-class economic ideas into practice. At the same time, Chans have a great need to be on their own, possibly to compensate for the dominance of home- and school-organised leisure. Almost as much time is devoted to being together with mates as to being with the family, doing homework, sports and working together.

The use of the media has a large and historically growing place in young people's lives. It is also an activity – not merely passive consumption, as is often claimed. The media are used voluntarily and their use is not organised (even if their production is controlled and professional). The media comprise a broad spectrum, in which TV is closely associated with the family, books with school, and music with the peer group. The media open up the world and, through it, young people acquire selective knowledge about the world – facts as well as fiction. The media are also used as an emotional outlet, to channel feelings of fear, tension, aggression, humour, tenderness, togetherness. (We shall discuss this later as regards music.) Through the use of media content offered by the cultural industries, young people's frames of reference are extended beyond their local parental and school environments and raw materials are discovered for the formulation of and experiments with dreams, ideals, identities and norms.

Betty: . . . The most vulgar right now is Madonna.
B-A: Yeah, OK, I thought she sang – OK, she doesn't sing badly and I thought she sang fairly well before she got famous, but that hysteria, that's . . . yuk. I hate people who don't have their own identity or personality and that [. . .].
Lots of people start listening to things just because everybody else does or because their mates do. But I don't, it has to be something I get hooked on by myself.

Jonna: I don't have no acoustic guitar.
Ove: But if music's so important to you, shouldn't you get an acoustic guitar so you could work on making songs?
Jonna: Yeah, but if I want I can just borrow somebody's guitar . . . lots of people have one.

Certain state or local authority-controlled institutions – from youth club discos to TV and radio monopolies – cannot be excluded when discussing unorganised leisure time, in particular the entertainment and media world, even though it is dominated by commercial interests. The requirements of the culture industry set limits and boundaries. One such requirement is to keep up to date and to relate to new trends in the various fields of the youth scene, which in turn places demands particularly on economic resources – to buy stereos, records, tapes, clothes, to attend concerts, etc. All three of our bands, however, are clearly reluctant to be trendy and to eradicate their own individual identities. They prefer to be selective, choosing what suits their own identities and needs – not to swallow everything that is placed in front of them. In our bands, there seem to be signs that commodity-fetishism is on the wane. It does not seem quite so important to *own* records and large stereos, but instead to know, have listened to and *experienced* various kinds of music.

Demands are also conveyed to young people by the leisure sphere. Organised leisure has firm rules and boundaries, set both by state or local authority recreational staff and by voluntary adult workers or older youth, for how such leisure activities should be conducted. Sports, music instruction, and organisation activities also have fostering and disciplining functions – from learning how to be on time to acquiring knowledge and competence related to particular aims and areas of use. Also included here is a type of performance demand that harmonises with the demands placed by school.

A career within the leisure/recreational professions (the media, culture, sports, politics, religion etc.), of course places the same sorts of demands on the individual as any other career. However, in the sphere of voluntary, leisure activities, it is another matter: these have a polar, complementary relation to work (school) and the family's reproductive necessities (sleep, household work). In many ways, to our young bands, leisure time contains life's real meaning and purpose, while school and work are necessary means for survival.[16] In this respect, there are relatively great similarities among the three bands' environments.

Having said that, a few differences can be detected. For example, the relationship between leisure and school is somewhat different in the three groups. Generally, school tends to buttress organised and scheduled leisure activities but ignores or opposes others that contain an implicit – or open – critique of school's coercion. In Chans' environment, where organised leisure occupies a greater space, there are many connections between school and that sort of leisure activity (the educational association, concerts, dances, films, etc.). In Lam Gam and OH, school has less influence over, and is less involved with, their free time.

Relations between the family and leisure are less polarised since young children and adults especially spend a great deal of their leisure time within the confines of the family. But during the teenage years more and more leisure time is spent away from the family environs. Teenagers enter a youth culture field, a sort of generational community that crosses local boundaries. This youth culture milieu, with its commercially distributed media products

Gösta: Now I've said that I *don't* want to be one of those who work flat out to . . . yeah, get to the top of whatever. What I want to do is have lots of friends, get to know masses of friends.

Ove: What do you think of working at Volvo?
Sigge: . . . it's OK, but it's nothing compared to music. It's more fun to be on tour with the band than working at Volvo. That's what I want, to play music and be in a band.

and other goods, with its lifestyles and subcultures, and shared subjects for conversation and contemplation, tends to be more open than either family or school. To a degree, it spans social class boundaries and definitely, gender, ethnic, geographical and national borders. Via the mass media, our three groups – despite all their differences – have been influenced and fascinated by in principle similar youth cultural styles and music (punk and, later, hard rock). Naturally, this has not meant the eradication of class differences or local traditions; youth culture discourses were assimilated in each band culture and acquired different tonalities. However, the fact remains that leisure and the media contain more opportunities for cross-cultural forms and communication, than do the family and school. Because they are a generationally defined public sphere, youth cultures open out to society but close ranks to parents and teachers. In addition, through the search for style and identity, new types of differentiations and boundary demarcations among youth are created – for example, between 'techno (synth) freaks' and heavy metal fans. These subcultures not only express class, gender or geographical differences, but also, at least in part, transgress them with other types of differentiation. This may be seen as a late modern phenomenon, since it means that creating style and choosing identity, more than ever involves individual and reflexive choice rather than an automatic incorporation in a given social role.

Leisure also has other important aspects – for instance, it is a kind of preparation for the future (here exemplified by Chans members' business activities and the Ark's 'workshop culture'). Experimenting with one's own identity, socialising in one's peer group and the more or less developed games with the opposite sex help to lay the foundations of a social and communicative competence which can have a critical influence on your future working life as well as the capacity to form a family of your own.

SPACES FOR IDENTITY WORK

A common feature of our three groups is that they are teenagers in a world largely structured by family, school, work, leisure organisations, the media and the peer group.

Ove: Why don't you like synth music?
Jonna: It's music for the wimps that live in Hovås [upper class area] . . . it's for those spoiled brats that live in ten-room houses with swimming-pools and with pappys that buy them cars when they're five.

Conny: . . . You could say that on the surface I balanced between the half-rich over there [the terrace house district he lives in] and the poverty here at the Ark . . . Inside I know this is where I want to be . . . I like it here. I'd rather be dressed in a pair of old, torn jeans and a horrible red T-shirt like this, and sit down here and listen to Clash and Sex Pistols smoking a fag, than go around in a nice jacket listening to some fucking synth pop on a hundred quid Walkman. I'm not happy with that.

Bamse: Before, I was in church on Thursday and out raving on Friday and Saturday. Then, next Thursday . . . the church youth group again. Then next Friday and Saturday . . . But nobody said to me: 'Now you've got to stop going out, right? Otherwise you can't be in the church.' They only said: 'Have you been out again?' Well, like yes. Then I began to be a bit ashamed, like you can't think for yourself. Like it doesn't go together, doesn't work.

Their worlds are pervaded by the same social, ethnic and gender hierarchies that inscribe the whole of Swedish society, but they have different positions in these hierarchies. Their relations to the various spheres and agents of socialisation also vary. They handle demands from these spheres and agents in different ways, depending on preconditions, and they have different prerequisites for utilising the resources offered by these spheres as fields of action. In these positions, in and between the different spheres, young people create their own, unique personal identities in which elements of socio-economic, ethnic, gender and geographical collective identities are included together with subcultural elements, combined through identity processes in which personal experiences and choices participate in a complex way.

There is an overall dynamic in that these spheres cooperate according to established patterns. Primary socialisation in the family has a reproductive and intimate character that stands in a certain opposition to the progression-oriented, disciplining and system-influenced processes in school and working life. During one's youth, leisure time acquires an increasingly clear and important function as a third pole, separated from the other two. Feelings, created but repressed in the other spheres, are acted out in leisure time in the peer group, in the use of media and entertainment, where things necessary for identity work but not accepted at school or in the family are tested. At the same time, the family and school have to deal with problems linked to the entertainment and leisure spheres such as uncertainty about norms, consumerism, drug abuse, etc.

Along with the family/school polarity, an important tension then arises between the media and school, a mutual distrust which, among other things, stems from conflicts between the state and market systems. However, also discernible in this pattern is an underlying tension between both systems and life world. Identity work occurs in the interchange between these poles, in the social and psychic space created by the different spheres.

SUBJECTIVE DRIVING FORCES

KURRE

Ulf: What is culture?
Kurre: To me? To be who I am.
Ulf: What do you mean by that?
Kurre: I don't care much about other people's culture. I've got my own culture [pause]. I think it's culture to smoke. It's culture to take snuff. It's culture to play music. Most of what you do is a bit of culture. That's what I think. I have problems with that stuff, like old things, like traditions. Old culture and that. [. . .] It's like bourgeois people are very big on old culture. Fine pictures and books and all that. It's like – not everybody can afford to keep up with that culture. So then you create your own culture. That's what we do. And that's what I do too.

The speaker here is Kurre, just turned 18, and OH's prime mover. One is struck by the self-awareness he expresses, and his lack of respect. He has little regard for tradition, our cultural inheritance, which he perceives from a defensive position as elitist. Against tradition he posits another, ethnological and relativistic concept of culture which permits more subjectivity. He has his own culture which is just as valuable as anyone else's. From a broader perspective, one could say that Kurre responds to late modern culture erosion by falling back on his own subjectivity, supported by an understanding of society in terms of class, which we know has been mediated by his family.

In general, Kurre appears very sure of himself. He can imagine being 'some sort of leader of something special', 'taking responsibility', 'changing things', 'communicating to others'. How all of this is to be implemented, he does not yet know, but that is of less importance: 'The day I figure that out is the day I'll really start to work'. In practice, he has already started to question normality, which is what it is about. Many of his hopes are linked to the band: 'It is a weapon.' And indeed, as time goes on OH becomes largely Kurre's project.

As an interviewee, Kurre gives a sympathetic impression

if one is not alienated by his (in due course modified) rebel image (see p. 48). He finds it easy to express himself, seems interested in other people, thinks for himself and has aspirations. He is by no means unaware of his charm, and views it as a resource: 'It is bloody easy for me to get into contact with other people – I know just about every type.' One side of Kurre's social competence is oriented towards his ambition to become something special. If he chooses to, he can manipulate others to satisfy his own needs – setting his stamp on OH is an example. Another side of Kurre is his sensitivity to and empathy with other people, expressed in a fear of hurting others and an inability to exercise physical violence. But to start with, one perceives Kurre as quite simply a person with a strong ego, who is sure of his parents' love ('they like me a helluva lot'), who thinks it is 'one of the easiest things in the world' to make friends, who respects everyone's right to be heard and engages himself in what is happening in the world and who cope with the risk of appearing somewhat odd. Not even unsatisfactory school results seem to have made inroads on Kurre's self-confidence.

When Ulf gets to know Kurre, he is up to the hilt in the role of young rebel. His ideal is a sort of projection of the present into the future, a prolonged adolescence equipped with some of the advantages of adult life – especially economic independence. Like so many young people, he wants to avoid the petit-bourgeois 'Svensson' life, which he perceives as a kind of petrifaction, and instead 'take up the struggle against the normal'. To Kurre, his parents' way of life symbolises a threat to his identity, separation from his mates and social isolation in a 'cell' (a couple). He seems to have a great need for autobiographical continuity. Getting away from everything, for better or worse, is tempting, but rejected as a kind of 'suicide'. Without mates, he would not survive: his mates, and especially those in OH, are more important than heterosexual relations, which always represent a potential threat: 'I'm scared of tying myself down, I'm shit scared of that [...] It's ...it like takes away some of your ... what you ... like your own ideas, right?' The opposite sex – from your mother to girls your own age – involves a risk of restricting your subjectivity, your ego development. These views are difficult to dismiss as rationalisations; there is no evidence that

Kurre: It's bloody hard to imagine myself hurting anybody [inaudible], like. Yeah, OK, if I go and get drunk – then I might not know what I'm doing and that. But I always get into a state, maybe not of anxiety, but I regret, you know those kinds of feelings the day after, like 'what the shit did I do that for?'
Kurre: I don't think I go on and on, nobody has ever said anything. There's just a lot of people who've said: 'What in the hell do you have that on for and why the hell ... and that?' It's my way of communicating, not to say anything about it, just ... dress different or behave a bit different.
Kurre: I've noticed with my mum and dad ... they've ... my mum's got a friend, dad has a mate at work and that. Then there's a few neighbours and relatives and that. But he's got no contact with any of his old pals at all. That frightens the shit out of me. That you can be separated. For that's the ... in the 18 years I've been alive, that's like been the basis in my life ... I'd never have survived without mates.

Kurre: But my great dream's to take off somewhere. Not to give a shit, just pack my bag and go. With a thousand in my pocket and see what happens. I often say to my mum, 'Tomorrow I'm going, I can't cope any more' [pause]. It's maybe a kind of suicide, right? [. . .] For them it is, they stay around, and maybe they miss you, right? But I don't want to do that really because I think I have it so good sometimes. Sometimes I think it's shit. *Kurre*: My mum says it's bloody egotistical to think of yourself all the time, but . . . I have to have my own, I've got to get my own thing across in some way. Like, now it's confirmation, you know, when you're confirmed you feel, like you've got to get a haircut, right? What the shit's that good for? Whether I go with a tie and shirt, expensive clothes, nice gear, right, or a junky outfit, I'm still the same person.

Kurre would have any problem finding a girlfriend if he wanted to.

However, there is also the risk of being rejected by society and losing control over your life if you depart too far from the norm: 'I could very well just sit down there on the square and hit the bottle [. . .] But I think it's better to do something proper.' Kurre refuses to be a victim; separation from society is no more desirable than separation from mates.

From this conflict issues a double strategy which Kurre shares with most of the members of OH. As we have seen, the strategy is to get an ordinary job but to put your true identity into your free time and especially into music; in other words, to choose to deviate but still live *in* society, possibly even to live *on* one's deviation – as an artist. With rock music, Kurre tries to build a bridge to the future, which means that he can keep his ego together. In the present, horizontally, his rebel role seems to fulfill the same function, but in addition, it encompasses several subordinate functions:

1) to *mark off* your own subjectivity from one's parents, particularly from your mother – as part of the liberation process,

2) to *be seen* generally, to be Someone,

3) to *provoke* discussion of what is important in life ('communicate to others') and

4) to *test* how much you can deviate and still be accepted by your mates.

Against the background of his position in the group, it is logical that the key values of the OH culture – authenticity, intimacy and control (see pp. 39 ff) – are crucial to Kurre. His 'rebellious' clothes style especially asserts the authentic. The style comes from 'below', from the poor and oppressed; the song lyrics' victims and the music's rawness correspond to political sympathies and the connotations of the clothes. Shit, rags and rock have something in common. On the other hand, something lurks under the façade. The surface is actually for show; what counts is what is inside – the feelings. Here the tension between form and content turns into a 'modern' paradox: if this is what Kurre's appearance wants to say, the message seems to negate itself. But rejection of superficiality recurs in Kurre's heterosexual relations and in his taste in music. He contrasts 'genuine' groups like Clash, Jam and Alarm with synth music, which is also associated with frightening technological advancements – robots only outwardly resemble humans. If the demand for authenticity is primarily communicated via a 'late modern' form – as style – its content has a humanistic, anti-modern slant.

This picture of Kurre is a reconstruction, based on early impressions and, above all, on the first interview with him. The depiction focuses on his self-awareness and rebel identity without actually questioning them. Consistency and homologies appear more clearly than tensions and contradictions between individual elements.[1] To a degree, this is probably a consequence of mutual projections. To Kurre, Ulf seemed to represent a sort of departure from the gap between the adult and youth world; he comprehended Ulf's response to his rebel role as positive and took it seriously. To Ulf, Kurre was, among other things, a possible heir to 1968, albeit in the conditions of a different time, and this doubtless contributed to certain difficulties in differentiating complications. In retrospect, with access to at least a provisional blueprint, it is much easier to see the cracks in the surface.

Kurre is hardly as secure in his rebel role as he seems. It is rather more defensive than offensive, and may be interpreted as an attempt to turn the experience of being an outsider into something chosen and exclusive. To see this one only needs to bring into relief what lies between the lines, the undercurrents in his speech. Behind the fear of being isolated as an adult lurks a powerful need for approval. Kurre knows he is odd: 'If I didn't play, I might be worried about what I think and believe 'cause it's so different from what other people think and believe.' The celebration of intimacy, the 'G' in OH, can be seen against the same background of awareness of how vulnerable the ego is when it is alone, isolated. Considering Kurre's lack of technical skill, the collective has to become a prerequisite for creating music. And the group offers the self protection against outside criticism: the ego is collectivised – One Hand Beats Five Fingers.

As long as Kurre is in school, social ostracism is a greater threat than he wants to admit. Antithetical to his great dreams of being a leader etc. are the fates of the many

Kurre: But . . . as it is now, there's too bloody many computers and that. I mean, I'd refuse to learn a computer [. . .] They're going to do in humanity, I think. And then, their music, like I think electronic music, synth pop and computers go together. Just because of that I think it's bloody scary.
Kurre: No, but you act like a mate. You're just like any old pal. For one thing, you're much more experienced. We . . . we respect you in a different way from a pal maybe. One could say you're in between a pal and a parent. And there's hardly anybody we know like that in between, there's only you that I know who's like that.

Kurre: You get a bloody sharp tongue, right, if somebody comes and says 'Christ, you guys are rubbish,' boy you learn to give it back. I mean, you know that you've done something that's yours [. . .] Then we're like solid together – to fend it off, like. Psychologically, you get mentally stronger when you're a 'G' like us.

Kurre: I think there'll be a nuclear war.
Ulf: You think so?
Kurre: Yeah, 100 per cent.

Kurre: For instance, I haven't got into any one subculture, I want to be more or less in all subcultures. I have wide music interests, but with others, it's trendiness, first this and then that. [From a school essay.]

victims described in the song texts. The future also inspires feelings of impotence; not only mechanisation (computerisation) but, even more, the threat of nuclear war elicits fear. However, Kurre is not pacified: dreams of freedom can be kept alive in music, you can try to engender a living utopia in the communality of the band, and you can support church charities. But the struggle is unequal.

In fact, Kurre is at once too smooth and too vulnerable to be a 'real' rebel. If he were, he might not guard himself against the failure of his dreams by getting himself an ordinary education. However, Kurre does not put all his eggs into one basket – evidence of this abounds. In 1984 he admired the punks' rashness, but did not join up with any manifested subculture. His relation to music is not absolute but utilitarian: like so many of his contemporaries, he accepts the idea that different kinds of music suit different occasions in varying degrees. His tolerance of different opinions, his fear of hurting others and losing control over his aggressive impulses are other characteristics not primarily associated with rebels. It is more a question of ambivalence. Kurre has contradictory needs: to gain approval versus influencing others, total engagement in the here and now versus instrumental visions of the future, authenticity versus style, security versus development, deviation versus normality.

What went on during the period Ulf was documenting the band confirms the transitional nature of Kurre's rebel identity. Put bluntly, he was gradually inclining towards normality; the rebel role was being questioned and toned down. It was proving largely dysfunctional in conjunction with the demands issuing from both his entry into working life and OH's success in the field of rock music. The double strategy mentioned above was assuming a stronger, goal-oriented import, and the dynamic and instrumental were gaining the upper hand. At his job, Kurre proved himself able to 'get on' with people as easily as he did in other situations and was quickly rewarded with independent responsibilities. In OH, he methodically established his musical ideas, became the group's 'slave-driver', was the prime mover in the expulsion of Bamse, and steered the music towards discipline and good sound – albeit at the expense of less immediate experiences of joy, more doubts and pangs of conscience.

Thus far, an attempt has been made to sketch two pictures of Kurre which have different emphases and which together indicate a fundamental ambivalence in his personality. Neither of these pictures is historical and so both are drastically curtailed. What follows is an attempt to interpret the driving forces behind Kurre's rock music and how his subjectivity is constituted. Methodologically, this involves a reconstruction, not so much of Kurre's real upbringing as of his *experience* of it. The reconstruction entails approaching a psychoanalytic viewpoint in which memories comprise 'screen memories' or projections, which acquire their value through the *significance* the subject ascribes to them. In the predominantly verbal actions which represent adolescent Kurre in our material, three aspects co-exist: the contemporary ('now'), transference and the infantile-biographical. At best, one will find patterns or lines of experience that are possible to relate to established general theories.

Kurre was born in 1966, the first child of the family. His parents were then 20 and 19 years old. His father is an immigrant ship's cook, with a fairly messy family background (alcoholism, abuse, divorce). His mother comes from a stable, Social Democratic working-class family demanding respectability. To Kurre, his maternal grandparents seem 'old fashioned', a judgement that seems also appropriate to his paternal grandmother, who is said to have thrown Kurre's father out of the house because of his hairstyle. Kurre has related that his mother has forbidden him to visit this grandmother with his hair long.

According to his mother, as a child Kurre was totally uninterested in cars (he later showed the same indifference to mopeds and real cars, and only got a driver's licence at the age of 20 after succumbing to pressure from his father). However, when he was small he liked to build things and do carpentry, activities which he now sees as illustrations of his desire to 'do it himself'. His mother made her children a priority – Kurre has two younger brothers – but also worked part-time as a cleaner and shop assistant. Kurre's father found a job as a cook in the army and gradually became head of the catering staff. However, on a couple of occasions he was absent from home: he went through his first crisis (which recurred several times), when Kurre was four, and did his one year-military service when Kurre

Kurre: ... if you can go ahead with other people ... not sitting on you but asking you to do this and that and you do it, you can go ahead with that, yeah at least for a while – I'm not saying always – then you can damn well be president. [...] Then you can be – you can get somewhere, for then people like you, they trust you and will let you do a lot of things.

Kurre's mother: We're all together, you might say, every evening. We meet every single birthday and ... sometimes in between [...] And it's true that if perhaps I have been and still am very positive to the family, to togetherness and all that, perhaps [my husband] has been a bit different, he maybe doesn't much like large gatherings ...

Kurre: I think you should be a youth for as long as you can. You should get into it, live it out. My dad has always said so too. He's always regretted ... that he, well, got kids so early.

began school. (This information comes from the mother; Kurre maintains he knows nothing about it.)

Throughout Kurre's childhood the family had frequent contact with his mother's family. Family outings and contacts replaced high cultural ambitions in a way characteristic of the working-class. According to his mother, Kurre's father was never keen on these family gatherings and preferred to withdraw. However, to Kurre it was his father, not his mother, who most often 'took the kids out'.

Ulf: If you didn't play music, what would you do?
Kurre: I'd travel, travel, travel everywhere. Not have a place to live exactly. Yeah, OK I'd come home too, but first of all I'd travel and support myself with odd jobs here and there.

Kurre: He works as a cook for the army. And he often has problems with his job. He began as a drudge and worked himself up. And then he starts working under the chef and is like the foreman, and so they all come with questions like 'Where's this go?' and 'Where should I put this?' and he thinks it's a real drag as he has to do his job too, yeah? And so often when he comes home, he doesn't say much, like he hasn't much more to say. He's simply done in.

The total picture of Kurre's childhood indicates that his mother functioned as a strong cohesive force while his father periodically at least seemed to have felt fettered by the family. Presumably he experienced his early marriage as an escape from one dependency to another. In any case, this is how Kurre understands his father and one may speculate about the extent to which Kurre feels unconscious guilt for shackling his father further by his arrival into the world when his father was so young. A little less speculatively, one would suspect that his father's fate plays a part in Kurre's ambivalent relation to girls. His father has had a dream of 'crossing the border', of living a freer life, travelling, being an artist, and this dream has been 'communicated [to Kurre . . .] the whole time, one way or another'. Kurre's own greatest dreams correlate well with those ascribed to his father.

Kurre's relations with his mother bear the imprint of the self-evident: 'She's just there.' She is experienced as dominant in the family, she is the one Kurre feels he resembles most and to whom he is closest. In relation to his father, Kurre is much more analytical and divided. Partly, his father seems alien: 'sometimes I think I know him, sometimes I think I don't.' Their relationship has not been improved by the fact that the father dislikes his job and his working hours have prevented them from seeing each other in the mornings. Partly, Kurre admires his father for not having given up, and partly he feels sorry for his father for what he has gone through (and willingly talks about).

Once when OH was discussing the Prince film *Purple Rain*, Kurre perceived his own father in the main character, the Kid's failed father, and tried to explain his fate with something that is either a projection or a cliché: 'He must have had a hell of a childhood.' At the same time, he asserted that the son was 'incredibly like his father' at the film's turning-point, the father's suicide attempt: 'When they die, you pull yourself together and like ... You never get a chance to show who the hell you are. They never know what the fuck you're about.' To 'show the old man' as the Kid does in the film, seems important to Kurre. One senses traces of aggression and bitterness under his words; but this is only one aspect of how Kurre is affected by his relation to his father. If this aspect emphasises separation, Kurre's need to be considered an independent person, another aspect draws father and son together: the inheritance syndrome – transference of the father's ambitions to his son. Kurre also reads this aspect into the film's father–son relationship: 'Just like a company. He takes it over and runs it.' And, just as in the film, it is in music that the father and son can meet and coalesce: '*He and I* [emphasis added] have succeeded with something'. Here, as on many other occasions, Kurre is keen to acknowledge his father's support and encouragement. At the same time, Kurre seems to want to imply that in practice he tries to live his father's life for him, to realise his father's failed dreams and set him up, or as Kurre himself says, 'brush him up' – a heavy responsibility for a teenager.

Kurre has led Ulf to believe that, to a significant extent, his father has made use of other family members for emotional compensation. He has tended to try to understand and empathise with the cause of his father's weakness, probably at the expense of his own need to be recognised. One suspects that this lies at the root of certain elements of Kurre's personality – his empathy, diplomatic talents and fear of aggression. But as has been indicated, there is also a basically tacit accusation of not having been seen, against which his affability may be interpreted as reaction-formation.

The contradictory father gestalt, here cloven into a 'failed Svensson' and an irresponsible 'adventurer', acquires its full significance first in relation to Kurre's secondary socialisation, particularly in school.[3] Kurre's experience of beginning school is very negative; in retrospect, he now thinks he was simply not mature enough. In his third year, at his mother's urging, the family moved to the Village. Changing schools was also difficult – a fact confirmed by his mother. In the intermediate school (years 4–6) Kurre had trouble keeping up, felt singled out as the dunce ('Mostly it

Kurre: When I started in the first class, I wasn't ... I was just not mature for school. I was just worthless, I didn't understand a thing. I ... I guess you'd say, my parents made a mistake, they should of made me repeat the class. [inaudible] Then I moved out here, and that was hard too. New mates and ...

Kurre: And then school ... well, it's a bit of an elimination process, I think. It's not like everybody should learn, but the ones that have trouble learning ... the teachers don't spend much time with them and their mates think they're like shit,

'don't know nothing' [...]
You have to be mentally strong
to handle that.

Kurre: Yeah, I didn't have a lot
of mates. I had a few, but when
you go to school you feel so
unsure, you never said hello to
anybody [...] The kid I was
always with when I was
younger, he was like the
world's bullied kid [...] They
bullied me too like hell when I
went to school [...] that's
why I went around with him so
much.

Kurre: I got a lot more influence
with people, I like became
Kurre, right? Before I was like
the one who was always around
[...] What happened was that
I got to know a lot of girls,
specially at school, and then the
guys want to know you, right?
[...] I often sat with girls and
talked and had a good time
[...] It was like I just turned
my back, you know, like I
dared do that.

was only me who didn't know'), and he sometimes cried
during lessons. His parents in part reacted in different ways.
His mother seems to have given him unconditional support;
she is still critical of the school's exclusion, which Kurre has
extended to a criticism of organised sports – to all situations
with mandatory competition. But Kurre could talk over all
his problems with his mother. In the way of most fathers,
Kurre's seems to have been more critical of his son's performance (which his mother explains by pointing to difficulties
adjusting to demands different from those placed by schools
in his father's homeland.)

Kurre himself thinks that both parents demand good
behaviour, but while his mother's dreams are of making
him into 'an honest person who can live a normal family
life', his father's are 'different' and more performance-
oriented. However, Kurre did not manage to live up to his
father's demands in school; on the contrary, it looked as if
the family had acquired another 'loser'. Neither could
Kurre find compensation with friends. Even though he had
a best mate, both he and his mate were so deviant that they
were bullied. Upon entering upper school (classes 7–9),
Kurre seems to have been considered a pathetic wimp, who
could not hit back, who was not interested in mopeds and
did not even get pocket money (since he delivered newspapers). To all appearances, circumstances were directing
him in the footsteps of his 'failed' father.

But in the eighth class came the turning point, about
which Kurre has already been quoted. His mother says he
matured fast. Kurre himself relates that he 'began to think'
and 'speak for himself'. He discovered it was easy to get
into contact with girls, which gave him a certain status
among the boys. He found the courage to act out his deviation and began to shape it into a style, the 'rebel image'.
He became more detached about school demands; he
would deliberately arrive late, but his marks improved. An
interest in the world at large found political expression,
affiliated with his 'red' maternal grandparents as well as
with his rebel role. He helped to start a Social Democratic
Youth group at school and became a sort of Robin Hood
to younger students who were being bullied. Protected by
his rebel identity, he set about dealing with his parents. His
liberation focused above all on his mother, the parent who
has taken most responsibility for his upbringing and most

single-handedly represents normality. It is illuminating that when on one occasion she refused to acknowledge him, he did not react negatively, but rather considered the episode as an affirmation of his independence.

From the viewpoint of developmental psychology, Kurre has now entered adolescence. Other libidinal objects replace his parents – peers and idols chosen from the media. Kurre's rebel style is punk-influenced, both as regards form (collage) and content, but it is not typical. The same is true of his choice of rock models: he does not stop with the punks but follows his own lights. When other boys in his class play Kiss and Sweet in school, Kurre counters with Gyllene Tider's *Billy*, a teeny-bop group song, because the lyrics deal with a fate that he can identify with. He discovers Clash, reads about Joe Strummer and sees in him someone else who advanced despite fairly ghastly circumstances. The same pattern appears in Kurre's identification with Allan Vega: the intended victim's ability to keep his head, 'brush himself up' and go on.

However, Kurre doesn't just dream; he also tries to bring the world around him into line with his dreams. The decisive step is taken when he begins to play the guitar – encouraged by his father. Three stages are now melded together. Fundamental is the contradictory father relationship: it is as if only Kurre knows who his father really is and he has taken upon himself to show it; but also as if only by succeeding with this can he show who he himself is and free himself from the shadow figure riding him. The conquest of love and self-realisation are here linked together with performance into a syndrome that one could call the Amadeus complex – referring to the constellation of problems presented in Milos Forman's film. The second stage concerns idols and Kurre's own music-making. In my opinion Kurre's ego ideal leans on the image of his 'border-crossing father', but this introjection merges with elements from certain rock stars. From this point onwards, Kurre consciously searches for recognition:

> *Kurre*: The old man's always wanted to be something, right. He is something, definitely, but he thinks he's nothing. He thinks you have to be like a giant to be something. And I do too. For better or worse. But that's why I mean if I become something, then I could like have him at my side. He's my dad, it's thanks to him that I . . . well . . . almost. He needs it. He needs to have . . . I mean, well like if he hasn't made it, well

Kurre: My mum is shit scared of . . . Once out at Väla [a supermarket], I went 20 meters ahead of my mother. She saw me but I didn't see her. She wouldn't know me 'cause I looked such a mess – looked like hell in her eyes, and that's . . . not quite the normal.

Kurre: [*Billy's*] about a guy that's [. . .] a junkie and that. Wrote a letter [inaudible] to his house . . . a mess. [Gyllene Tider] were good then.
Kurre: Allan Vega's a really cool type that once . . . someone threw a bottle at him, he was on stage, right? He took the bottle and – it missed him, right – anyway, he took the bottle and banged himself in the head, pang . . . [inaudible] Then he just stood and shouted, 'Do it again, try to hit me!' Like that . . . even if the music's not good, that's a bloody cool person, his personality I mean.

he'd like to see one of his kids do it [. . .] Now I think that's
a must, I'm going to do it. I think it's cool, I want to do it. I
want to be something, yeah? Because, well it's almost not even
for my own sake really.
Ulf: But?
Kurre: But for his and everyone else's who . . .
Ulf: Are put down?
Kurre: Yeah. So it's both/and like. The ones that have thrown
shit at me, I don't want to throw shit back, I'll just brush it off
and . . .
Ulf: Don't you want a little revenge?
Kurre: No, not revenge [. . .] It's a cruel word, but I want
[. . .] to do like . . . shake it off, and then they'll look at me
and they won't shit on me again [. . .] same as my old man
[inaudible], yeah I want to brush him off too . . .

Theoretically, Kurre's plans may be understood in more
than one way. The coming to terms with one's parents,
mandatory in adolescence, is often a painful experience,
plunging the young person into loneliness and depression.
An impoverishment of the ego occurs with consequent feelings of emptiness, unreality and death. What Kurre does is
to defend himself against the danger that all energy is
directed towards the self, which would result in a
paralysing narcissism. Instead, he manages to handle the
typical narcissistic re-evaluation of the self productively.
His omnipotent self-glorification is by no means unique;
rather it is typical of adolescents finding themselves in the
midst of a transformation of their inner world. The ego is
weak and threatened, but it seeks a foothold by cathecting
objects in the external world and having great ambitions to
transform and give life.

One interpretation might be based on this convulsive
process of liberation from parents – the motive force here
being a sort of bereavement. During adolescence, infantile
conflicts are reactivated, including sadistic impulses
directed towards the parental object. In small children, such
impulses leave guilt feelings and the desire for reparation of
the imagined or unconsciously damaged object. This desire
constitutes the foundation for subsequent creative activity;
reparation is in essence symbolic, and symbol-formation is
creative. In the future, situations requiring that something
be given up will produce symbolisation: in this sense,
creativity can be equated with bereavement. Attempts at
reparation strengthen the subject's ability to survive object
loss without being overwhelmed by aggression, and to
accept the real object as it is. If reparation does not remain

only in the imagination, the lost object is given an objective existence as 'text' (the work of art) and thereby the possibility of surviving outside the ego.[4]

From a psychoanalytical perspective, adolescent liberation from the parents primarily concerns coming to terms with the child's internal psychic parent-representatives. Parental bonding can remain and be expressed in transference long after the parents have disappeared. Total liberation may almost be considered utopian. Kurre's reduction of the parent figures to 'Svenssons' does not exclude deeper enduring bonds, as I have tried to show in the case of the 'border-crossing father'. (We shall return to the mother figure later on.) This hypothesis may help to explain Kurre's turning to rock music as reparation. In this case it is reasonable to focus on his relation to his father mainly because Kurre himself talks about 'rehabilitating' him. One could imagine, as has already been implied, that the increased pressure of the drives in early adolescence activated a complex of guilt feelings and suppressed the aggression in their relationship. When his father begins gradually to appear in a more realistic 'Svensson' guise, this is unconsciously associated with aggressive impulses and Kurre's guilt increases; living his father's life for him becomes his way of trying to get rid of his guilt. Kurre's rock music project is to revive his destroyed father object, immortalise it in music and in this way liberate himself from it.

Another interpretation has to do with Kurre's own notions of what creative activities are for. To him, creating something involves working with something that seems dead, worthless, seeing it as a sort of challenge, finding potential life in it – 'brushing it up', putting one's stamp on it, giving it life and through this, living on in it in the eyes of others. In short, to create something expressly involves conquering one's own mortality.

Given Kurre's adolescent processes, his 'do-it-yourself' syndrome becomes more comprehensible: controlling the entire creative process means that one ensures that the product becomes an image of oneself. Other bits of Kurre's puzzle fall into place as well. He claims that he, like many others, is afraid of dying. But dying has a special meaning for him: to be unable to develop into what he could be (or actually is). Rock's bridging function between youth and adulthood corresponds to a survival strategy. To be a

Kurre: But, to take care of something that's *dead*, I think that's cool [exemplified by an old tape recorder in the Barn]. I scrounge in skips for stuff that's basically dead. When we came here, it was basically dead, and I thought, 'Wow! Here we can do what we want.' You can just create something out of something that's dead for others.

Kurre: What means most to me is that I can move about free and still play something safe and have this feeling the whole time that I'm living, I'm doing it. It's me doing it, dammit – look at me now, mum and dad and mates and – no, but like various people who've thrown shit at you 'cause you've played music.

Kurre: I'm not afraid of growing up any more but I want to be grown up in the right way [. . .] I'm scared to, I'm always scared of dying. Now.

Kurre: I got a shock, I was completely ... [...] I don't ever want to say to mum and dad that shit 'cause then I know they'd say 'Why aren't you more serious in school, blah blah blah'. [...] And I'll never forget when I got that envelope where it said: 'You have been placed there,' like. I thought I was in ...

'Svensson' is to many teenagers tantamount to being No One, that is, dead – the end of childish dreams of greatness, infinite possibilities, unthwarted mobility. It is, like literal death, a narcissistic violation.[5] The majority of the threats thematised in OH's lyrics – war, environmental destruction, drugs, and so on – may be seen in the same terms – as narcissistic violation. And on the other side of the coin, life and authenticity are linked to the narcissistic need to be seen. The person who keeps his eye glued to the surface of things misjudges life, gets no 'chance' to 'be himself', accepts death. Life presumes that the Other sees you, it is inter-subjective. In this way, everyday communication to Kurre also contains a creative aspect. In his own eyes, his ability to 'take on people', to lead and direct, is a way of drawing out (or 'brushing up') the intact core of humanity which he believes exists in everyone, even in racists. He can then be confirmed by the other, see his mirror image in the other and erase the differences which were initially present. This seems to be about

> a projective selection in perception of the objects that promise narcissistic reinforcement so that it may be presumed that these objects are 'always already' like oneself; not an 'incorporation' of the outside, but rather *a tendency towards an 'extension' of the self.*[6]

Keeping the question of narcissism in mind, let us return to Kurre's development. When he was 16 and applying to go to gymnasium, he suffered an unexpected blow. He did not get into the food technology course and thus could not be a cook like his father and eventually Someone in that profession. This shock brought back memories of previous school failures and provoked a temporary relapse into infantile behaviour. But this new narcissistic violation did not stymie Kurre; rather, it contributed to an even closer association with the 'border-crossing father' inside him and to self-realisation outside of school.

A year and a half later OH was formed. As in all groups united around an external project, OH also had inbuilt conflicts between the project itself – demands for results, and the collective being, the absorption into a security without demands – and between progression and regression needs.[7] It has already been mentioned how emphasis was shifted during the documentation of this book so that progression demands increased successively – largely because of Kurre. However, and in this perhaps lies the utopian element in OH, the desired success was still seen in terms of 'G', of solidarity and communality, of the original peer group: the goal should be attained through unity. It cannot be claimed that OH has been 100 per cent successful, but by the spring of 1987, the original gang was still intact, only increased by one member (on keyboards).

Without anticipating the discussion of youth gangs and rock music later in the book, a particular aspect of the gang will now be examined. Other researchers have indicated a transference mechanism[8] in referring to the gang as a 'social womb.'[9] Extending the metaphor, one can see 'maternal' and 'paternal', regression and progression demands continually clashing in young music groups. This is particularly true of OH since its members all have fathers who are experienced as alien in some way or another. And the results are similar: not only does Kurre play to 'show the old man' – but the 'Amadeus complex' applies generally in the group.[10] It is also worthwhile viewing the Bamse conflict in the light of transference: his irrationality (with clear origins in oedipal conflicts) activated father conflicts in the others and the transference in turn produced counter-transference – withdrawal etc. – which Bamse experienced as attempts to ostracise him.

The narcissistic elements in Kurre are bound up with the group in an equivocal way. The group not only satisfies his dynamic needs – his attempts at working out narcissistic infringements through learning to control the world at large, accept different challenges, perform.[11] Another of Kurre's mirroring needs belongs in the Barn's attic. There, in the heart of the idealised 'G' you can confirm what you *are*, there it is not about *becoming*. There you can 'be yourself', withdraw from the demands of the world and be absorbed into the collective. Just like a good mother, the group gives protection and warmth without requiring the same in kind – or at least so it seems if, like Kurre, you have a relatively unchallenged position in its 'heart'. Similar notions are linked to the attic as a gathering-point. According to Freudian psychoanalysis, a house or a room represents something feminine in the unconscious. Kurre's maternal transference to the Barn is very striking: he not only personifies it, but also praises it in terms recalling

Kurre: To do something that, that you do with your . . . yeah, what should I say, your absolutely best mates, that you can live on, what a dream! And you know, we're not, like we don't play the buddies game – we're brothers.

Kurre: Stuff like that's a bit disturbing, 'cause you think, 'What the hell's up with him?' And you had to ask him all the time like 'How's it going, how is it with you?' You always had to take it easy so he wouldn't have a bloody fit and just disappear.

those he uses to refer to his mother (compare 'It's always there for us, always' with 'She's simply there'). Also here there is a narcissistic element, a yearning for fusion which recalls primary narcissism's 'oceanic' feelings. This contact with early symbiotic relationship patterns may be considered an important form of regression when these early levels of experience have not yet been coloured by incestual cathexes and therefore have a more immediate ability to reinforce the ego.

There are no implications of abnormality in the above references to narcissistic elements. Such elements are normal during one stage of adolescence, and most researchers into the human psyche tend to agree that a dose of narcissism is a necessary ingredient in all creative activity. It is, of course, tempting in Kurre's case to speculate on a new kind of adolescence; a phase, whose qualities would correspond to the altered conditions of primary socialisation in late modern society as described by some scholars such as Thomas Ziehe, who discusses tendencies towards a 'narcissistically-coloured structure of needs'. What we can say is that Kurre is in no way unique among our youth – with reference to narcissistic elements that can be linked with discussions of altered personality patterns. However, we cannot comment on how these elements in Kurre – apart from the possibility of tracing them to adolescent development as such – could be related to a new 'structure of needs'.

THREE THEMES

Altered personality characteristics may stem 'from below', which means that they are established during family social-isation. As a mass phenomenon among modern youth they can be linked to the changes in the family situation which we have already sketched. Parents have been marginalised as educators and made uncertain in their role as guides. The mother especially transfers this insecurity to the chil-dren and binds them to her. The introjected shadow of the great mother then falls over future relations and leads the child to search for similar fusing experiences and to avoid demands that would expose the unrealistic in this omnipotent ego ideal. The goal becomes to sustain and empower the wavering sense of self.

However, narcissistic features can also be established 'from above', as reactions to late modern conditions in general. In this sense, narcissism applies not only to youth; middle-aged people may also have difficulties 'loving them-selves', establishing deep and durable relationships – 'becoming adults' – even though it is primarily the young who are exposed to such problems. Today, Western youth comprise a distinct group, unproductive and dependent, pressured by the conflict between all the promises of the commodity-world and the lack of fixed orientation points, by unemployment, competition for education, nuclear arms and environmental destruction. Blocked life perspec-tives and cultural erosion throw young people back upon themselves and their peers, make identity problematic and create a crisis in the subjective base of society. The 'maternal' aspects of narcissistic features then entail taking the impact of the mother-symbiosis into the unconscious, not as disturbance but as a kind of diffuse, somewhat utopian recollections which the subject mobilises as a defence against the premature shouldering of 'Father's

Law', the de-mystification of the surrounding world, the colonisation of the life-world by the system etc.[1]

If it is true that changes have indeed occurred in personality patterns, these changes must have spread into what we have called the third stratum of the modernisation process and they should be detectable in certain attitude shifts traceable in our informants: Kurre's resistance to becoming an adult could be seen as an example. In the following we shall try to widen our spectrum. We shall leave deep psychic structures for the level of symptoms and concentrate on three themes: our youths' relationships to authority, work, and sexuality and living together.[2]

Ulf: Do you often think of yourself as a youth, or don't such boundaries mean very much?
Bobo: No, it doesn't matter much.
Ulf: Was that the case two years ago?
Bobo: [pause] No. Then, well you maybe looked down more on adults, or whatever [laughter]. Then you probably thought most of them [adults] were rotters, all of them – no, I don't know, but nearly all. But now, you're more, now you've got to accept it [inaudible]. Before, you didn't have to be with them, but now, well, workmates and that – you move around more and more with adults.

Kurre: I've said to the man that I work with now that there's nothing worse than some shit complaining when I work [...] If I do something and he says I do it wrong, well it'll damn well turn out right, yeah, like holding a spanner wrong [...] – oh boy, then I just blow up, like 'What the hell do you mean, what the hell are you getting at?' [...] Like he's experienced and he knows a lot more, right?

Micke: We said we'd try, right? Then people noticed it was great in the studio. Then, like it's him [the producer] and yeah, we've kept in contact with him and he wants us [...] OK, there's an authority, I look up to him 'cause he's so good.

AUTHORITY

Micke: Well, you don't exactly look up to any older person, do you?

Are we living in a time of the dissolution of authority as public debate on the subject, referring to among other things, violence in the schools and on the streets, would have us believe? Judging by the youth in our bands, the picture is more nuanced. The young Kurre challenges authority with his rebel image, which distances him not only from the adult world but also from his conformist peers. However, as we have seen, this does not mean he lacks authority figures: words of wisdom from his mother may find their way between his lips, his 'border-crossing' father pushes him, and Kurre himself seeks idols in the rock world. These more or less rebellious models are then played off against each other. It is about adolescent liberation, in which established social institutions (the family, school, the law, the military, etc.) are allied with the large parents of childhood, and subjectivity finds support in the culture industry's offerings of alternative points of identification. During this period Kurre had to claim the right to choose his own identity and erase previous school experiences. Entry into working life normalised conflicts with authority – for Kurre as for many other youth: what then became vital was not to become adult in the wrong way. Thus Kurre learns to develop his diplomatic talents for tactical reasons and to master the aggression which superiors still prompt in him, and this at the same time as OH finds support from an outside authority – a producer.

There are of course different nuances of the attitudes represented by our three bands and the individuals in them. However, their attitudes may be summarised in the contention that one must qualify oneself to be an authority: a position of power does not automatically elicit respect. Two elements are particularly required: to be 'fair' and to possess knowledge which is deemed usable. The sensitivity to adults' power is highly intensified. An adult must appear sympathetic, more a mate than a superior. The young must be awarded a certain amount of autonomy. Bullying counteracts identification. In short, social insights into the young and their needs are required. Knowledge *per se* does not necessarily help; knowledge must also be considered subjectively usable, such as that possessed by the music teachers at the Ark or by OH's producer. In these instances, knowledge can, to a degree, compensate for social deficiencies, in which case a classic exchange can occur: subjection now against a higher position later. Even so, this still seems to be an exchange which is easier to carry out if one comes from a higher social group: Chans has an easier time coping with school obligations than does Lam Gam. These principles also apply within the groups: the leaders are informal and watched over.

Jonna: The teachers you had in ordinary school, they were really dumb, but the ones we have now, they're like people who've been out working, like in restaurants and such places . . . They're not like teachers, they're more like ordinary people . . . They talk like us . . . yeah, they're more ordinary people who've worked on ships and restaurants and such.

Håkan: I think that school, well you should learn something there, and one thing you should learn is democracy – it's incredibly important! If you don't learn it, then it'll never work in the long run [. . .] But I've noticed that if a teacher's fair, then it's easier for the whole class to be fair back [. . .]

Johan: What is a teacher who's fair like?

Håkan: I think it's like putting yourself at the same level as the students – neither under nor over.

WORK

Johan: What sort of life do you want to avoid when you grow up – in the future?

Olof: Working round the clock [laughter]. [We want to] have free time. To do what you want and no work from morning to night.

In recent years, a declining work ethic has been highlighted as a social problem, referring to high sickness rates and resistance to industrial jobs – the 'flight from the factories' – among the younger generation. It has been suggested that the old-fashioned, capitalistic, Lutheran work ethic, with its admonitions to 'do a good job', is dissolving. Youth do not take any old job, not even during economic crises, and if they do, they have difficulties accomplishing it. The oppo-

Frasse: Why do you work? [. . .] It shouldn't be dead boring, though at the same time, I can imagine – it doesn't need to be a rave either. I mean, you work to support yourself [. . .] Meet people – I think that's important. [. . .]

Johan: Are you someone who wants to do something big and get known and famous?

Frasse: No, I wouldn't say that [. . .] I wouldn't want to be a prime minister or anything. [. . .] No, no, that sounds heavy. I'd rather . . . a little company maybe, with somebody employed and have a good income and . . .

THREE THEMES 193

Kurre: When we're sitting up here rapping it's totally different from being at work. They never talk about such stuff there, they talk, yeah well, it's bloody dull to listen to, like [about] their fucking home distillers and such shit and 'What did you do at the weekend?' and 'I was out and got laid'. – that sort of talk, right? It's crap. I usually go out, ... just leave and have a cigarette by myself [...] And so it's fucking important we have this group.

Micke: I can like see it, like right in front of me, when we're out touring, we have a great time in the bus ... [inaudible] You might think it gets fucking dull in the end but still, you sit and talk and ... get to a place and set up the gear or maybe we help, don't set up the gear ourselves. Do sound and light checks ... yeah, turn them on and check them out. Should be a real buzz. And then a few fans afterwards, should be a few girls coming up ... autographs and that [laughter]. I think it sounds fantastic.

Finn: At the moment ... it's more slog and practice than fun [...] Micke's never up for it. He comes up here and rests. Then I'm not up to it either. It's really hard, right, but OK, when the song's done, then ...

Betty: Even if I find a good job, I might go around worried, 'just think if there's an *even better job* that I don't have' ...

Kurre: And then I develop myself, by God I develop myself so much more by working. In school, as I wasn't particularly interested in school, I just fooled around.

sition between leisure time hedonistic acting-out and ascetic work discipline seems to have sharpened and produced ambivalences. Youth either make qualitative demands on work – demonstratively difficult to fulfil – or cultivate an instrumental attitude which means that at least for a time, they will accept dull but relatively well-paid jobs in order to augment leisure consumption. The result is that the central role of work in identity is no longer equally self-evident.[3]

This ambivalence is clear in our groups. Generally, to them work is nothing more than a necessary evil: life begins outside the factory gates and office doors. Not even the members of Chans seem to entertain any great hopes of self-realisation within work; work merely represents possibilities for a comfortable life. At the other end of the spectrum, Lam Gam perceive work as a bridge to adult privileges. Among the members of OH, most of whom now work, hardly anyone can conceive of working at a manual job his whole life long and thus hardly identifies himself with his job – with the possible exception of Kurre. What counts is music, activities having to do with music, and group solidarity, which are sometimes expressly pitted against workplace experiences.

Kurre's dreams of being a musician are bound up with efforts to turn work into leisure or to dissolve a seemingly entrenched dichotomy. It is easy to see a social reproductive mechanism, the 'freak syndrome' behind the orientation to the world of rock, but that would be misleading if it obscured the radicalism of the work utopia that dreams of rock music contain. Music-making satisfies needs for autonomy, responsibility, solidarity or communality, learning, creativity, recognition and, possibly, social advancement. What conventional occupation within Kurre's reach can supply all that? In OH and Lam Gam utopias are kept alive, even though their members safeguard themselves with ordinary jobs for the time being, and some of them could contemplate occupations other than in music. At the same time, at least in OH, rock music dreams create problems with balancing regression and progression interests. If Kurre has his black moments, the costs of commitment in terms of deferred satisfaction of immediate needs are even greater for Micke and Finn. Free time tends sometimes to be engulfed by alienating work.

However, the threat of unemployment naturally increases the importance of having some sort of job, a consideration which is less immediate for Chans members but very much present for Lam Gam members, who consider living on benefit extremely degrading. Among the members of OH, the fear of being rejected by society does not necessarily disappear because you have obtained a permanent job. One consequence of Kurre's efforts to come to terms with normality in the guise of a number of 'challenges' is that it becomes important to do his best with all the tasks presented to him: even drudge jobs can teach you something. The fear of social separation is held in abeyance by a subjectively functioning morality which distinguishes Kurre from the others in OH: on the one hand Finn, who professes to have nothing against living on benefit when and if such an occasion would arise (he is also the one in the group who succeeded best in school); on the other, Micke and Bobo, who tend to have an hereditary work ethic to counteract their fears of landing on the scrap heap. To Micke and Bobo, taking a day off and staying home from work would be a kind of fraud – in addition to the fact that it could become a dangerous habit. School obligations were a different matter: the serious business of life begins after school.

Bobo: Yeah, then I'd rather've tried to pray myself free. And if I hadn't got free, well that would've been that. [. . .] I don't know, I think it feels wrong. It's strange, 'cause when I went to school then I could very well [. . .]
Ulf: Now, you've actually not been at this job all that long, but don't you think that . . .
Bobo: No, I don't. . . [. . .] It feels wrong [. . .] both for me and for the job [. . .] I think when you've got a job you're obliged to go there. You're employed there to work and get your wages. Then you're just there, like that . . .
Ulf: Does it feel like you're deceiving somebody?
Bobo: Yeah, it does. If you're healthy and stay home, I think that's cheating. I'd never dare go out [. . .]
Ulf: It's not that if you gave in, so to speak, to the urge to stay home it might become a bad habit?
Bobo: Yeah, that's very possible. That it could be [a bad habit] is a real worry too. It was like that sometimes in school.

SEXUALITY AND LIVING TOGETHER

Conny: We're such close pals too, it's not only the boy–girl thing, it's like being good mates too, so we can just be with each other [. . .] like two boy mates, two girl mates.

In this area, the effects of cultural release are both tangible and publicised. Women's growing demands and their refusal to sacrifice themselves have put sexual roles in something of a crisis. The nuclear family has had to make adjustments in favour of looser cohabitation arrangements or single-parent families. Divorce has become more common. Long-term sexual relationships are entered into early, but family formation is delayed. However, the question is how genital youthful sexuality actually is. Perhaps such pairings primarily satisfy needs for closeness and approval

Bobo: Yeah [laughter], I wouldn't've thought it would work. Don't think so. I mean, shit if she'd been pretty, it'd never have worked, then everybody would've had a go. But then if somebody had been together with her, it'd also have gone to hell, it'd never have worked. Come up here and rehearse maybe and they'd have sat here and mucked about on the sofa and us there talking about something else [. . .].
Ulf: So in a way, it's good that you're five boys?
Bobo: Yeah, I think so, I think it's easier to talk when you're five boys.

Ove: You're doing it all night so you can't cope with getting up in the morning?
Ola: Ha, ha . . . no, but it's often a problem to get up . . . and then you think, don't give a shit. I've got a bit sloppy with school lately . . . this term, absent too much.

B-A: He's more animal than human! [. . .] Sometimes he growls and runs around on all fours, then you begin to wonder . . . But then when he comes out with something really civilised, you get terribly shocked! I mean, I've known him almost a year and he can still shock me.
Karl: I think it's right that *we* are together a lot but that you can have others too.
Olof: Mmmm. They can sort of come and go a bit.
Gustav: I think that they [the girls] *can* be with us, but not like . . .
Björn: Not in the inner circle, so to speak.
Håkan: You shouldn't shut yourself off.
Karl: But I don't think we should lose track so we suddenly get to be 10–15 people who are always together, we should keep it at us seven.
Björn: It should be this little circle [. . .]
Gustav: But then we shouldn't live in each others' pockets.

and are only distinguished from friendships by their depth. Hence it is logical that there is nothing abnormal about having mates from both sexes; sexuality has been deflated.

Kurre reflects central aspects of this development. To a large extent, he represents the softer male role dominating in OH – at least on the surface. (In practice, this by no means excludes casual sexual exploits and thus is consistent with a traditional distinction between good girls and sluts.) Like the others in the group, Kurre has experienced fairly long-term heterosexual relationships, considers intimacy rather than sexuality to be the core of relationships, and consequently advocates monogamy. However, at the same time, heterosexual relations entail bonds which can jeopardise the OH project and Kurre's self-imposed task of reliving his father's youth for him. In fact, musical ambitions create tensions around not only Kurre's but the whole group's relations with the opposite sex. Taking a girl into the band would seem inconceivable as it could create rivalry and splits. Only as an audience do girls fill an important role: their response confirms sexual identity, a postulation also voiced by Lam Gam. Several Lam Gam members, in the manner of working-class lads, happily partake of the early fruits of adulthood but have more problems managing everyday demands: Ola and Jonna live together with their girlfriends but do not always manage to get up to go to school in the morning. Chans appear somewhat more 'old-fashioned'. Their sexual experience seems more limited; their environment hardly encourages such activity and they have an inner resistance to going the whole way. The conflict between suppressed sexuality and self-discipline in Chans is expressed in, among other things, their common fascination with Olof's pubescent 'animality'. Forming a family, which Chans members view as inevitable, is to be deferred to a distant future – to the age of 30 or even 40.

Even though, unlike OH, Chans and Lam Gam do not try to exclude girls, they still represent male enclaves, similar to those of hunting parties or barrack-room fraternities.[4] Single-sex groups are less demanding even if they may feel confined and cannot satisfy certain needs. In fact, it seems more important for the youth in our bands to have mates than to have girlfriends. The uncomplicated male conviviality is idealised. It is no accident that the members of our groups recall their shared childhoods with some nostalgia, even though those childhoods are rather recent. Group members are 'brothers' (Kurre). Nevertheless, comradeship sometimes seems more of a dream than a reality, even for the members themselves. Under the surface lurk fears of causing or being the victim of separation. The members of our groups give the impression that the worst that could happen to them is to be left on their own; their self-esteem sometimes seems totally dependent upon relationships. Consequently, the sexual preserve is exposed to a double threat.

Ulf: Good friends are important, yes? [agreement] Almost more important than having a girl?
Finn: Yeah, that's true. Anyway, with a girl there'll always be arguments – 'And what've you been up to tonight' [in a distorted voice] and that . . .
Ulf: So it's less heavy with mates?
Finn: Oh yeah, you're so relaxed . . .

The attitudes of the young band members towards authority, work, sexuality and living together may be described generally as 'modern', despite certain differences, mostly class-determined, between the groups and even within them. If we compare them with the generation we (the authors) ourselves represent, it is very apparent that in the bands, subjectivity is given greater latitude. This is evident not least in the demand that the situations you land in must be emotionally rewarding: in other words, it is more difficult for band members to subordinate themselves to abstract power and to differentiate between things and their contexts. Thus authorities are evaluated very concretely according to their abilities to confirm the ego by establishing a friendly relation to it, which seems, at least in the groups with a lower social base, to be a prerequisite for learning. Dependence on relationships is also reflected in the high value placed on leisure or free time in which plans and projects and personal relations comprise an indivisible unity, and in the close relationship between love and friendship, which means that the satisfaction of sexual needs is subordinated to intimacy and being received or simply confirmed as a sexual being. What is at stake throughout appears to be the sense of self.

If the above is true, it lends credibility to the hypothesis of a new, narcissistically toned adolescence in modern youth. However, on the basis of our methods and our material we cannot verify this hypothesis. In general it is difficult to pinpoint changes in fundamental psychic structures.[5] We can say, though, that notions of permanent deep psychic structures do not seem very valid as they presume an ahistorical and asocial belief in an 'authentic' human nature. We would also add that among our youth one can see how subjective psychic structures rooted in early childhood interact with secondary socialising effects in a way unfamiliar to us from our own teenage years.

THE GROUPS
AND THEIR
ROCK MUSIC

THE BAND AS A GROUP

Gurkan [from the Ark's house committee]: Yeah, well, it's a home . . . you're here more than at home.

Jonna: Why I'm never home – well, I go home and eat after school and then I go to the Ark, come home about 11 or 12, eat and go to bed.

Ola: . . . but, true, they [parents] think I'm away a lot . . . 'Oh, so that's what you look like', they say when I come home . . . ha, ha . . . 'Boy, how you've grown' . . . ha, ha, ha.

Ove: What would you do if the Ark didn't exist?
Magnus [like Freddy and Putte, a member of the Ark house committee]: I'd commit suicide [giggles].
Freddy: If they closed it down, we'd blow the place up . . . if we can't have it, we'll make sure nobody else does either.
Putte: Yeah, if we didn't occupy it, we'd set a fire that'd be seen all over Gothenburg.
Ove: How does it feel when you think that one day you'll leave your mates and sit in a flat with a wife and kids?
Putte: Shit, feels horrible . . . Sunday walks in the park with the kids . . . and to get old and start to work, be just work, home, sleep, work . . . damn it, don't want that.

Gurkan: I won't do that!
Ove: What are you going to do?
Gurkan: Go out and have fun . . . I'll be going to the disco till I'm 80.

Young people forming themselves into groups is no recent phenomenon.[1] Historical examples include medieval roving journeymen and apprentices, the bands of children and youth in the seventeenth century in large cities like London, or in the Swedish countryside before the advent of industrialisation.[2] When in everyday speech we talk about youth groups and gangs, we are usually thinking of the type of male-dominated group formations which began to crop up in working-class areas in conjunction with the growth of modern industry. In Sweden, as early as the 1890s, a so-called boy gang committee was appointed by parliament to investigate what could be done with the large groups of 'depraved and immoral' youths who more or less lived on the streets. Hence the concept of youth has long been associated with young men and social problems – an association confirmed by research. The studies made during the 1920s and 1930s by the Chicago School also influenced discussion of youth in Sweden.[3] According to these studies, the gangs that developed in the slum areas of large cities were responses to a socially and culturally unstable society in which social control and the given forms for the transference of norms had collapsed.

After the Second World War and during the growth of a youth-oriented consumer goods industry, the view of youth and youth groups gradually changed. Gangs became less and less a phenomenon closely connected with young, rowdy working-class boys. Gangs began to be formed in other social strata, especially in the expanding middle strata, and girls began to appear in the gangs, albeit with peripheral roles. Even though groupings of middle-class youth had naturally existed before, they were never characterised as gangs. It was in conjunction with the growing mass culture in the 1950s and 1960s that youth from different social strata first began to enter a common 'scene'. However, this is not to say that such youth culture comprises a class-conciliating consumer culture: cultural and class oppositions cut deep into the youth scene, and have a decisive influence on the constitution of the gang groups.

The group constitutes a pivotal part of young people's social world; they often spend more time in their gangs than they do with their parents.[4] In contrast to a school class, for example, the gang is a self-selected group of individuals of the same age, and consequently of greater emotional value for its members. Life in the gang primarily takes place in its members' free time and usually without adult participation. In the gang a way of relating to society is developed and a style cultivated via the system of symbols which the gang refers to. To a high degree, gang membership is decisive for the individual member's identity and relation to the surrounding world. In modern society, young people's orientation to and need for groups of their own age must be seen against the background of the special problems of discontinuity in the teenage years. Being a child and being an adult constitute two social roles which place utterly different demands on the individual. Youth is a transitional phase between childhood and adulthood, a time of liberation from parents and seeking for and testing one's own identity. During the late modern period, identity formation has become a rather complicated task (we shall return to this later). We should bear all this in mind when we look at the need for groups as a transitional medium, in which much of the arduous, painful liberation efforts and identity experimentation can occur, but in which one can also be shielded against heavy demands from parents, school and the culture industry. The group can thus function both as a platform for an offensive relationship to the surrounding society and for searching, questioning and criticising, and as an authority in which membership craves conformity and can actually restrict and check individuation.

With certain reservations, we may consider our three bands as small gangs. There is one critical difference between them and ordinary youth gangs, however. In ordinary gangs, a fairly unplanned and unformalised co-existence forms the basis for their group relations. Our three bands have a clearly articulated project, an activity

Johan: Is it difficult to be adult in a way?
Karl: Yeah. I think that it's like an incredible difference to suddenly be 18, not 16. I think that's *scary* almost, if you think about it a lot . . . It's not exactly that you're afraid of the future, but time goes too fast.

Kurre: Yeah, dreams are . . . big dreams and little dreams. One little dream is that we can keep together for a long time, yeah? That's a dream we all have. A bigger dream is, well, that we could get a record contract, that we could support ourselves on it, and an even bigger dream is that we want – like everybody else – we want peace and that, we're trying to do something for peace, a little at least . . .

Conny: . . . .KSMB's great, I think, really cool, that was a fucking cool band. Hated by lots of adults . . . I saw that myself the other day when I put on *Jag vill åka till Harrisburg* (I'm going to go to Harrisburg) and my mum just stopped, just like that, and said 'What's that he's singing . . . you can't sing that' . . . and she went on and on like that.

Jonna's mother: . . . every time they talk about an amateur talent show on TV, I nag him to try it out, I mean, you never know, they might win. I've even taken it upon myself to send in cassettes and that, to help them.
Ove: So if the band would get a record contract you wouldn't advise against, try to get him on to something else, like finishing school first or whatever?
Jonna's mother: Hell no, I'd be bloody glad. I'd like to be in it myself, think it would great fun [. . .] If Jonna'd come home and say, 'Now I'm just going to play, I'm quitting school tomorrow,' I wouldn't oppose it.

Ulf: Was it difficult in school, at times?

Kurre: Mmm. I even cried sometimes in school.

Ulf: Was that because it was difficult?

Kurre: I . . . I couldn't handle it . . . you were pressured. Often it was only me who couldn't hack it. And then . . .

Ulf: So that made you feel dumb?

Kurre: Yeah. I guess that's what makes me want to give it back, in the music, right? Like, 'Look now' – understand?

Chans' teacher: It's unusual to have a band at school, but then it's an unusual group too.[. . .] Chans and the boys there, they're unusually unaffected [. . .] They give me an impression of being natural in a way, they've preserved a curiosity, a playfulness in this society, which is so hard, so stressed and ruled by perform-ance and competition.

Ove: But you've got long hair and always wear torn jeans. What are you trying to say with that?

Lollo: Yeah, that I don't have some asshole over me, who's controlling me, that I'm myself, that no shit's gonna tell me what to do.

Ove: What do you think of people who go round with attaché cases in the academic subjects in your school?

Lollo: I think they want to say that they think they're better people.

and a vision which links the individuals together. This also leads to certain complications, to which we will return. However, although our bands may be considered as 'pro-ject groups', they nevertheless fulfil for our youth a number of functions also found in ordinary gangs.

In order to be able to consider a number of youth as a gang they must form a fairly stable grouping which dis-tinguishes itself from its surroundings. Of our three bands, Lam Gam and OH most sharply mark themselves off from their parents. This is not to say that they dissociate them-selves from their parents in general; to some extent both OH and the Ark culture have roots in their parental cul-tures' values and attitudes. The members of Chans avoid provoking their parents, which is not to say that they are uncritical or totally subservient. Generally, in all three bands, the parents regard their childrens' playing positively, but they also tend to have a 'sober' attitude, which includes expressed scepticism towards too high aspirations which could jeopardise a 'real' career. Only in Lam Gam is there a parent who supports her child's fantasies of being a rock star.

Demarcation from school is also most obvious with Lam Gam especially, and with OH. The Ark may almost be viewed as a gathering-place for youth who have not done well in school. Negative experiences in school are central factors behind playing rock music for both OH and Lam Gam, for whom playing rock offers the possibility of raising themselves out of the rather unattractive future for which school lays the foundations. Chans members show no tendencies towards oppositional boundary-setting in relation to school; but even so, they demarcate themselves in various ways in relation to their teachers and school mates by playing in a band, publishing a paper, being an exclusive group with their own inside jokes and rituals, and by dismissing school-like demands for progress in their playing. However, by bringing the individuals in the bands together, school has played a decisive role: both Lam Gam and Chans started as school bands.

In relation to then-accessible youth cultural styles, Lam Gam and OH in several respects clearly share a basic atti-tude. Both groups are influenced by hard rock and punk, musically and as regards image. Their identification with hard rock and punk and their disregard for other youth cultural styles involve above all underlining a generation-based distinction, a demarcation in relation to school and the adult world. Punk's sensitivity to social evils and injustices to an extent corresponds to values embraced by the bands' parental cultures. Lam Gam and OH's lyrics support the weak – against power and 'them up there'. Chans' relation to the youth cultural scene is more complex: there is no clear subcultural orientation, instead what is stressed is the importance of distance and flexibility. Chans has developed an active and reflective attitude to what is happening in the youth scene as regards music, fashion, film, etc., but no need for a common identification object: there is no counterpart in Chans to Lam Gam's Ebba Grön and Imperiet or OH's U2 and Clash.

Gender demarcation is important, particularly to OH. The tendency to keep girls at a distance, which indeed all three bands have or have had, expresses a need to test and experiment with one's own masculinity in peace. As has already been noted, in principle all the youths in our bands come from homes where the mother is the emotionally dominant parent. Given that, their male solidarity may also be an attempt to liberate themselves from strong maternal bonding, to keep the 'feminine' at a distance, while at the same time in practice their bonding recreates aspects of the original symbiosis with their mothers.

To the boys in the single-sex gangs, the 'feminine' is something radically alien – the 'Other'. To the feminine is ascribed everything that their own male identity has rejected or repressed. This projection is facilitated by the fact that their own identity is in accord with society's norms and, in particular, with the dominant male norms of the rock world. Betty and B-A's incorporation into Chans has involved a certain shift: it has become more apparent that the boys' picture of the feminine as the 'Other' *vis à vis* their own identity may not be the same as concrete female identity. Such questioning learning processes in the world of rock have become seriously possible because of the relative breakthrough of female musicians in mixed-gender groups appearing in conjunction with punk. Prior to punk, female rock musicians were practically inconceivable; today, even if only every tenth rock musician is a woman, the proportion is much greater than previously, and the women are no longer relegated to a stage decor-vocalist

Conny: I remember Lollo when I met him, yeah, not a day went by without him being stoned. I think that music and the Ark help him more than some old lady down at the social. That's the way it is, like somewhere along the line it's society. And this division between the rich and the poor, that's society, too, and rules and laws that are wrong as hell, and that's also society, right? Yeah, that's about it, what I can write about, I think.
Ove: How've you come to all these insights about society?
Conny: Well, it's the music [Ebba Grön, KSMB] I've come in contact with.

Gösta: We've created something special in some way, and we've our own humour too.

Ulf: What does it mean that you're five boys, could you think of . . . or that there aren't any girls?
Micke: That wouldn't've worked, I don't think. No, but in any case we would've had to know the girl a long time. It would have been even worse than with Bamse in the group.

Karl: Then it was the first Rock in Storby [. . .] Then it was like there, conflicts between Villaholmen and Storby and so we were like pretty scared . . . [. . .]
Gösta: We were afraid that they'd boo us out, but it didn't happen.
Björn: Yeah, and get beaten up and that [. . .]
Gustav: We said like this to the man who was going to do the programme: 'Oh no, don't say we're from Villaholmen . . . ' [giggles and noises]. 'Say we're an Oasis band!'
Gösta: And they listened a lot to hard rock and that, so we did rather sort of hard rock songs and that, a little popular . . .
Gustav: It was the first time Frasse had on a sweatshirt and trainers, I believe [laughter].

Ubbe [old Ark regular]: It's only good – the less they [social workers] are involved, the better . . . and the aim with the Ark from the beginning was that we should take over totally. *Only kids, no involvement from the social or the recreational* or *nobody else* . . . but it seems like somebody doesn't want to let go.

Conny: Maybe somebody is getting tired, who knows, that's the way it is with everything. But I still think the core will stay and we'll stand on the stage in Ullevi [a big stadium] some day [laughter]. No, but if we aim to maybe we'll get to the Student Union or something.

Ove: Do you think you'll be a band that'll get gigs in town too?
Conny: Yeah, I think so, I think – yeah, for sure.

Gösta: . . . .the main thing is that we're together. That's what, I think, we have each other for. Not just to sit and play, that'd be boring. I think it should be fun.

Kurre: I liked Bamse, we got on well, but musically, we were at opposite ends. Sometimes it worked and it sometimes didn't. Now it always works [. . .] For me, privately, I got a lot more space to play – not on the guitar – but to be able to express myself in the band without always being forced, always so leaned-on by bloody Bamse. That can seem like 'what a fucking ego trip', but I knew Finn and Bobo and Micke before, when Bamse was around, and I knew what they wanted and they wanted the same as me. [. . .] I don't want to be a dictator in the group . . . but I talk a lot about ideas, right, but I take everybody in the band seriously, everybody's ideas seriously.

combination (for example, the many competent female musicians in Prince).[5]

The three bands may also be described as havens or 'refuges', where you can be granted respite from societal demands by melding together and becoming one with the group through activities such as playing music. For all three bands the gang functions as a fortress against pressures from school and parents. Independence is maintained in varying degrees in all groups; even if the gang by definition involves demarcation, it is still part of a social context related to its surroundings – to other gangs, youth culture styles, school, other groupings (societies, associations), parents, etc.

The need for autonomy is particularly evident in Lam Gam and OH, not least in their fondness for their respective quarters – the Ark and the Barn. To the boys in Lam Gam, the most important thing about the Ark is that they are left in peace there – 'leave us kids alone'. The band itself has a more progression-oriented function; the band permits you to show yourself, the music facilitates contact with youth from other areas through gigs, etc. If the Ark means security and entrenchment, the band is something of a spearhead towards the outside world. The core of OH is autonomy and intimacy, but the band also has an important outer-directed function: via the musical project which forms the basis for togetherness and solidarity, OH wish to convey the 'G' ideology to others and make it a model for society. For Chans, the gang as haven is primarily linked to the need to 'have fun'. In the gang you are fairly freely permitted to show sides of yourself which neither school nor parents would sanction. However, for Chans members as well, the band functions as a link to the world at large – with other youth, the music industry and the media.

Like Lam Gam and OH, Chans is an instrument to orient its members out of the protection of the family and towards their individual identities and their own adult existence. In general, relations to and between individual members seem to be subordinate to the need for bonds with the group. In all the gangs, there is also, at least sporadically, a climate that makes it possible for the individuals to work with and test their dreams and conceptions of who they are. This, however, is not to say that these examinations occur on equal terms. Particularly for Kurre and later, for Finn, OH has had an important individualising function; the band has become a sort of laboratory in which they test and develop their own abilities and in which the limits for the expansion of their egos are set, partly at the expense of Bamse's individuation possibilities. A similar conflict became apparent when Lam Gam split up: in particular Sigge and Seppo's subordination ceased and their creativity was released.

To share a project, as our bands do, to play in a group, also entails the members being forced to be taken as the individuals they actually are. The collective project places demands that provoke conflicts and oppositions which in turn compel individuation and function divisions in a wholly different way from what is commonly the case in ordinary youth gangs. On the other hand, new problems can arise; for instance, the project and its concomitant progression efforts may collide with the group's need for security and community. Chans never truly backed the project, which was subordinated to togetherness. However, in OH, the dream of 'taking a peer group to the stars' contained a fundamental conflict. This 'both/and' met with real opposition when Bamse was excluded from the group for a year because his presence was at odds with the need for progression.

Ove: How has your role as guitarist changed in the new band?
Sigge: I get to do more things . . . more advanced stuff, you could say . . . more fun. I like this music a lot more.
Ove: What was it that made you change bands?
Sigge: I want to learn to play better . . . learn more.

SEARCHING THROUGH
SYMBOLIC PRAXIS

SEARCHING

Barbara-Ann: The type I'll be in a year's time is roughly the type that, a year ago, I thought I would become. [. . .] I think everything's going according to plan, actually.

Finn: What am I afraid of? Well, war, of course [pause]. And I'm afraid of, yeah, of being a failure in life, of like not attaining the ideals I've set myself [. . .], humility, trying to be nice to others, not running around being bossy.

In times when everything is in a state of flux, you are compelled to become a seeker. There is nothing new *per se* about this for youth: youth is the time of life when you are expected to come to terms with fundamental questions about the ego, existence, and society. It is easy to forget that not long ago few people were able to concern themselves with such questions; instead, most were occupied with heavy physical labour. However, we would postulate that the search in the late modern era not only entails a quantitative difference but also new conditions which are set by cultural erosion.[1]

If identity was formerly something you grew into more or less obviously, today it is something you have to acquire. Neither is identity permanent but, like everything else, subject to change and thus it has less and less to do with nature or destiny. In this lie both liberation and pressure to perform. What is not already given is feasible, possible to come to grips with. Whatever happens is your own responsibility, whether it has to do with career, relationships, your own body or personality. Among the youth in the three bands, notions of makeability are present in OH with a heavy stress on the inner world, and accompanied by feelings of inadequacy: it is difficult to be or to find oneself. Through presuming an 'authentic' end, OH's position may seem less modern than Chans' programmatic flexibility, but in fact, it presumes a modern context of self-awareness. One might also distinguish between a 'vertical' (OH) and a 'horizontal' (Chans) way of handling the modern world, which are joined together by the demand for mobility.[2]

Later, as accumulated social knowledge penetrates the recesses of the life-world, access to objectivised self-references increases. The result of this reflexivity is as double-edged as that of feasibility: on the one hand, new forms for self-understanding, on the other, the removal of opportunities for primary experiences since the territory is already colonised by others, and difficulties of living up to the norms. With our youth, forced reflexivity is sometimes very evident, and it not only includes references to the music scene and biographical writing. Lam Gam refer to the Ark as a 'refuge for the working-class' (Conny). In his descriptions of himself, OH's Bamse indicates a fairly advanced awareness of socialisation ('Oedipus complex'). Among the youth in Chans, the girls particularly, even though they are younger, express themselves in similar analytical terms and have a somewhat adult perspective on themselves.

Today, when choices of urban lifestyles are made available by the media to the imagination virtually everywhere, considerable demands are placed on individuals to orient themselves and find a balance between the inner visual explosion and the scope of the outside world. Your origins still provide support, as is demonstrated in the differences between Lam Gam's and Chans' cultural styles, but the tendency towards *individualisation*, breaking away from the family's lifestyle, still penetrates. A number of examples of this have already been given: from Kurre's view of culture, which overrides his family's them-up-there criticism of established culture and seizes upon an ethnological concept of culture and lands in a self-assertive subjectivism, to the commonly shared criticism of parents' modes of living, which has been inspired by media culture. Self-image is not determined by the past but by the here and now and dreams of the future.[3]

It is this fund of makeability, reflexivity and individualisation which sets the conditions for identity work and gradually supercedes previously valid patterns of action. This has to do with finding ways to handle the lack of warmth and meaning and the emptiness of late modern existence.

One response is *subjectivation*, searching for closeness and intimacy in order to balance the system world's cold anonymity. Correlated to this is a striving after expressiveness, understood as authentic expression, and an inclination to decide questions through referring to what one 'feels'. In the three bands, subjectivation roughly corresponds to what has previously been denoted as an absorption into the

Bamse: Yeah, like when [my dad] died [...], it's a bit like, you know, the Oedipus complex [...] now when the old man can't fill mum's place, or it's empty now after [him] and mum, um, she's alone [...] and well, you'd sort of like to take that place to fill her life up.

Barbara-Ann: All that economy stuff, [my stepfather] has got me interested in that. [...]Before they got married, there wasn't anybody to identify with. [. . .] Really, but I don't think I've ever had a real liberation process, OK, *I* shouldn't really say that, but . . .

Betty: I think about things a helluva lot. It's a bit difficult to explain. It's like what they say, that you have a little of that identity . . . no, but when you're a teenager . . .

Conny: It's true that it can sound dicey, that I don't belong anywhere, but you can say that I belong in many places . . . *and that's bloody wonderful, that is.*

Bamse: Just strumming a chord on the guitar, that's . . . that just opens your heart. It does for me. And it does for Kurre too, I know that. And I do so want to be in that group again. I want to show that I belong to them, I want to show that I'm the same person as them, think the same.

Jonna: I'll be here as long as I can [...] I mean you can be here even if you're 30, drop in sometimes and that [...]
Ove: Will the gang keep together even though you live in different places [...]?
Jonna: Yeah, I think so.

Barbara-Ann: He [Frasse] asked me a rather personal question about girls in general. And then I asked: 'Who knows you best, me or Olof?' – 'Yeah, you, yeah definitely you, you know that, like I've told a whole lot of things to you that I'd never dream of telling Olofsson!'

Finn: What do I get out of it? Yeah, you know – but there, there, togetherness is incredible, it's super, and you haven't got it like on just one level, you have it on all levels.

Bamse: I wanted it to be like a hobby from the beginning, 'cause I'd already decided what I wanted to be, right? But of course you can compromise there, like Finn's done. It's just as important. But then, if the music takes over what I think is most important now, what's given me such an incredible amount, then I'd leave behind something that's helped me and I don't think that's right. [...] The church's given me an awful lot.

Olof: I think people who can't figure anything out for themselves are a bit boring.
Johan: But is it fair to them? Should they be sitting there doing those boring jobs then?
Olof: No, but they can find their own thing.

Lollo: But always, when there's a party at my place, it's always like 'Come in and wreck the place.' On the ninth floor. The biggest I had, now when was that, yeah, that was in the winter break, then there were two calls to the cops . . . and the whole fucking yard was a mess of cans and stuff, a smashed record player and telephone that'd been chucked out [laughter]. The beds were broken, they'd collapsed and there were screwdrivers in the doors [. . .]
Sigge: Don't you remember that it was you who kicked in the door to your brother's room [laughter] or when you were gonna turn out the light and you took the hammer and smashed the switch . . . whap, the whole fuckin' thing fell apart.

'maternal', into the collective ego – the community, 'G'. However, this absorption is permeated in varying degrees by 'paternal' development demands, compelled reflexivity and individualisation. These tendencies are in part carried by the members into the group, and in part, give the group project new framework. The consequences may be that, as in OH, the individual's own ego is transformed into a project. Security in the group becomes conditional: the threat of being cast out into the cold can be experienced as being forced to remain 'the same person'. In short, the fear of separation, described earlier, evokes a deep awareness of the impermanence of the here and now. The members of Lam Gam have access to the Ark and are therefore not equally exposed as a group, but the need for closeness and warmth is, as we have seen, no less palpable with them. The same is also to some extent true of Chans, but it is demonstrated more indirectly – for example, in the desire to 'work with people'. To what extent the group members really open up to each other remains unclear; some of them indicate that true intimacy is reserved for heterosexual relations. The group rather gives access to a zone where pressures are eased and where the members can act-out together.

Another response or attempt at orientation may be mentioned summarily, since it seems not to be equally widespread in our groups. We are referring to *ontologisation*, the striving for certainty, defending oneself against loss of meaning through a new spirituality or fundamentalism. Among our groups, this inclination actually only exists in the OH culture as remnants of a couple of members' Christian beliefs. However, at the same time it is clear that the striving for a fixed point competes with a longing for subjectivating closeness and is actually subordinate to it. The position of Finn and Bamse particularly in the question of committing themselves to the church or music may be described as vacillating, which allows the modernity of the context to arise: there are always alternative possibilities, certainty can never be as absolute as it was before, retrieving Christianity must be an individual decision.

Possibly, these two types of responses have already peaked. In any case, a third type of orientation, the striving for *empowerment* – suffusing everyday life with intensity – seems more in the spirit of the 1980s in its connections with aesthetic self-presentation, graffiti and computerised signs. Empowerment affirms what is modern in a different way and tries to sharpen it in order to keep feelings of emptiness at bay. The striving for empowerment occurs in all three groups, most markedly in Chans and least in OH. Essential to the Chans culture is, as we have seen, 'to have fun', to fill time with bold, cocky jokes, to find something 'ballsy' in the most trivial chart or schlager music or event. But also, more than the others, Chans members are fascinated by façades, styles, aesthetics, and in certain cases, their search for intensity inclines towards neo-conservative political ideologies, with commercial aesthetic labels such as 'excitement' and the like. The doing-nothing culture of the Ark leaves greater latitude for subjectivation, but this is complemented by setting high value on 'wreaking havoc', 'having a rave-up', and Lam Gam goes at least as far as Chans in acting-out on stage. For all the groups, music intensifies the feeling of life: you 'create something together' (Bamse), you get charged up for concerts, you are someone just by being in a band. Striving for empowerment increases individualisation, and in the process, the parental culture can be perceived as meagre and static.

Bobo: Like now, when you work and that, yeah, like before, when you went to school . . . always otherwise if I'd be up to near midnight on a Thursday and had to get up on Friday, then I'd think: 'Bloody hell, I'm tired, gotta get home and sleep'. But when you play, then [. . .] like if it's a Wednesday and you're working, you think, 'Oh great, I'll be home soon, then it's just up and play tonight.' You've got something to look forward to.

ROCK AS SYMBOLIC PRAXIS

What is special about the three gangs is that they play rock; their search is conducted around a specific symbolic praxis. We shall now look a little closer at the function of rock in their identity work.

If the search for identity is considered as a kind of production process, which largely takes place on a pre- or unconscious level, we can also talk about raw materials and tools, or, more simply, about three types of sources: objective, socio-linguistic and subjective. These sources meet and combine in the activities of all gangs, and the form and results of the search are determined by how they are combined. This makes each gang unique and unpredictable.

OBJECTIVE SOURCES

The three gangs are coeval, but they live under different geographical and socio-economic conditions. They are the

Micke's father: They were here the first year, so it was a bit difficult. Just practice, and couldn't do this and couldn't do that, just banging back and forth [. . .] And then, there was the divorce and . . . I thought it was better they were here than they didn't have anywhere to go, and so many times I just cut out [inaudible], when I couldn't stand listening anymore [laughter].

Ove: What do you think of the other bands that practise here at the Ark and live here in Bergslunden? What are you like compared to other bands?
Ola: Better. No, [laughter], the other bands are often shit boring on stage [. . .]
Ove: But musically are you . . . if you compare with Banal Oktav . . .
Ola: Banal Oktav's definitely much better than us musically. But they've played a lot longer too.

Conny: It's good stuff, but [sigh], yeah, I don't know, lots of people come here who don't know anything. Sit here and bang and thump. And the ones that can, like Lollo, like they go in once and sit and hammer with a hammer in one hand and a microphone stand in the other.

children of a crisis, but this crisis penetrates the life world of different groups in different ways, and in fact is not experienced as a crisis by the youth themselves but as a given framework. Living conditions set limits for what is feasible and simultaneously provide young people with possibilities to act. These limits also apply to something as concrete as the physical and technical prerequisites for playing rock music.

To play rock requires a place to be, a truism which nevertheless contains great problems as regards conflicts with family and neighbours and between generations. If you live in a rental block like the members of Lam Gam, you are clearly handicapped, but living in a detached house may not be much better, and few landlords will rent premises to a young rock band. Without the Ark, Lam Gam would hardly have existed, and it is questionable how the other two bands would have fared had they not had access to a few families' residential space.

Equally, to play rock requires equipment – instruments, amplifiers, etc. – a potentially expensive investment. Only one member of Lam Gam owns his own equipment; the parents of Lam Gam do not feel they can afford the expense, however much they might want to buy instruments for their children. In 1986, OH, the only band with employed members, assessed the combined value of their equipment at about SEK 70,000.

These differences have several significant effects. If, like Lam Gam, you play – and rehearse – in a public youth project, the rest of the world is continually present in the form of other representatives of the Ark culture, many of them also musicians. This makes it more difficult to cultivate visions of greatness and entails strong local pressures to conform. However, the Ark culture is also stimulating and offers an alternative to the commercial rock scene. Disputes in the band, even splits, are absorbed and conducted rather undramatically. OH, with their ambitions, their own quarters and equipment, are exposed in another way. Chans are protected from trendiness basically by a lack of will to commit themselves to music.

Another effect is linked to the limits set by the individuals' technical competence. What is remarkable about rock as a popular movement is that its practitioners tend to be self-taught to such a great extent, through imitation, advice, etc. – in other words, informal processes. At least since punk, in principle anyone can play rock. None of the bands contains any brilliant musicians, which is one reason why the punk style was adopted, at least for a time, by all three bands. However, differences among the bands emerge here as well. Access to its own quarters and instruments most certainly increases a band's potential to develop technically and advance. It must indeed be trying to arrive for a rehearsal and find that someone has made a mess of the equipment, which is what happened to Lam Gam at the Ark. And if you do not own an instrument, you cannot practise at home.

SOCIO-CULTURAL SOURCES

This heading refers to two levels of inter-subjective resources: the norms or behaviour dispositions which we carry with us, and the world of signs, the system of symbols or, in short, the language which surrounds us and which we lay claim to.[4]

The dissolution of tradition, cultural release, involves precisely these resources being turned into something of a battleground: against the system's successful rational discourse the life-world mobilises individual subjectivity. The following section concentrates on the linguistic level, and in particular, the sign system of rock.

In contrast to other animals, human beings use signs not only to point out phenomena but also to represent them, using symbols. Through the symbolic order of verbal language, we take our place among others. According to Lacan, the subject arises from the child's giving up the interplay with the 'other', primarily the mother in the mother–child dyad, but preserving a life-long language-dependent need for confirmation by others. Language thus enables you to master the surrounding world only at the cost of a 'constitutional lack'. This lack becomes part of discourse. Being discursive, verbal language forces a linearity – a first then – on our ideas, which restricts what is signified. The original pre-linguistic unity between the signified and signifier, between the child and the mother, has been lost. Through this 'castration', which at the same time means that other acoustic expressions are undifferentiated and become music (song), the physical need of the 'other' becomes desire, something that can only be articulated in the metaphors surrounding the signifier like a shadow but transcending it. The unconscious is established in tandem with the conscious. From now on, reminiscences of the pre-linguistic, 'maternal' field of the drive, the 'semiotic', will wage war on the 'symbolic', the controlling patriarchal structure – 'father's law'. This is the war waged in socially accepted forms within the area of art.[5]

Artistic symbols are 'presentative' rather than discursive. A symbol unites communicative and expressive, rational and instinctive aspects, form and content. However, in societies, where verbal language dominates and has exclusive ties with power, the public and the rational, certain experiences will be suppressed or never symbolised. Presentative symbols articulate such experiences which are unaccessible for discourse. They thereby avail themselves of the surplus of meaning which wafts around the linguistic symbols. This surplus of symbolic primary forms, 'proto-symbols', may be described as sensual-symbolic forms of interaction – unconsciously socialised ways of relating or patterns of action, which have been left in the background of consciousness. Proto-symbols constitute a treasure-trove for the imagination. New artistic expressions always involve a dissolution of conventions – including the unarticulated – followed by a new unity that rests on the mobilisation of proto-symbols through creative regression to a pre-language stage. Thus twentieth-century modernism's 'semiotic' praxis may be seen as a symptom of a crisis in people's relationship to social intercourse and a turning-point in terms of the concept of meaning.[6] However, it would also seem that, at least in certain historical periods and certain social strata, puberty, with its release of instinctual impulses, is open to similar processes. The role of rock music in present-day young sub cultures encompasses an area where 'the barbs of the non-identical towards the generally accepted'[7] are kept sharp. Consider some of the patterns of movement that punk introduced and denoted as dances:

> The pose is [...] the only one of the dances allowing pair relations. One partner poses in extremely parodying positions while the other moves around the first with a fictive camera, taking snapshots of the beautiful poses. The pogo consists of simply hopping up and down in place without moving the arms [...] The robot has almost imperceptible small

movements with the head and hands, which can suddenly go over into a whole body twitch ('Frankenstein's first step').[8]

Among the arts, music comprises a special case in that it is based on 'unconsummated' symbols, 'significant form[s] without conventional significance'.[9] This gives the content of the language of music a fundamental ambivalence, which is thought to facilitate contact with deeper levels of feeling. By means of certain specific characteristics, rock music seems to be inordinately suitable for such contacts.

Rock is a mass-produced commodity, and it would be naive to believe that this would not affect what rock stands for. However, it is equally naive to imagine that being a commodity eradicates rock's use value as an expression of the common needs of large numbers of people all over the world, or compromises its radical criticism of ruling forms of rationality and socialisation.

One important aspect of this radicalism is the ability to bring together areas which are fragmented in modern everyday life: the individual and the emotional, the social and the rational. This aspect is tangible in the foundations of rock – beat and sound. The beat is the perceptible, physical pulse, associated with ancient drums, rocking, or the mother's heart beat. Yet it is also connected with big-city sounds, the machine rhythms of working life and other mechanical pulsating sounds. In this way, the beat mediates between the body's own and the de-humanizing rhythms inflicted by the modern environment. Against this background stand out solo voices, most often singing, the guitar and synth, which sometimes follow, sometimes depart from the basic pulse – to test their identities, so to speak, in relation to the collective foundation. You control the 'machine' instead of being controlled by it. The unique, 'dirty' sound of rock also links it to the body. Voice quality tends to be ordinary rather than trained, what counts is intensity rather than beauty, and the acoustic tones of the instruments are modified by overdrive and various kinds of added effects. The end result resembles the beat: on the one hand, sounds reminiscent of the cries of children and the strong voices of parents, on the other, artificial everyday sounds, reminiscent of everything from revving motors to pipping computers.

These basic elements are overlaid by the composition

structure and the song's words. To understand rock and pop music's attraction for young people, you must recognise the power of beat and sound, rhythm and force, the need for idols as transitional objects and musical environments as total experience. With its Afro-American roots, rock also represents a sensuality which sharply contrasts with European classical music and older generations' musical styles and tastes. But this sensuality responds to expressive needs during adolescence and carries associations with black subcultures, which may seem tempting alternatives in the search for identity.

However, the lyrics are not unimportant. Many rock lyrics from recent decades express primary processes in young people's life situation; they have represented a reconquest of the verbal language from corrupt adult institutions. Moreover, rock offers remarkable possibilities for collective communication and the sense of community: it draws people together. Rock continues to provide a platform for an artistic communication which is more accessible than other art forms to working-class youth who lack high cultural capital and who tend to be oriented towards the collective.[10]

Ove: What do you think you get out of playing?
Ola: Well, what I get out of it, is that it's fun and that I can tell people things I can't say in any other way . . . You can't just stand up in a square or something and say things straight out, like into the air.

The recent development of rock reflects in our three bands, at least to an extent, tendencies which could be called late modern. These musical expressions of late modernity encompass several levels.

Breadth and development of genres. On this point, it is difficult to generalise. As regards our groups, Chans responds 'horizontally' to cultural release, with a basic openness or lack of faithfulness that contains elements of both freedom – working on conflicts of the superego – and fear of conflicts within the band. The other two bands explore 'vertically' within a narrow niche of punk and hard rock filtered through local music traditions. Lam Gam could not hold the two styles together within the framework of the band, while OH gradually eased into another niche – synth rock. On the level of signs, this genre development involves 'modernising' on the part of OH, which is also more congruous with the group's scale of values. Their style develops in tandem with the 1980s in a way that goes beyond punk references while hard rock elements are modified. In Lam Gam, hard rock and vertical progression interests collide with a status quo in which punk prevails.

Frasse: I'd never, like imagine going to bed and listening to hard rock, 'cause it's really *terrible* . . . But, like when you're cleaning the house or are little pissed off, then I could very well put it on, yeah, really loud, so that it really bashes my head.

Jonna: No, not heavy metal, I don't want to play that. . . no, a little more soft . . . but we can't do that . . . we can't play so fierce [. . .]
Ove: What do you like?
Jonna: Yeah, we like 'most everything except van Halen [laughter], Whitesnake and that.

Punk and hard rock are combined primarily by an emphasis on *aggressive male acting-out*. Thus the two styles become attached to a tradition harking back to Elvis Presley and the Rolling Stones. At present, hard rock stands somewhat alone for the continuation of the aggressive element, or rather, one of the currents within hard rock, since it has not escaped being affected by either the synth or masculine role crises. For teenage boys, who still comprise a majority of the hard rock public, it provides the opportunity to act out one side of their egos through identifying themselves with a grotesquely exaggerated masculine sex role. In other kinds of hard rock, like the type played in Europe, another, softer and more androgynous, and possibly characteristic division is cultivated. Lam Gam are more strongly oriented towards traditional hard rock, whereas OH incline towards a more diffuse masculinity.

Punk and hard rock bands also come across strongly as *groups* and thereby offer appealing dreams of male togetherness and being subsumed in a collective ego – this is particularly true of punk bands. Within the framework of the collective, hard rock also leaves room for individual performance, especially on solo guitar and singing, and consequently responds in a more multi-dimensional way to audience expectations. To identify oneself with a guitar virtuoso may be seen as a longing for a strong ego control of the world. These tendencies are particularly illustrated in our bands by Bamse in OH and Sigge in Lam Gam.

Punk and hard rock have associations with *protest from below* directed towards both generation and class. In punk the protest is verbalised in an explicit way which has been exemplary for Lam Gam and OH, but hard-rock lyrics do not lack elements of protest. From a position of inferiority, broad 'macho' hard-rock lyrics strike out against a masculine ideal which is considered middle class, and 'rock cultism' may be interpreted as a response to terrorising rationality. Punk-oriented Swedish groups strive to assert the lyrics' content by singing them in Swedish; it is characteristic that after the group had split up, the hard rockers in Lam Gam began to work in English – in accord with the conventions of the genre. OH's fondness for English and Chans' vacillating are more difficult to explain. Apart from questions of formal competence in the language, English is easier to deal with in certain ways. It is rock's original

Sigge: Yeah, that was cool that was [Magnus Uggla's *I Don't Give A Shit*]. We played it at school so that the teachers really suffered . . . they came up and turned down the amplifier, they did, you know . . . just went up on stage and turned it down. The bloody creeps, sat there holding their ears . . . so dumb. Shit, they can keep out then if they don't want to listen.

Jonna: I thought it was pretty cool, everybody started to go in jeans in one piece and cotton trousers and that. And there was me in my tatty jeans [. . .], only me I, think, in the whole school. Long hair and torn jeans. Then you were feared in school.

Sigge: Yeah, but that's important too, if it's Swedish words it must be something that means something, like that has a meaning . . . but if it's English, then all you have to do is sing it out.

Conny: There was only one week left before this competition [. . .] So we said we'd write a song that's about like *Kickar* [Kicks] with Imperiet . . . So then we took the bass in that song, it's more or less lifted direct . . . and then, if you listen to the first melody in the song, it's also from *Kicks*. Then there's the middle 8, that's from another Imperiet song called *Vad tror du hon vill ha* [What Do You Think She Wants]. So there's two songs from Imperiet that we put together – with some of our own stuff too, of course. But 'cause we play it our own way, it becomes another song anyway . . .

language and provides a number of ready-made clichés, and the demands placed by listeners on English (as a second language) are not as great as those placed on Swedish. A foreign language offers possibilities for new lines of thinking through its phonetic associations and English links all groups with the truly great musicians in the genre. Another aspect of the protest is represented by the cultures' clothes styles, which emphasise the sub-proletarian and bohemian elements and which appear as a kind of modified suburban style, through which you denote your affiliation with an anti-school culture and disaffiliation from the 'squares' or 'wets'.

However, the most important expression of protest is aggressiveness in musical and physical performance, even though it is a restrained and ritualised protest that runs the risk of turning into gesture and cliché. Hard rock can be reduced to an amorphous mass of endless riffs, songs in a monotonous high register, technical displays on the guitar, speculative stage shows, hippy hairstyles and jeans or leather jackets, decorated with names of idols or symbols. However, being so bound to recognisable formulas, is also conducive to security and clarity, which perhaps are prerequisites for vertical progression – investigating the possibilities of the genre – for many youth just beginning to play.[11]

Expressions of heterogeneity in lyrics. In the wake of cultural release, one might theoretically expect a growing pressure to keep within the confines of already existing music, a strong intertextual awareness as well as a certain freedom in one's relations with these 'proto-texts' and tolerance towards the combining of disparate elements. In the present case, an analysis of the status of the three groups as amateur rock bands is complicated; it is difficult to distinguish the effects of insufficient ability from the impact of a late modern mentality. No such problem exists as regards intertextual awareness, which is obvious in all three bands; and what Lam Gam, for instance, loses in scope on this point, is made up in depth. More problematic is Lam Gam's tendency to assemble rather than compose songs. Not just individual sentences or melodies, but whole verses or choruses from various Imperiet or Ebba Grön songs constitute the easily recognisable raw material of several of Lam Gam's songs, so that the whole more or less becomes an unexpected combination – bricolage.[12] The distinction between covers and their own original creations is fluid. We are dealing here with a confluence of causes. In part, the composer/bricoleur Conny considers his needs for expression well channelled via his two models so that the impulse to demarcate ego boundaries is not so strong; in part, he has not developed the habit of writing songs. The latter may seem crucial, but it is worth noting that he stands by what he has done and seems not to have any scruples. OH's attitude to musical appropriation of this kind is definitely more rigid and has been so from the beginning. The punk do-it-yourself ideology, which seems to stem from Kurre, safeguards ego identity and makes authentic expressions incompatible with the use of pre-existing lyrics. This does not mean that OH refrain from borrowing but that it is more covert, possibly often unconscious, and hence more difficult to detect. Chans occupy a sort of middle position: their music contains many and varied style references, from children's songs to Bauhaus. Chans' attitude towards these references seems as offhand as Lam Gam's, but Chans work them into new contexts to a greater degree than do Lam Gam. *Teheran* contains open borrowings from Bauhaus and the Swedish band, Lustans Lakejer, but has also been influenced by the theme music from the film *Goldfinger* as well as by calypso, ska and oriental melodies. The song may have international references but the text is very characteristic of Chans.

Excepting OH, and with certain reservations made for unknown factors, the three bands exhibit a fairly palpable heterogeneity in – and with Chans, within – the songs. The raw materials come largely from the media, music, films, serials, in other words, from indirect experiences which acquire a mirroring function. Conny understands Lam Gam's *Solen* (The Sun) in this way; according to its creator, the song is inspired by a TV programme on Latin America, but unlike another Lam Gam song about Bergslunden, *The Sun* does not contain a single reference to historical time or geographical space.

Focus on beat and sound. To 'let rip', to be 'loud', to have a 'beat' are considered fundamental and crucial to music, especially by Lam Gam and the early OH. It seems reasonable to associate these demands for intensity with needs for regressive forms of experience, subjectivation and

Conny: No, but I think I express my own thing through Imperiet, or maybe most with the help of Ebba . . .

Ove: Why isn't that good [Blå Tåget, *Staten och kapitalet*/Blue Train, *The State and Capital*]?
Lollo: To us it's old music.
Jonna: There's no beat in it.
Lollo: There's no beat, that's it.
Jonna: It's that crappy Totte Wallin music and all that.

Finn: It feels good in the whole body, you're in it, in every note.
Ulf: It in the body?
Finn: Yeah, it does, you tremble and you hop and you dance and you think everything's just fucking great [pause]. And everything just blazing out, it's fantastic [. . .] You feel, yeah, just like you're in nirvana or something. – Especially when we play a gig . . . then we're just like one person playing everything . . . all the instruments.

Kurre: That it – the rock feeling disappears? It doesn't, Uffe, not with two guitars.

Ove: What do you feel now? Do you feel that the bass is your instrument? It's OK?
Jonna: No, it isn't OK, I'd rather play guitar. But it's just that it's a bit better than bass. All bass players are always in the background and the guitarists, they're always the ones that get famous, and it's always been that way if they don't have a singer with them. It's always him or the guitarist who gets famous but never the bass player.

empowerment. Overcharged sense organs, physical elation in conjunction with spontaneous movements or special sounds, the absorption of the ego in the group as in a womb and the subsequent related experience of expansion and omnipotence make rock an activity which has been related in an almost exemplary way to a narcissistic structure of needs.[13]

Historically, during the 1970s a white and a black reclamation can be discerned of the basic elements of rock by punk and disco's preliminary street stages. The white elements were dominant in our three bands – albeit less clearly in Chans – and are based on an energetic assertiveness and a high, raw and even sound, dominated by the guitar (the electric guitar signifies rock for many young people). These characteristics make it possible to describe punk as an expression of a kind of offensive narcissism. Contemporaneous rock and pop have been more heavily influenced by the disco culture's rhythmical machinery, with drums and bass fronting the sound. Here the musical monotony creates a static room whose walls make a projection screen for grandiose fantasies – a more defensive expression of narcissistic needs.[14]

Rock's narcissistic appeal can be understood as an inducement to symbolising the pre-linguistic mother-child interaction in presentative symbols.[15] The structure of narcissistic needs – the reference here is to narcissism 'from below' – is premised upon the subject's being 'preserved' in the arms of an omnipotent, archaic representative of the mother. This means that the interaction exists on a proto-symbolic level, deprived of discursive symbolising. However, it is accessible through presentative symbols, which to a certain degree exist between proto-symbols and discursive language and thus can acquire a bridging function: converting 'the speechless into speech' (Lorenzer). In short, by reviving the early stages of symbol organisation, rock 'awakens' the 'slumbering' proto-symbols and thereby becomes therapeutic.

For those who are actually beginning to play rock music, there may be the following chain reaction: from the contact established with deep structures, primarily through beat and sound, grows a secondary need to verbalise your experiences. In this connection, rock's collectiveness initially may be a hindrance – fears of exposing to others the gap between the 'real me' and the grandiose 'ideal me'. Beginning to produce your own lyrics is something of a breakthrough, a victory over fears of separation.[16] After this, the collective can more clearly become a resource, which under happy circumstances involves increased closeness to primary processes. When the censor weakens and the unconscious is released the lyrics become more about 'shared daydreams'.[17] The released 'semiotic' expressions can leave multifarious traces alongside the text's main line. In our three groups they take the form of more or less articulated screams and shouts, semantic as well as phonetic qualities in certain repetitions, specific use of antitheses, etc. OH's *Living for Weekends*, for example, relies almost exclusively on the diphthong /ai/ as an end rhyme and its lamenting sound would seem to represent both longing, collective feelings of impotence in the OH culture, and the songwriter Micke's subjective separation problems. Chans' use of nursery rhymes recalls childhood and criticises aspects of the adult world in a way that also implies separation problems. The nonsense in the chorus of Lam Gam's *The Sun* ('Na-na-na-na-na-') connotes a threatening mumble as well as a humming to infants and thereby captures not only a fundamental ambivalence in the Ark culture, but also a desire for narcissistic satisfaction which is underlined by the final verse's repeating that people can think and believe 'just as they want'. For those who remain in the role of listeners the same primitive elements in the music may help to hold together an ego which is experienced as so empty that it is threatened by fragmentation.[18]

Post-tonal harmonic structures. The tonal structures, in primarily major–minor tonalities, that have dominated Western art and popular music for several centuries, have built upon particular tensions which are resolved upon returning to the tonic. This has given the music a clear progression and goal-consciousness which, like aspects of the realistic novel, have been linked to the high bourgeois epoch's ego-strong individuals. Rock music often lacks this goal-consciousness: the final resolution is replaced by a fade-out, the boundaries between verse and chorus becoming more vague and the harmonic progression less tied to clear tonal relations. Together with other tendencies – the focus on beat and sound, the explosive encroachment of machine rhythms – this would seem to indicate a radical

Monday dark and I leave home at five/Tuesday why, the sergeant screams and I don't know if I'm wrong or right/And nothing seems to better, I have five more months to climb/But soon we'll be together, my friends and you and I/Living for weekends. Yes its then I'm flying high/ I'm living for weekends but the rest is an awful time/But soon we'll be together, my friends and I/and then it will be over and I don't know if I should cry.
        OH: *Living for Weekends*

transformation in the subjective structures of the kind that we have dwelt upon earlier, tending to result in individuals with less rigid ego boundaries.[19]

It is possible to trace certain inclinations toward less rigid tonal thinking in our three groups. Although a functional tonality dominates in their music, ordinary or plagal cadences are alternated with others – Aeolian, mixed Lydian, mediant, and in some cases, Dorian. As far as we can tell, it has seemed quite natural to deviate somewhat from the European and to do this without landing in the fold of the undesired avant-garde.

The advent of the synth. With the revolution in information technology, the possibilities of making music have also radically changed. Various synthesisers now enable you not only to create a virtually infinite variety of sounds but also to pre-programme whole concerts. The German group, Kraftwerk, are famous for placing doll models of the band members on the stage to perform pre-programmed concerts, which is one way of commenting ironically on late modern de-humanisation while at the same time making use of it. Clattering, pipping, hissing and other sounds have become common elements in modern rock music. A new kind of equality between the mechanical and the physical is being established, which seems to leave less and less space for the subject to manifest his or her presence. Against synthetic sounds that express an altered sense of time the bass drum's heartbeat ('discothump') stands increasingly alone.[20]

The three bands have both resisted and adapted to this development. Adaptation has meant that the synth has become part of the groups' equipment, even though the synths used are neither very advanced or expensive nor employed in altogether conventional ways. After OH acquired a synth, it became increasingly dominant under the singing; the other bands use it more for effects or background. However, in none of the bands has the incorporation of the synth been followed by the use of pre-programmed mechanical rhythms. To an extent, this might be due to lack of economic resources, but primarily it is a choice involving the defence of a craft, a resistance to machine-produced music which is particularly marked in the two groups coming from lower social backgrounds.

Lollo: They sit there with their computers and play, it's disgusting . . . it's not cool. [song starts up – Kraftwerk's *Radioaktiv*] That's enough! God!
Jonna: Turn it off, for Christ's sake! Turn it off.

SUBJECTIVE SOURCES

Here we shall consider the inner world: subjective structures, the motive forces of creativity – instinctive impulses,
defence mechanisms, activated infantile conflicts, etc.
Traditionally, adolescence represents a breakdown and
reformation of the psychic organisation which results in a
more or less stable adult character. Late modern life conditions are prone to complicate this consolidation of the ego:
objectively, adolescence is prolonged, while at the same
time, it is invaded by impatient dreams of an independent
life, which subjectively truncate it. The striving for adult
privileges goes in tandem with the desire for narcissistic
satisfaction, so that the boundaries of the adult world are
erased in a never ending search for identity. Instead of
being successive and phase-specific, conflicts are super-
imposed on each other in the 'new' adolescence. Liberation
from parental representatives, a secondary narcissistic
charging of the self, and entrance into heterosexual relations impinge upon each other.[21]

From our perspective, the defence mechanism called
regression is particularly interesting. Adolescence represents
certain tendencies to flee the discursive. Youth resuscitate
the language of the body and action, they do not 'talk properly', while at the same time, they develop new symbolising
needs and load their internal as well as external objects with
new meanings. Not least, media products acquire specific
use value in this way.

The older generation usually has some difficulty understanding why rock music must be played so loud that it can
be felt as physical vibrations. The use value in this instance
need not have anything to do with protest; the high volume
can be a way to try to cope with the feelings of emptiness
that arise as the self becomes depleted during the break-up
from childhood's parental figures. To the extent that a
narcissistic maternal introjection dominates over the representatives of the self among modern youth, these feelings
of unreality are reinforced. Stimulating or exciting the
senses creates the experience of existing surrounded by a
greater being; it makes it possible to regress to a symbiotic
stage in a controlled way. The culture industry's supply
of sensations often provides similar compensations. The
spectacular violence in videos or hard rock shows thus

Jonna: I don't know . . . I just
know I just get lost when I
listen to music.

Ulf: How does watching nasty
videos go together with
Christianity?
Bamse: I don't know, I've come
. . . I've always been, like blood-
thirsty before. Maybe I miss it
[laughter]. No, I don't know, I
really don't know why. It
stimulates me, you know, I
want to be frightened sometimes. I like to become . . . I
can't live such a dull life as it is
at home.

mediates not only between the ego's own aggressive impulses and an incomprehensible everyday violence – somewhat like the representatives of evil in folk tales.[22] It also contributes to the consolidation of the ego through an empowering which banishes emptiness. However, detachment is transitory, the hunger for objects craves new sensations and so consumption is intensified.

Perhaps it is possible to distinguish in more detail the musical levels responsible for different psychic tasks.[23] When Kurre talks about the experience of standing 'under coloured lamps' and 'pouring out' a song at 'high volume', it seems justifiable to relate it to the release of id impulses via the basic elements of rock. It is only when the music is played at full volume, when it has a heavily marked and regular basic beat and the correct timbre that Kurre – as both listener and guitarist – can release his inhibiting self-control and let his feelings loose. All the talk about music being 'feelings', the significance of 'power' and high volume, and talk about the panic that arises when it is the 'wrong' sound and when the sound environment becomes alien, refers to precisely this level. Volume, pulse or beat, and timbre are decipherable in infancy and they affect an adult in a strong but often barely conscious way (for example when department store music (Muzak) makes customers move more slowly and increases their desire to buy without their being aware of the music, or when the beat and sound of film music steers our emotional experience of the film without our noticing it). This is one of music's essential functions; the layers in texts and visual arts which have similar functions are often comprehended as musical – the phonetic qualities of words, voice timbre, poetic metre, regular rhythmic dance movements, etc.

Beyond this level are other musical parameters with different functions. Melodic, harmonic and rhythmic structures, for example, require more concentrated listening to be noticed and also provide more possibilities for experiencing an ego-oriented mastery than an id-oriented acting-out. The construction of a melody is a kind of challenge, a problem that the listener as well as the musician must solve. How should a melodic movement be continued and rounded off? The solution of such problems strengthens the ego's sense of control over the acoustic environment and expands the ego's boundaries. Coming up with good songs and working out successful solos or arrangements belong to this level (OH, for instance, became increasingly fascinated with 'accents'). In rock the group is of great importance here: on these levels an interaction occurs between the individualities of the singer and solo instrumentalist and the collective accompaniment. When musicians, listeners or dancers enter into this interplay it becomes a way of handling and processing modern individuation.[24] On a corresponding level, verbal (semantic) and visual (process) parameters occur: text content to be construed and examined, significant aspects of clothes and styles to be interpreted, etc.

There are also musical aspects which have more to do with demands from the superego to follow given rules. Fidelity to genre and the fact that songs have formal structures that fulfil the requirements of the genre satisfy such demands. In this a complex interplay between levels occurs. For example, rigid choice of genre can be a way to create a stable framework for the acting-out pursued on the beat and sound levels (Lam Gam), while flexible style experiments can indicate either a strong ego-oriented search or an intensive revision of the strict superego demands which provoke that type of stylistic upheaval (Chans). The psychic function of the music for groups and individuals should be understood in its concrete contexts. Our examples rather indicate possible contexts than offer a complete catalogue of music's psychic functions.

In the discourse on youth, the dominant tendency has been to simplify young people's complex relations to the culture industry by avoiding questions concerning the products' use value. The discussion focuses on producer and goods and views youth as the misled objects of a huge manipulative machine: kids as victims of commodity aesthetics. Against this, it may be argued that people in general choose their symbols more or less consciously but always meaningfully, and that the meanings of such symbols are realised in particular use situations.[25]

Consumption does not necessarily involve passive devotion. On the contrary, the act of symbol consumption should be seen as a confrontation between different subjective structures. The producer is represented to the receiver as discourse, and just as the former constructs an absentee receiver, the latter reconstructs an absentee producer in such a way that previous object relations are reactivated. This means *inter alia* that the act of consumption is always selective: only what can respond to the receiver's immediate needs is realised by the universe of discourse. Each 'reading' is unique. There is never a single 'text', but always a variety. There are, however, preferred readings which may be related to age, gender, class, etc. This explains why many youth do not perceive 'barbaric' values in a 'text' as problematic the way adults do – assuming the expressions are perceived at all. They have quite simply sought something else.[26]

The victim theory has difficulty explaining why some youth become skinheads or discofreaks while others play religious rock or listen to classical music. Neither does it help anyone understand why, despite all the resources, it is so difficult for the music industry to programme a hit. Worse still, the victim theory most probably contradicts its own expressed aim of fighting 'the negative effects of commercialism' by excluding the use value arguments which could point to putative alternatives. Young people use the products of the culture industry because they think they get something significant out of them. There are no grounds for assuming that they would willingly allow themselves to be deprived of a source of enjoyment. The established culture is not a credible alternative: it is neither as indiscriminately open nor as unique as its advocates would have you believe. If you persist in drawing boundaries between the 'good' established culture, 'our cultural inheritance' and the 'evil' mass culture, you simply push the young into the arms of the culture industry. It and it alone will then appear as immaculate, unsullied by incest.[27]

Relations between youth and the culture industry have to be perceived as a complex interplay in which one group of youth functions as an avant-garde or 'trend-setter', while the vast majority, the 'mainstream', are forced to keep to stylistic innovations after they are filtered through the media and labelled. Not all young people are unconventional and independent seekers in the late modern universe. Neither do they all achieve a symbol production of their own which transcends mundane models for their personal appearance and domestic environment. Individual differences aside, our three rock groups represent an avant-garde which has been infiltrated by commercial impulses, but which on the whole makes fairly free and (self)-conscious use of the world of signs.[28] Kurre's motive for playing rock, for example, was originally determined by his bonds to the introjected 'border-crossing' father in combination with problems with school; his choice of Strummer and Co as idols reflected a desire for liberation and redress. There are, of course, a number of other circumstances which can steer youth towards rock: Bamse, Kurre's antagonist in OH, comes to mind here.

Bamse's motives for getting involved in rock recall Kurre's: an Amadeus complex at bottom, the desire to be seen by his father as Someone, a relationship with his father loaded with guilt feelings and need for reparation, reinforced by poor school performance. However, this familiar pattern of conflict also contains differences. Kurre has grown up in a matriarchal family with two caring parents. These differences seem to have led to different oedipal phases and different male roles. Kurre seeks a part in the patriarchal structure through identification with the 'border-crossing' idealized father; Bamse, through attempting to identify with a rigid, potentially castrating and repudiating father in a likewise otherwise strongly female-dominated environment. As far as we can tell, Bamse's efforts have been doomed to failure and have led to superego conflicts in his teenage years, manifested in macho tendencies, minor criminality and aggressive behaviour. The propensity for confrontation may be taken as a struggle for psychic survival – striving for elementary experiences of self-reality. With Bamse, the conflicts have gradually diminished through the influence of alternative father figures, girl friends, the church youth and not least, OH. Bamse's interest in rock and his choice of idols are also different from Kurre's. Bamse's interest and choices are centred around the guitar's potential symbolically to control the world at large and its immediate expressiveness, instrumental virtuosos and hard-rock groups. Corresponding needs in Kurre are channelled through the group rather than an instrument. This indicates a verbal and social ability that Bamse lacks, the foundations for which were presumably laid in close interaction with his mother.

Ulf: If you think of your dad now, what do you feel for him?
Bamse: That he was wonderful [pause]. But I didn't think so then. I've wished for him to be dead many times [. . .] But in '80 when he got sick [. . .], I closed my hands in prayer then and said, Dear God, if you make dad get well – then you know, you promise a lot of things – like then, I'll behave at home, I'll be better in school, yeah, I'll be a good Christian, I said. And . . . I'll really show my dad who I am, I said. My dad got better, but I didn't change [. . .] In school I was truly brilliant [. . .] Didn't give a shit about anything, except broads and mopeds. [. . .] Hell, if my dad had died then, in '80, then he'd never have got . . . then he'd have got a completely negative picture of my development. He'd never have seen how I'd develop. And I really wanted him to. Because dad said, you're an asshole, you'll never be good for anything . . .

Bamse: I always got it from both of them. I've been scared of my dad [. . .] He had a temper, just like me. I want to change, get away.
Ulf: [. . .] Why don't you want to be alone?
Bamse: No, it's no good. Because I think being alone is not strong.

Bamse: [. . .] It's hard to play, it's competitive. He's so good, I want to be better. [. . .] It's because I've never been able to do anything else. [. . .] But [with] music I can show what I know, I can identify myself – as a guitar, you might say.

EXCURSUS: ADOLESCENCE AS A SECOND BIRTH

Can late modern adolescence be seen as a subject's second birth or second entry into language? It has become so much more difficult to become an adult. Again, it is a matter of coming to terms with a capricious higher authority that sometimes stimulates subjectivity, sometimes dampens it. Society pays homage to youth as myth while at the same time it marginalises real young people; it prolongs youth but simultaneously fills it with knowledge about and pictures of adult contradictions which reach far down into childhood. The dissolution of tradition together with technocratisation expose the subject to pressures of reality which invade the finest pores and render the preservation of the self into a question of survival.[29]

In the adolescent struggles with identity, the gang fills the function of a cocoon which recreates or revives memories of early mother–child symbiosis and protects against the pressures of the system. The gang is also a medium for forays into the adult world that can acquire experimental and sometimes avant-garde qualities. While adults' privileges are tempting, their ways of life seem repugnant, lacking in subjectifying and empowering elements to the degree that this lacuna can seem lethal to subjectivity. In any case, 'father's law' involves considerable costs in the form of a choice between 'Svensson' isolation (subservience to an alien father) and being an outcast (the father's repudiation of the son), a restriction of the open 'now' identity and consequently a narcissistic violation. In short, one aspect of adulthood encompasses a reactivated compulsion to abandon the breast-mother for good and to consummate 'weaning' in order to be able to function in a patriarchal structure.

Late modern life conditions foster a tendency towards increased resistance on the part of the subject to this consummation. The maternal object is preserved as a resource in the unconscious, which is used for symbolic praxis, and artistic creativity. Making rock music mediates between the maternal and the paternal, the wild and the civilised, the physical–semiotic and the linguistic–discursive. This mediation can be understood in a Kristevan way as the maternal questioning the name-giving paternal, which in its turn socialises the maternal. Learning to play rock repeats the language-learning process that follows the first phase of the unification of mother and child – but with a difference. If the motive force of verbal language learning is the need to control the separation from the mother by symbolising it, modern youth seemingly learn to master rock's presentative symbols as a response to societal demands to complete that separation once and for all. This, in turn, suggests Kleinian reparation theories: rock music becomes a work of mourning sparing object representatives that would otherwise be devastated.

However, rock, as a pocket of resistance for the maternal, lives dangerously. Greater mastery of rock's discourse and its possibilities of capturing a position in the field also increases the probability of the symbols being transformed into accessible but empty signs and of commodity qualities taking over. This means that young people who play rock run the risk of becoming captives in a system structure, hostages of the father. But the outcome is by no means certain; it will be determined by the geographical, social and historical context.

LEARNING PROCESSES IN MAKING ROCK MUSIC

One aspect of our three groups' quests and creative efforts concerns *learning processes* that are very different from the pedagogical activities of school. Playing music develops and changes individual and collective identities and socialises individuals in particular kinds of knowledge and skills, norms and social fields, lifestyles and modes of expression.[1]

Socialisation is often thought of as upbringing: parents and teachers within a fixed institutional framework (the family and the school) teach knowledge and rules to children who are to become well-adjusted citizens. However, this view is far too narrow and superficial. We are continually being socialised by daily life experience, not least in adult working and family life, and thus socialisation is not limited either to youth or to institutions. Moreover, socialisation is not a passive, pliant labelling process. It is a process whereby we encounter new external impulses and transform them into new subjective structures – bodily and mental.[2]

In our bands' 'micro-cultures' new types of interaction are developed out of outer and inner 'preconditions' through new learning processes. These preconditions are decisive, for the processes are incomprehensible without their contexts.[3] In the present case, learning processes take place in the areas of tension between different fields of action (spheres) and the subjective structure of needs described in the previous section.

Learning processes are always both *individual* and *collective*. Learning occurs in individuals and these individuals are involved in various forms of learning groups, but there are differences of degree. Sometimes people are part of social groups (such as family, school class or peer group) learning things together in shared activities. Sometimes learning is more individualised, as when you are reading a book alone.

Learning processes may be *obligatory* or *voluntary* (see the previous section on leisure). To be initiated, voluntary processes presume individual choice. Learning processes can also be *institutionalised (formalised)* or *spontaneous (informal)*. In school, learning is highly institutionalised and formalised. To be sure, because of their social rules, gangs of mates hardly achieve total freedom, but they lack formally sanctioned hierarchies and their use of time is not as strictly regulated as it is in school. There are status hierarchies within and between gangs, but they are more fluid and lack written and authorised regulations.

In addition, learning processes may be *closed* or *open*. Those in school are most often goal-oriented – closed, with already given aims, curricula and study plans. The pupils, of course, do not know the details of the goals, or answers, in advance (otherwise there would be no learning), but they know or believe that someone – the teachers, the head-teacher or the school board – has established plans and aims for their instruction. What knowledge and competence are to be acquired is well-defined. In peer-group learning, however, no actor usually believes such fixed goals exist; it is an open learning.

In summary, learning processes in peer groups' spontaneous activities (including playing music) are *different* in several respects. They are voluntary, informal and open where school normally builds on enforcement, institutionalisation and goal-orientation.[4] The authors believe that these differences apply to many self-selected youth cultural activities and to most peer groups' modes of living. As has already been pointed out, this means that having a common project at all is special, and in particular, playing rock music provides different possibilities from other shared activities. Learning processes in our three groups thus stand as examples without any claims to be general.

Ove: Did you learn [how to play] here at the Ark?
Jonna: Yeah, but I didn't learn anything.
Lollo: Nah, they're worthless, the teachers.
Jonna: It was after we started up the band that I started to learn anything. Before, it was about one song a year.

LEARNING TYPES

When one of the bands meets together to compose a new song, rehearse or perform, a great deal happens all at once. When a new song is to be put together, for example, all the musicians must find and memorise their parts, and get an idea of the progression of the song and what the others do.

Conny: Yeah, first you get to know a helluva lot of people when you play in a band, and you learn a helluva lot, you know ... Not just how you set up an amp – and lots of people don't know that – but you learn everything, like you learn other instruments even though you don't play them ... you just listen to them ... learn how they work, what you do with a PA system, electricity and technology ... you learn that you have to put together and take apart all the stuff at gigs ... you know, things like lights too and how you connect the amp to the PA system and all that ... But most of all, you meet masses of new people ... I think you really get together over music. Masses of people play music in town who you wouldn't probably meet unless you played yourself ... Like every new place you play in, you get to know the people in a single night ... And then when you meet them again somewhere, you recognise each other and talk ... And you talk about music the whole time, you listen to each other and learn from each other. That's bloody important.

Kurre: But it's more fun to play that type of music – it's more of a challenge, right? Those accents and the rest – like one, two, three, four, one, and then the accent on two ... It's got more complicated but it's a lot more fun – you can go into the song more and fiddle with it and change.

Finn: [My singing] has got a lot better [...], much more sure now. Like when we play a song or a chord, a verse, I know exactly what chord will come after, so I'm right on it [...] The singing has got stronger too; I think I can like build it up from below more than I could before. But I've still got a lot to learn [...] We've gone over and over and over these songs till you're like up to here by the time you bike home, but it's paid off.

The sound equipment has to function, cords and flexes perhaps repaired. Study circle attendance lists have to be filled in and the latest musical, local, or international news discussed. Someone comes up with new song ideas and must express them so that the others understand. Someone else stubbornly practises a difficult passage several times on his or her instrument. Timbres and parts for the song, guitars and synth must be worked out. Perhaps someone refers to other songs familiar to the band in order to explain how something should be done. They all borrow ideas from other bands, but are often anxious not to copy; they want to be original as well. Conflicts may arise between different musical tastes within the group, but these are conflicts to which everyone seeks acceptable solutions, so that everyone participates, no one is ignored and the band retains its distinctive character. All this occurs through lively discussions in which the decision-making structure is constantly tested, and through which a strong communal feeling is attained, expressed in a shared euphoria when the song comes together for the first time: 'It's us who did that!' Throughout this work each band member gradually begins to realise his or her previously unforeseen possibilities and limits and learns to adjust his or her ideals by confronting both the others in the group and an imagined audience. In both ephemeral innovations and scheduled solos, the individuals finally have opportunities for more or less spontaneous and unhampered acting-out, supported by the group's fascinated engagement: 'Give it everything, let it rip!'

At least as much happens in the other situations, for instance, in the preparations for and performance in a concert, when relations with the audience also play a part. We shall now try to distinguish and develop different types or levels of learning, in light of what they are aimed at and what skills are attained.

LEARNING IN THE EXTERNAL WORLD

Certain aspects of learning are directed from the individuals and groups outwards toward a world which is taken as given: objective life conditions – on the one hand, nature, on the other, societal institutions that are experienced as a given 'second' nature.

Traditionally, school pedagogics focus on this type of learning and it is an important element in the three groups. In part it concerns music-making itself – handling instruments for example; in part it applies to activities around music, from knowledge of electronics to dealing with study circle economy.

This first type of learning has three subtypes:

Practical competence, directed towards things in the material world. The band members learn technical skills: mastering their instruments, handling sound technology, etc. One important part of practical competence has to do with the creation of a physical space around the group (rehearsal quarters, the stage). The practical handling of things in the physical world is, of course, at the same time an 'inner' ability, anchored in one's own body's psychophysical skills. But things remain external (that they also can be symbolically or expressively charged through activities is referred to in the dimensions given below).

For OH, striving to set their stamp on the music market, the desire for musical competence is significantly greater than it is for Chans, to whom music is play which, aristocratically, must not be turned into work. Chans also seem less interested in physical work with their rehearsal quarters: there is an enormous difference between their messy and impractical cottage and OH's neat and tidy 'home'. To those who want to turn physical labour into a professional identity, practical skills are more highly valued and more self-evident.

There is also a traditional 'male' element in the practical aspect of rock-playing. Electronics, guitar and drumming techniques are considered male specialties. The type of technology involved in rock-playing links it to other traditionally male areas of interest (sports, motor vehicles, computers, etc.), but is somewhat distant from the areas traditionally occupied by young girls. The girls in Chans care less for the instruments and the 'equipment' than do the boys. This is a result of the fact that male gender socialisation places men closer to the dominant instrumental attitudes to external nature prevalent in our culture.[5]

This practical learning tends to become goal-oriented or instrumental, to relate to things through power and manipulation in a rigid subject-object relationship.[6] However, this instrumentality is not unavoidable. By means of

Håkan: I think it's cool, all the gear, at least a bit [...] I think music gear – like there's something special with it. Amps, boxes and that [...] Specially the guitar [...] To test different instruments, that's really cool.

Gösta: And during the recording sessions, we've learned that we should try to do things a little more exactly [...] If you're going to make a record, for instance, you need to know everything and exactly how everything should go.

Ola: Yeah, I started a fan club. [...] A fun thing, thought it was cool, so I sat down and started writing membership cards and then we went round and chivvied everyone to become a member, so in the end I got about 70 members.

Finn: For instance, Bobo takes care of selling the band. That's like his task. So if we get to do a recording, or if Bobo gets wind of a gig, and he [...] follows it up, then the whole gig's Bobo's. He has to keep up the contacts, inform us about everything. And if it's me who comes up with something, then I do the same. So we manage gigs personally, like make them into a personal thing.

Johan: Was it you who worked with the fan club?

Karl: Yeah, it was Håkan and me who put together the paper. [...] We've got 30 members now. But at its peak, we had 120 members.[....]

Johan: But how could you get so many people? Were they relatives?

Gustav: Yeah, it's relatives, mainly.

Olof: I've a lot of contact with [Karl] through We Youth [educational association] too [....] I'm only treasurer there, and he's in it. He *is* Chans, like [...]

Johan: You take care of the reports for the study circle and that?

Olof: Yeah, I make it up [laughter]. [...] What I do is

see to it the reports agree more or less with what we do, sort of.

Ove: Can you say a little more about your message, what it is you want to get across?

Conny: It's basically in the words I've already done, it's society that's going to hell [. . .] It's fucking well not Lollo's fault that he's like he is [. . .] And this division, rich-poor, that's society too, rules and laws that are fucking wrong . . . Yeah, that's mainly what I can write about, I think.

Ove: How've you come to these insights into society?

Conny: Well, it's because of the music I've come in contact with.

Ove: Obviously, you've been listening to music critical of society, music by Imperiet and Ebba . . .

Conny: Yeah, but it like began, really, if you just look at that part, it began with [Magnus] Uggla [. . .] What I started to think about then, think about in the same way like, were things like society. Like 'Can it be so awful, is everything always so crazy?' School and everything, yeah, and then I thought, 'What do I like think myself,' like 'Shit, it's all so bloody bad.' I was so young, I don't know, yeah, but so I began to think. [. . .] Wasn't long ago, around '80–'81 or so. But I started to buy a few records. And like there was always someone who opened a door for me, and so I started to think about that too and suddenly, yeah, suddenly I began to see there was something else too.

Bamse: We are – everybody in the group is a bit of a peace – you know, those activists, right? I wasn't so much before, but become one, yeah? I was inspired . . . began to think a lot how it'd be if we had peace, what you could do together. [. . .] So we've started to do a lot of songs and that now. And we can play gigs and communicate it.

playfulness and communicative interest, and in combination with the other learning types, practical learning can also assume a different, more 'open' basic character.

Practical learning in gangs differs from more formalised learning processes because of its context – its relations to other learning types and to the life situation of the young. Rock-playing is a self-selected activity within the framework of the peer group's social network; this increases motivation and satisfaction at the same time as skills are 'legitimised' by their status in musical life and among other mates. (In school, a hierarchical status system legitimises the skills taught there, but also reduces motivation.) Lam Gam express this well when they relate how learning was intensified – or even first became possible – in their peer group.

Administrative abilities, directed towards surrounding institutions. This concerns learning to handle society's agencies (those relating to the state and the market) by means of power and/or money. Societal institutions are seen and treated here in terms of systems, as rigid, impersonal structures – as 'second nature'. These institutions tend to turn administrative learning into strategic action, in which you manipulate rules in order to achieve self-serving goals.

In this way band members handle their local radio, societies and associations, manage their economy and develop methods for marketing. Webs of strategic actions are woven around the bands, contacts are made with the media before gigs in order to attract attention to demo tapes or records.

There are, however, marked class variations. As a middle-class group, Chans has a significant advantage in administrative capabilities. They incline towards the private sector, but had they been more oriented towards the sphere of cultural capital and education, voluntary associations and/or public, state-supported cultural life would likely have been more accessible.

It is not mandatory that administrative learning be strategic. It is intimately connected with social learning processes (which we will return to later) that can give it a less manipulative and more communicative direction; but this also depends on how the surrounding institutions relate to young people. When the institutions are heavily influenced by system demands, they elicit single-minded, goal-rational responses. If, for example, societies and associations are strictly and impersonally formalised, youth are tempted or forced into a manipulative stance. This helps explain our groups' cunning methods of marketing themselves or making off with study circle subsidies.

Knowledge of nature and society. This ever-present aspect involves acquiring conscious, cognitive concepts for things – knowledge rather than skill. To learn concepts for guitar-playing or social organisations may very differ from being able to deal practically with the electric guitar or administratively with study circles.

Working with music provides knowledge of the world through intensive listening to and writing of lyrics. Several of the bands' songs deal with ethical or social problems. The bands develop a conceptual understanding of the world, as well as a more specialised knowledge about artists and music styles – that is, knowledge of the narrower field of music. In their shared activities, they form concepts for various 'external' relationships having to do with the world-at-large, knowledge which is usable also outside the confines of the group.

However, this knowledge can also assume an instrumental character and become congealed into a sort of reified factual expertise. Chans' knowledge of pieces of music and artists sometimes appears to function in this way: it seems to be desirable to parade as much detailed knowledge as possible without relating it to other experience.

On the other hand, making music is designed precisely to develop the search for knowledge in a more communicative way. Music groups themselves place great weight on communicating different kinds of knowledge to the public (as regards our bands, this is particularly true for Lam Gam and OH, for Chans, only during their early punk-influenced period). This communication overlaps the expression of the bands' or their members' own feelings – an aspect to which we will return.

LEARNING IN THE SHARED WORLD

Not all learning processes, however, are directed towards something external. Certain aspects of learning presume

Finn: Sometimes I get mad at the world, get despairing about it. It's a shitty world we live in. [...] A few days ago I read in the paper that Ronald Reagan might get the peace prize from Nobel. Just that makes you want to puke. Things like that just put me right off. I want to come out with a message, that, that's about how in the hell can such idiots, like manipulate me just ... however they like.

Sigge: Sure you're affected ... I try to be as good as them playing on the records.
Ove: Do you practise at home ... what do you do then?
Sigge: No, but I sit at home and try to come up with new songs, and sometimes I sit and play along with records ... really cool that.

Jonna: The music you played, you've got to like that music too ... that's bloody true. But ... that music I could listen to here at the Ark, yeah, Ebba Grön and that ... but then, when I came home, I always put on Maiden or something like that.
Ove: So at home you listened to hard rock?
Jonna: Yeah, I've always listened to it [...] First, in the beginning, you thought it was cool hard rock, but then, when you started to play yourself and started to understand music, you didn't only listen to how cool or tough it sounded but how they played and that. Like him ... or like the new song that starts with the bass ... I mean, it takes a lot from hard rock ... It's him in Maiden, he began with things like that sometimes ... We've got a lot from him.

Conny: What in the hell should we do – there was only one week left till the contest. So then Ola said: 'We gotta write a song,' right in the middle of a practice. OK then, we said we'd write a song that's a bit like Imperiet's *Kickar* (The Kicks). So we took the bass line from that song – it's almost lifted direct – and then if you listen to the first melody in the song, it's also from Kicks, then the middle 8's from another Imperiet song called *Vad tror du hon vill ha* (What Do You Think She Wants) ... So we put two songs from Imperiet together, with something of our own, of course. But because we play it our own way, it becomes a totally different song anyway – we don't sound at all like Imperiet, thank God. [...] I think I express my own thing through Imperiet, or maybe most with Ebba ...

Kurre: We must produce our own material that *we* can play, that no one else can play. Not go after somebody else and try to be just as good as them, because that already exists, they can do it, and we'll be just a bloody bad copy of it.

Ulf: But when you listen [to other groups] then, what do you get out of it? [...]
Micke: I try to compare it a bit with our group, what they're doing that's so good.

Gustav: Well, we don't exactly imitate, we don't do that. We get inspired. [...]
Gösta: We don't *take*, but when we're working with something, we maybe get some inspiration from other bands.

Frasse: We're not going to get into any particular genre; I think then you can get stuck after a while. It's better to experiment, do a bit of everything. I think that's cool. [...] At the same time, you don't, like stay in one place and become *totally* original just because you're *supposed* to.

Ove: Do you think you'll fall out with them [Sigge and Seppo] if you quit?
Jonna: No, I don't think so, but I'd say what I think in any case. I think it's so bloody off. If Seppo quits, then he's just used us – that's what I think. Like he's just learned to play the drums, he's not meant to quit then. We've worked fucking

another relationship to what one learns, an inter-subjective relation, in which what is investigated is something that must be or become both external and internal, shared by the learners themselves, in order to exist at all. This is the genuinely social world.

The social, 'shared' processes have two sides. In part, they go on between and among individuals in groups, in part, they are directed outward, towards the audience and the surroundings. In both cases, it is difficult to distinguish exactly those processes emanating from music-making itself from those based on general interaction in and around the groups. However, we shall focus on a third division, based on the object of these learning processes. Its first aspect could be called cultural; its second and third together form the truly social aspects of the intersubjectively shared world.

Cultural skills, aimed at the communicative symbol systems used for the interaction of individuals.[7] Young people encounter a number of symbols, texts, genres and styles, all of which presume inter-subjective validity in order to function. Linguistic symbols can only work if they are at once external and internal – in other words, if they are valid in some social sphere and within the individuals. Every cultural, symbolic communication assumes a language system valid both for (some) others and for oneself. Symbols must have significance equally for an interpretative community and for the individuals communicating within it.

Naturally, you can learn a musical style in a purely instrumental/practical way (corresponding to the learning dimension 'practical competence' above), but in order to understand and correctly manage it as a style (genre, meaningful discourse, etc.), you must gain the competence to interpret meaning and significance, which requires that you 'enter into' the cultural system, participate in it and anchor it in your own experience. From the entire cultural stock of different language systems (styles, forms of expression, etc.), language is internalised in the individual (and the group). But at the same time, this never occurs as passive copying, as a 'simple reproduction'. It always requires a productive agency, in which language itself becomes transformed in an 'expanded reproduction'. Language is recreated and renewed by the individuals in the groups on the basis of both objective and subjective conditions (demands and resources).[8] (The way this takes place has already been indicated in the previous section on the social sources of creativity.)

To this type of learning belong all the bricolage techniques by which the bands create new meaning through placing different symbolic elements in new relations with each other. The bands choose and appropriate various musical genres and playing styles. The different genres prescribe certain ways of expression (hard rock, for example, requires particular types of guitar and bass riffs, ways of singing, guitar solos, etc.). By absorbing elements of other genres in their music, bands create openings for their own experiences – for impulses and expressions rooted in their unique objective and subjective life situations. Our three groups' (especially Chans') wild patchwork of different stylistic fragments may be seen as articulating such a need. It also expresses the late modern tendency of the cultural sphere increasingly to place symbols and styles at the disposal of those wishing to communicate experience.

Music-making is not consistent or homogeneous. It encompasses a wide spectrum of symbolic forms: music, texts, speech, visual expressions in clothes, hairstyles, attributes and gestures, etc. This level is extremely complex, especially since several of these symbolic systems are particularly rich and often lack the 'discursivity' of written verbal language (see previous section). Like visual expression, music is multi-layered and not organised by a series of discrete, meaningful terms – other than to a limited extent when the music contains obvious signals of various kinds, such as melodic motifs which refer directly to other music or to extra-musical sounds.

This multifariousness makes the appropriation of these particular symbolic systems especially complicated and gives them an important expressive potential for young people. However, it also causes problems for a reconstructive analysis, which mainly uses the medium of the written word. All language experiences cannot be immediately verbalised. Given a little distance, the band members may later be able to formulate in words why they chose certain genres and not others.

Normative capabilities, aimed at rules for social interaction. Included here are learning to deal with conflicts and to cooperate. Like symbolic systems, the norm systems

hard with him [. . .] We've bloody backed him all the way. So I don't think he should quit.

Ola: We like said last year, like we thought Seppo was fucking awful, completely tactless, but like we never said anything to him, it was kept secret from him what we thought. I don't know, maybe they talk just as much shit about me too.

Kurre: I've learned to socialise with other people in different ways. I've learned to adapt . . . to other situations than school and all that. I've learned . . . like there's another life. [. . .] In school you're more or less forced to learn. But we're not. We have fun, we learn something that we think's fun. In school, it doesn't need to be fun . . . You learn an incredible lot. You get more mates as well. You learn to get to know them, that's also important. You learn to do things with your own body, like you know that you're good at something, right? Which gets you self-confidence and that. You get a big mouth too. [. . .] And you get mentally stronger when you're a G like we are.

Finn: What you learn . . . .well, I think you learn, like Kurre said, to adapt – and develop yourself too. You get new ideas, exactly what new ideas you get is hard to say, but you get . . . you get more sensitive, like to good music. [. . .] If anything happens, then you're a group together. We stand together.

Ulf: This increasing messiness you talk about, what do you think that's all about?
Micke: That we've become too . . . like we demand too much of each other. [. . .] We get all up tight about getting ahead and . . .

Håkan: [Apropos criticism from certain quarters against the band's vocalist]: It feels a bit wrong, because if one person goes, you can't trust the others either, in a way. So there's a bit of threat there, a little.

Ove: Why do you play rock music in a band? Why is it important to you?

Seppo: What's important, I don't know . . . I suppose it's having fun . . . fun together and doing things together, like, that's cool too . . . that you get to build up something together . . . to play, like.

Kurre: Togetherness, solidarity [G], is most important.

Bobo: You only get somewhere by keeping together.

Finn: I think that when we stand on stage, which we've done twice, yeah? on a real stage, then you feel more togetherness, I think you feel the G more then.

Bobo: Mmm, then you feel that you've done something together or you're doing something together.

Kurre: To do something that, that you do with your . . . yeah, how can I put it, your absolutely best mates, that you can live on, what a dream! And you know we're not, like we don't play the buddies game – we're brothers, like Bamse wrote in his farewell note. [. . .] I would say that one reason it's this way is the Barn – that's a big part of it.

Ulf: You mean bringing you together?

Kurre: Yeah. The Barn's always been there for us, backed us.

Håkan: We've been together since we were in the first class, like nursery, we've known each other. And like we've built this up together, built up a special personality or whatever it is. [. . .] You can never make a fool of yourself, no . . . [. . .] No, I've never experienced getting embarrassed or anything. Yeah, if I've done something really dumb or something, but not for little things. You laugh that off [laughter].

Ola: Nah, I can't sing, but I sing anyway.

Ola: No, Conny – he writes so you don't know what he's on about . . . He writes like about

must be 'shared' – inner and outer, self and others – to function and be valid. Rules for behaviour which only one person recognises or which are not internalised by individuals do not constitute real norms for social relations.

In the three groups several different normative learning processes were observed at work. Learning often occurs when the youths' own experiences are related to the social group through empathy with others: both Håkan in Chans and Ola in Lam Gam can reason from another position, a point of view other than their own. Attitudes that from a strictly egotistical point of view were initially acceptable later seem wrong and a need for authoritative inter-subjective norms arises.[9] This sort of learning also interacts with the fear of conflict and separation which exists in the gangs.

Our groups have a number of different social conflicts to cope with. Outside interests must be weighed and measured against each other and against the individuals' own needs. Disputes also arise around the more or less recognised leadership which, at least temporarily, exists in the groups. Conflicts can range around questions of competence as well as around individual deviations from the group's common modes of living. All these conflicts call forth attempts at solutions; for example, discussions (when each band member tries to understand the other's motives and to arrive at compromises that satisfy all parties), denial (avoiding the problematic area, trying to suppress the issue), or more formalised procedures (for instance, voting or casting lots). Group cooperation and mutual support are developed in these processes. As a result, the group's set of specific norms emerges: to award high priority to the band, to be in time for rehearsals and concerts, socialise in their free time, give each other practical assistance, commit time and resources to music, keep together, avoid having a single leader, manage on their own as much as possible and/or be autonomous. In addition there are particular norms in each group: OH wants to be progressive, to 'be themselves' and not be 'macho', for example, while Chans tries to be funny and original, and to balance enjoyment with school and career.

Two late modern aspects of this normative learning are that it is so open, and that it occurs to such a high degree in the peer groups' self-chosen and self-governed context. The young have – and are permitted – to experiment and find a structure of norms valid for them, which also to a high degree becomes explicit and reflected; in other words, they can discuss their own moral precepts with each other and with outsiders.

Relationship skills, directed primarily towards the group community. In music groups, there is an extremely strong feeling for what the melding of the group's individuals involves. This has to do with an ability which does not principally entail rights and wrongs but rather the ability to associate and engage with other individuals. For such relations and groups to arise and continue, relationships must be both internal and external, made by both parties. In this sense, this level is also truly 'shared'. Relationship skills are practised throughout your life and change character in different life phases. Boys and girls develop these skills differently in different social strata and cultural circles.[10]

We have observed in our groups a complicated interplay of various types of relationship and affiliation. Not least important are relations with parents (affiliation with the family), with single individuals (friends), and with the peer group as a collective (gang membership, 'G'). These three develop in a complicated interaction. Thus, group community may be seen as a means to separate from original family bonds, while such solidarity in its turn may be threatened by new and 'too strong' friendships or emotional ties (for example, with someone not belonging to the gang). However, group solidarity can also contain and reinforce pair relationships.

Today, cultivating mutual relationships is extremely important, albeit difficult. Early conditions for growing up establish strong needs for group affiliation and fears of separation. It is not difficult to see how the members of the three groups grapple with such fears.[11]

LEARNING IN THE INNER WORLD

Learning is more than the sum of the two aspects discussed above. Certain learning processes have mainly to do with the inner world, to which each person has unique access. People may show their feelings, needs and motive forces to others through various kinds of language and behaviour,

things he believes . . . he flips out when he writes lyrics . . . He writes about like he's some sort of Communist who's so poor and all . . . Himself, he lives in a house – and has it good, and he writes that we're so poor and can't cope and that . . . I think it's a load of crap when he writes about politics and that . . . Yeah, it puts me right off . . . No, I don't want to sing that shit. I think I have it pretty good compared with other people.

Conny: You might say that outwardly I could choose between being half rich over there and poor down here, in a way. Inside myself I know it's here I want to be . . . I like it here.

Finn: There's one thing I haven't dared say before. It's still a bit painful. [. . .] Sometimes, when I've been at home, when I haven't thought there was anybody else home . . .
Micke: Stood in front of the mirror.
Finn: Stood in front of the mirror. Taken a mike and stood in front of the mirror and seen how I look. [. . .]
Kurre: But sure, you want to see yourself – you can never do that up on a stage, up there you don't know what you look like. Or in the Barn, you can't ever see yourself.
Micke: Put up a wall-to-wall mirror in the Barn.

Björn: I started to play to get in contact with – mostly with girls . . . I wanted to be noticed and I wasn't: I thought I was little and boring. But then . . . Now most people know who I am. And that's cool. So now it's not *the* reason why I play but it was why I started. I wanted attention! I've always tried to get as much attention as possible. [laughter] And that's been good. You meet a lot of people when you're out playing. [. . .]
Johan: Do you still feel the need to be noticed?

Björn: Yeah, but it's not so strong any more. Now I feel that I can get it outside. Now it's that yearning to be on the stage, that's still as strong as it was. When there's lots of people [. . .] and you go up on stage – that's fantastic!

Jonna: They get off on it when you play. You automatically become a better person. 'Do you play football?' they say to somebody, 'Yeah, I play football.' – 'What a bloody turd,' they think. 'Do you play in a band?' 'What a cool guy' – that's how a lot of people think.

Ove: So you rise in status when you play in a band?
Jonna: Definitely, you're cooler than almost anything else.

Ove: What's so much fun about playing? Why do you do it?
Lollo: Because it's so great . . . yeah, it's a lot better than just hanging out. It's ballsy. To feel that, like . . . Yeah, it's fun, for yourself like, just to feel that you create something . . . Then it's cool with the whole band, like we're a collective . . . you feel that you're doing something together and that you're doing something yourself and that you're doing something good.

Finn: It's cool to work with something not everybody else works with. It's – OK, I'm exaggerating again . . . No but, not everyone does music. Millions do football. [. . .] Right, it's like fantastic when you're – like now, when was it, yeah, May Day it was, when we came down and there were some girls who asked wasn't it me who sang in that group, yeah, and who thought it was good, and when was our next gig [laughter]. Well, like you grow ten metres, don't you. But it's bloody cool anyway.

Kurre: I like to play outside [the Barn], like to an audience. [. . .] Because then you're like a hero – 'Here I am' and they think, 'Wow!' I like that. [. . .] You grow as a person. It's fun

but each person is alone when confronting these feelings, needs and forces in their own body. This learning that relates to the subjective world may also be divided into three dimensions.

Self-knowledge, reflexive insights into the individual's own identity. By means of valid language (cultural skills) and conceptual knowledge of the world, as well as by testing ideals (see below, ability to form ideals) and releasing your feelings in the group (see below, expressive ability), you can learn to know who you are. You can reflect upon your social positions (gender, class, age, place of residence, ethnicity and time period) and perceive your boundaries – what you can and cannot do.

Reflexive ability utilises many 'discursive' forms of language. A person formulates his or her identity by relating already existing concepts or images to each other as verbal language arranges words and sentences. But identity/discourse also develops in, for instance, visual styles, where you attach to yourself particular attributes or identify yourself through choice of clothes. Buttons and inscriptions indicate who you think you are – but so also do a red scarf and torn jeans. These visual elements function as signals that carry meanings which combine to convey a new 'message' about an individual's identity.

Melodic, rhythmic and harmonic progressions in music sometimes create particular units of meaning that stem from their previous fields of association.[12] By correlating such existing units of significance, the bands create 'utterances' about their subjective identities. Like visual expression, music thus possesses a kind of semantic-discursive level, not only in the groups' song lyrics.

The reflexive ability has increased in our late modern period.[13] Identity is considered problematic and becomes the object of conscious work. There are also modern elements in the ways our groups express their identity; for example, the post-tonal harmonic structures in the songs of all three bands, which, together with the use of synths and electronics, are expressions of modern conceptions of time and space.[14] OH's striving for authenticity – to be themselves, to be genuine – is made feasible only through modernisation, for authenticity is not naturally given but an historically and socially created option. To focus reflexively on the agreement between symbolic signs (language, music) and a subjective, inner feeling – that is, between style and identity – is possible only after the modernisation process has sundered the immediate unity between them that existed in more tradition-bound, pre-modern societies.[15] When Kurre and the others in OH actively construct their own authentic identity and 'naturalness', it is done in an interplay between demands from the stylistic fields (cultural skills) and inner feelings (expressive ability).

Ability to form ideals, directed towards desires and goals for individual identity.[16] By using socio-cultural images and language – for example, via idols – individuals express their own ideals. Empathy with these stars becomes a method of developing and altering identity. One achieves self-awareness and pride through forming ideals which are gender- and class-specific, but also deeply unique for each individual, depending upon each person's combination of objectively, subjectively and socially determined experience.

Ideals are closely associated with learning types discussed above, normative capabilities and relationship skills. The formation of ideals contributes to the production of norms and they may be associated with feelings of belonging. To be included in a group may require both certain norms and certain ideals, and the latter can be developed through group solidarity. However, we are dealing here with a subjective aspect of the process previously observed on the social level. Through identity ideals, the self acquires significance – you 'become someone'. Lollo in Lam Gam and Kurre and Finn in OH clearly possess such ideal formations: they see themselves as unique, even 'chosen' in some way. In these cases, there is also a strong connection to a psychodynamic need to outdo their fathers or at least show them that they too are competent (the 'Amadeus complex').

In music, choice of genre and form may demonstrate a way of relating to an ideal. Lam Gam chose a rather narrow genre, which from one perspective may seem like a kind of rigidity – a stubborn adherence to a given identity. However, this narrow genre framework provides enough security to act-out and release sensitive feelings on other musical levels (see below). And conversely, Chans' prolix experiments with many different genres may either indicate flexibility and freedom or insecurity. Their constant style changes are at once symptoms and causes of uncertain

to see if there's anything in the paper, on the band in the paper. The greatest, most fun thing in the world is to play in public.

Micke: If we got famous, what I'd do is tap my old man on the shoulder and say, 'Hey! look at us – it was possible to make something out of that too.' That's actually one of the things that would have been best about us getting somewhere – that he sees that we haven't busted our asses for nothing.

Betty: Everybody's looking at me. I think that's cool. [. . .] We're on stage, doing a song, and it feels great and has been really cool. And then the song's finished and people shout, 'Oh, fantastic! More, more!' Then it feels like: 'Christ, that went well! And the audience thought so too!' [. . .] Everybody's happy about everything, because. . . if it works . . . it's not just *me* who did it – everybody does something for a song to be really good.

Ola: It's about a boy that had problems at home 'cause they were going to move. He didn't think that was cool at all so he protested and that.
Ove: Where'd you get that idea from?
Ola: Well, I thought a bit about what could happen, so I thought of it.
Ove: Was it something that you'd felt yourself?
Ola: Yeah, sort of, when we were going to move. I've always lived in a house and then suddenly we're going to move to a flat.

Conny: Music, like I get absorbed in it, listen to some words and I like live in it, all my feelings rise up, I've sniffled through many lyrics I've heard. [. . .] Now it's some Imperiet song that's stuck in the same way – you get sort of despair if you can't get it out, like you get prickly, pissed off – all tearful even! Like in Sweden a man isn't meant to cry, everybody knows that, but it . . . [. . .] Like everyone thinks the same, right? and then the only way for me to get it out is to stand on stage and sing it all out, right? Then it goes, disappears, and I can communicate to others what I feel – if you hold it inside it just grows and grows. Sometimes you feel like standing up and shouting and screaming, that helps, but it's better to write down some lyrics (inaudible) and then get up on stage, and sing it yourself.

Kurre: . . . music for me, it's, it's feelings. . . . To stand with a guitar in your hands, yeah, under coloured lights, high volume, pouring out your own song, with your own lyrics, that's . . . that's a helluva feeling. It just tingles all over your body.

Bamse: In our place, there you say, you do – yeah, just as you feel like. [. . .] I turn up my amp all the way and play and play. I can't do that anywhere else. [. . .] When you [Ulf] play in your group, don't you feel liberated then? [. . .] Like when you're mad, then you play hard and loud . . . [. . .] Music's meant a lot to me. I've been able to create something. It's that creativity in me that's made me experience . . . instead of talking about experiences, how I feel, I can show it on the guitar.

Håkan: Sometimes, when you play, it all like feels good, then you're willing to sacrifice all your spare time then. Like, you always have fun, but anyway . . . You don't *always* get shivers up and down your spine because the music's good. Sometimes you do and then it feels extra sweet. [. . .] When you're working with a new song, especially then . . . if you feel it's starting to work, that it's a good tune. [. . .] Those are times you can't really describe it – that feeling. [. . .] You go all quiet, like, in the face, you feel as if you get all hot in some way. And so you like start to feel all goose

identity; a fear of conflict in the group, which leads to a preference for compromise instead of shaping a stable group identity, and a compulsive restlessness in the search for something to believe in, a continual need to test and reject ideals that are too strongly associated with intolerable constraints.

Breadth of genre and development between songs (which is even clear in Lam Gam, for example, in conjunction with the formation and dissolution of the band) may be a response to the withering away of tradition in modern society. Intensive work is required in the search for and creation of ideals; they are not simply given by a consonant cultural tradition. This modern aspect gives rise to various responses: both rigidity and flexibility may be interpreted as ways of coping with the late modern plurality of ideals.

Expressive ability to articulate one's own feelings. Acting-out and expressiveness always occur by means of different social languages (music, etc. – cultural skills), but cannot be reduced to the purely social. They always presume a subjective identity, that is, the individual possesses and experiences inner conditions and impulses.[17] We have already examined what subjective impulses the groups' creativity responds to. In making music, previously repressed or censored feelings and impulses are released – for instance, those of a sexual or aggressive nature. By being released in music, they are given a language and attain social recognition. Several of our band members have articulated this expression of feelings as a joyful 'liberation' from inner pressures. This aspect is perhaps most vital to boys, who in music are allowed to display feelings of weakness, sorrow, tenderness, intimacy and frustration which would otherwise be shut off or not considered legitimate for men. Girls are allowed other validated means of intimate expressiveness (crying, reading romantic books, caressing animals, etc.).

Thus it is not a question of a pure, unadulterated opening of one's inner life but of connecting a language to its impulses in a way that reshapes them. The inner and the cultural can only be analytically separated. Such separation, however, corresponds to the youths' own perceptions as they elucidate the expressive aspects of music-making.

The musical aspects most clearly related to and usable

for these expressive actions are volume, beat (pulse) and tone colour (sound).[18] By singing and playing instruments one can act out feelings in a way similar to that of the phonetic ('musical'[19]) aspects of spoken language. These aspects are also experienced as important by the groups themselves and are subjected to a great deal of reflection.

The differentiation of expressiveness is itself a modern phenomenon; traditionally, expressive elements were incorporated in and subordinated to social–normative elements. The revaluation of beat and sound in contemporary rock music renders these levels even more central. Rock's beat and sound meet late modern narcissistic needs for voluntary, instantaneous, ego-dissolving experiences. Expressive learning is also something that the ordinary school tends rather to ignore, but for that very reason, it is extremely important in peer group gangs.

THE COMPLEXITY OF LEARNING

We have studied various aspects of learning and sketched a model of three sets of three (nine) learning types:

Worlds	Constituents	Types of Learning
Objective	Nature	Practical skills
(outer)	Society	Administrative organisation
	Concepts	Cognitive knowledge
Inter-subjective	Symbols	Cultural style
(shared)	Norms	Normative ethics
	Groups	Relational affiliation
Subjective	Identities	Reflexive self-knowledge
(inner)	Ideals	Ideal formational motivation
	Desires	Expressive acting-out

Figure 11 Types of learning

In reality, the different learning types are never separate, even if young people themselves in their thoughts and actions and we in our analysis focus attention on one aspect

pimply. [. . .] It's the same when you hear a good song, sometimes. [. . .] It's a little kick, like . . . you get a little high.

Björn: Before I was really unsure of myself, off stage . . . I think that's why I like to be on stage – you can act out, go the whole way there without . . . in a way I didn't dare to when I was off stage. But I think I can do it now. Now there's not *such* a big difference. You can act out totally on stage without people thinking you're totally weird. Do whatever you like, almost. But I think I can do that now in ordinary life too, but I certainly couldn't before.

Betty: I've learned to be more assured on stage. [. . .] Partly, it's to do with performing things in public. Partly it's a bit more inner security, I dare show myself, I dare let go a little. Then you feel good inside yourself.

at a time. It is possible for them and us to treat technical skills or group togetherness as separate entities, even though they do not exist apart from knowledge and language. The systematised overview is of course ours and our analyses go further than the groups' self-comprehension. But in embryonic form, similar differentiations exist in the groups' own practice.

It is clear that the learning types often not only presuppose but also counteract each other. In many of the quotations from OH, for example, feelings of solidarity are linked to expressiveness, and this, in turn, requires technical as well as stylistic abilities. When someone talks about acting-out in a guitar solo it is simultaneously associated with the group's collectiveness and is viewed as a sign that the demands placed by the rock genre are fulfilled. Rock relates to many life areas and links them together in an activity: outer, divided and inner worlds, thoughts and feelings, knowledge and acting-out.

These learning processes qualify the individual for the field of music and for life in general. Music-making carries the groups into the field of music, whose rules and processes, demands and resources, lead to learning processes that mediate between individuals and society. To learn to compromise, take account of others, handle group relations, defer satisfaction of needs, act out feelings, experiment with different styles and languages, develop flexibility and identity, all prepare for a) personal relations in a future family (the family-based intimate and reproductive sphere), b) education and future working life (the school and work-based production sphere), and c) cultural life, creativity and recreation (the leisure and media-based sphere of consumption and aesthetics).

Through early interaction in the family, school and peer groups, individuals' subjectivity develops. These individual subjects are part of peer groups in new interactions, under pressure from those demands levied by the spheres and with the resources offered by them. Group interaction entails a continued (secondary) socialisation and is enacted in learning processes in the three worlds. These learning processes provide qualifications which are later used in the interaction between individuals within the various spheres.

EXCURSUS: COMMUNICATION

Aesthetic expressions have various types of functions. 1) Objective (material) functions in production and distribution. These functions warrant an economic or technical analysis. 2) Inter-subjective (socio-cultural) functions in the sense of creating and sharing meaning and belonging through symbols 'pointing to' something else. These functions lend themselves to hermeneutic and semiotic investigations. 3) Subjective (acting-out) functions having to do with expressiveness. These functions require pschyo-analytic study.

Thus, an Afro-American-influenced singing style in rock music can be analysed from several perspectives simultaneously. On the material level, can be noted the worldwide dominance of the imperialist American music industry. On the level of symbol and social relations, it is important to white European youth to find style elements which counter those of their parental culture, and in this regard, the Afro-American style provides a clear contrast. Furthermore, Afro-American culture carries social significance as the culture of resistance of an oppressed group, which gives its appropriation a special symbolic meaning. On the subjective level, Afro-American influence relates to certain psychic experiences, which this type of music encapsulates and works upon, and whose roots are in white youths' childhood and upbringing.[21]

Music (and all aesthetic praxis) is, of course, in one sense communication from the sender (composer/musician) to the receiver (listener). But there are also other communicative aspects that the explosion of mass communication has made impossible to disregard. The use of music (consumption, reception – which, however, indicate nothing of the productive activity it is always about) is part of people's lifestyles, together with appearance, performance and language. In the choice and identification with music styles, the individual signals his or her true and/or desired identity (individual or collective), sets boundaries and marks differences, demarcates position in a socio-cultural field. Moreover, music is also functional for the users themselves, not only as regards their surrounding world. It provides space for inner impulses, to experience and act out, and possibilities for collective social processes within the user group.

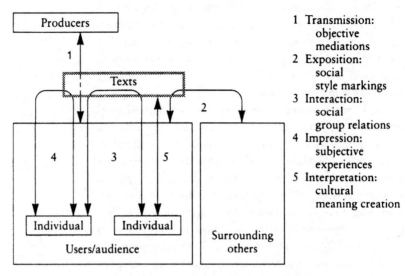

1 Transmission:
  objective
  mediations
2 Exposition:
  social
  style markings
3 Interaction:
  social
  group relations
4 Impression:
  subjective
  experiences
5 Interpretation:
  cultural
  meaning creation

Figure 12   Functions of aesthetic expressions

Culture always marks status positions in social hierarchies, but it does more.[22] For example, by listening to hard rock, you become able to show who you are and how you relate to other tastes in the music field and to enjoy powerful experiences, develop social contacts – for instance, with the opposite sex – and experience solidarity, a sense of belonging to a collective.

It is important what music as a language *says* and points to through its symbolic function, and what it *does* – objectively in the context of production and distribution, and subjectively through the psychic and social processes of those using the music in question.

MODERN POSSIBILITIES

Musical learning processes in groups by no means constitute an harmonious whole. Neither are they all 'positive': power, coercion and suffering exist in groups as they do in families, school, etc. Learning processes are not unproblematic; shared activities may be educational – giving knowledge and skills – but they also engender new problems. We have outlined aspects of learning that often only exist in inhibited or embryonic forms and whose full realisation is hindered by a number of obstacles.

Sometimes various aspects of learning compete with each other; concentrating on technical perfection, for instance, can collide with group cohesion if it involves dropping a band member. Playing in a group can also conflict with individual interests in other areas – with other spheres (family, school, work, sports, etc.).

The learning processes described here are not universal and eternal, general human learning types. They arise out of specific problems imposed on youth by late modern life. Some are easy to deal with and consequently do not become a focus of attention. However, in particular periods, places, societies, classes or genders, certain relationships are felt problematic enough to compel attempts at resolution. Thus the above delineation of learning types is based on what 'stands out' in the authors' material. Sometimes it is a matter of explicit verbalisation of the problem area, sometimes we have analysed underlying patterns by studying the groups' behaviour and non-verbal expressions.

The learning processes of music comprise an exemplary model for how late modern challenges can be dealt with. The technocratisation which enables instrumental and strategic actions to dominate over communicative actions threatens learning in the shared and inner world – social and expressive learning processes. This engenders counter-movements when groups are actively exploring just these dimensions of learning. Such movements compensate for lacunae in the dominating institutions with which they often openly collide, and consequently conflicts arise.

Late modernity sharpens the conflicts between the altered needs (subject structures) developed in primary socialisation (the family) and the altered possibilities of satisfying these needs offered by society's established organs of secondary socialisation (school and work). The result is crises on the one hand and potential for change on the other. This change is effected by the establishment of differently organised social forms such as peer groups, in which different learning processes are developed.

Playing rock music contains seeds of resistance,[23] critique and alternative utopias. Its learning processes are different from those found in school and working life, and have been developed as a reaction to them. Rock's learning processes lack permanent leaders and permanent goals; they are voluntary, non-hierarchical, open and spontaneously developed. They allow collective play, and involve cultural, normative, social and expressive learning. Within late modern life conditions, these learning processes are inquisitive and experimental, and are used as touchstones for identity-formation and resistance to the coercion exercised by dominant institutions. The potential resistance, critique and alternative utopias are simply possibilities existing in embryonic forms in micro-processes in youth groups' daily lives, and their expansion and development depends on their context. Most often, under the pressure of the system world's demands, they gradually submit to ordinary adult, class and gendered family and working life. But they remain viable as embryonic memories and possibilities. In memory they can function like sparks of inspiration in future contentious situations. The alternative learning processes in peer group rock bands contain the potential for resistance. Members of gangs have experienced working with their identities, collective searching, symbol production and shared acting-out. Throughout their lives the memory of these experiences will continue to intimate the possibilities of a different life praxis.

RESISTANCE AND ALTERNATIVE PUBLIC SPHERES

All of society is riddled with oppositions. The capitalist music industry as well as the state music institutions prioritise instrumental and strategic skills. The dominant public agencies, with their 'ordinary' learning processes, rest on institutionally supported traditions and are pervaded by demands from the system world.[24] In the production of aesthetic styles and symbols, for instance in the field of rock music, which our groups have made their primary project, different demands collide head-on. In this sphere, conflicts stemming from oppositions between system and life world, between systems and between different spheres and institutions are carried on. For example, the demands of music life steer OH towards strategic behaviour towards the audience and contravene the group's former Clash-influenced, engaged, communicative and expressive ideals. Chans' playfulness collides with the record studios' demands for perfection.

An important aspect of playing has to do with creating order out of chaos, mastering the material and the instruments, handling the public and having power over time and space. These activities, rooted in the first learning type (practical, administrative and cognitive), can raise self-awareness and provide narcissistic satisfaction (that is, function in interaction with the ability to form ideals, and expressive ability). They provide models for strengthening the ego and for seizing power over one's own life conditions. However, an ambivalence is also embedded here. Under systemic pressure, these activities can assume goal-oriented and manipulative characteristics and reduce the surrounding world – including other subjects and one's own body – to objects. This occurs when these aspects are uncoupled from and made dominant over the social and expressive aspects.[25]

This risk may be exemplified by the significance of equilibristic solos. Managing a long and difficult solo expresses and augments ego strength (in both soloist and listener), but such an accomplishment can also take on traces of manipulative control reminiscent of instrumental (wage) labour. The groups' efforts to establish a delicate balance between various aspects thus may be seen as attempts to seek a different, communicative ego strength, to establish an identity in and influence over the world without mastering it. Their ways of coping with the problems of leadership may be interpreted in this light. The bands avoid rigid authority structures and strive for mobility and free communication within the group, and in such efforts, for the inter-subjective, communicative and subjectively expressive aspects central to counter the goal-oriented skills. Interaction within the group and with the public is, like acting-out, important for developing richer and non-repressive ways of handling modernity – that is, without reducing its dimensions.

It is neither necessary nor indeed feasible to eliminate goal rationality or the system world, but they need to be controlled and restricted lest they deform communication in the life world. You can try to master your instrument and still seek communicative relations with other band members and with your public.

The three groups' predispositions for this vary. Their attempts, particularly as regards school, to develop different learning processes encounter varying amounts of support or obstacles in the public spheres the groups move in. When they find themselves in a tight network of system-dominated public institutions, as Chans do, they become surrounded and have difficulty in the long term in countering demands for integration from the bourgeois public sphere. Music-making has to surrender and be reduced to either a strictly privatised hobby or a regular professional career.

In other cases, for instance, Lam Gam, there is an accessible oppositional or counter public sphere to relate to (the Ark), in which local subcultures with alternative scales of norms and values cultivate different learning processes that transform social and expressive needs from problems into resources.[26] Social movements, sub- and counter-cultures construct networks of public structures (premises, media, societies or organisations, etc.) which, more effectively than single groups, resist system demands and develop communicative alternatives. The modes of living in such groups and alternative public spheres naturally contain differentiations and conflicts as in society as a whole, but they establish different relations between the various aspects. For example, expressiveness need not lead to new repressions but instead to innovative symbolising in the interchange between acting-out and curiosity about the outside world. The Ark environment made it possible, even desirable, for Lam Gam to prioritise the voice's rawness and intensity over its purity and brilliance. Such counter-cultures or alternative public spheres are always provisional and experimental, never totally 'liberated islands', since the dominance of system demands can never be permanently resisted other than by constant movement.

CONCLUSION

Our study has led us to conclusions which point to various issues for further consideration. We shall now proceed to formulate some of our views on the debates, work and research on youth. But first, a summary of our preliminary answers to the initial question: Why rock?

Why has music, especially rock and pop music, become so crucial to contemporary young people? Why did the adolescents we studied play rock? How were their motives related to adolescence and to late modernity? When sketching some of the reasons for playing rock we are well aware that they may be extended to the use of other media products and cultural symbols as well.

First, it is necessary to underline that there is no single, uniform answer to these questions, only a cluster of answers on different levels which track some of the many polydimensional connections between youth, modernity and rock music. Second, playing rock must be viewed not only as a reproductive but also as a transformative activity. It not only shapes skills required by and preserving existing social forms, it also contributes to processes of change. Playing rock reproduces power hierarchies while at the same time it contains elements of defensive reactions to systemic pressures as well as offensive experiments with new life forms. We must not lose sight of the fact that rock is an ambivalent phenomenon with affirmative, critical and utopian aspects. Rock's field of action stretches between life-world and systems, and it would be a mistake to focus only on one end of the spectrum. This book has tried to concentrate on life-world processes in their interaction with systemic pressures.

Third, rock-playing must be understood as first and foremost a cultural activity. It belongs primarily to the cultural end of the inter-subjective level, albeit also being connected with the social end as well as the external and internal levels. Rock-playing in peer groups uses resources and meets demands from the external and internal worlds as well as from the socio-cultural field itself. It cannot be reduced to merely an instrument for learning processes, necessary for social, reproductive or psychic identity formation, even though it clearly has such functions. It is undeniably also an aesthetic activity in its own right, subject to the rules of its own, relatively autonomous field.

WHY ROCK?

Bearing all this in mind, let us return to our initial question and divide the motives for playing rock into at least three main groups in order to capture if not the essence, then at least important use values of rock.

COLLECTIVE AUTONOMY

Playing rock, you can do things together with your best friends on your own terms. On the one hand this collective autonomy concerns the need for autonomous play, for a free space, separated from adults in family and school. In its activities, the peer group establishes an autonomous sociality which defensively sets limits for the demanding encroachments of family and school. Choosing rock to gather round delimits this group of peers from surrounding adults and from other youth styles – regardless of whether you play yourself or just listen to a tape recorder at full volume. No outsider tells you what to do in a rock band.

On the other hand, rock music suits and fortifies peer groups, especially the normally larger groups formed by boys (the traditionally tighter and smaller groups of girls are not as easily transformed into rock groups). The need for group communality is satisfied by music because of its collective form (the visual arts or writing cannot really offer the same possibilities). Group collectivity is obvious in that rock music is based on the band rather than on soloists or big orchestras. The reception of rock is also mainly associated with peer relations.

These needs are augmented in late modernity because of

rapid generational changes and increased system demands – for instance in and from school. System rationalisation and colonisation of the life-world produces tensions within institutionalised spheres such as school and creates the need for autonomous spaces for peer group collectivity. This pressure is felt most by adolescent boys in the middle of a long education and discipline process who are ill at ease in family life. Male peers can function as an alternative family, aiding individual growth but also steering and restricting it within definite boundaries. The reverse of autonomy can be a certain marginality: young people are often not integrated into socially productive and reproductive structures but exist in a suspended position, which the autonomous peer group may confirm. The reverse of collectivity can be conformist group pressures. Both of these risks increase if groups are pushed into strictly defensive positions because of the lack of material, social, cultural or psychic resources. Even so, collective autonomy has a great use value for late modern adolescents as it meets objective system pressures and gives latitude for social group relations and for more offensive learning processes different from those of school by being voluntary, spontaneous, non-institutionalised and self-governing. In this way, peer group rock-playing develops social group structures in reaction to objective forces.

ALTERNATIVE IDEALS

It is possible to find different stylistic models and even become 'something' – namely, a rock musician – via other than conventional means. The socio-cultural world of rock offers alternative ideals to those offered by family and school, and rock playing can channel a problematic relationship with achievement demands for which there is no suitable outlet within the framework of a 'normal' career – for example in school. Like sports, music can give (chiefly male) working-class youth who dislike or do badly in school an emergency exit, an alternative opportunity for success and recognition. Granted, most amateur musicians never achieve real careers in rock, but they are at least able to play with that thought in mind and inspired by that socio-cultural field.

The need for such alternatives could increase as the cultural erosion of traditions renders normal or ordinary careers and conventional ideals less secure and widens the gap between desires and reality. And alternatives are certainly needed in the adolescent testing of ideals, so important in the break from adult domination in family and school and in the formation of identity. The reverse side here could involve an elitist pursuit of status or investments in cultural capital if the pressure from the economic market system becomes too strong. However, by avoiding fixed leaders and power hierarchies, rock groups can test late modern norms in a democratic and flexible way. Peer group rock-playing develops social norms relating to objective as well as subjective levels.

NARCISSISTIC ENJOYMENT

You can express things in music that cannot be expressed in other ways; you can have fun and create something, express your feelings and identity by standing in the spotlight, mirrored and amplified by a band and an audience. Through several conjunctive symbolic channels – words, tones and visual styles – adolescent conflicts can be symbolised, partly in opposition to system-tainted verbal language. The restricted instrumental rationalisation of late modernity intensifies these needs, since the communicative aspects of life are forced out of school and work and this must be compensated in leisure, for instance, in youth cultural activities. This aspect is perhaps most vital to boys who, by playing rock, are allowed to display feelings of weakness, tenderness, intimacy, sorrow and frustration which would otherwise be stifled. Girls seem to find other legitimate outlets for such feelings.

There are three sub-aspects or sources of such narcissistic enjoyment (satisfaction, pleasure or jouissance).[1] Music-making as an aesthetic activity in general gives creative pleasure by enabling the individual to leave some trace of him- or herself in the world. Further, the volume, beat and sound of the music form parameters that facilitate, for both listeners and musicians, a temporary and voluntary dissolution of ego-boundaries and a 'regression' to pre-verbal, 'narcissistic' forms of experience, feelings of life, involvement and wholeness in your own body, which can be therapeutic. Finally, the individual self is experienced as greatly enlarged by merging with the band (teamwork) and being mirrored by the response of the audience.

The more rapidly the world changes, the more the young feel unproductive and anonymous in their own modern environment and hence the stronger are the needs for creative pleasure. The creative, expressive and reflexive aspects of self-expansion respond to the increasing late modern needs for self-reflection and self-appreciation caused by changes in socialisation and in everyday life. The great interest in and use of music (and a few other aesthetic forms such as diary-writing) in adolescence proves that such needs are strong in that phase of life, in which rapid identity development produces an insecurity that has to be countered by ephemeral self-confirming experiences. Experimenting with new languages can also be part of a cultural expropriation and colonisation process if the elements of personal and collective creativity are thwarted and the reproduction of commercial images becomes too unoriginal. The enjoyment of being communally involved in music may then lock the individual into a state of group dependence, a sort of ecstatic imprisonment, where no strong ego identity or intellectual capacity can develop. This risk is, however, highly exaggerated by the current youth debate; rock's new languages and self-expanding experience generally aid rather than hinder the development of a strong personal identity in late modern adolescence. Thus peer group rock finally develops cultural symbolic expressions that meet subjective needs.

All in all, rock contains elements of and potential for a different kind of learning, which is more open, flexible and multi-dimensional than the institutionalised learning at school, and which focuses upon relational, normative and symbolic levels that counter objective system colonisation and fulfil new subjective needs for reflection, expressiveness and ideals. Therefore, rock is important for growing up in late modernity, for inspiring resistance to system demands from both state and market, and for enriching the quality of late modern life.

Much of this, albeit in different proportions, is valid for other forms of cultural activity as well, but the combination outlined above is unique for rock and pop. Of course, the rock scene will continue to develop and perhaps even change its name, but the constellation of needs and forces satisfied by peer group rock will not disappear that easily, only transform, as long as late modern social, cultural and socialisation forms survive.

THE YOUTH DEBATE

This study has shed new light upon a number of important aspects of youth culture. We shall examine three of them below.[2]

SERIOUS PLAY

We have investigated only a few youth groups' involvement in rock music, but we postulate that we would find parallel processes in other youth groups and in other types of youth cultural activities – for example, those oriented around dance, cars, horse riding, etc. Youth culture – the cultural activities and uses of symbolic expressions by young people – is much more serious and important than the conventions of the public debate on the subject would sometimes have us believe.

These youth cultural activities are based on leisure, they are voluntary and chosen, and they contain strong elements of play and enjoyment, and they are far more profound than may be first assumed. There is a connection between modernity, youth and cultural means of expression. The wealth of cultural creativity that exists in youth may be linked psychologically to the development of identity in adolescence, socio-culturally, with young people's special place in society, and historically, to the transformation of adolescence and the position of youth brought about by late modernity. Young people's symbolic praxis may be taken as a response to these transformations – a response that affects everyone's future.

In our empirical examples, we have examined several of the complex links existing between and within youth culture, the life conditions of youth and late modern society. Playing rock in peer group gangs expresses the all-embracing work with identity, which not only the young are forced into today: it is a modern form of working with conflicts which is a response to demands and which utilises resources from all areas of life.

ACTIVE SEARCHING

Young people's relations with the resource that is the commercial, mass media conveyed, popular culture is more active than is usually claimed in youth debates. Youth culture has to do with seeking, and often, with re-creation. Young people choose styles and expressions from a contradictory, in part mass-mediated, market; they seek expressions that function and are usable in relation to their own objective, social and subjective prerequisites.

The media provide access to expressions and experiences which open up the local living environment to the surrounding world. This is significant for identity development, not least in adolescence, when the testing of subjectivity – formed by parental and school environments – is all-important.

Access to different sorts of resources involves class and gender demarcations – despite late modern openings. Youth cultural styles not only mirror such boundaries, but also provide meeting-points – all three of our groups periodically were attracted to punk, hard rock – and new types of differentiation in other dimensions.

Among the various types of cultural and social resources, rock music occupies a pivotal place. Rock's learning processes are not unique; they have counterparts in many other kinds of activities. But rock offers a particularly effective combination of social, communicative and expressive learning for late modern youth – in contrast to the dominating institutional learning processes at school. Rock opens up unusually wide doors to deep psychic levels and needs structures.

NECESSARY NORM EXPERIMENTS

The openings and insecurities of a multi-cultural society are examined and dealt with subjectively through self-controlled experiments with modes of living. Young people's lifestyle experiments being often re-creative as well as innovative, they contribute to the further development of society. One important result of peer group learning processes is the development of norms and language. The combination of collectivity and symbolic praxis enables necessary seeking for and testing of norms for relations and behaviour.

It is neither feasible nor desirable to return to a uniform system of morals. Our mutable and multi-cultural society renders experimenting with norms in the various subcultures necessary. Moreover, these experiments facilitate resistance to the oppression which exists in all dominant traditions.[3]

That norm experiments are needed is not to say that all the norms experimented with are equally desirable. You can accept fundamentally experimental ways of responding to modernisation without approving all their concrete expressions. In the youth culture arena, questionable responses flourish also – for example, fundamentalism and neo-conservatism, misogyny and racism, elitism and consumer hysteria, or fascination with barbarism and violence.

Such problems are not solved by resorting to authoritarian prescriptions or by forcing the undesirable expressions under ground through censorship, but rather through a flexible combination of discussion and struggle. Public arenas are needed in which different subcultures and orientations can meet in normative conflicts without relinquishing their special character and in which they can communicate freely, uncoerced by state authorities or market forces.

YOUTH WORK

It is common to see learning as connected to certain institutions, but we have shown that this is not the whole story. Young people's involvement with rock music (or dance, cars, etc.) contains various types of learning processes, which contrast with those of school by being voluntary, open and spontaneous. They are quite simply different. But these learning processes can also inspire productive renewal of institutional youth work – provided the adults involved respect the unique qualities and autonomy of youth cultural expressions.

THE COMPLEXITIES OF LEARNING

Both institutional and other learning have various aspects or levels. Learning processes are always directed towards the external as well as the shared and inner worlds, and for each world there are several learning types. All learning is complex, but often only certain aspects are focused upon in different contexts and, consequently, learning types develop unevenly. Learning in institutions under heavy pressure from the system world (state and market) tends to focus on the external world, and has a goal-rational, instrumental character. The ordinary school, for example, stresses practical and cognitive learning. Schools also pursue learning aimed at the formation of ideals, norms, relationships, but this tends to be covert, part of a 'hidden curriculum'.[4] If our three gangs' learning is directed towards some learning types more than others, it still takes account of the different worlds in a more balanced way.

It is important to be aware of the complexities of this sort of collective learning when working with youth (and in a wide sense, in all pedagogical efforts). Learning is never just the acquisition of knowledge, but to ignore this aspect would be misguided. Both the official and the hidden curriculum are real. School and all youth work encompass learning in the external, the shared and the inner world. No aspect is 'truer' than any other, but some dominate or attract due attention while others are hidden or allowed to atrophy.

COMMUNICATIONS BETWEEN DIFFERENT SPHERES

Learning goes on in a number of different contexts which for young people may be seen metaphorically as different rooms: the family, school, work, the media and peer groups. Each room has its own language, norms and relationships. The rooms are often isolated from each other. It would be useful if each room could open onto the others, not to raze walls (it is good to have different rooms to go between) but to enable youth work, for example in school, to demonstrate some understanding and respect for other learning processes in other contexts.

We advocate neither a subjectivisation of school (school imitating youth culture) nor a system-controlled subsuming of leisure (through incorporation in school). It is neither feasible nor desirable to abolish the particular position of school: the systematic learning processes produced there require a certain detachment from other areas of life and they may have utility value for those involved in them. On the other hand, it is also dangerous if school's relations with leisure culture become dominating and controlling, or, for example, if the world of rock becomes colonised by school-like, system-dominated structures. Tendencies towards such institutionalisation of youth culture can easily be detected; in Sweden there is a growing interest in rock music on the part of educational associations, music schools and traditional clubs and associations. What we would advocate is communication between the different spheres (or 'rooms'), each retaining and using its integrity and individuality. It is important, for instance, that school and other spheres of youth work function on a level *between* that of the technocratic apparatus and family intimacy.[5]

Opening doors between rooms can also take place on different levels. School can be inspired by or take note of different aspects of youth culture: on the objective level, the content of teaching can be revitalised; on the social level, working methods can be appropriated; and on the subjective level, personal relations can to a degree be inspired by peer group relationships. This would be a way to increase the possibilities for the identification and involvement asked for by present-day youth.

LEARNING TO RESIST

In addition, learning processes entail an intrinsic duality. Learning, socialisation and youth work invariably involve a degree of absorption in pre-existing structures, but they can also help to transcend these structures. Since dominant traditions and social structures give rise to suffering and repression, resistance and change are needed. Work with youth should therefore always involve a commitment to 'double qualification' – combining adaptive and integrative aspects with liberating and critical ones.[6]

Functioning learning processes also require that 'progression' (learning new things) interacts with 'regression' (living out deep feelings). A schooling for resistance and emancipation comes about via learning processes that develop a non- (self-) repressive and flexible ego, open to experiments with *different* forms of experience: 'discursive', and 'presentative', 'symbolic' and 'semiotic' ('proto-symbolic').

There is no totally unintegrated resistance, which is not to say there is no resistance. Modernisation continues to produce emancipatory potential in tandem with new forms of repression – resistance as well as power. Learning for resistance takes place primarily in social movements (counter-cultures, alternative public spheres), but in some cases it can also be developed within institutions for youth work.[7]

YOUTH RESEARCH

As we mentioned in the introduction to this book, to conduct research on youth is problematic. Youth researchers, like teachers and social workers, have their own system demands to deal with, and the desire for 'solidarity with the research subject' does not erase these problems.

POLYDIMENSIONAL CONTENT

Youth research needs polydimensionality. Regardless of what youth cultural phenomenon the researcher begins with, he or she invariably encounters multi-layered processes. The scientific illumination of such processes must therefore also be polydimensional. It is necessary to encourage cooperation among different disciplines in order to conceptualise several dimensions of youth culture, for it is only when blinkered reductionism is avoided that the important dynamic of youth culture appears. We need research on youth which keeps doors open instead of sealing itself hermetically around a limited approach.

We have seen how playing rock (like, for example, squatting or patterns of consumption) embraces aesthetic, social and psychological levels, as well as several interwoven dimensions such as age, gender, class, place of residence and ethnicity. Even if individual researchers may have to concentrate on certain levels or dimensions, combining them gives a richer understanding of the processes of youth culture.

In the present work our selection of informants has taken account of the influences of social milieus. We see many important dimensions to pursue further, future studies which will illuminate the limitations of the work we have already carried out.

One important question in this regard has to do with reception, the use of cultural expressions. We have touched upon this, but there is a strong need to focus more directly on it.[8] There is a wealth of quantitative information on mass media consumption, but few qualitative analyses of the functions and significance of the media and popular culture. What learning processes occur (with different young people and in different contexts) in the listening and dancing to music? And what subjective driving forces lie behind aesthetic reception? In the present study, we have had to content ourselves with examples of how the motivation to perform – as prompted by a father or father-figure and not satisfied by success in school – gives rock a compensatory function in the formation of identity.

Another urgent task is to give priority to gender. This is of great importance in the present era when rapid and fundamental cultural changes have begun profoundly to affect sexual roles and relations, a phenomenon that is extremely significant in youth culture. Young people's work with identity has a great deal to do with their sexual identity, and in this, the effects of the de-traditionalisation of adult society are strong. We have indicated several mechanisms involved in these aspects, but they need more thorough testing in studies in which researchers of both sexes cooperate with male, female and mixed-gender youth groups.[9]

A third task is to examine more broadly and systematically the entire spectrum of learning processes undergone by youth, giving particular attention to the relations between learning processes in the spheres of the family, school, work, organised and unorganised leisure. To some extent this has been done in quantitative investigations but rarely in qualitative in-depth studies, which normally concentrate on either the family, the school, or leisure, but rarely extend to all spheres simultaneously.[10] Such broad studies should be able to clarify the picture of the tension-filled relations between different forms of activity and their contributions to identity development, learning and socialisation. It would also be instructive to follow groups over a longer time span in order to trace lengthy processes better and gain insights into the long-term significance of youth cultural learning.

THEORETICAL OPENNESS

The demand for multi-dimensional youth research has certain consequences. Different theories direct attention towards different aspects, for example, cultural change or the continuation of traditions, class or gender oppositions, the influence of the media, the reproduction of social power relations, or aesthetic creativity. These divisions and specialisations are legitimate and necessary; but it is also important to retain a non-sectarian modesty and openness towards research directions and approaches other than one's own. No single aspect will do justice to all of youth culture. It is necessary to try to perceive several aspects simultaneously without reducing them to a single entity or assigning greater importance to one. Young people's rock-playing is never nothing but an investment of cultural capital, a compensatory pubescent activity, or a creative acting-out. It is several things at once, and each 'nothing but' analysis is barren, a dogmatic reductive analysis.

The present work has been inspired by several different theoretical traditions, and through 'bricolage', we have tried to construe fruitful connections between these traditions guided by our empirical material. We would hope for more inter-disciplinary efforts in future; for instance, closer cooperation between qualitative and quantitative methods could give interesting results. As it is now, they lie rather far apart.[11] Closer exchanges between theories of social fields, cultural reproduction, adolescence, modernity, symbolic praxis and alternative public spheres would be worthwhile – including fierce battles between such theoretical traditions.

STRATEGIC SELF-REFLECTION

Along with an internal, methodological and theoretical openness in research, a strategic opening in a somewhat different direction is needed. This has to do with taking note of the position of the researcher's own sphere, that is, the relations between research institutions, systems and life-worlds. It is tempting to incline towards a traditional research role which reduces youth to objects and in which theories and methods are taken as given. Researchers must reflect over the functions of their own research and seek ways to counter mechanisms of dominance inherent in their academic institutions, to keep a tight rein on system demands and strive for a more *dialogic* relation to the youth who must tolerate being repeatedly examined and checked.

This task is not wholly separate from the arguments conducted in the previous chapter on resistance and the alternative public sphere in the youth cultural arena. Researchers must also try to handle power and resistance, to develop possibilities for double qualifying and establish new, flexible *meeting places* in which different groups and interests can communicate with each other with as little coercion as possible.

There is a great deal left to do. Where, for example, can researchers communicate their theories and results with other than system-dominated authorities (representatives of the commercial media or bureaucratic state agencies)? It is difficult to establish direct channels to young social movements; possibly action research offers more opportunities in this regard. On the other hand, there are important tasks for critical, self-aware research in contact with youth workers (teachers, social workers, etc.). Such tasks might include querying relationships that are usually experienced as self-evident, showing that youth workers' 'own' institutions not only solve problems but also help to create them, and understanding that the youth cultural fields they work in are not only full of problems but also contain unique experiments that explore responses to the challenges of cultural modernisation.

NOTES

INTRODUCTION

1 See Sernhede (1982, 1984).
2 A Nordic form of what could be called alternative upper secondary boarding-schools for adults, started in the late nineteenth century.
3 *Krut* 1982, no. 26. The article in *Dagens Nyheter*, 12 March 1983, 'Du har inte en chans – ta den!' (You Haven't a Chance – Take It !), was published in an extended version in *Zenit* 1984, no. 84.
4 See the above-mentioned texts and also Fornäs (1979, 1980 and 1981) ; Fornäs and Sernhede (1983) ; Sernhede (1984).
5 For details about the bands see 'Three Bands – Three Cultures'.
6 See Fornäs *et al.* (1984b) who presented texts by Willis, Hebdige, McRobbie, Hartwig and Ziehe to the Swedish public; and Donald Broady's introduction of the works of first Ziehe and then Pierre Bourdieu.
7 Bennett (1980) is a valuable source which puts the professional career in focus. Finnegan (1989) contains interesting chapters on the learning and composition models of local rock bands, but stays roughly within ethnographic limits, not going into deeper cultural or psychological interpretations. Both are inspired by Howard Becker's ethnographical model of 'art worlds' (Becker 1982). Cohen (1991) deals with the local Liverpool rock culture. Within Scandinavia, other relevant new studies of rock groups include Arvidson (1987), Öhlund (1988), Berkaak (1993) and Berkaak and Ruud (1992).
8 Trondman (1989) and other Swedish sources indicate that between 6 and 10% of teenagers play in rock/pop groups and that in total, over 100,000 people (of all ages, out of a total population of 8.4 million) play rock/pop, 10–15% of them women. Seca (1988) is a statistical study of Paris rock bands. Wills and Cooper (1988) examine the health and working conditions of professional pop musicians.
9 This applies to otherwise very useful histories and analyses of rock such as Gillett (1970), Salzinger (1972), Sandner (1977), Jerrentrup (1981), Durant (1984), Street (1986) Wicke (1987), Pattison (1987), Hatch and Millward (1987), Redhead (1990) and Reynolds (1990). They all acknowledge the existence and importance of rock's amateur basis in everyday life, but do not penetrate it empirically or theoretically. The lacuna in empirically underpinned and theoretically qualified literature on the reception of pop seems to be even larger than the one on the production of rock. Media researchers have published many statistics on music use and some good figures and analyses are contained in Feilitzen *et al.* (1989), but few qualitative pop music reception studies exist.

However, recently, some works have been published that connect modernity and pop discourses in interesting ways. The arguments on sampling, reflexivity and authenticity in the articles by Perry, Savage and Harron in Frith ed. (1989) are good examples of this as are works by Frith, Shepherd and Mowitt in Leppert and McClary (1987), as well as many of the innumerable texts on rock published since then.
10 Comp. Hebdige (1987, p. 14).
11 Concepts of subjectivity in cultural analyses are not new. Lorenzer (1981, 1986) and Nylander (1986) provide several exciting examples. However, one important difference in our work is that we were working with living people and not with aesthetic artefacts. We have had the opportunity to study subjectivity in living speech and in the flesh, not just in texts.
12 Lam Gam's ambivalence towards Ove reflected the functions that, at least in the beginning, he was associated with: on the one hand, social worker, on the other, rock musician (see band descriptions). A great many methodological problems are revealed in, for example, the interview segments, but here we take up only a few issues.
13 This is partly because in the end the material did not seem to be all that usable. This is the price one pays for endeavouring to be open to unforeseen insights instead of seeking answers to prepared questions. The relative absence of this material in the book is also due to the fact

that the demand for anonymity prevented a complete presentation of the bands' music.

14 We have come across and been inspired by similar method reasoning on the part of e.g. Willis (1978 and 1976/1980), Broch *et al.* (1979), Christoffersen and Andersen (1982), Holter and Kalleberg (1982), Jacobsen (1982), Ehn and Löfgren (1982), Berger (1982), Bietau *et al.* (1982), Eneroth (1984), Heitmeyer (1986), Jensen and Pittelkow (1986) and Hughes and Månson (1988).

15 See *inter alia* Groeben (1980) and Olsson (1986).

16 The concept of 'culture' is problematic: we use it as a concept for symbolic aspects of life forms, which has to do with both consciousness and communication. This is narrower than that of aesthetics: in effect it bridges both. When we talk about 'youth' or 'peer group' cultures, we lean towards 'manners and customs', whereas terms like 'cultural expressions' lean more towards 'art'. See Hannerz (1992).

OH – IN BETWEEN

1 Statistical Report, Helsingborg 1985: 8 and 1983: 6.

2 Statistical Report, Helsingborg 1985: 8 and 1983: 6. Since the electoral districts and the housing areas do not quite correspond, our survey of political sympathies must be taken with a pinch of salt. According to our findings, the municipality has not bothered to obtain socio-economic data corresponding to the old divisions into social groups.

3 The following description is of the situation in the autumn of 1985.

4 The following presentation is based on notes of observations made on 15 September 1985.

5 From observation notes taken 20 September 1985.

6 The eighth year, with its feeling of a breathing-space, seems to be particularly given to such maturation processes. See also Holmberg *et al.* (1982).

7 For Kurre, it would seem that history is in the process of repeating itself. He has returned to the idea that playing must be fun and has difficulties subordinating himself when working with the group's producer in the same way that he had felt suffocated in [the band] Basic (conversation 10.10.86). In addition, at the time of writing (late 1986) OH has agreed to reincorporate Bamse into the band.

8 Interview with H and A, 06.10.85.

9 See Murdock (1973, p. 57).

10 Schönström (1986, p. 94).

11 See Møller (1984, p. 94). The concept originated with the psychiatrist Hanns Sachs.

FROM THE SUBURBS – LAM GAM

1 The introductory pages of this section are taken from Ove Sernhede's notes from 1 September 1985.

2 All information on Bergslunden is taken from the Gothenburg Municipal Administration office's statistics for 1965–1984 and the Gothenburg social services' area description for 1984.

3 The following presentation is based on interviews with young people, social workers and parents.

4 See Willis (1977).

5 See Corrigan (1976).

6 See Willis (1977).

7 Ibid.

8 This section derives from observation notes taken in November 1985.

9 The following is from observation notes taken in November 1985.

DETACHED – CHANS

1 The following is a reconstruction of notes taken by Fornäs on various visits to Chans during summer and autumn 1985.

2 The facts in the following sections are taken from *Områdesdata för Stockholms län* (Area Data for Stockholm County) (1985); Statistics Sweden: Population and Income Statistics (1985); Election Statistics (1985); the National Census (1985) and various other official sources.

3 Most band members came from homes with more economic and cultural capital. See Bourdieu (1986), Broady and Palme (1986), Zinnecker (1986), Rasmussen (1987) and Roe (1987a).

4 According to Nordberg (1984), young people's language is above all more emotional and complicated than that of adults. This is well-illustrated by Chans' language.

5 According to a questionnaire concerning band members' use of time.

LIVING IN THE LATE MODERN PERIOD

1 This argument is inspired by Habermans (1981, 1984 and 1988) and Negt and Kluge (1972).

2 See Rasmussen (1987). The various fields may have different degrees of institutionalising: the concepts of 'fields' (Bourdieu 1979/1984), 'the public sphere' (Habermas) and 'institution' (Berger and Luckmann 1966/1984) are not all synonymous.

3 See Gillis (1981), Bjurström (1980) and Mitterauer (1986 pp. 92ff., 249ff.).

4 Information on the history of the Swedish school has been obtained from *Krut* 10, 1979. See also Mitterauer (1986, pp. 83ff. and 142ff.).

5 Boëthius (1989).

6 See also Keniston (1970).
7 However, the word seems to have been used in Swedish as early as 200 years ago.
8 The Million Dwelling Programme was a comprehensive housing programme, initiated by the Social Democratic government.
9 Brolinson and Larsen (1983), Bjurström (1980), Mosskin and Mosskin (1969).
10 The concept of 'late modernity' was developed by Fornäs (1987), inspired by the way Jameson (1984) relates to the postmodernist analysis of contemporary culture to Ernest Mandel's concept of late capitalism. Jencks (1986/1989) refers to 'late modernism' in a slightly different sense. Cahoone (1988), Willis (1990) and Giddens (1990) later used similar concepts. Our discussion here is based mainly on Habermas (1981, 1984 and 1988) and Ziehe (1982 and 1991). Parallel diagnostics of our cultural period can be found in postmodernist works, in media research (e.g. Reimer 1989) and in some works on recent psychic changes, for example Keniston (1968 p. 259 and 1970). Habermas' work lends itself to our needs because it tries to flexibly synthesise some important theoretical traditions and levels of analysis: social, cultural and psychological dimensions of historical development. We find it important to retain a fundamentally ambivalent openness towards modernisation and (late) modernity and to be neither apologetically optimistic nor narrowly pessimistic. The view of the modern project fettered by the one-sided and repressive form of capitalist modernisation, with its double systematic colonisation of the life-world, offers a useful way out of this dilemma. And Habermas' way of differentiating various levels of modernity allows space for different theories to contribute to our understanding in a non-reductive way. Our discussion of youth culture in late modernity would not have been possible without Thomas Ziehe's insights into the ambivalent and polymorphous dimensions of young people's (late) modern life-worlds.
11 See the subcultural analyses of the Centre for Contemporary Cultural Studies (Cohen, Willis, McRobbie, Hebdige et al.).
12 The following passage is directly inspired by Jürgen Habermas' and Thomas Ziehe's arguments.
13 Ziehe and Stubenrauch (1982) depict the demise of norms as an erosion crisis causing cultural release and cultural expropriation which involve the life world being pervaded by reflexivity, 'makeability' and individualisation (Ziehe 1991). Habermas (1981/1984 pp. 339ff.) says that the rationalised life world entails more and more subjectivity, reflexivity and mobilisation. See also Negt (1984 pp. 53ff.), Mitterauer (1986 pp. 39f) and Beck (1986). Beck, like the present writers, also dis-

cusses on the one hand individualisation, defusion and dissimulation and, on the other, reflexivity.
14 Not least, this process affects gender identities, roles and relations, which are variously expressed by youth cultures. See Beck (1986), Mitterauer (1986 pp. 54 and 95) and Drotner (1985).
15 On the special role of the media in this, see Hannerz (1992), Beck (1986/1992) and Fornäs (1987, pp. 31ff.).
16 Already during the 1960s, this was a theme of various psychological theories, especially in the psychoanalytical tradition.
17 On punk, see Hebdige (1979), Bay (1982) and Laing (1985).

THREE SPHERES

1 This accords with much other recent research, for example on media use, where both lower working-class and upper middle-class youth watch television much less than the groups in the middle – though for different reasons (see Roe, 1983).
2 Our linking of work with school, and the media with leisure organisations possiby needs explanation. Even if work and school are most often influenced by two different systems (market and state) and can be in opposition to each other (which we will deal with when we come to that sphere), they both have an obligatory and disciplinary function in young people's lives. They also place similar demands on competence and knowledge, efficiency and goal rationality. In principle, the school precedes and prepares for working life. The media and leisure spheres are equally influenced by the above-mentioned systems, but for our young people they still comprise a recreational, voluntary and pleasurable field of action – experienced as a compensation for school/work. They are also in part interchangeable: media consumption functions and can be described as a subdivision of leisure activities as a whole.
3 See Stroh (1984), Mitterauer (1986), Rasmussen (1987), Hurrelman and Neubauer (1986). In Bourdieu-inspired studies are mentioned 'resources' which families administer. See also the concepts of 'social' and 'cultural capital'.
4 With the three concepts of individuation, intimisation and privatisation, Holter et al. (1976) have described how the social changes of the twentieth century have affected the family. See also Björnberg and Bäck-Wiklund (1987).
5 The family type, a concept referring to internal role distribution, can vary enormously within a social class. An instrumental father role is, however, more common in higher social

classes. The lower the class, the more the mother is likely to dominate. See Kälvesten and Meldahl (1972) and Prokop (1976).

6 With the breakthrough of capitalism, the father's presence in the home diminished. The concept of the absentee father, however, refers not only to physical absence but also to evasive or repelling behaviour on the part of the father. The extent to which this creates problems for the boys' gender role orientation seems to largely depend on the mother's ability to fulfil instrumental functions and on the availability of other father figures in the family's social network. See also Nettelbladt (1984).

7 See Ziehe and Stubenrauch (1982).

8 See Broady (1981), Thavenius (1981) and B.-E. Andersson (1982, pp. 18ff.).

9 Ottomeyer (1977).

10 Broady (1984).

11 See Ziehe and Stubenrauch (1982) and Beck (1986/1992). The technocratizing tendency of the late modern period has thus been pitted against a tendency towards intimacy – even in relations between teachers and pupils. While the technocrats would transform school into a well-oiled knowledge machine – in accord with the instrumental requirements of the two societal systems – the advocates of intimacy would transform the classroom into an almost family-like haven. Both tendencies generate problems since there are significant advantages with a school that is neither machine nor intimate sphere but something in between – see Ziehe's discussion of a desirable level of 'sociability' (1991).

12 Ziehe and Stubenrauch (1982).

13 The structuring effects of school on leisure have been studied in a Danish investigation of gymnasiums by Adrian et al. (1980).

14 Czaplicka (1987) and von Feiltzen et al. (1989).

15 Bjurman (1981).

16 See Hartwig (1980) for a discussion of different development perspectives on teenage aesthetic practices for boys and girls of different social strata.

KURRE

1 If one wishes to consider Kurre's rebel style as a variant of the OH culture, one could refer to homologies between the central values of Kurre's ideology, dress style and musical tastes (see Willis 1978). Homology entails a culture value manifesting itself on several levels in a system. Or, the reverse – an object acquiring a collective meaning without contradictions.

2 See Gammelgaard (1980, p. 49).

3 On this point, we would acknowledge Roe (1983) who has shown how difficulties in school can compel youth to seek a compensatory counter-identity.

4 This line of reasoning has been inspired by the Klein school of psychoanalysis. See Segal (1964), Møller (1984, pp. 120ff.) and Laufer (1966).

5 See Møller (1984, pp. 119ff.).

6 See Ziehe (1979, p. 130). The emphasis is in the original.

7 Progression entails the enlarging of the ego – to change, develop, take risks. Regression is the reverse: the ego is consolidated through the repetition of a previous experience. Progression and regression concern tendencies that are always psychically active in the subject and fundamental in all learning processes. The person who cannot let himself/herself go suffers separation anxieties, and the person who cannot handle change cannot let him or herself go completely either. In a somewhat different and stricter psychoanalytical sense the concept of regression is used to denote *inter alia* a regression from secondary to primary processes in the psychic apparatus and regression to past development stages. Controlled, voluntary regression comprises an essential element in aesthetic reception and production and it is sometimes described as 'regression in the service of the ego'. The notion of 'retrogression' recalled by the concept is problematic and indicates a need for theoritical review (this is particularly true of American ego psychology – see Erikson, for example (1968). See also Ziehe and Stubenrauch (1982, chap. III), Laplanche-Pontalis (1967/1988 under 'Regression') and Kris (1952/1977).

8 In psychoanalysis, transference denotes a realisation of infantile prototypes (father, mother or other psychic representatives), especially in the relationship between analyst and patient, where the term describes infantile reactions directed at the analyst. See Laplanche and Pontalis (1967/1988) under 'Transference'.

9 Ziehe (1975).

10 The 'Amadeus complex' may be defined as the child's efforts to realise the father's unfulfilled dreams; thus it is an aspect of the Oedipus complex, focusing on achievement as the heir to rivalry. It should be recalled that it concerns paternity as a function. Mothers too with an instrumental role in the family can be agents of the Amadeus complex as is the case with Betty in Chans. On W. A. Mozart's relationship with his father, see Hildesheimer (1977).

11 Ziehe (1979, pp. 131ff.), inspired by Grunberger, *Le narcissisme* (1971) refers to an 'anal' narcissism which is associated with the experience of capability. See also Freud's 'narcissistic types' in *Über libidinöse Typen* (ref. Møller, 1983, p. 38).

THREE THEMES

1 Ziehe has suggested both of these hypotheses: Ziehe (1975) and Ziehe and Stubenrauch (1982).

2 The choice of Kurre as a point of departure for the study of subjective forces in playing rock music has nothing to do with the notions of representativeness. It has been based on the limited possibilities of including *everything* in our analysis, and on Kurre's accessibility: he is the one we have known longest and the one who has talked most openly with us. We suspect that aspects of his particular identity also exist in other youth both within and outside of our groups; we have implied as much in our attempts to connect our analyses with psychoanalytical theories of adolescence and narcissism, which we believe also relevant for Betty, Håkan or Lollo. Nevertheless, we have tried to keep our analysis of Kurre specific and avoid general conclusions, partly because we understand that our picture may contain very specific class and gender elements.

3 See also Brückner *et al.* (1981), Gorz (1980 and 1983), Negt (1984) and Lindberg and Lundberg (1983, pp. 25ff.).

4 The need for male preserves may be seen as a defence for a laboriously acquired and vulnerable masculinity. See Liljeström (1973/1983), Dinnerstein (1976) and Chodorow (1979).

5 A tendency towards an increasing number of diffuse disturbances and borderline cases has been clinically established (Kristensen and Nielsen 1978, pp. 281 ff.). Researchers such as Riesman with his 'other-directed personality', Fromme with his 'market-oriented man'. Horney with the 'neurotic personality of our time', M. Mead with 'the American national character', Mitscherlich with his 'fatherless generation', Brandt-Humble with 'the Aniara man' and Keniston describing youth as a 'new life phase' all tried to put their finger on conjectured changes in consciousness before concepts such as 'the new socialisation type' (Ziehe 1975) and 'narcissism' provoked debate (see Häsing *et al.* 1979, Ziehe and Stubenrauch 1982, Lasch 1979, Nielsen 1982, Frimodt 1983, Møller 1983 and Fornäs *et al.* 1984b).

THE BAND AS A GROUP

1 See Gillis (1981, pp. 61ff.) and Mitterauer (1986, pp. 29 ff., 59, 162f., 206ff. and 236ff.).

2 See Ambjörnsson (1978), Bjurström (1980) and Wennhall (1987).

3 See for example, Thrasher (1927) and Jonsson and Kälvesten (1964).

4 For discussions on the functions of the gang as regards individuals see, for example, Hartwig (1980), Baacke (1982) and B.-E. Andersson (1982, pp. 34ff.).

5 It would be very interesting also to investigate female gangs and mixed gangs in which the girls occupy more central positions than they do in Chans (see contributions in McRobbie and

Nava, 1984, *Kvinnovetenskaplig Tidskrift* 1986: 1, and Mannheimer, 1975). On womanliness as 'the other', see Harding (1986, pp. 163 ff. and 1987, pp. 14ff.), and Moi (1985, pp. 163ff.). Compare also how Willis (1977) describes 'the lads'' relations with girls on the periphery of the gang and how H.-D. König in Lorenzer (1987, pp. 189–345) analyses the social-psychological foundations of the cowboy myth.

Simonsen and Mow (1984) quite rightly criticise Ziehe for not focusing enough on the gender aspects of ongoing cultural release. To us it is obvious that the social gender is one of the most central areas for the expression of cultural modernisation and this is continually evident in youth cultures' style experiments and in rock music (see Chambers 1985, Drotner 1985 or Ganetz 1987). Many comprehensive investigations of youth confirm this (Czaplicka and Ekerwald 1986, Fischer 1982). Ulrich Beck (1986/1992) awards gender relations a primary role along with the self-critical reflections which modernisation's own destructive risks compel. He sees two current social themes in the foreground: the threatening aspects of the global risk society and the conflicts between men and women, hitherto melded into the family. According to Beck the centre of the conflict is expanding in that while women have strengthened their position in the family and in education greatly, their possibilities in work and politics do not correspond to their ideals of equality nor their growing expectations. In our gangs, too, it is obvious how and ideology of equality in the family, school and leisure activities collides with an economic and political reality in which power relations between the sexes are preserved.

SEARCHING THROUGH SYMBOLIC PRAXIS

1 See Zinnecker in Baacke and Heitmeyer (1985, pp. 24–25). In the following we are indebted to Ziehe and Stubenrauch (1982). It is worth noting that the search has no final goal in postmodern society. Not only the young but also adults can and must seek and change their identity today to a greater extent than in more traditional societies. See Fornäs (1987, pp. 34f.) and Mitterauer (1986, pp. 40 and 252): 'In the background lies a static idea of the adult role which is placed against the dynamic of youth. The adult is '"complete"', not able to change. [. . .] Considering the increased pace of the processes of social change, the question arises whether this static notion of the adult role can be maintained. A new notion could be offered: life-long learning, which involves being prepared to incorporate in one's own personality development changes which occur

in one's surroundings. Learning in its tra-ditional sense is certainly a facet of the role of youth; however, with the new formulation of the boundaries between youth and adults would be erased as would their oppositions.'

2 Keniston (1970) has noted the extreme stress on mobility on the part of modern youth: one places oneself in movement (self-transformation), one places others in movement ('engaging one-self'), moves through the world (geographically – travel, socially – up or down, and psycho-socially – through identification with the powerful or the oppressed). The opposite pole, stagnation, is associated with death and it strongly affects the view of the adult world; see the portrait of Kurre.

3 This accords with other research results. Keith Roe (1983, pp. 49 and 142), for example, refers to 'anticipated socialisation' as an important mechanism, where school results more than the home environment determine young people's cultural tastes because marks point to the social future that young people have already prepared themselves for and identified themselves with.

4 The concept of 'language' here should be taken in a broad sense, as symbol-mediated interac-tion. It includes musical, pictorial and physical as well as verbal (spoken or written, discursive) language. Interaction thus covers all actions in which more than one individual participates. Communication stands for that aspect of interaction which concerns some form of trans-ference or exchange between individuals or groups. Language means communication through symbols, and verbal language is con-fined to the spoken or written as opposed to other languages or symbolic forms.

5 This survey is based on Langer (1958), Lacan (1973/1977), Nylander (1986), Kristeva (1974/1984) and Kristeva (1980).

6 See Kristeva (1980), p. 40.

7 Lorenzer (1972). This presentation is also based on Lorenzer (1981) and Kris (1952/1977).

8 Nielsen (1981, p. 34).

9 Langer (1942, p. 204).

10 We follow here Fornäs and Sernhede (1983). We do not claim that working-class youth play more rock than others but that rock is more accessible to them than most other aesthetic activities.

11 See Bjurström (1985) as regards the hard-rock genre.

12 Bricolage harks back to the 'anarchistic dis-courses' of surrealism and Dada and was systematised by the punks who could trans-form a flag into a jacket, a steel comb into a knife, etc. – in general, cultivated heterogenity. See Hebdige (1979).

13 See Baacke (1968).

14 See Frandsen et al. (1982).

15 In this section we follow Ziehe (1975, pp. 233ff.).

16 Compare Sernhede's experiences of the project Let a Thousand Stones Roll; Sernhede (1984).

17 This was discussed above when describing the music of OH.

18 See Klausmeier (1973), Nielsen (1977) and Wirth (1984, pp. 88ff. and 115).

19 See Fornäs (1980 and 1984), Middleton (1983), Rasmussen (1983), Björnberg et al. (1983) and Björnberg (1984).

20 See Lilliestam (1984).

21 See Blos (1962), Ziehe (1975), Ziehe and Stubenrauch (1982).

22 See Bettelheim (1976).

23 See Kohut (1957), Klausmeier (1973), Nielsen (1977), Fornäs (1980 and 1982), Brolinson and Larsen (1981) and Middleton (1983). Kohut elaborates Kris's (1952/1977) concept of 'regression in the service of the ego' and connects in an ingenious but somewhat mechanical way various levels of conscious-ness (id/ego/super ego) to levels in music as we have suggested in this passage.

24 See Bradley (1980) and Tagg (1981).

25 See Broady et al. (1979).

26 One problem that deserves attention is the putative (narcissistic) tendency of modern youth to seek approval but avoid confronta-tion. Among other things this inability to deal productively with what is new could involve the risk that aesthetic works are reduced to projection screens.

27 See Fornäs et al. (1984b).

28 This 'avant-gardism' recalls the expansion of boundaries in artistic creation and presumes being open to psychic regression, being pre-pared to release impulses which adapted and normative language usually suppresses. This is not about total opening but about trying to find new, unconventional symbolic expressions in a confrontation between narcissistic impulses deriving from maternal symbiosis and the language-making 'father's law'. Adolescence is a creative life phase in which the possibilities for such reappraising experiments are particularly great; such experiments exist in all heuristic creativity, but seem unusually explosive in youth movements and subcultures. See Kristeva (1974/1984), Bürger et al. (1981), Lorenzer (1972, 1981 and 1982), Ziehe (1975, pp. 238 ff.), Erdheim (1982), Wirth (1984, pp. 23ff.) and 'Excursus', below.

29 Wirth (1984) stresses adolescence's character-istic of 'second chance' (healing previous psy-chic wounds). This aspect is implicit in the idea of 'second birth'.

LEARNING PROCESSES IN MAKING ROCK MUSIC

1 See Ziehe and Stubenrauch (1982), Negt (1971) and Döbert et al. (1980). T. Bennett

(1980), Spengler (1987), Öhlund (1988) and Cohen (1991) all deal with young rock groups' learning processes.

2 See Lorenzer (1972, 1981 and 1986), Krovoza (1976).

3 See Ziehe and Stubenrauch (1982).

4 Are learning processes in peer groups also *unusual* in Ziehe's sense of the word (1982)? In other words, do they lack the support and limitations provided by traditions? Ziehe's concept does not refer to any sort of 'alternative pedagogics' but to learning in a new, uncommon (late) modern context in which habits play a smaller part. As will be seen, in our three groups there are strong 'unusual' elements, as well as traditional aspects. On modernity and pedagogics, see Bjerg (1987). Essential in unusual learning processes is what we have called openness, that is, the lack of previously given goals. The last part of Ziehe and Stubenrauch (1982) emphasises this aspect.

5 See Frith and McRobbie (1978/1990) and Shepherd (1987).

6 The concept of goal-rational action encompasses both instrumental (directed towards external nature) and strategic action (directed towards people). See Habermas (1981/1984 and 1988).

7 In this, music occupies a special position, not least in relation to written language. Compare the section in the present book on social sources.

8 In *Capital*, vol. 2, Marx refers to simple and expanded reproduction of (economic) capital. With simple reproduction, a given amount of capital is renewed at the same level; with expanded reproduction, surplus production is utilised to increasse the size of total capital through accumulation. The French sociologist Pierre Bourdieu has used the concept of capital in a metaphorical sense within the area of culture – referring to economic, as well as social and cultural capital. However, it seems to us that Bourdieu sometimes tends to reduce capital reproduction to the simple type. In any case, we have observed a tendency in many current structural and post-structural cultural theories to overemphasise the constants of reproduction and socialisation. Thus when we assay the terms simple and expanded reproduction *vis à vis* symbolic communication, it is to stress that symbol systems are never constant, static structures into which individuals are simply incorporated. The term 'expanded reproduction' in this sense does not refer to any quantitative growth but to a continual qualitative change and development of the symbolic system itself. See Lorenzer (1986), Frank (1983), Kristeva (1974/1984 and 1975/1986) for similar points of view.

9 We shall not go into a detailed analysis of norms in our groups. Neither shall we enter into the discussion conducted around Kohlberg's moral development theory. See Döbert *et al.* (1980), Wellmer (1986) and Gilligan (1982).

10 See Liljeström (1983), Sørensen (1985 and 1986).

11 See Ziehe (1975 and 1982) on how narcissistic tendencies affect peer groups.

12 See the musical semiotic concept of 'museme' (Tagg, 1979, 1981 and 1987). The connection of musical levels to functions on different levels in the psyche has been discussed by *inter alia* Kohut (1957).

13 See Ziehe's concept of 'cultural expropriation' and 'reflexivity' (Ziehe, 1991). See also the section on late modern life conditions in the present volume.

14 See Björnberg *et al.* (1983), Björnberg (1984 and 1987) and his references and sources.

15 See Habermas (1981/1984), Ziehe and Stubenrauch (1982) and Fornäs (1987). Analyses of African rhythm in Chernoff (1986) clearly underline how modernisation has affected contemporary African drumming. Formerly, the subjective level was totally subordinated to the social, but now individual improvisation has begun to break through. Subjectivity, authenticity and expressiveness (see the learning type expressive ability) are not self-evident but comprise socially produced possibilities for differentiating between and within the inner, shared and outer worlds. See also Frith (1986) for a productive analysis of how authenticity in popular music has become possible through modern technology. In the analysis of Kurre's subjectivity in a previous section, these elements are discussed more concretely.

16 See psychoanalytical concepts having to do with the superego and here, particularly ego ideals in, for example, Blos (1962).

17 Expressivity is an important (and problematic) concept in Habermas (1981/1984). See, for example, the discussion in Bernstein (1985) and Honneth and Joas (1986). Expressivity concerns psychic processes on the id and primary process level. We consider it important – against both essentialism and postmodernism – to see subjectivity as something created and formed in a socialisation process. But equally, it is not pure illusion, reducible to an empty play between signs. See Moi (1985).

18 See the section above on the subjective sources.

19 See Kristeva (1980) who, in accord with a long tradition, describes the deepest and pre-semantic levels of verbal language as musical. The description is revealing but at the same time somewhat misleading as music too, albeit not in the same way as verbal language, functions on all psychic levels. Music is not a pure 'language of feeling' – related to what Kristeva

calls the 'semiotic'. But it obviously has a certain ability, in relation to the cognitive rationality that, via discursivity and semantics, is generally associated with verbal language.

20 See Habermas (1981/1988, chapter VI), where he divides the life-world's reproduction and the crises (pathologies) which can arise there into nine fields. The three main types of learning processes are somewhat parallel to the three main types of language – 'constative', 'regulative' and 'expressive' – which Habermas (1981/1984) has taken over from speech-act theory (Austin, Searle, *et al.*). But the placement of what we call cultural aspects is not entirely clear.

21 On the first level, see, for example, Chapple and Garofalo (1977); on the second, Tagg (1979) and Shepherd (1982). Klausmeier (1973) has worked on the third level.

22 Pierre Bourdieu, with this concepts of taste and habits, and Paul Willis and other British subculture researchers in their style analyses, focus on the second of these communication aspects.

23 See Sernhede (1984), Fornäs *et al.* (1984a and b) and Fornäs (1993).

24 See Thavenius (1981, p. 50), who characterises the main oppositions with the concept of system versus communication, inspired by Habermas (1976, 1981/1984 and 1988). Habermas (1962/1989) and Negt and Kluge (1972) lie behind the concept of the public sphere which we use here. See also Bürger *et al.* (1982).

25 Adorno and Horkheimer (1944) depict well this repressive tendency in (bourgeois) subjectivity. Habermas (1981/1984 and 1988) confirms our argument that this tendency is not inherent in all rationality (as a tragic mandatory dialectic of enlightenment), but is linked to a 'pathology' in capitalistic forms of modernisation in which system demands deform inter-subjective communication.

26 Negt and Kluge (1972) discuss this as 'counter-public spheres'; the closest term in British subcultural theory is 'counterculture' (Hall and Jefferson 1976). See Fornäs (1987). Note that our bands comprise unique examples which cannot support hasty generalisations. Working-class gangs can also lack networks and middle-class groups can have them. Both the Swedish music movement of the early 1970s and the punk movement around 1980 provided Swedish youth groups with access to such networks – as do the trash metal, hiphop and house cultures of the early 1990s.

CONCLUSION

1 The choice of terms is complicated as different theoretical traditions define them differently. The distinction between ego-oriented *plaisir* (lust, pleasure) and bodily *jouissance* (bliss, ecstasy, orgasm) made by Lacan (1966/1977) and Barthes (1973/1976) seems to make both these terms too specific for our purpose. The narcissistic enjoyment we discuss has elements of both pleasure and *jouissance* as well as need satisfaction, but a full treatment of these concepts is beyond the scope of this summary. See also in Laplanche and Pontalis (1967/1988) under 'Experience of Satisfaction' and 'Pleasure Principle'.

2 Fornäs *et al.* (1984b) argue not only against uncritical liberalism, but also against two prominent types of neo-authoritarian points of view – aristocratic and romantic proletarian. They also discuss the two main pillars of the debate: commercialism and lack of norms. Today, the power relationships between the different positions have shifted somewhat.

3 See Benjamin (1968).

4 See Broady (1981).

5 Habermas' ideas concerning 'non-coercive communication', the system and life-world are most pertinent in this context. Ziehe (1991, pp. 164ff.) warns of a 'loss of sociality' through the destruction of possibilities of handling the unfamiliar in a socially productive way, and argues in favour of a voluntary introduction of unfamiliar elements. This would require self-imposed limitations on both verbalisation, profanation and intimacy, and an emphasis on a 'third moment' ('the unspoken, the symbolic, the non-symbiotic'). Sociality seems to be associated with the preservation of such a third moment. Compare Negt and Kluge's development of the concept of the public sphere (1972).

6 See Illeris (1981) and Broady (1981) on counter and dual qualification.

7 Fornäs and Sernhede (1983) and Sernhede (1984) examine more exhaustively the limits and possibilities of social youth work.

8 See Roe and Carlsson (1990). Radway (1984) is an interesting study of reception, but it deals with adult women's reading romance literature. In youth and/or rock music there is so far only rather superficial empirical material and badly founded speculation.

9 It would, for example, be interesting to test feminist, psychoanalytical cultural theories here. See Kristeva (1974/1984), Moi (1985) and Harding (1986).

10 For example, Andersson (1982), Roe (1983) and Czaplicka (1987) are interested in the relations between school and leisure.

11 See, for example, Roe (1985) and Czaplicka and Ekerwald (1986). They both give valuable quantitative data on young people's use of the media and consumption respectively. Very few projects are conceived as a combination of the two traditions.

BIBLIOGRAPHY

Adorno, T. W. and Horkheimer, M. (1944) *Dialectic of Enlightenment*, New York: Social Studies Association.

Adrian, H. *et al.* (1980) *–tretton års erfaring* . . . : *Gymnasieelevers lektielæsning, fritid og fremtidshåb*, Copenhagen, published by the Authors.

Ambjörnsson, R. (1978) *Familjeporträtt. Essäer om familjen, kvinnan, barnet och kärleken i historien*, Stockholm: Gidlunds.

Andersson, B-E. (1982) *Generation efter generation. Om tonårskultur, ungdomsrevolt och generationsmotsättningar*, Stockholm: Liber.

Andersson, D. and Larsson, O. (eds) (1987) *Va' säjer dom? ungdomsforskarna*, Stockholm/ Malmö: Socialstyrelsen/Utbildningsproduktion.

Arvidson, A. (1987) 'Rockmusiken i lokalsamhället', *Nord-Nytt*, 24: 5–16.

Baacke, D. (1968) *Beat–die sprachlose Opposition*, Munich: Juventa.

—— (1982) 'Peer-groups und Jugendkultur: Formen des Gruppenlebens und seine Funktionen', *Neue Sammlung*, 5: 468–480.

Baacke, D. and Heitmeyer, W. (eds) (1985) *Neue Widersprüche. Jugendliche in den 80er Jahren*, Weinheim/Munich: Juventa.

Barthes, R. (1973/1976) *The Pleasure of the Text*, London: Jonathan Cape.

Bay, J. (1982) 'Dadada–is all I want to say to you, Om punk i Danmark', *Grus*, 6: 4–28.

Bay, J. Drotner, K. , Jørgensen, B. B., Nielsen, E. and Zeuner, L. (eds) (1985) *Ungdomskultur. Årbog for ungdomskulturforskning*, Copenhagen: Borgen.

—— (1987) *Ungdomskultur. Årbog for ungdomskulturforskning 2*, Copenhagen: Nyt fra samfundsvidenskaberne.

Beck, U. (1986–1992) *Risk Society. Towards a New Modernity*, London: Sage.

Becker, H. S. (1982) *Art Worlds*, Berkeley: University of California Press.

Benjamin, W. (1968) *Illuminations*, New York: Harcourt Brace.

Bennett, H. Stith (1980) *On Becoming a Rock Musician*, Amherst: University of Massachusetts Press.

Berger, A. A. (1982) *Media Analysis Techniques*, Beverly Hills: Sage.

Berger, P. L. and Luckmann, T. (1966/1984) *The Social Construction of Reality. A Treatise in the Sociology of Knowledge*, Harmondsworth: Penguin.

Bergman, H. (1923) *Jag, Ljung och Medardus*, Stockholm: Bonniers.

Bergryd, U. (1987) 'Den hemliga rationaliteten – moral och livsvärld', in *Den sociologiska fantasin – teorier om samhället*, Stockholm: Rabén & Sjögren.

Berkaak, O. A. (1993) *Erfaringer fra risikosonen – opplevelse stiludvikling og rock*, Oslo: Universitets-Forlaget.

Berkaak, O. A. and Ruud, E. (1992) *Den påbegynte virkelighet. Studier i samtidskultur*, Oslo: Universitetsforlaget.

Bernstein, R. J. (ed.) (1985): *Habermas and Modernity*, Oxford: Basil Blackwell.

Bettelheim, B. (1976) *The Uses of Enchantment. The Meaning and Importance of Fairy Tales*, New York: Random House.

Bietau, A., Breyvogel, W., Helper, W. and Schroder, H. (1982) *Subjektivität, Selbstreflexion und Handlungsplanung im Forschungsprozess*, Essen: Universität Essen.

Bjerg, J. (ed.) (1987) *Pædagogik og modernitet. Nye etingelser for en gammel diskussion*, Copenhagen: Hans Reitzels Forlag.

Bjurman, E. L. (1981) *Om barn och barn. Om barns olika vardag*, Lund: Liber.

Bjurström, E. (1980) *Generationsupproret. Ungdomskulturer, ungdomsrörelser och tonårsmarknad från 50-tal till 80-tal*, Stockholm: Wahlström & Widstrand.

—— (1982) 'Kulturproduktion och medvetandeformer', in U. Hannerz, R. Liljeström and O. Löfgren (eds) *Kultur och medvetande – en tvärvetenskaplig analys*, Stockholm: Akademilitteratur.

(1985) 'Hårdrockens myter möter myterna om hårdrocken', *Socialnytt*, 2/1985: 56–63.

Björnberg, A. (1984) 'There's something going on – om eolisk harmonik i nutida rockmusik', in *Tvärspel*: 371–385.

—— (1987) *En liten sång som alla andra. Melodifestivalen 1959–1983*, Gothenburg:

Department of Musicology, University of Gothenburg.

Björnberg, A., Brette, K., Fornäs, J. and Lilliestam, L. (1983): 'Skräck och fascination–två hit-analyser', NordiskForum 39–40: 40–44.

Björnberg, U. and Bäck-Wiklund, M. (1987) Vardagslivets organisering i familj och närsamhälle, Gothenburg: Daidalos.

Blos, P. (1962) On Adolescence. A Psychoanalytic Interpretation, New York: Free Press.

Boëthius, U. (1989) När Nick Carter drevs på flykten. Kampen mot 'smutslitteraturen' i Sverige 1908–1909, Stockholm: Gidlunds.

Bourdieu, P. (1979/1984) Distinction. A Social Critique of the Judgement of Taste, London/ New York: Routledge & Kegan Paul.

—— (1986) Kultursociologiska texter. I urval av Donald Broady och Mikael Palme, Stockholm: Salamander.

Bradley, D. (1980) The Cultural Study of Music, Birmingham: CCCS (unpublished paper).

Brette, K. (1986) '"The Curse Has Been Lifted". Om tjejer och hårdrock', Kvinnovetenskaplig Tidskrift, 1: 48–53.

Broady, D. (1981): Den dolda läroplanen. Krut-artiklar 1977–80, Stockholm: Symposion.

—— (1984) 'Om bildning och konsten att ärva', Krut, 35/36: 4–15.

Broady, D. and Palme, M. (1982): 'Den oregerliga rockmusiken', Krut, 26: 4–6.

—— (eds)(1986) Kultur och utbildning. Om Pierre Bourdieus sociologi, Stockholm: UHÄ.

Broady, D. , Weyler, S. and Östling, B. (1979) 'Fyra teser om ungdomskulturen', Krut 9: 4–13.

Broch, T., Krarup, K., Larsen, P. K., and Rieper, O. (eds)(1979) Kvalitative metoder i dansk samfundsforskning, Copenhagen: Nyt fra samfundsvidenskaberne.

Brolinson, P. E. and Larsen, H. (1981) Rock . . . Aspekter på industri, elektronik & sound, Stockholm: Esselte Studium.

Brückner, P., Bott, G., Knödler-Bunte, E., Negt, O., Ortzen, Peter V., Vester, M. and Ziehe, T., (1981) 'Industrialisierung der inneren Natur: Kapitalismus und bürgerliche Gesellschaft', in E. Knödler-Bunte (ed.) Was ist Heute noch Links?, Berlin: Ästhetik & Kommunikation.

Bürger, C., Bürger, P., and Schulte-Sasse, J. (eds) (1982) Zur Dichotomisierung von hoher und niederer Literatur, Frankfurt am Main: Suhrkamp.

Cahoone, L. E. (1988) The Dilemma of Modernity. Philosophy, Culture, and Anti-Culture, Albany: State University of New York Press.

Carlsson, A. and Ling, J. (eds) (1980) Nordisk musik och musikvetenskap under 1970-talet. En kongressrapport, Gothenburg: University of Gothenburg Department of Musicology.

Carlsson, U. (ed.) (1987) Forskning om populärkultur, Gothenburg: Nordicom-Sweden.

Chambers, I. (1985) Urban Rhythms. Pop Music and Popular Culture, London: Macmillan.

Chapple, S. and Garofalo, R (1977): Rock'n'Roll is Here to Pay, Chicago: Nelson-Hall.

Chernoff, J. M. (1986): African Rhythm and African Sensibility. Aesthetics and Social Action in African Musical Idioms, Chicago: University of Chicago Press.

Chodorow, N. (1979) The Reproduction of Mothering: Psychoanalysis and the Sociology of Gender, Berkeley: University of California Press.

Christoffersen, M. N. and Andersen, B. H. (1982) Åbent interview, Copenhagen: Social-forskningsinstituttet.

Clausen, C. (ed.) (1985): Ungdommens historie, Copenhagen: tiderne skifter.

Cohen, S. (1991) Rock Culture in Liverpool, Popular Music in the Making, Oxford: Clarendon Press.

Corrigan, P. (1976): 'Doing Nothing', in Hall & Jefferson: 103–105.

Czaplicka, M. (1987) Tonåringar och fritid. Hur skolungdomar använder sin tid, Stockholm: Konsumentverket.

Czaplicka, M. and Ekerwald, H. (1986) Ungdomars konsumtion –85, Stockholm: Statens ungdomsråd/Konsumentverket.

Dinnerstein, D. (1976) The Mermaid and the Minotaur: Sexual Arrangements and Human Malaise, New York: Harper & Row.

Döbert, R., Habermas, J. and Nunner-Winkler, G. (eds) (1980) Entwicklung des Ichs, Königstein: Verlagsgruppe Athenäum, Hain, Scriptor, Hanstein (2nd edn).

Drotner, K. (1985) 'Piger og ungdomskultur – eller historien om at sole sig i usynlighedens skaer', in Clausen: 226–259.

—— (1989a) 'Intensities of Feeling: Emotion, Reception and Gender in Popular Culture', in M. Skovmand (ed.) Media Fictions, Aarhus: Seklos.

—— (1989b) 'Girl meets boy: Aesthetic production, reception, and gender identity', in Cultural Studies, 208–225.

Durant, A. (1984) Conditions of Music, London: Macmillan.

Eco, U. (1980/1983) The Name of the Rose, trans. WilliamWeaver, New York: Harcourt Brace.

Ehn, B. and Löfgren, O. (1982) Kulturanalys, Stockholm: Liber.

Eneroth, B. (1984) Hur mäter man 'vackert'? Grundbok i kvalitativ metod, Stockholm: Akademilitteratur.

Erdheim, M. (1982) Die gesellschaftliche Produktion von Unbewusstheit. Eine Einführung in den ethnopsychoanalytischen Prozess, Frankfurt am Main: Suhrkamp.

Erikson, E. H. (1968) Identity, Youth and Crisis, New York: Norton & Co.

Feilitzen, C. von, Filipson, L., Rydin, I. and Schyller, I. (1989) Barn och unga i medieåldern. Fakta i ord och siffror, Stockholm: Rabén & Sjögren.

Finnegan, R. (1989) *The Hidden Musicians. Music-making in an English Town*, Cambridge: Cambridge University Press.

Fischer, A. (ed.) (1982) *Jugend '81: Lebensentwürfe, Alltagskulturen, Zukunftsbilder*, Opladen: Leske & Budrich.

Fornäs, J. (1979) *Musikrörelsen – en motoffentlighet?*, Gothenburg: Röda Bokförlaget.

—— (1980) 'Till kritiken av myterna om den populärmusikaliska konspirationen', in Carlsson & Ling: 40–59.

—— (1981) *Den svenska musikrörelsens organisering*, Gothenburg: University of Gothenburg, Department of Musicology.

—— (1982) 'Rockmusikens kraft', *Krut* 26: 40–45.

—— (1984) 'Framtiden i det som hittills varit', in *Tvärspel*: 197–213.

—— (1985) *Tältprojektet–Musikteater som manifestation*, Stockholm/Gothenburg: Symposion.

—— (1987) ' "Identity is the Crisis". En bakgrund till kulturella uttrycksformers funktioner för ungdomar i senmoderniteten', in Carlsson: 29–39.

—— (1990) 'Moving Rock. Youth Culture and Popular Music', in *Popular Music*: 291–306.

—— (1991) 'Thinking about More Than One Thing at a Time', in J. Ehrnrooth and L. Siurala (eds) *Construction of Youth*, Helsinki: VAPK-Publishing/Finnish Youth Research Society.

—— (1993) ' "Play It Yourself": Swedish Music in Movement', *Social Science Information*, 32, (1): 39–65.

Fornäs, J. and Sernhede, O. (1983) 'Ungdomskultur, rockmusik och ungdomsarbete', *Nordisk Forum* 39–40: 124–128.

Fornäs, J., Lindberg, U. and Sernhede, O. (1984a) 'Pink Freud – kulturklyftor och ungdomsproblematik', *Zenit*, 84: 29–37.

—— (1984b) *Ungdomskultur: Identitet och motstånd*, Stockholm: Akademilitteratur (later edns: Stockholm/Stehag: Symposion).

—— (1990) 'Under the Surface of Rock – Youth Culture and Late Modernity', *Popular Music and Society*, 14(3): 1–25.

Frandsen, J. N., Gleerup, J. and Petersson, E. (1982) 'Erfaringer i klemme. Narcissistiske tolkninger i ungdomskulturen', *Bidrag*, 16: 144–175.

Frank, M. (1983/1989) *What is Neostructuralism?*, Minneapolis: University of Minnesota Press.

Frimodt, J. (1983) *Narcissisme: Freud, Kohut, Ziehe*, Copenhagen: Unge Pædagoger.

Frith, S. (1981) *Sound Effects. Youth, Leisure, and the Politics of Rock 'n' Roll*, New York: Pantheon Books.

—— (1986) 'Art Versus Technology: The Strange Case of Popular Music', *Media, Culture & Society* 8 (3) 263–279.

—— (1988) *Music for Pleasure. Essays in the Sociology of Pop*, Cambridge: Polity Press

—— (ed.) (1989) *Facing the Music*, New York: Pantheon Books.

Frith, S. and Goodwin, A. (eds) (1990) *On Record. Rock, Pop, and the Written Word*, New York: Pantheon Books.

Frith, S. and McRobbie, A. (1978/1990) 'Rock and Sexuality', in Frith and Goodwin (1990): 371–389.

Gahlin, A. (1983) *Levnadsvanor i Sverige: Barn och ungdomar*, Stockholm: Sveriges Radio PUB.

Gammelgaard, J. (1980) *En kamp for det rigtige liv*, Copenhagen: Rhodos.

Ganetz, H. (1987) 'She was only sixteen. Om ungdomskulturforskning ur kvinnoperspektiv', *Häften för Kritiska Studier* 4.

Giddens, A. (1990) *The Consequences of Modernity*, Cambridge: Polity Press.

—— (1991) *Modernity and Self-Identity. Self and Society in the Late Modern Age*, Cambridge: Polity Press.

Gillett, C. (1970) *The Sound of the City*, London: Sphere Books.

Gilligan, C. (1982) *In a Different Voice*, Cambridge, Mass.: Harvard University Press.

Gillis, J. (1981) *Youth and History*, London: Academic Press.

Gorz, A. (1980) *Adieux au prolétariat, au delà du socialisme*, Paris: Editions Galilée.

—— (1983) *Le chemin du paradis*, Paris: Editions Galilée.

Groeben, N. (1980) *Rezeptionsforschung als empirische Literaturwissenschaft*, Tübingen: Gunter Narr Verlag.

Grossberg, L. (1992) *We Gotta Get Out of This Place: Popular Conservatism and Postmodern Culture*, New York/London: Routledge.

Habermas, J. (1962/1989) *The Structural Transformation of the Public Sphere. An Inquiry into a Category of Bourgeois Society*, Cambridge, Mass. : MIT Press.

—— (1976) *Zur Rekonstruktion des Historischen Materialismus*, Frankfurt am Main: Suhrkamp.

—— (1981/1984 and 1988) *The Theory of Communicative Action*, 2 Vols., Cambridge: Polity Press.

—— (1985/1988) *The Philosophical Discourse of Modernity*, Cambridge: Polity Press.

Hall, S. and Jefferson, T. (eds) (1976) *Resistance through Rituals. Youth Subcultures in Post-war Britain*, London: Hutchinson.

Hall, S., Hobson, D., Lowe, A. and Willis, P. (eds) (1980) *Culture, Media, Language*, London: Hutchinson.

Hannerz, U. (1992) *Cultural Complexity. Studies in the Social Organization of Meaning*, New York: Columbia University Press.

Harding, S. (1986) *The Science Question in Feminism*, Milton Keynes: Open University Press.

Hartwig, H. (1980) *Jugendkultur. Ästhetische Praxis in der Pubertät*, Reinbek bei Hamburg: Rowohlt.

Häsing, H., Stubenrauch, H., and Ziehe, T. (eds) (1979) *Narziss–Ein neuer Sozialisationstypus?*, Bensheim: päd extra buchverlag.

Hatch, D. and Millward, S. (1987) *From Blues to Rock. An Analytical History of Pop Music*, Manchester: Manchester University Press.

Hebdige, D. (1979) *Subculture: The Meaning of Style*, London/New York: Methuen.

—— (1987) *Cut 'n' Mix: Culture, Identity and Caribbean Music*, London: Methuen.

—— (1988) *Hiding in the Light. On Images and Things*, London/New York: Routledge.

Heitmeyer, W. (ed.) (1986) *Interdisziplinäre Jugendforschung Fragestellungen, Problemlagen*, Neuorientierungen, Weinheim/Munich: Juventa.

Hildesheimer, W. (1977/1985) *Mozart*, Stockholm: Norstedts.

Holmberg, O., Lindberg, U. and Lundberg, F. (1982) *Tonår. Ett projektarbete i åk 8*, Lund: Pedagogiska gruppen.

Holter, H., Gjertson, A., Henriksen, H. Ve. and Hjort, H. (1976) *Familjen i klassamhället*, Stockholm: Bonniers.

Holter, H. and Kalleberg, R. (eds) (1982) *Kvalitative metoder i samfundsforskning*, Oslo: Universitetsforlaget.

Honneth, A. and Joas, H. (eds) (1986) *Kommunikatives Handeln. Beiträge zu Jürgen Habermas' 'Theorie des kommunikativen Handelns'*, Frankfurt am Main: Suhrkamp.

Hughes, J. A. and Månsson, S-A. (1988) *Kvalitativ sociologi*, Lund: Studentlitteratur.

Hurrelmann, K. and Neubauer, G. (1986) 'Sozialisationstheoretische Subjektmodelle in der Jugendforschung', in Heitmeyer: 157–172.

Illeris, K. (1981) *Modkvalificeringens pædagogik*, Copenhagen: Unge Pædagoger,

Jacobsen, J. K. (1982) *At interviewe. En bog om at spørge meningsfuldt*, Copenhagen: Hans Reitzel.

Jameson, F. (1984) 'Postmodernism, or, The Cultural Logic of Late Capitalism', *New Left Review*, 146: 53–92.

Jencks, C. (1986/1989) *What is Post-Modernism?*, London/New York: Academy Editions/St. Martin's Press (3rd, revised and extended edn).

Jensen, E. F. and Pittelkow, R. (eds) (1986) *Det ukendte publikum – nye metoder i medieforskningen*, Copenhagen: CA Reitzels Forlag.

Jerrentrup, A. (1981) *Entwicklung der Rockmusik von den Anfängen bis zum Beat*, Regensburg: Gustav Bosse Verlag.

Jonsson, G. and Kälvesten, A-L. (1964) *222 Stockholmspojkar: en socialpsykologisk undersökning av pojkar i skolåldern*, Stockholm: Almqvist & Wiksell.

Kälvesten, A.-L. and Meldahl, G. (1972) *217 Stockholmsfamiljer: psykodynamisk bearbetning av ett intervjumaterial*, Stockholm: Tiden.

Keniston, K. (1968) *Young Radicals. Notes on Committed Youth*, New York: Harcourt, Brace & World.

—— (1970) 'Youth: A 'New' Stage of Life', *American Scholar*, 39: 631–654.

—— (1971) 'Psychological Development and Historical Change', *Journal of Interdisciplinary History* 2 (2): 329–345

Klausmeier, R-G. (1973) 'Pubertät und Beatmusik', *Psyche*, XXVII.

Klein, M. (1930/1975) 'The Importance of Symbolformation in the Development of the Ego', in *Love, Guilt and Reparation*, London.

Kohut, H. (1957) 'Observations on the Psychological Functions of Music', *Journal of the American Psychoanalytical Association*, 5: 389–407.

Kris, E. (1952/1977) *Psychoanalytic Explorations in Art*, New York: International Universities Press.

Kristensen, P. and Nielsen, E. (1978) 'Heinz Kohut's narcissismeteori. Introduktion og perspektivering', in Nielsen and Nielsen: 281–322.

Kristeva, J. (1974/1984) *Revolution in Poetic Language*, New York: Columbia University Press.

—— (1980) *Desire in Language. A Semiotic Approach to Literature and Art*, New York: Columbia University Press.

Krovoza, A. (1976) *Produktion und Sozialisation*, Köln/Frankfurt: EVA

Krut (1979) Stockholm, 10.

Kvinnovetenskaplig Tidskrift (1986) Gothenburg, 1.

Lacan, J. (1966/1977) *Ecrits. A Selection*, London: Tavistock.

—— (1973/1977): *The Four Fundamental Concepts of Psychoanalysis*, London: Penguin.

Laing, D. (1985) *One Chord Wonders. Power and Meaning in Punk Rock*, Milton Keynes: Open University Press.

Langer, S. K. (1942) *Philosophy in a New Key*, Cambridge, Mass. : Harvard University Press.

Laplanche, J. and Pontalis, J.-B. (1967/1988) *The Language of Psychoanalysis*, London: Hogarth Press.

Lasch, C. (1979) *The Culture of Narcissism*, New York: Warner.

Laufer, M. (1966) 'Object Loss and Mourning During Adolescence', in *The Psychoanalytic Study of the Child*, XXI.

Leppert, R. and McClary, S. (eds) (1987) *Music and Society. The Politics of Composition, Performance and Reception*, Cambridge: Cambridge University Press.

Liljeström, R. (1973/1983) *Uppväxtvillkor. Samspelet mellan vuxna och barn i ett föränderligt samhälle*, 3rd edn, Stockholm: Liber.

Lilliestam, L. (1984) 'Syntharnas intåg', in *Tvärspel* (1984)

Lindberg, U. (1982) ''Man känner takten i hela kroppen och liksom ryser'. Erfarenhetspedagogik i en verkstadsetta', *Krut*, 26: 9–19.

Lindberg, U. and Lundberg, F. (1983) *Arbetsliv. Ett projektarbete i åk 9*, Lund: Pedagogiska gruppen.

Löfgren, M. and Molander, A. (eds) (1986) *Postmoderna tider*, Stockholm: Norstedts.

Lönnroth, L. (1978) *Den dubbla scenen. Muntlig diktning från Eddan till ABBA*, Stockholm: Prisma.

Lorenzer, A. (1972) *Zur Begründung einer materialistischen Sozialisationstheorie*, Frankfurt am Main: Suhrkamp.

—— (1981) *Das Konzil der Buchhalter. Die Zerströng der Sinnlichkeit. Eine Religionskritik*, Frankfurt am Main: EVA.

—— (ed.) (1986) *Kultur-Analysen*, Frankfurt am Main: Fischer.

Lundmark, L.-E. and Stridsman, K. (eds) (1985) *Sen' kommer en annan tid. En antologi om barns och ungdomars livsformer*, Stockholm: Socialstyrelsen/Liber/Allmänna Förlaget.

McRobbie, A. and Nava, M. (eds) (1984) *Gender and Generation*, London: Macmillan.

Malmberg, C. -J. (1979) 'Något om Jacques Lacan', *Kris*, 11–12: 17–25.

Malmgren, G. (1985) *Min framtid. Om högstadieelevers syn på framtiden*, Stockholm/Lund: Symposion.

—— (1992) *Gymnasiekulturer. Lärare och elever om svenska och kultur*, Lund: Lund university.

Mangs, K. and Martell, B. (1982) *0–20 år i psykoanalytiskt perspektiv*, Lund: Studentlitteratur (3rd edn).

Mannheimer, E. (1975) *Idématerial kring ungdom och sexualitet*, Gothenburg: Gothenburg University, Department of Sociology.

Marx, K. (1893/1978) *Capital*, 2, London: Penguin/New Left Review.

Melucci, A. (1989) *Nomads of the Present. Social Movements and Individual Needs in Contemporary Society*, London: Hutchinson Radius.

Middleton, R. (1983) ' "Play It Again, Sam": Some Notes on the Productivity of Repetition in Popular Music', *Popular Music* 3: 235–270.

—— (1990) *Studying Popular Music*, Milton Keynes: Open University Press.

Mitterauer, M. (1986) *Sozialgeschichte der Jugend*, Frankfurt am Main: Suhrkamp.

Moi, T. (1985) *Sexual/Textual Politics: Feminist Literary Theory*, London/New York: Methuen.

Møller, L. (1984) *Freuds litteraturteori*, Copenhagen: Akademisk Forlag.

Møller, M. (1983) *Narcissisme – sygdom eller skældsord?*, Copenhagen: Dansk Psykologisk Forlag.

Mosskin, L. and Mosskin, P. (1969) *Ungdomsupproret*, Stockholm: Bonniers.

Murdock, G. (1973) 'Struktur, Kultur und Protestpotential', in D. Prokop (ed.): *Massenkommunikationsforschung 2, Konsumtion*, Frankfurt am Main: Fischer.

NAVF (1984) *Barnekulturens ytringsformer*. Senter for barneforskning (seminar report), Trondheim: NAVF.

Negt, O. (1971) *Soziologische Phantasie und exemplarisches Lernen. Zur Theorie und Praxis der Arbeiterbildung*, Frankfurt am Main: Eurpoäische Verlagsanstalt.

Negt, O. (1984) *Lebendige Arbeit, enteignete Zeit*, Frankfurt am Main: Campus.

Negt, O. and Kluge, A. (1972) *Öffentlichkeit und Erfahrung*, Frankfurt am Main: Suhrkamp.

Nettelbladt, P. (1984) *Men pappan då? Vad forskningen säger om småbarnspappor*, Lund: Studentlitteratur.

Nielsen, B. S. and Nielsen, E. (eds) (1978) *Socialisationsforskning: Senkapitalisme og subjektivitet*, Copenhagen: Borgen.

Nielsen, E. (1977/1984) 'Narcissism och rockmusik', in Fornäs *et al. (1984b)*: 235–256.

—— (1981) 'Ungdomskultur – klassekultur', *Kontext* 42: 20–37.

Nielsen, H. K. (1982) 'Problemer i Thomas Ziehes narcissismeteori', *Kontext*, 43: 70–87.

Nordberg, B. (1984) 'Om ungdomars samtalsstil', *Nysvenska Studier* 64: 5–27.

Nylander, L. (ed.) (1986) *Litteratur och psykoanalys – enantologi om modern psykoanalytisk litteraturtolkning*, Stockholm: Norstedts.

Öhlund, T. (1988) *Rockbandet. Kultur och läroprocess hos en kamratgrupp i yngre tonåren*, Umeå: Umeå Universitet, Institutionen för Socialt Arbete.

Olsson, A. (1986) *Den okända texten*, Stockholm: Bonniers.

Ottomeyer, K. (1977) *Ökonomische Zwänge und menschliche Beziehungen*, Reinbek bei Hamburg: Rowohlt.

Pattison, R. (1987) *The Triumph of Vulgarity. Rock Music in the Mirror of Romanticism*, New York/Oxford: Oxford University Press.

Prokop, U. (1976) *Weiblicher Lebenszusammenhang*, Frankfurt am Main: Suhrkamp.

Radway, J. (1984) *Reading the Romance. Women, Patriarchy, and Popular Literature*, Chapel Hill: University of North Carolina Press.

—— (1988): 'Reception Study: Ethnography and the Problems of Dispersed Audiences and Nomadic Subjects', *Cultural Studies*, 2 (3) 359–376.

Rasmussen, P. (1987) 'Unge med kulturel kapital – om drenge med høje karakterer i gymnasiet', in Bay *et al*: 100–121.

Rasmussen, P. J. O. (1983) 'Rock og regression', Copenhagen: Musikvidenskabeligt Institut (unpublished paper).

Redhead, S. (1990) *The End-of-the-Century Party. Youth and Pop Towards 2000*, Manchester: Manchester University Press.

Regionplanekontoret (1985) *Områdesdata för Stockholms län*, Stockholm: Stockholms läns landsting.

Reimer, B. (1989) 'Postmodern Structures of Feeling. Values and Life Styles in the Postmodern Age', in J. R. Gibbins (ed.) *Politics and Contemporary culture. Politics in a Postmodern Age*, London: Sage.

Reynolds, S. (1990) *Blissed Out. The Raptures of Rock*, London: Serpent's Tail.

Roe, K. (1983) *Mass Media and Adolescent Schooling: Conflict or Co-existence?*, Stockholm: Almqvist & Wiksell International.

—— (1985) 'Swedish Youth and Music. Listening Patterns and Motivations', *Communication Research*, 12 (3): 353–362.

—— (1987a) 'Culture, Media and the Intellectual. A Review of the Work of Pierre Bourdieu', in Carlsson: 17–27.

—— (1987b) 'The School and Music in Adolescent Socialization', in J. Lull (ed.): *Popular Music and Communication*, Newbury Park: Sage.

Roe, K. and Carlsson, U. (eds) (1990) *Popular Music Research*, Gothenburg: Nordicom-Sweden.

Rosengren, K. E. (ed.) (1986) *På gott och ont: Barn ochungdom, TV och video*, Stockholm: Liber.

Salzinger, H. (1972) *Rock Power oder Wie musikalisch ist die Revolution? Ein Essay über Pop-Musik und Gegenkultur*, Frankfurt am Main: Fischer.

Sandner, W. (ed.) (1977) *Rockmusik: Aspekte zur Geschichte, Ästhetik, Produktion*, Mainz: Schott.

Schönström, R. (1986) 'Den befriade människan Pär Lagerkvists besvärjelse av kastrationen', in Nylander: 277–297.

Schütz, V. (1982) *Rockmusik–eine Herausforderung für Schüler und Lehrer*, Oldenburg: Verlag Isensee.

Seca, J-M. (1988) *Vocations rock. L'état acide et l'esprit des minorités rock*, Paris: Méridiens Klincksieck.

Segal, H. (1952/1986) 'A Psycho-Analytical Approach to Aesthetics', in *The Work of Hanna Segal*, London: Free Association Books/ Maresfield Library.

—— (1957/1986): 'Notes on Symbol Formation', in *The Work of Hanna Segal*.

—— (1964): *Introduction to the Work of Melanie Klein*, London: Hogarth Press.

Sernhede, O. (1982) 'Låt tusen stenar rulla. Om rockmusik och ungdomsarbete', *Krut*, 26: 28–39.

—— (1984) *Av drömmar väver man . . . Ungdomskultur, socialisation, ungdomsarbete*, Stockholm/Malmö: Socialstyrelsen/Utbildningsproduktion.

Shepherd, J. (1982) 'A Theoretical Model for the Sociomusicological Analysis of Popular Musics', *Popular Music 2*: 145–178.

—— (1991) *Music as Social Text*, Cambridge: Polity Press.

Simonsen, B. and Mow, E. (1984) 'Fordi du ikke er en rigtig mor, kan jeg ikke blive en rigtig mand', *Unge Pædagoger*, 8: 18–29.

Sørensen, A. S. (1985) 'Pigekulturer – intimitet, forførelseog skønhed', in Bay *et al.* : 119–135.

—— (1986): 'Längtan efter skönhet –om flickkultur förr och nu', *Kvinnovetenskaplig Tidskrift* 1: 34–47.

Spengler, P. (1987) *Rockmusik und Jugend. Bedeutung und Funktion einer Musikkultur für die Identitätssuche im Jugendalter*, Frankfurt am Main: Brandes & Apsel.

Statistiska Meddelanden Helsingborg (1983–1985), Helsingborg (1983: 6, 1985: 8, 1985: 9).

Steward, S. and Garratt, S. (1984) *Signed, Sealed and Delivered. True Life Stories of Women in Pop*, London: Pluto Press.

Street, J. (1986) *Rebel Rock. The Politics of Popular Music*, Oxford: Basil Blackwell.

Stroh, W. M. (1984) *Zur Psychologie musikalischer Tätigkeit. Musik in Kellern, auf Plätzen und vor Natodraht*, Stuttgart: Marohl.

Tagg, P. (1979) *Kojak – 50 Seconds of Television Music Toward the Analysis of Affect in Popular Music*, Gothenburg: University of Gothenburg, Department of Musicology.

—— (1981) *On the Specificity of Musical Communication – Guidelines for Non-Musicologists*, Gothenburg: University of Gothenburg, Department of Musicology (unpublished paper).

—— (1987) *Musicology and the Semiotics of Popular Music*, Gothenburg: University of Gothenburg, Department of Musicology (unpublished paper).

Thavenius, J. (1981) *Modersmål och fadersarv. Svenskämnets traditioner i historien och nuet*, Stockholm: Symposion.

—— (1987) *Kulturens svarta hål*, Stockholm/Lund: Symposion.

Thrasher, F. (1927) *The Gang*, Chicago: University of Chicago Press.

Trondman, M. (1989) *Rocksmaken – Om rock som symboliskt kapital. En studie av ungdomars musiksmak och eget musikutövande*, Lund: Department of Sociology (unpublished paper).

Tvärspel–trettioen artiklar om musik. Festskrift till Jan Ling (1984), Gothenburg: University of Gothenburg, Department of Musicology.

Voullième, H. (1987) *Die Faszination der Rockmusik. Überlegungen aus bildungstheoretischer Perspektive*, Opladen: Leske & Budrich.

Wellmer, A. (1986) *Ethik und Dialog*, Frankfurt am Main: Suhrkamp.

Wicke, P. (1987) *Anatomie des Rock*, Leipzig: VEB Deutscher Verlag für Musik.

Willis, P. (1976/1980) 'Notes on Method', in Hall *et al.* : 88–95.

—— (1977) *Learning to Labour*, London: Gower Publishing Company.

—— (1978) *Profane Culture*, London: Routledge & Kegan Paul.

—— (1990) *Common Culture. Symbolic Work at Play in the Everyday Cultures of the Young*, Milton Keynes: Open University Press.

Wills, G. and Cooper, C. L. (1988) *Pressure Sensitive. Popular Musicians under Stress*, London: Sage.

Wirth, H.-J. (1984) *Die Schärfung der Sinne.*

Jugendprotest als persönliche und kulturelle Chance, Frankfurt am Main: Syndikat.

Ziehe, T. (1975) *Pubertät und Narzissmus. Sind Jugendlicheentpolitisiert?*, Frankfurt am Main: EVA.

—— (1979) 'Gegen eine soziologische Verkürzung der Diskussion um den neuen Sozialisationstypus', in Häsing *et al.*: 119–136.

—— (1991) *Zeitvergleiche. Jugend in kulturellen Modernisierungen*, Weinheim/Munich: Juventa.

Ziehe, T. and Stubenrauch, H. (1982) *Plädoyer für ungewöhnliches Lernen*, Reinbek bei Hamburg: Rowohlt.

Zinnecker, J. (1986) 'Jugend im Raum gesellschaftlicher Klassen. Neue Überlegungen zu einem alten Thema', in Heitmeyer: 99–132.

INDEX

activity 73, 74, 75, 122, 250–1
administrative abilities 233–4
aggression 89, 91, 106, 153, 217, 241; One Hand
    Beats Five Fingers (OH) 46, 47, 49, 50
Alarm (band) 52, 178
alcohol 65, 98, 123
alienation 150
Alphaville (band) 100
Amadeus complex 184, 188, 226, 240
ambitions 108, 176
antagonism 37, 73
Anti (band) 34, 35
approval, need for 178
Ark 56, 59, 60, 63, 64, 67–77, 208; concerts
    76–7; culture 67–76
Arts and Cultural Administration Institute 6
aspirations 123
atmosphere 100
Attentat (band) 59, 80, 82, 88
authenticity 41, 177, 178
authority 191–2
authority, challenge to see rebel image
autonomy 205, 251–2

beat and sound, focus on 218–20
behaviour dispositions 78, 212
Bergman, Hjalmar 95
Bergslunden (suburb) 63–71, 155; youth situation
    65–7
Berman, Marshall 8
Bourdieu, Pierre 7, 8, 9
Byrne, David 135

Camouflage (band) 76, 77
Chans 6, 14, 94–139, 155, 157, 265; activity
    122; authority 192; clothes 96, 99, 100;
    cottage (rehearsal venue) 95–101; cover
    versions 100; cultural tastes 124–8; culture
    111–24; economic resources 161; employment
    193, 194; empowerment 210; family
    backgrounds 156, 160; flexibility 207; genres,
    breadth and development 215, 216; having
    fun 205; history 104–11; image 97; and late
    modernity 143; learning processes 232, 233,
    234, 236, 237, 240; leisure 167, 168, 169,
    170, 171; Longing for Peace (song) 134, 137;
    love songs 135, 136, 137; lyrics 105, 135,
136, 219, 220; objective sources 211; original
    music 128–38; parents 114, 121–2, 162, 164,
    193; project aims 206; qualitative methods
    11, 12, 13; resistance and alternative public
    spheres 247, 249; school 114, 121–2, 123,
    164, 165; security 209; sexuality and
    cohabitation 195; socialisation 208; solidarity
    131; songs 131–4, 136, 137, 138, 218;
    stagnation 107; style 96, 120; subjective
    sources 224; Summerland (song) 136;
    synthesisers 135, 137; Teheran (song) 132–4,
    136, 218; Totte (song) 131–2, 136;
    Villaholmen 101–4; vocals 137; Whata
    Dream (song) 136; youth cultural scene 294
Chicago School 201
childcare 148–9, 154
church and religion 36, 41, 42, 45, 66, 154, 209
Clash (band) 178, 184, 204, 247; and Chans 105,
    106, 127, 136; and One Hand Beats Five
    Fingers (OH) 28, 30, 32, 33, 34, 52
class see social
clothes see under individual bands
cohabitation 194–7
commercialisation 40, 145
communication 39, 129, 145, 244–5, 258–9
competence 108, 232–3; social 176; verbal 71
competitions 86, 87
comradeship 196; see also friendship; 'G' ideology
concerts 76–7; see also stage shows
conflicts 157, 177; Chans 108, 110, 112, 120;
    One Hand Beats Five Fingers (OH) 38, 50,
    187; social 237
conformity 116, 252
control 46
cover versions see under individual groups
creativity, artistic 227
criminality 74
criticisms 108
culture 67–76; see also under individual bands

daily life 144–5
dance pop 35
de-traditionalisation 154
Dead Kennedys (band) 105, 106, 128
Def Leppard (band) 52
demands, external and internal 114–15
dependence 40

detachment 117, 128, 138
deviant tendency 74
deviation, fear of 120
Dire Straits (band) 97, 127, 134
discipline 46, 47, 163, 165, 179
disco music 219
disputes see conflicts
dominance, male 114, 195
Downtown (band) 82
drugs 40, 65, 74, 118, 123, 133

Ebba Grön (band) 204, 217, 218, 233, 234, 235;
    and Chans 101, 105, 106, 127; and Lam
    Gam 59, 80, 81, 82, 84, 85, 88, 90
Eco, Umberto 22
education 148, 154; see also school
Ekseption (band) 127
emigration 22, 23, 64, 102
employment 172, 177, 179, 192–4
empowerment 209–10
ethnic/nationally mixed backgrounds 156, 159
expectation gap 152
expressiveness 241, 242
external world, learning in 231–4

Fältskog, Agneta 52
family 147, 148, 157, 158–63, 172, 238;
    background 156, 159; single-parent 64, 78,
    102; see also father; mother; parents and
    under individual bands
fan club 83, 107, 108, 122, 124
fan magazine 97, 99, 106, 108, 122, 124, 128,
    139
father, estranged 161
father and son relationship 182, 184, 186, 191,
    226
feelings and instincts, acting out of 106
flexibility 115–16, 128, 166
Forman, Milos 184
Fornäs, Johan 4–5, 10, 11, 192, 239; and Chans
    95, 110, 111, 114, 117, 118, 121, 122, 123,
    124, 127, 134; and family 159, 162; and
    learning in the external world 232, 233, 234;
    and school 164, 165, 166, 167
'freak syndrome' 193
free time see leisure
friendship 83, 87, 176, 195, 238; loyalty 35
fun see having fun

'G' ideology 36, 37, 38, 45, 178, 188, 209, 238
Ganetz, Hillevi 4
gang phenomenon 201–6, 227, 268; girl members
    70; Lam Gam 65, 66, 69, 70, 72, 75; see also
    'G' ideology
gender 204, 261; see also mixed; single
generation gap 149–50
genres, breadth and development of 215–17
Gessle, Per 106
gigs 131; see also concerts
growing up 46, 227–8; fear of 44, 124
guitars 88, 89, 91, 135
Gyllene Tider (band) 105, 106, 184

Habermas, Jürgen 7, 8, 9, 150
Hall, Stanley 146
hard rock 171, 217; Chans 107, 136; English and
    American 81; influence 193, 215, 216; Lam
    Gam 59, 68, 73, 79, 83, 86, 91; One Hand
    Beats Five Fingers (OH) 34, 35, 38, 53, 56, 57
harmonic structures, post-tonal 220–1
having fun 36, 37, 205, 210; Chans 100, 105,
    117–19, 130, 138
Hebdige, Dick 9
Helsingborg (town) 21, 22, 39
Hendrix, Jimi 33, 52
heterogeneity, expressions of in lyrics 217–18
Hildebrand, Staffan 26
hobby band see Chans
home districts comparisons 156
homogeneity 114, 115
HSFR see Research Council for the Humanities
    and the Social Sciences
humour 50, 58; see also having fun

ideals 82, 240, 252–3
identity 70, 72, 79, 171–2; see also sexual
idols 184
image 48; see also rebel; style and under
    individual bands
immigration 147
Imperiet (band) 127, 204, 217, 218, 233, 235;
    and Lam Gam 84, 89, 90
impressions 34
independence 42–3, 184, 205
individualisation 152, 206, 208, 209, 210
individuation 224
inheritance syndrome 182
inner world, learning in 238–42
institutionalisation 107
inter-subjective functions 244, 245
interaction 243; One Hand Beats Five Fingers
    49–51
interpretation 14, 15
intimacy 44, 195, 205
Iron Maiden (band) 59
isolation, fear of 178

Jam (band) 178
Jameson, Frederic 8

Klein, Melanie 10, 228
Kohut, Heinz 10
Kraftwerk (band) 221
Kris, Ernst 10
Kristeva, Julia 10, 227
KSMB (band) 204; and Chans 105, 106, 127,
    128, 136; and Lam Gam 81, 90
Kurre 175–89

Lacan, Jacques 10, 212
Lam Gam 6, 59–93, 155, 157, 265; authority
    192; autonomy 205; beat and sound focus
    218; Bergslunden suburb 63–71; conflict
    songs 136; cover versions 82, 84, 85, 88,
    89, 90, 91; dissolution 86–8, 206;

Lam Gam *cont.*
economic resources 161; employment 193, 194; empowerment 210; family backgrounds 156, 159, 160; genres, breadth and development of 215, 216; history 77–88; *How Did We Get Here?* (song) 89–90; image 84; and late modernity 143; learning processes 233, 234, 237, 240, 241; leisure 167, 168, 170; lyrics 86, 217; male dominance 114; *Money and Dead Nature* (song) 90, 92–3; music 88–93; objective sources 211, 212; ownership, strong feelings of 71; parents 162, 164, 193; qualitative methods 11, 13; rehearsals 85–6; resistance and alternative public spheres 249; school 164, 165; security 209; sexuality and cohabitation 195; as single–sex band 113; solidarity 62; songs 82, 88, 89–90, 92–3, 136, 218, 220; style 68; subjective sources 224; synthesisers 82, 88, 90; *The Sun* (song) 88, 90, 218, 220; vocals 88; wasting time 118; youth cultural scene 204; youth situation in Bergslunden 65–7; *see also* Ark
language 41, 70–1, 118; bad 50; discursive 219; of theory 14; of youth 15
Låt Stenar Rulla project (Let a Thousand Stones Roll) 4, 5–7, 66, 80
late modernity 143–54, 156, 171, 175, 227–8, 265–6; children of the boom 147–50; crises 150–4; prehistory 143–7
leadership 42, 248
learning complexities 258
learning processes in rock music 229–49, 261, 269–71; learning types 230–45; modern possibilities 245–7; resistance and public spheres, alternative 247–9
learning types 230–45; communication 244–5; complexity 242–3; external world 231–4; inner world 238–42; shared world 234–8
leisure 170, 177, 193, 196, 202; activities 104, 124–5, 167–71; organisations 157; organised/scheduled 168, 170; spontaneous 168
Let a Thousand Stones Roll *see* Låt Stenar Rulla project
liberation 183, 191
Lindberg, Ulf 3–4, 7, 10, 11, 13, 158; and authority 191; and employment 194; Kurre 175, 176, 178, 179, 181, 182, 185; and learning in the shared world 235, 236, 237; and One Hand Beats Five Fingers (OH) 26, 30, 31–2, 33, 38, 40, 42, 46, 57; and searching 218, 222, 226–7; and sexuality and cohabitation 195, 196
Lindgren, Astrid 100
living conditions 211
living standards 75
Lorenzer, Alfred 10, 219
love songs 39; Chans 135, 136, 137
loyalty *see* friendship
Lustans Lakejer (band) 218
Lyotard, J.F. 8
lyrics 38, 43, 215; antitheses 54, 56; heterogeneity 217–18; naive 137; and politics 137;

solidarity 45; *see also under* individual bands

makeability 207, 208
managers 99
marginality 252
market 144–5
materialism 41
mates *see* friendship
media 157, 169, 172
melody 223
micro-cultures 156–7
middle-class 14, 111, 155; area 102, 103; criticism of 151; culture 114; and economic resources 162; gangs 201; and leisure 168, 169; teachers 164; *see also* Chans; Lam Gam
migration 155
mixed gender bands 23, 69, 109, 110, 111; *see also* Chans
modernisation 8, 151–2
modernity *see* late
money, importance of 74
mother, importance of 161, 183–4, 204; *see also* transference
motives for playing rock 251–5; autonomy, collective 251–2; ideals, alternative 252–3; narcissistic enjoyment 253–5
music 88, 135; abilities 108; ambitions 195; background 79; beat and sound 218–20; guitars 35, 88, 89, 91; harmonic structures 220–1; listening 51–2, 125–6; melody 223; percussion 135; signature tunes 27, 30; taste 51–2; technology 40; theory 79; *see also* lyrics; songs; synthesisers; vocals *and under* individual bands *as* cover versions; music; original music

narcissism 187, 188, 189, 190, 196, 219, 222, 253–5
narratives 135, 136
naturalness 39–41
nature and society, knowledge of 234
Negt, Oskar 8
new wave 106, 136
norm experiments, necessary 256–7

Oasis rock 100, 101, 107, 205
objective functions 244, 245
objective level 12
Oedipus complex 208
OH *see* One Hand Beats Five Fingers
One Hand Beats Five Fingers (OH) 6, 21–58, 155, 175, 265; appearance 48–9; autonomy 205; Barn (rehearsal quarter) 21, 24–8; beat and sound focus 218; chaos 46–8; conflict 177; conflict songs 136; culture 39–48; economic resources 161; ego, individual 209; employment 193, 194; empowerment 210; family backgrounds 156, 159, 160; 'G' ideology 117; genres, breadth and development of 215, 216; Helsingborg (town) 21, 22, 39; history 32–9; individualisation 206;

One Hand Beats Five Fingers *cont.*
    interaction 49–51; *Just a Dream* (song) 53–4,
    57; language 118; *Last Fight* (song) 47; and
    late modernity 143; learning processes 232,
    234, 237, 239–40, 243; leisure 168, 170, 171;
    Living for Weekends (song) 220; lyrics 187,
    218; makeability 207; male dominance 114;
    music 51–8; musical development 56; musical
    taste 51–2; naturalness (being yourself)
    39–41; objective sources 211; *Oh Yea* (song)
    47; order and chaos 46–8; original music
    52–8; parents 162, 164, 193; power and
    powerlessness 41–3; producer 192; qualitative
    methods 11, 13; resistance and alternative
    public spheres 247; *Right or Wrong* (song)
    52–3; role models 121; school 164, 182–3;
    sexuality and cohabitation 195; signature
    tune 42; as single–sex band 113; solidarity
    188; songs 40, 42, 43, 45–7, 52–7, 136,
    220; *Streetman* (song) 45; style 48–51;
    subjective sources 224, 226; synthesisers
    57, 178, 221; *The Rain* (song) 40, 45, 55–6;
    Toni's (song) 43, 46, 53; *Too Young*
    (song) 45; 'us and them' attitude 43–6;
    vocals 55; youth cultural scene 204; *see
    also* Kurre
ontologisation 209
openness, theoretical 262–3

parents: aspirations 123; attitudes 34; culture
    151; demands 162; intervention 108;
    liberation from 42, 185–6; support 105, 183;
    see also father; mother *and under* individual
    bands
passivity 73, 75
patriotism, local 72
peer-groups 165, 167
percussion 135
Pimple (band) 107
playfulness *see* having fun
politics 84, 85; dissociation from 45, 75, 138; in
    lyrics 137; problems 91
pop music 250
post-punk 136
power/powerlessness 41–3
producer 192
professionalism 56
projects 4; articulated 202–3; details 5–7; *see also*
    Låt Stenar Rulla
protest 216–17
proto-symbols 213, 219
puberty 79, 146, 213
public, contact with 83
public spheres, alternative 247–9
punk 154, 171; advent 151; beginner's 89; Chans
    99, 101, 105, 106, 111, 128, 135, 136;
    influence 193, 215, 216; Lam Gam 59, 68,
    73, 84, 85, 91; One Hand Beats Five Fingers
    (OH) 32, 35, 43, 53, 55, 56, 184; rebel image
    90; and recession 153; street stages 219;
    tradition 38; *see also* Swedish
Purple Rain (song by Prince) 11, 181–2

qualitative methods 10–16
quality, demand for 35

radio 125–6; *see also* media
rebel image 48, 49, 191; Kurre and One Hand
    Beats Five Fingers (OH) 176, 177, 178, 183,
    184
rebelliousness 105, 179
reception 261
recession 153
reflexivity 207–8, 209, 239–40
regeneration, social 110
regresssion 222
rehearsal space 42, *see also* Ark; Barn *under* One
    Hand Beats Five Fingers (OH); cottage *under*
    Chans
rehearsals 85–6, 129–30
rejection 177, 194
relationships 71; with opposite sex 79–80, 98,
    112; skills 238, 240; *see also* sexual relations
release, emotional 130
religion *see* church
Research Council for the Humanities and the
    Social Sciences (HSFR) 6
resistance 247–9, 259–60
resources, economic 160–1
restlessness 115–16
revenge, social 79
rock 73, 75, 97, 111, 250; blues 34; progressive
    90; sign system of 212; traditional 37; *see
    also* hard rock; Oasis; rock as symbolic
    praxis; Swedish
rock as symbolic praxis 219–28; adolescence, late
    modern 227–8; objective sources 210–12;
    socio-cultural sources 212–21; subjective
    sources 222–6
roles, fixed 51
Rolling Stones (band) 60, 61, 216
Roxette (band) 106

Saga (band) 52
school 157, 163–7; authority 192; bands 193;
    central role 146; demands 108; demarcation
    193; and leisure activities 170; negative
    attitude 67–8; positive attitude 103; primary
    socialisation 172; rejection 69; role 36; *see
    also under* individual bands
searching through symbolic praxis 207–28, 256,
    268–9; rock as symbolic praxis 219–28;
    searching 207–10
security and control 44, 118–19, 209
Segal, Hanna 10
self-appreciation 254
self-awareness 178
self-control 165
self-determination 41
self-discipline 40, 195
self-image 72
self-reflection 254, 263
self-respect 79
Sennett, Richard 8
sensitivity 62, 176

sensuality 215
serious play 255–6
Sernhede, Ove 4, 5, 7, 10, 11, 12, 158, 163, 170, 171, 195; and 'G' ideology 201, 203, 204, 205, 206; and Lam Gam 60, 66–71 *passim*, 73, 74, 78, 79, 81, 84, 85, 86; and learning processes 230, 233, 234, 237, 239, 240; and school 165, 167; and searching through symbolic praxis 211, 214, 215, 218, 219
sexual feelings 241
sexual identity 113
sexual relations 44–5, 50; *see also* relationships with opposite sex
sexual roles 41
sexuality 153, 154, 194–7
shared world, learning in 234–8
signature tunes 27, 30, 42
Simple Minds (band) 52, 57, 97
singing *see* vocals
single-sex groups 195
skills, cultural 235
smoking 98
social class 119, 150, 164, 202; *see also* middle; upper; working
social life 109, 154
social movements 150
social position 114
social problems 65, 91, 201
socialisation 10, 146, 154, 157, 208, 229; changes in 254; Chans 112, 113; family 190; primary 172, 246; secondary 243, 246
socio-cultural sources 212–21; beat and sound, focus on 218–29; genres, breadth and development of 215–17; harmonic structures, post-tonal 220–1; heterogeneity, expressions of in lyrics 217–18; synthesiser, advent of 221
sociology, cultural 9
solidarity 28, 35, 37, 42, 43, 44, 45; *see also under* individual bands
solos, instrumental 135
song-writing 88
songs: camp 35; commercial 52; horror and fantasy 137; with messages 38; protest 53, 90; recordings 107, 110–11; repetition 135–6; rhyme 135; satirical 135, 137–8; victim 43, 45; *see also* love songs
special effects 91
spontaneity and rawness 46
stage shows 47, 82, 84
stagnation 109
state 144–5
status 13, 71, 80
Strummer, Joe 34, 184
style 37, 39, 150, 217; *see also under* individual bands
subjectivation 208–9, 210
subjective functions 244, 245
subjective level 12
subjectivity theories 9
subordination 112
Super Natural (band) 76
superficiality rejection 177–8

Swedish punk 34, 79, 81, 88, 90
Swedish rock 73
symbolic praxis 227; *see also* searching
symbols: artistic 213; consumption 224–5; cultural 250; linguistic 235; presentative 213, 219; unconsummated 214; *see also* proto-symbols
synthesisers 38, 40, 46, 215; advent 221; dominant 55; jagged 89; *see also under* individual groups
systems, symbolic 235

Talk Talk (band) 97
Talking Heads (band) 97, 98, 126, 127, 133, 135
Tältprojektet (Tent Project) 4
tastes, cultural 124–8
technical skill 211–12; Chans 111, 120, 138; Lam Gam 71, 83, 91; One Hand Beats Five Fingers (OH) 38
tensions 74
Tent Project *see* Tältprojektet
Thåström, Joakim 81, 84
theoretical fields 7–10
togetherness *see* solidarity
Toto (band) 52, 57
tradition 152, 153
transference, maternal 188–9, 190
transference mechanisms 13, 180, 188

U2 (band) 28, 52, 53, 55, 127, 135, 204
Uggla, Magnus 82, 88
unemployment 64, 194
upper-class 155
'us and them' attitude 43–6

vandalism 65
variety 138
Vega, Allan 184
victim theory 225
videos/films 107
Villaholmen (suburb) 101–4, 155
vocals 55, 88, 135, 137

wasting time 71
Whitesnake (band) 59
Willis, P. 9
Winnicott, D.W. 10
working-class 23, 48, 159; culture 69; dichotomy 45; and economic resources 162; families 181; gangs 201; ideology 42; Lam Gam 64; and leisure 168; musical taste 52; parents 67; population 155; sexuality and cohabitation 195; youth 252; *see also* One Hand Beats Five Fingers (OH)

youth clubs 66
youth cultures 146–7, 149, 151, 152
youth debate 255–7; norm experiments, necessary 256–7; searching, active 256; serious play 255–6
youth festivals 104
youth organisations 104

youth and parents, experience of 153
youth research 260–3; openness, theoretical
    262–3; polydimensional content 260–2; self-
    reflection, strategic 263
youth work 257–60; communications between

different spheres 258–9; learning complexities
258; resistance 259–60

Ziehe, Thomas 7, 8, 9, 10, 150, 189
ZZ Top (band) 50

Lightning Source UK Ltd.
Milton Keynes UK
UKOW040442061012

200145UK00002B/73/A

9 780415 085021